SCHOOL CHOICE
AND SOCIAL
CONTROVERSY

SCHOOL CHOICE AND SOCIAL CONTROVERSY

Politics, Policy, and Law

STEPHEN D. SUGARMAN
FRANK R. KEMERER
Editors

BROOKINGS INSTITUTION PRESS
Washington, D.C.

Copyright © 1999
THE BROOKINGS INSTITUTION
1775 Massachusetts Avenue, N.W.
Washington, D.C. 20036
www.brookings.edu

Library of Congress Cataloging-in-Publication data
School choice and social controversy : politics, policy, and law /
   Stephen D. Sugarman, Frank R. Kemerer, editors.
      p.   cm.
Includes bibliographical references and index.
   ISBN 0-8157-8276-4 (alk. paper)—ISBN 0-8157-8275-6 (pbk. : alk. paper)
   1. School choice—Social aspects—United States.   2. School choice—Law and legislation—United States.   3. Education and state—United States.
I. Sugarman, Stephen D.   II. Kemerer, Frank R.
   LB1027.9 .S352 1999   99-050418
   379.1'11'0973—dc21   CIP

9 8 7 6 5 4 3 2 1

The paper used in this publication meets the minimum requirements of the American National Standard for Information Sciences—Permanence of Paper for Printed Library Materials, ANSI Z39.48-1984.

Typeset in Sabon

Composition by Oakland Street Publishing
Arlington, Virginia

Printed by R. R. Donnelley and Sons
Harrisonburg, Virginia

Contents

v

Preface

This book presents the results of a cooperative endeavor. Behind the rhetoric about school choice lie important legal and public policy issues that so far have received little attention in the choice debate yet have critical implications for the drafting and implementation of school choice programs. For example, to what extent can and should the government control the admissions process in choice schools to ensure equality of opportunity and a diversified student body? Will choice plans encompassing religious private schools pass muster under the Constitution, and, if so, can these schools favor faith members in admissions and employment? Will schools of choice be required to observe student and teacher rights generally recognized in traditional public schools, either through the direct application of the Constitution or through enabling legislation? How will the expansion of school choice affect the funding of public schooling generally? What will be the unionization and collective bargaining rights of teachers in public charter schools and private voucher schools? How can school choice win the support of teachers when the teachers' unions have so strongly opposed it? Is expanded school choice a threat or an opportunity for children with disabilities? Even if there is strong demand for new schools of choice, will they be created? Can choice schools be accountable to the public without re-creating all the regulation of public schools that the choice movement seeks to escape?

Having identified these and other key issues for research and analysis about school choice, the editors commissioned a team of distinguished law and policy scholars to explore them. Draft chapters were presented by team members for roundtable discussion and debate at a symposium held at the School of Law at the University of California—Berkeley on April 17 and 18, 1998. Additional school choice scholars were invited to attend as commentators to enrich the discussion. Thereafter, team members revised their chapters in light of comments from participants.

The authors owe a debt of gratitude to the outside commentators who attended the symposium: Marcus Cole, Stanford Law School; John Coons, University of California—Berkeley School of Law; Chris Edley, Harvard Law School; Steven Gilles, Quinnipiac College School of Law; Kenneth Godwin, University of North Texas, Department of Political Science; Margaret "Peg" Goertz, University of Pennsylvania, Graduate School of Education; Jane Hannaway, Education Policy Center at the Urban Institute; Terry Moe, Hoover Institution at Stanford University; and Janet Weiss, University of Michigan, Department of Public Policy.

We are also grateful to the Spencer Foundation of Chicago for providing the major funding for the project and to the Bank of America—Texas and the Chancellor's Office at the University of North Texas for providing supplemental funding. The University of California School of Law provided space for the symposium, and the Earl Warren Legal Institute at the law school provided logistical support, as did the Center for the Study of Education Reform at the University of North Texas. To each, we express our deep appreciation.

SCHOOL CHOICE
AND SOCIAL
CONTROVERSY

Introduction

STEPHEN D. SUGARMAN

FRANK R. KEMERER

Giving parents the right to choose the schools their children attend is an increasingly popular idea, both in practice and in public opinion. So far, the debate has centered primarily on whether school choice is a good idea. Supporters argue that it is the only way to improve the quality of schooling. Critics claim that choice will destroy public education. Competition is played off against extremism. Family preference is portrayed as either caring or selfish. Public education is at risk either because of choice or unless we try choice. The battle is waged in newspaper and magazine columns, radio and television talk shows, professional journal articles, and a steadily increasing number of books.

This volume goes beyond debating the merits of school choice to address matters of policy, politics, and law that are typically ignored in other books and in debates about the issue. Simply put, the book does not seek to make the case for or against school choice, even if some readers may detect in the chapters that follow the underlying preferences of some of the authors. Rather, it provides analysis designed to be helpful to those on all sides of the school choice debate as well as to those charged with designing and implementing school choice programs. Careful attention to these latter issues is essential if choice programs are to both improve schooling and withstand legal challenge.

Readers will learn in part 1 of the book how much choice now exists in both the public and the private sectors and where charter schools and school voucher plans (the most controversial forms of school choice) fit in that overall pattern. Policy development is influenced by the exercise of political power. Those entrenched educational interest groups representing school boards, administrators, and teachers opposed to choice may shape the form and extent of school choice programs as much as interest groups supporting school choice. Part 1 includes an examination of how theory and politics combined to influence the ebb and flow of school choice programs throughout the United States from the early flirtation with vouchers in the 1970s onward. Policy development is also influenced by systematic data gathering, evaluation, and presentation. This part of the book closes out with a look at what is known (and how much is still unknown) about the consequences of school choice, claims that advocates and opponents of choice frequently overstate.

Crucial school choice design issues that could make a world of difference in how a plan functions and who might benefit or lose from its operation are addressed in part 2. Since traditional public school finance is based upon local taxpayers funding the local public schools that local resident children attend, what lies ahead for the financing of elementary and secondary education in America if the schools that many children attend are not traditional local public schools? If there is demand for schools of choice, will schools that families want their children to attend just spring up? If not, can policy interventions overcome the obstacles to their creation? If schools of choice are to be held accountable to parents and to the state other than merely by the choices of families to enroll or withdraw their children, what are the accountability measures that will serve important public objectives but will not threaten to undermine the basic goals of school choice itself? Can legislators ensure that school choice serves equity interests, thus staving off the emergence of schools that are segregated by race and class? These issues, to which school choice supporters all too often pay scant attention, are explored in depth in part 2.

Broad legal rules are relevant to many of the most controversial aspects of school choice plans and yet are little discussed in the school choice literature. Part 3 of the book examines these underlying rules closely. They include constitutional provisions, labor laws, and civil rights laws that will be instrumental in shaping the outcomes of school choice policies and programs as public policymakers seek to avoid or to respond to litigation. If our society moves toward more experimentation with charter schools and school voucher plans (with or without the inclusion of religious schools), what are the legal rights of students and teachers already in, or seeking to study or work in, those schools? What are their constitutional and civil rights? What collective bargaining rights will teachers have? Constitutional law is a primary concern for voucher programs encompassing private religious schools. While the U.S. Supreme Court in 1998 rejected an opportunity to decide whether such programs violate the Constitution, the matter will come before the Court again in the future. At stake are the rights of families to seek religious schooling for their children as well as the rights of the private schools that seek to educate those children. Racial isolation in our public schools continues even though it has been nearly fifty years since the Court decided *Brown* v. *Board of Education*. During this period, school choice has been used both to resist desegregation and to promote integration. How can the newer forms of school choice be regulated to further racial justice? Finally, how are the legal rights of children with disabilities to be protected, and advanced, in school choice regimes? Part 3 analyzes in depth the answers to questions like these, illustrating how the development of public policy is inevitably linked to legal rules.

In chapter 1, Jeffrey Henig and Stephen Sugarman lay the groundwork for the rest of the book by describing the current dimensions of school choice. They note that, by one measure, upward of half of American families already exercise choice to some degree. The most common way is through the choice of where the family lives. Perhaps 5 million additional children are sent to a public school of choice rather than being assigned to a neighborhood school. In most cases, the family selects a specialty, alternative, magnet, or thematic school located in its district. Some families, especially of late, opt for a school in another district; and a small but very rapidly growing number select a charter school for their children. Outside the public sector, about 5 million children attend private schools, and perhaps a million more are home schooled. There is only very modest public subsidy for this latter school choice, although public funding of small-scale school voucher programs now exists in Milwaukee and Cleveland. Henig and Sugarman emphasize that families do not have an equal opportunity to choose: low-income families are more likely to be locked into an assigned public school, often in a neighborhood in which they would prefer not to live. Expansion of choice could broaden their options considerably, although the net social outcomes of expanded choice are uncertain and will probably depend importantly upon the design of any scheme—for example, whether it is focused on the poor or extends to all families and how large a financial subsidy is provided.

Robert Bulman and David Kirp describe in chapter 2 how shifting racial and educational politics have opened windows of opportunity for the implementation of choice programs rejected in the past as ideologically extreme. For example, they describe why it was not possible to include private schools in the school choice experiment undertaken in Alum Rock, California, in the early 1970s and why plans that award vouchers for private school use resurfaced twenty years later. In the contemporary setting, Bulman and Kirp examine the political factors that produced success for vouchers in Milwaukee and Cleveland but failure in California and Jersey City, New Jersey. They then turn their attention to the fastest growing segment of school choice, charter schools. The origin of charter schools, they note, stems less from ideology than from pragmatism. Together with state-level politics, this fact has led to considerable variation in legislative design. As examples, they describe the development of charter schools in California and Arizona. Unlike California, charter schools in Arizona operate more like private than like public schools, even though the Arizona plan was initially intended to stave off movement toward private school tuition vouchers. Bulman and Kirp conclude that the growing institutionalization of school choice, coupled with a continuing favorable political climate, augurs for its endurance but that charters may well play a far larger role than vouchers.

Jeffrey Henig provides in chapter 3 a comprehensive review of the research literature on school choice. Henig shows that, as empirical studies have become more numerous and more sophisticated, some trends are beginning to emerge. For example, demand appears to grow after choice plans are in place for awhile. Yet inadequate information remains a problem, and self-segregation is common. Henig describes a number of research findings regarding supply-side consequences of choice. Included among them is the potential of private schools to reduce the unit cost of education and to stimulate innovation in public schools. Private schools, he notes, also appear to afford a greater sense of community than public schools. Further, he observes that school choice in general can serve the needs of the hard-to-educate student. Finally, Henig describes the conflicted state of the research on the impact of school choice on student achievement. He concludes his chapter by suggesting that the absence of ideological consensus on the functioning of the market in education, and on the role of the government in the design and regulation of choice programs, has so far prevented the research findings from having as great an impact as they perhaps should have upon the direction that public policy takes.

Stephen Sugarman argues in chapter 4 that school choice may dramatically change the financing of U.S. public education in general. He begins by discussing why and how public schools are currently funded. Because that funding is so dependent upon wealth, significant disparities in resources available per student exist among states, school districts, and schools. Sugarman then turns to the funding of public school choice and illustrates how interdistrict choice plans and charter schools serve to expose the inequities in the current system and may eventually make them intolerable. In the latter part of the chapter, he explores the potential funding of private education. He describes and critiques the traditional concentration of public subsidy on public education and then focuses on recent efforts to increase the flow of public money to private schools through vouchers. Should the trend continue, he observes, subsidized private school choice that is favorable to low-income families may also sharply increase the pressure to change how we fund regular public schools. In short, it is possible that school choice could do for school finance reform what thirty years of school finance litigation has failed to achieve.

In chapter 5, Paul Hill shows how a lack of attention to school choice start-up problems will limit the availability of distinctive, consistent, and reliable schools, regardless of how much demand exists for such schools. Hill argues that because today's public schools are too bureaucratically organized and too committed to a reform-by-investment, one-size-fits-all mentality, they are unlikely to provide an adequate supply of the new schools that families would want. He also explains why demand alone will not generate a rapid increase in supply from the private sector. Hill concedes that charter schools represent a good start on increasing supply, but he contends that, because of the inexperience of charter school operators and their misguided acceptance of undesirable accountability arrangements, this movement as it now stands will also fail on the supply side. As a solution, Hill emphasizes the need for new enabling and facilitating entities. These bodies, which should be developed through public-private partnership, can be organized to provide training and expertise that will help replicate successful schools, make school facilities fairly available to all providers, and provide start-up and ongoing management services to ensure that interested educators can take full advantage of whatever new choice arrangements emerge.

Previous writers have commented on the significance accountability plays in the outcomes of school choice. Too much regulation to ensure accountability undermines the potential of school choice to improve education. Too little leaves the way open for abuses. In chapter 6, Frank Kemerer presents a model accountability system for public policymakers that serves the interests of the family and the state without unnecessarily intruding on institutional autonomy. His model focuses especially on the roles of information provision, achievement testing, financial auditing, and the promotion of tolerance. His proposals are based on both empirical findings and legal and policy considerations. Kemerer shows that, like traditional public schools, school choice programs tend to be ethnically and economically segregated. In response, he proposes requiring all choice schools to comply with a 20 percent set-aside for low-income families. Constituting both a sanction and an incentive, the set-side is designed to further school integration across race and class without running afoul of federal law.

In chapter 7, Robert O'Neil examines whether the Constitution imposes on choice schools the obligation to recognize the constitutional rights of their teachers and students just as traditional public schools must do. The answer, he shows, depends upon whether the school's conduct constitutes state action under the Fourteenth Amendment. First, O'Neil discusses the relatively easy cases involving charter schools (which do meet the state action requirement) and parents educating their children at home (which do not). Then he examines the hard case of publicly funded private schools. O'Neil explains why the U.S. Supreme Court decision in *Rendell-Baker* v. *Kohn* does not necessarily provide the definitive answer, even though in that case the Court concluded that the Constitution did not apply to decisions made by a private school that was almost entirely publicly funded. By drawing upon other precedents, he presents a set of circumstances under which a federal court might well conclude that private voucher schools are subject to racial and gender discrimination law, due process, and possibly free speech constraints after all. Finally, he points out that while constitutional standards might simply be imposed as a legislative condition of participation in a school choice plan, it is nonetheless uncertain whether the full imposition of the Constitution on private schools of choice would be socially desirable.

Jesse Choper takes up the question in chapter 8 of how the religion and speech clauses of the First Amendment affect the participation of religious private schools in school choice programs. After reviewing the major U.S. Supreme Court rulings on aid to religious private schooling, Choper concludes that, while Court decisions since the early 1980s have opened a window of opportunity for programs that channel money to parents for underwriting the costs of religious private school tuition, the constitutional viability of school voucher programs is by no means clear. This is especially so because the uncertain views of a single Supreme Court justice (Sandra Day O'Connor) may well be determinative, at least if Court membership does not change. Assuming that it would not violate the establishment clause to include religious schools in a school choice scheme, Choper then explores whether it would be unconstitutional to exclude them from a plan that includes other private schools. His analysis demonstrates that the resolution of two pivotal, but divergent, Supreme Court rulings in the free speech area are key to the answer of this question. Finally, Choper addresses, on the one hand, whether religious private schools participating in a publicly funded choice program could constitutionally impose religious restrictions in such areas as admissions and employment and, on the other hand, whether states could forbid such discrimination. Again, he points out the somewhat inconsistent implications of existing case law but, in the end, concludes that parents might well successfully challenge substantial government intrusion into the autonomy of religious schools.

One of the most sensitive and controversial issues associated with school choice is its impact on racial and ethnic minorities. In chapter 9, Betsy Levin explores whether school choice will enhance opportunities for racial justice or aggravate the separatism that already exists in American education. She examines the history of school choice during the 1960s in perpetuating a dual school system and its relevance to the attitudes of racial and ethnic minority leaders today. Levin discusses the politics of choice that has brought about an alliance between conservatives and inner-city minority groups and notes an apparent divergence in the attitudes of national civil rights leaders and local community activists about the potential of school choice as a school reform measure. Then she explores the extent to which choice now is exercised by racial and ethnic minorities and what conclusions, if any, can be drawn from that experience. Additional topics discussed in this chapter include the perceived advantages of choice to minority communities, whether the supply of choice opportunities will grow to meet the demands of racial and ethnic minorities at the same pace as for nonminorities, whether the quality and experience of teachers will be similar, whether admissions criteria will operate to limit access for racial and ethnic minorities, and whether adequate resources will be available to facilitate equality of opportunity for minority parents to choose. Levin concludes by reviewing school choice design features that may minimize some of the risks and enhance opportunities for achieving racial, ethnic, and economic justice without undermining the opportunity for school choice to improve education and without disadvantaging those left behind in traditional public schools during the transition to a broader choice system.

Because unions represent the vast majority of American teachers, there is no question that they are key players in the design and implementation of school choice programs. In chapter 10, William Buss analyzes how school choice affects the role of unions and the collective bargaining process. Buss first examines why teachers' unions are generally opposed to school choice and the actions they have taken to shape school choice legislation. He then explores the possibility that school choice could pave the way to a new form of teacher unionism. Next, Buss relates the existing federal and state legal framework to issues involving collective bargaining in the context of charters and voucher schools. Will the teachers in those schools be represented by unions at all? If so, how will the development of school choice affect who is in the bargaining unit? For example, are teachers who serve on charter school governing boards or in a managerial capacity eligible for union membership? How will the union's influence over school operations be different in the choice setting than in the current setting, in which the union is often responsible for the election of the officials who oppose them at the bargaining table? Does union involvement leave room for individualized incentives like merit pay or increased teacher autonomy?

In the book's final chapter, Laura Rothstein examines how children with disabilities are likely to fare in school choice programs. She lays out the essentials of federal disability law, including amendments enacted in 1997 that affect choice schools. Rothstein describes the experience of children with disabilities in older forms of public school choice, such as alternative and magnet schools, and then she examines how federal disability law affects charter schools. She identifies potential barriers to equal access for children with disabilities and suggests some possible solutions. Then Rothstein examines the role private schools have played in serving children with disabilities in the past and identifies potential problems that voucher programs pose for children with disabilities. Included among them are limited funding, lack of expertise, student selection, and the tension between mainstreaming and the development of specialty schools targeted to children with disabilities. Though skeptical of voucher plans, Rothstein concludes by identifying ways in which public policymakers could improve their design so that children with disabilities are not left behind.

Is school choice a threat or an opportunity? We think the right answer is not yes or no but rather "It depends" or, perhaps, "Both." For example, the politics of school choice to date has been especially contentious with respect to the impact of choice on minority children from low-income families. Many people are concerned that choice will yield racially and ethnically distinctive schools, even when those schools are filled with minority children whose families happily chose to send them there. Others, of course, want these families to have the same range of choices now practically available to wealthy white families who elect to live near each other in exclusive suburbs and use the public schools.

Furthermore, some of those liberals who favor school choice for inner-city, poor children view with unease the support they receive from conservatives. These liberals like the idea of narrowly focused choice schemes but fear that, once such a voucher program is in place, conservatives will seek to transform it in ways that submerge, rather than enhance, the interests of minority group families. For example, Polly Williams, a key legislative backer of vouchers for low-income families in Milwaukee, has expressed misgivings about the recent expansion of school choice there to include both charter schools and religious schools in the voucher plan, worrying that the system will now most benefit white churches, white-run private schools, and white students. "Affluent folks are going to take it all on as their own," she told *Education Week*. "Yuppies who have choices are going to be the beneficiaries now."

This dispute reveals at least two central points. First, sometimes principles are at stake in the school choice debate that are little affected by facts or program design. Second, the consequences of school choice will vary greatly depending upon what sort of plan one has in mind and which children one looks at. The chapters of this book demonstrate the importance of the second point. If future political debates about choice include much more careful attention to the legal and policy issues canvassed here, we will be content that this book will have made a useful contribution.

PART ONE

Emerging Patterns

CHAPTER ONE

The Nature and Extent of School Choice

JEFFREY R. HENIG

STEPHEN D. SUGARMAN

Advocates of charter schools, school vouchers, and sim-ilar school reform ideas often talk as though American families today have no choice as to where they send their children for elementary and secondary schooling. These critics of the traditional public education bureaucracy typically portray it as an unresponsive and inefficient monopoly that simply assigns children to a school based upon their home address.[1] This description fails to capture the very considerable degree to which families already select the schools their children attend.

This chapter describes the nature and extent of school choice currently available and exercised. Accurately tallying up the choosers is difficult for several reasons, which we explore below; but it is worth noting at the outset that, by one plausible way of counting, more than half of American families now exercise school choice. Considerably more of that choice occurs in the public sector than in the private sector. Further, some families have more choice than others.

That the current system provides more opportunities for school choice than is typically acknowledged does not directly speak to the question of whether altering the access or allocation of school choice would be a good idea. It does suggest, however, that there is grist for empirical analysis of issues that have tended to be debated in abstract and theoretical terms.

Public School Choice

Most American children attend a public school to which they are assigned, usually on the basis of where they live. This is hardly the same as saying families have no choice. A world of no choice would be one in which families were told where they had to live and in which children in each neighborhood were required to go to school together; or in which the federal government gathered up all of America's young and sent them off to boarding schools based upon, say, a lottery or what a team of professionals thought was best for the children or for the nation. Our world, however, is very different. Put simply, by deciding where they live, families can generally determine which public schools their children will attend.

Choice of Residence

Given that reality, one might be tempted to say that all or nearly all parents are making a school choice for their children. After all, if their children are enrolled in neighborhood public schools, then merely by deciding *not* to move somewhere else, the parents are choosing to retain those assignments. It is probably fair to say that, at the extreme, if their lives depended upon it, or if their children's lives depended upon it, nearly all families could, and would, move. Surely most people would agree that the decision not to move is a far too expansive notion of what constitutes making a school choice for one's children. Inequities in the distribution of income and wealth, along with racial discrimination that persists despite open-housing legislation, mean that residential mobility is an option that is far more available to some families than others. On the other hand, it would just as surely be a mistake to say that no one chooses their child's school by deciding where to live.

Clearly, the residential choices made by a large number of families are very much driven by school choice. Many families first decide precisely where they want their children to go to school, and having done that, they find a house or apartment in the right location. So many a household changes residence in anticipation of the eldest child heading off to kindergarten. Cross-national evidence suggests that the rate of moving among households with young children is especially high in the United States.[2] Other families take schools generally into account when deciding where to live. For example, when moving into a metropolitan area many families opt for the suburbs, or for a specific suburb, because of the reputation of the schools. Realtors typically provide information about the schools near the homes they are trying to sell. There are books and consultants available to provide advice about the schooling consequences of a new place to live. Still other families deliberately move to get away from a poorly performing school or a bad school experience their children have had.

It is also clear that many families pay little or no attention to the local schools when deciding where to live. Some families can only afford to live in one or two parts of town, and they will take the first adequate home or apartment that comes their way. Indeed, poor families seeking subsidized housing often have no choice at all as to where they live; they just take the one apartment offered to them by the local housing authority. Other parents may feel unwelcome in a new neighborhood or find it uncomfortable or otherwise undesirable to move away from where they were raised. Some families in this broad category might well wish to make a different school choice for their children but feel constrained to accept the local public school because of a sense that their residential opportunities are so circumscribed. It is important to remember too, of course, that for some poor families residential mobility may be imposed, not selected. Changing rents, job loss, or marital breakup can force parents to relocate against their will. One study found that children living with only one parent move twice as frequently as those living in two-parent households.[3] Largely involuntary mobility in some low-income areas creates tremendous barriers to learning, both for the students who move and for the schools that must accommodate them.[4]

Other families could take schools into account when making a choice of residence, but they do not. Some, for example, move to new communities for employment opportunities and make their housing choices at a time when they are uninformed about the schools. Many couples move into a house or apartment before they have children, oblivious to the schooling situation, and simply stay on when they become parents, never really considering moving for schools that might be better for their children. There are those who put their own convenience (say, proximity to work) or taste (say, the kind of house they live in) ahead of any consideration of the local schools. Indeed, some parents may care little about their children's education, and still others may believe that they would not be very good at selecting a school if they tried. What all of these families know is that, wherever they live, there will be a public school available for their children. For some, that is good enough—just like the comfort many people take in knowing that there is a fire department somewhere in the neighborhood.

There are no reliable data on how many families fall into these categories. It is not even clear which types of family described above ought to be counted as intentionally choosing their children's schools by deciding where to live. Is it enough that they thought at all about the neighborhood schools? Must the school have been decisive in determining where they live? What if the local school was really their second choice but the house was wonderful and that is why they made the decision? About the best we can do for now is report what parents say when asked in surveys. For example, in the National Household Education Survey conducted in 1993 by the National Center for Education Statistics, about half the parents whose children were assigned to the local public school claimed that "their choice of residence was influenced by where their children would go to school."[5] This, of course, is a very vague statement. Nevertheless, if all of those families were counted as intentionally making a school choice through their housing location, then we are talking about something like 18 or 19 million schoolchildren, a level that would swamp all of the other school choices now occurring.[6]

Even if only 25 percent of all public school–using families were said to be making deliberate school choices through residential selection, that would cover more than 11 million children—approximately equal to the aggregate of all other sorts of school choice. Regardless of what the "right" number is, surely it is true that, for upper-middle-class and wealthier families who have considerable residential flexibility, school choice through housing choice is a potent and much-exercised option. The 1993 study noted above found that, in households with income of $50,000 or more, 60 percent of the parents whose children attended an assigned public school took the schools into account in deciding where to live, in contrast to parents of just over 40 percent of the children in households with less than $15,000 in income. Race, partly because of its correlation with income, but for other reasons as well, also can be associated with differential access to residential mobility as a vehicle for school choice. There is at least some evidence, though, that such racial barriers are diminishing. Relocation from central cities to suburbs by young white families with school-age children was a familiar pattern in older metropolitan areas during the 1950s and 1960s; there is convincing evidence that there exists a new pattern of black suburbanization that mimics the early white pattern in important respects.[7]

It is perhaps also worth noting that living in a specific place does not always guarantee access to the closest, or most convenient, public school. Sometimes quirks of attendance-area boundary drawing or problems of school overcrowding have caused certain homes or blocks to be connected to schools in less convenient locations (although families may well learn about this before they move in). In addition, some children are assigned to out-of-neighborhood schools for reasons of racial balance, either pursuant to a court order or because of a school district's own decision, although this sort of busing appears to be very much on the decline. Again, families might well be aware of what sort of busing may be in store for them before they make their residential choice.

From time to time, public school attendance areas are redrawn, perhaps because new schools are opened or others are closed. These decisions often generate considerable local resentment, suggesting that the objectors care very much about their children's current school or at least are quite unhappy about the pending disruption.

Intradistrict Choice

Even when we exclude those who exercise choice via their housing location decisions, about half of the school choice now being exercised by American families is taking place in the public education system. Around 10 percent of elementary and secondary school students appear to be enrolled in public schools that were not assigned to them by virtue of where they live.[8] The most common type of public school choice is intradistrict choice. That is, a significant number of children (perhaps 4 or 5 million) attend public schools run by their local school district that have been deliberately selected by their families in response to some sort of choice opportunity (that is, other than by mere assignment based on residence). Often, but not always, these schools are not the ones located nearest to where the family lives. These intradistrict choice schemes come in several varieties.

NONNEIGHBORHOOD SCHOOLS. About one in seven school districts, and more than one in three districts with more than 10,000 pupils, has identified one or more schools as nonneighborhood schools.[9] These schools might be termed alternative or experimental or thematic or selective, and they have been created for a variety of reasons. Sometimes admission is on a first-come, first-served basis or by lottery. Sometimes selection criteria are imposed by districts that operate talent-based schools in math and science, the arts, and so on. Some districts impose racial criteria on these programs—for example, by giving preference to those children whose presence will promote racial balance. In any event, students only attend because of family choice, with no preference given to those who happen to live closest. Of course, some families may enroll their children in such a school precisely because it is near to where they live.

Some of the earliest examples of school choice of this sort can be found among the various specialty schools that offer innovative or accelerated programs for students whose high-level aptitude or creativity are not well or easily served by the conventional curriculum. The oldest among these have roots in the progressive education movement dating from the 1920s. Walnut Hills High School in Cincinnati, for example, was established in 1918 to serve academically gifted children; similar programs have long existed elsewhere, including the Bronx High School of Science in New York City, Lowell High School in San Francisco, and Boston's Latin School.[10] Specialty schools providing technical and vocational training and special schools for troubled youngsters also have deep historical roots.

A second major wave of alternative school formation occurred in the 1960s and early 1970s, often in response to parental and teacher pressures for a nontraditional curriculum. Because there is no universally recognized definition of what constitutes a specialty or alternative school, estimates of their prevalence necessarily are imprecise, but one source indicates that there are more than 2,200 of these choice schools in more than 1,000 districts.[11] Amy Wells puts the number at between 3,000 and 6,000 public alternative schools.[12] One study found that 3 million children attend such schools; another put the number even higher.[13]

Magnet schools are another important source of intradistrict choice, although they currently serve fewer students than do specialty and alternative schools. The magnet label is usually attached to choice schools that were intentionally developed as part of a school district's plan, sometimes in response to a judicial order, to achieve school integration without relying exclusively on mandatory reassignment. These schools generally use racial balance criteria in selecting among those who apply. Beginning in the mid-1970s, the number of magnet schools expanded rapidly for about ten or fifteen years. A 1982 study found 1,019 magnets in 138 districts, an increase from 14 districts in 1975. A 1995 study estimates that 1.2 million students were attending magnet programs in 2,433 schools located in 230 districts.[14] Magnet schools are, for the most part, an option limited to urban areas, especially large and racially heterogeneous central cities. Based on the 1990 National Educational Longitudinal Survey (NELS), Adam Gamoran found that city students were almost three times more likely than the national average to attend magnet public high schools.[15]

School choice in the magnet school setting is meant to serve the opposite function than was intended by some school districts in the South that were engaged in "massive resistance" in the early years after Brown v. Board of Education.[16] Rather than dismantle their previously all-white and all-black schools, some public school officials merely adopted the rule that students of either race could voluntarily transfer to any other school in the district. Unsurprisingly, this failed to generate a rush of white students to the black schools, and African American families claimed that their children would not at all be welcome at the hostile white schools. The U.S. Supreme Court held this pseudochoice regime unconstitutional in *Green v. County School Board*.[17] The legacy of that strategy is that some advocates of school integration have been leery of choice ever since.

NO NEIGHBORHOOD SCHOOLS. In a relatively few public school districts, all of the public schools are choice schools. Cambridge, Massachusetts, developed this scheme in 1981, followed later by cities such as Buffalo, New York; Montclair, New Jersey; and Berkeley, California. Children are not assigned to schools on the basis of neighborhood or given an entitlement to attend the school located closest to where they live. Every family must make a choice; many in fact opt for their neighborhood school. These communities generally impose racial balance criteria on the school selection process. Indeed, they have generally adopted this so-called controlled-choice approach as a way of eliminating racial isolation in their schools, often in the face of real or threatened judicial intervention. In a legal current environment in which judicial intervention for racial balance purposes is less probable, large-scale, controlled-choice plans now appear to be relatively rare, although some smaller districts have voluntarily adopted this scheme in recent years.[18] Possibly because of its Cambridge origins, this approach appears to be most popular in Massachusetts, where, for example, at least nine districts adopted controlled-choice plans between 1987 and 1991.[19]

Some districts have moved toward districtwide choice, less as a tool for integration and more as a vehicle for encouraging educational innovation and accommodating families and children with diverse interests and needs. Indeed, in some places school authorities aggressively promote the obligation of families to choose among schools. New York City's District 4 is a prominent example. The community school district in the East Harlem area of the city began experimenting with public school choice around 1974, and in 1982 it eliminated attendance zones for all junior high students. This reform was the outcome of a coalition of renegade teachers, entrepreneurial bureaucrats, and a core of dissatisfied parents and community activists.[20]

INDIVIDUAL TRANSFERS. Some families would like to enroll their children in a neighborhood school that is located inside their district but in another neighborhood. In other words, they seek to add choice on top of what is otherwise basically a system of assignment by place of residence.

Traditionally, public school districts have been highly reluctant to grant these requests as a matter of course, even if there is room in the desired school. In recent years, however, some districts have begun to welcome transfer petitions, or at least they welcome them if they promote, or do not undermine, racial balance. New York City is one example. Based largely on the perceived success of District 4, the New York City Board of Education, in 1993, established a general program to facilitate choice across all of its thirty-two community school districts. With New York City public schools currently serving well over a half million children, this policy, in theory, provides choice to a huge potential clientele, albeit in an attenuated form.

Yet while nominally allowing students to transfer freely, the New York program restricts cross-community district transfers to cases in which space is available. In other words, neighborhood children still have first priority. Moreover, due to the high-enrollment pressures on New York City schools, space for outsiders usually is not available.[21] The New York City choice plan is very different from mandatory choice schemes, such as Cambridge's controlled-choice plan, but when out-of-neighborhood schools they prefer have spaces available New York parents are allowed to enroll their children in them.

In most districts, as noted, there are no such entitlements. Instead, individual transfer requests are still generally granted only for good cause—typically because the child is having a serious problem in the neighborhood school that cannot be readily solved there. To be sure, school districts vary quite a bit in the rigidity and uniformity with which they apply their attendance zone policies. Some districts have clear and explicit provisions for transfers—for example, when a child wants or needs a special program not available at the home school. Others have an informal process by which aggressive parents can obtain exceptions, sometimes by working with local principals and sometimes by lobbying their school board representative. In some communities, there are formal mechanisms with appeals processes that families seeking transfers may utilize. Washington, D.C., for example, combines some formal choice options (for example, an academic high school, a school of the performing arts, and special vocational skills programs) with a largely sub-rosa process in which principals in charge of neighborhood schools are given enormous discretion about whether to accept children seeking entry from outside their attendance zone. The official records on discretionary out-of-boundary enrollment deal only with transfers that have been officially sanctioned, and the official count indicates that there were more than 9,900 such enrollments in March 1994, accounting for about one in eight of the District's pupils.[22] This leaves out the many reputed cases of students using addresses of friends or relatives in order to gain access to a more desirable school.

Interdistrict Choice

Some families wish to enroll their children in public schools located in other districts. Again, the public schools have traditionally opposed these requests except when very convincing reasons are given. School finance arrangements often discourage such transfers, especially if the rules of the game require both districts to approve, since it is often to the economic disadvantage of one of the districts. In some places, districts are willing to trade—that is, they will approve these requests on a one-for-one basis. Recently, however, interdistrict choice has expanded. According to one report, eighteen states have adopted choice plans that give children rights to enroll in public schools outside their district of residence.[23] Minnesota's open-enrollment program, phased in between 1987 and 1990, allows students in grades kindergarten through twelve to apply to schools anywhere in the state. Home districts may not prevent a student from attending school in another district, and receiving districts may not deny applications to enter their schools unless space is unavailable.[24] Although the Minnesota example has sparked a wave of copycat legislation, these plans differ somewhat from state to state. For example, in some states, school districts have the option of participating or not; if they do not, then neither may their students leave, nor may others enter. Ohio's experience, for example, has been that the major urban school districts have opted not to participate for fear of losing far more students than they could expect to attract.[25]

The key change brought about by interdistrict transfer plans is that students may leave without obtaining the permission of their home district. Nonetheless, children of families already living in the desired district have priority rights to attend their own district's schools. This means, in practice, that receiving districts can probably block in-transfers they oppose by refusing to acknowledge that they have space available. Other interdistrict voluntary transfer schemes have been adopted as part of metropolitan school desegregation efforts. In some of those plans, inner-city magnet schools are open to both in-district and out-of-district pupils on terms that will help further the community's racial balance goals. A few suburban districts have voluntarily opened their doors to inner-city schoolchildren as a way of promoting integration, but these programs tend to be very small in scale. Broader participation of the suburban schools has depended upon the forceful intervention of federal courts or state officials. Federal courts have very occasionally overseen the establishment of widespread interdistrict choice arrangements as a means of addressing metropolitan racial segregation; but in light of the Supreme Court's refusal to order integration of the public schools throughout the Detroit metropolitan area absent a showing of intentional exclusion of African American children from the suburban schools,[26] they have been much less likely to get involved in cross-district remedies than those restricted to local district lines.[27]

According to one survey, about 200,000 children nationwide (fewer than 0.5 percent of all public schoolchildren) were participating in various interdistrict choice programs in 1993.[28] Since this study, more states have enacted interdistrict choice schemes, and the opportunity generally has probably become more widely known. For example, in Iowa 2.6 percent of the public school pupil population was participating when the plan reached its seventh year of operation in 1996–97; Minnesota's grew from 1.2 percent in the first years to 2.3 percent; and Washington had 2 percent participating after four years.[29] This is to be contrasted with a participation rate of less than 2 percent in states with such programs in 1993–94.[30]

One additional phenomenon worth attention is the giving of a false address. Some families either so much dislike their neighborhood public school or so prefer another public school, or both, that they pretend that their children are living other than where they really are. By providing school officials with a false address, they seek to gain admittance to a different school. This is a highly motivated form of school choice. Informal inquiries suggest to us that sometimes school districts are very casual about this matter, especially when the parents are jumping from one school to another within the district. Perhaps officials are happy that parents care so much; and in some cases officials may be eager not to have public attention drawn to the reasons that some parents are fleeing certain schools. Occasional news accounts suggest that other times school districts try to be very strict, especially when the false address is outside of the pupil's home district. Often money considerations lie behind this rigidity. Either a district does not want to lose its children to other districts because of the state funds it will forfeit, or the receiving district does not want to have to pay to educate the children from other districts even if it were to get some extra state funds for additional enrollees. Not surprisingly, there are no reliable data as to the number of families who exercise choice by giving false addresses. Washington, D.C., school officials have estimated that about 4,000 to 7,000 students (as much as one in ten) attending schools in the school system actually live in surrounding jurisdictions.[31]

Charter Schools

Charter schools are the latest development in schools of choice, and at the moment, they are the most rapidly expanding form of school choice. These schools are deliberately designed to straddle the line traditionally distinguishing public from private schools. That is, they are officially public schools, but the charter concept envisions that they are to be quite independent in their management. (A great deal of attention is given to them in later chapters of this book.)

In many states, public authorities may provide charters both to existing public schools (often termed conversion schools) and to new schools (often formed by entrepreneurs of various sorts).[32] Charter schools receive public funding on a per student basis, are often responsible for achieving educational outcomes defined by their chartering body, and are subject to public oversight. Yet their charters are usually designed to exempt them from many of the rules and regulations that bind regular public schools to specific standards and procedures. States vary as to whether a would-be charter school is to seek its charter from the local district, a state agency, or either.

Minnesota, the national leader in public school interdistrict choice, also took the lead in the charter school movement, enacting the first legislation in 1991. By July 1996, charter laws were in place in twenty-five states and the District of Columbia. As recently as 1993–94, however, there were only an estimated 32 charter schools actually in operation, all but 6 of them in California. By 1995–96 that number had increased to about 250, and in January 1997 there were 428 charter schools in operation nationwide.[33] In the 1997–98 school year, it has been estimated that as many as 170,000 to 200,000 students attended about 700 charter schools.[34] Going into the 1998–99 school year, Arizona, California, and Michigan together accounted for more than half of the nation's charter schools.[35] At this rate of increase, charter schools could easily be serving more than a million pupils in the near future. Whether this growth rate can be sustained is another matter, however, and is explored in depth in Paul Hill's chapter in this book.

So far, charter schools typically draw pupils from the district in which they are located, although some charter schools draw generally from the broader community, and this may be a growing phenomenon in the future.

Generally speaking, charter schools admit on a first-come, first-served basis or by lottery, without giving preference based upon where pupils live. In this respect, charter schools are much like those magnet, alternative, and other such choice schools that many districts have been operating for years.

Private School Choice

Although there is a great deal of debate right now about voucher plans that would facilitate greater private school choice, nonpublic education has long been a matter of controversy.

A Little History

What we think of today as the Catholic school system came about because of Catholics' religious differences with Protestants, who effectively exercised political control over the public school system as it came into its own during the last half of the nineteenth century.[36] Although the public schools in that era were not formally religious schools, Protestant prayers were usually said; Catholics created their own system as a way to preserve their religious identity. In later years, with even larger numbers of Catholic immigrants, the Catholic school system grew. Following World War I, however, the nativism movement that swept the country sought, among other things, to force all Catholic children into public schools by prohibiting families from sending their children to private schools. In two famous decisions from the 1920s, *Pierce* v. *Society of Sisters* and *Meyer* v. *Nebraska*, the U.S. Supreme Court struck down these controls on parents' rights to direct the education of their children.[37] Families won the constitutional right to send their children to private schools, subject to the reasonable regulation of those schools by the state.

Renewed controversies over the use of private schools broke out again in the late 1950s and early 1960s, as some southern families, seeking to avoid the requirements of *Brown* v. *Board of Education*, turned to private white academies to educate their children. Although the earlier *Pierce* decision ensured families the right to private schooling, the U.S. Supreme Court hemmed in these clearly racially motivated endeavors. First, the Court said that districts could not simply close down their public schools in order to avoid integrating them.[38] Then it barred the payment of publicly funded tuition assistance to families attending the white academies.[39] In 1976 it held that a post–Civil War era statute provided the legal grounds by which an African American child could successfully challenge a private school's racially discriminatory admissions policy, although it was never clear that anyone suing such a school would actually want to attend.[40] Along the way, racially discriminatory private schools also lost their right to tax-exempt status.[41]

Attendance at private schools in the South has not become widespread: fewer than 10 percent of the pupils attend private schools in every southern state except Louisiana, which has a substantial Catholic population.[42] Nonetheless, this experience with open racism in private education continues to make many people nervous about nonpublic schools. Indeed, racial, religious, and social class exclusivity—three things that private schools have stood for at various times in our history—are exactly what they see themselves as fighting against.

Some Numbers

About 5 million children, or around 10 percent of the approximately 50 million children in school, attend private schools; about 85 percent of these attend religious schools.[43] In contrast to the past, however, Catholic schools are no longer as dominant. In 1970, about 70 percent of private schools were Catholic.[44] In 1998 Catholic schools accounted for about half of private school pupils; other religious schools accounted for about 35 percent.[45] The largest growth in private education over the past thirty years has been among conservative Christian schools, which enrolled around 14 percent of all private school pupils in 1995–96. Although only 15 percent of private school enrollment is in nonreligious schools, these get considerable attention in nearly every urban area because some of them are well patronized by elites. Some of these nonreligious, private schools specialize in the education of children with substantial disabilities (numbering perhaps 100,000).

Most private school enrollment is, of course, the result of individual family decisions. There was a time when many families sent their children to private school essentially unthinkingly—that is, as though there really was no question (or choice) about it. Imagine Catholic families in certain Catholic neighborhoods where everyone used the local Catholic school. For such families, as a practical matter, having their children attend the local parish elementary school followed as directly from the family's place of residence as did local public school attendance follow for most non-Catholic families. Moreover, for many of those Catholic families it was by no means a deliberate choice to live in a particular place in order to enroll their children in a particular Catholic school. Today, however, it seems very much the case that the decision to send one's children to a religious school is a deliberate one. In the early 1960s more than 40 percent of Catholic children attended Catholic schools (and surely the numbers were much higher in certain parishes), whereas by the early 1990s that proportion appears to have dropped to less than 20 percent.[46]

Home Schooling

Over the past thirty years there appears to have been a huge increase in home schooling—that is, keeping children out of formal schools and educating them at home.[47] This does not mean that these children are completely isolated from other children. Home school parents often band together for group activities; sometimes they share a church affiliation, sometimes they go on field trips together, sometimes their children play together when young and later play on the same sports teams (although they often find it difficult to get official school teams to play against them).

In some places, home schoolers have formed cooperative schools, with some shared teaching. Some have formed charter schools, thereby obtaining public funding. In a few places, home school parents have signed on with public school districts as carrying out independent study. This arrangement typically gives the school district another pupil for state financial aid purposes, while giving parents some tangible assistance from the district in the form of books and materials, visitation and advice from a teacher or curriculum specialist, perhaps funding for a computer, and so on. In other places, home schooling may be counted as part of the private school tally, and some home school parents officially form schools for their own children to attend in order to comply with state compulsory education laws. Sometimes home schooling is separately counted. Public officials often do not know the extent of home schooling going on (especially with the decline in an effective truancy officer corps), so many home-schooled children are not counted at all. Nevertheless, one home school organization claims that some 1.23 million children were being home schooled in the United States in the fall of 1996.[48] (This number might be very inaccurate, although the authors claim it is correct within 10 percent.) Patricia Lines, who has tracked home schooling for the U.S. Department of Education, estimates the number of home-schooled children at roughly 1 million.[49]

School Vouchers

Publicly funded vouchers (or scholarships) that may be used by parents to pay for their children's education at private religious and secular schools remain the favored choice vehicles for many school reformers. (Like charter schools, this idea is given considerable attention throughout this book.) School vouchers have gained academic and political support from some economists and business leaders, who predict great things from the competition that vouchers are meant to inject into the existing system, and from some pluralists, who believe that families, rather than the government, should decide what sort of education their children should receive. Although vouchers are often characterized as a conservative or libertarian and Republican idea, certain regulated school voucher plans have won the support of some Democrats who think of themselves as progressives.

Milton Friedman, the Nobel laureate economist, has favored providing unregulated school vouchers to all families, but his proposal has not enjoyed widespread political popularity and is nowhere in place in the United States.[50] Moreover, despite some recent court decisions favorable to school vouchers, doubts remain about the legality of including religious schools in such plans. Conversely, some observers doubt whether the government may legally permit vouchers to be used exclusively at private, nonreligious schools. Nevertheless, there have been some important developments on this front over the past several years.

Without question, the most visible and intensely examined school choice program is Milwaukee's experiment with vouchers for low-income students. Since 1990, Wisconsin has permitted a limited number of Milwaukee families to attend private, nonreligious schools at public expense. In 1996–97, about 1,600 students took advantage of this program. The state legislature's decision in 1995 to permit the vouchers to be used at religious schools was tied up in court for several years. In June 1998 the Wisconsin Supreme Court upheld the extension, and in the fall of 1998 the U.S. Supreme Court declined to review the case.[51] Hence religious schools are now participating in the plan, and the number of participating students grew to 6,000 by 1999. (These legal issues are discussed extensively in Jesse Choper's chapter in this book.) Following in Wisconsin's footsteps, the Ohio legislature instituted a voucher program for low-income students in Cleveland. Cleveland's program was designed to be somewhat larger than Milwaukee's and included religious schools right from the start. As of April 1997, about 2,000 students were enrolled in fifty-five participating private schools, forty-six of which were religious schools; by the end of the 1998–99 school year, 3,500 pupils were in the program.[52] Cleveland's inclusion of religious schools is also under legal attack. (Later chapters of this book, especially Jeffrey Henig's, address what lessons, if any, may be drawn from these two rather small experiments.)

In the middle of 1999, Florida adopted a plan to provide school vouchers of substantial value to children otherwise assigned to the state's worst public schools. Fewer than 1,000 children were scheduled to be eligible in the first year, but the numbers could quickly grow to as many as 25,000. The vouchers could be used in both religious and nonparochial schools. Opponents immediately challenged the plan in court.[53]

While the Milwaukee and Cleveland plans have been dogged by legal and political controversy, a privately funded movement has quietly grown that provides scholarships to children from low-income families. This movement now has programs in cities across the country, and far more children are attending private schools of choice with these vouchers than in the Milwaukee and Cleveland plans combined. According to the Center for Education Reform, a prochoice group, at least sixty-five private sector scholarship programs were operating by the summer of 1999.[54] Partners Advancing Values in Education (PAVE), which claims to be the largest privately funded kindergarten through twelfth grade scholarship program in the country, provided more than 4,300 scholarships, worth $3.5 million, to Milwaukee students in 1995–96.[55] PAVE receives funding from nearly forty-nine foundations and fifty corporations and businesses. Other important private scholarship programs include the Indianapolis program initiated by the Golden Rule Insurance Company, the Children's Educational Opportunity program begun in San Antonio in 1992, and the School Choice Scholarships Foundation program begun in New York City in 1997. Of these, the San Antonio program has been the most extensively and systematically studied.[56] In 1999 a substantial additional step in this direction was taken with the beginning of a nationwide private school voucher plan, when 40,000 pupils (of more than a million applicants) from low-income families in cities around the country were awarded scholarships from a $170 million fund raised in large part by financier Theodore J. Forstmann.[57]

These private scholarship plans are promoted by many of the same organizations and individuals that favor publicly funded vouchers. Although these plans face none of the legal problems, and many fewer of the political problems, that have so far limited the expansion of public voucher systems, it is currently unimaginable that private charity could sustain a nationwide private scholarship scheme that would provide choice opportunities for all the low-income families wishing to pursue them. Indeed, even where they are in place, these private scholarship plans so far have provided partial and modest funding that, as a practical matter, permit recipients, often at great effort, to seek enrollment only in low-tuition, often

Table 1-1. *Nature and Extent of School Choice Programs in the United States*

Program	Number	Percent
Total elementary and secondary schoolchildren	50.0 million	100
Schoolchildren privately educated	6.0 million	12
Tuition-paid private schools	5.0 million	10
Home schooling	1.0 million	2
Using publicly funded vouchers for private schools	a	
Using privately funded vouchers for private schools	a	
Schoolchildren in public school choice programs	23.5 million	47
Intradistrict choice programs (specialty, alternative, and magnet schools; choice districts; individual transfers; false addresses)	5.0 million	10
Interdistrict choice	0.3 million	0.6
Charter schools	0.2 million	0.4
Choice through choice of residence	18.0 million	36
Total schoolchildren in choice schools	29.5 million	59

a. Less than 0.1.

religious, private schools. In addition to doing what they see as good deeds, the supporters of these plans presumably seek to demonstrate that low-income families are interested in choice and will make sensible choices for their children by getting them into schools that better serve their needs.[58] Whether this movement will play out in that way remains to be seen.

Summing Up

Nearly 60 percent of all schoolchildren in the United States attend schools of choice (table 1-1). Some of the numbers in the table are of questionable reliability; for example, the number of families said to be making choice through choice of residence should be used with great caution. But even if we put aside completely school choice through choice of residence, nearly a quarter of U.S. schoolchildren attend schools that were picked out for them. Clearly, this is a great deal more choice than many people realize or acknowledge.

On the other hand, one should keep in mind that even those making a choice may not be getting their first choice. In some cases, the family might have applied to its first-choice school, but the child was not admitted. Perhaps the school was full or the child did not meet some admissions criterion. This outcome, of course, is inevitable in any school choice regime. In other cases, the family did not apply to its first-choice school because limitations on the family's range of choice automatically ruled that school out.

For many, it is a matter of money. The family simply could not afford to make its first choice: it was too costly to pay the required tuition in the desired private school or to buy a house in the neighborhood of the desired public school. Unaffordability is sometimes an absolute: the family is living in poverty. Other families would have to make a financial sacrifice of some magnitude. Often what leads them to say that they cannot afford their first choice is that they do not have to pay for the schools made available through a public school choice plan or by moving into a neighborhood they can afford.

Even putting aside paying tuition or moving, many families who make school choices do so in a second-best world. For example, they may opt for an alternative school inside the district but would have preferred one in a neighboring district. Yet no interdistrict transfer program was available to them. That many Americans do not get their first choice of schools does not mean that the system is a failure, of course. Limited options and limited resources mean that most people do not get their first choice for most things—vacations, houses, computers, cars, as well as schools.

It goes without saying that a substantial expansion of school choice would mean that even more children would attend other than neighborhood public schools. Yet it is very difficult to make any reasonable estimate as to how many. A 1992 study predicted that 15 percent of public school pupils would switch to private schools if no tuition were required of parents.[59] Surveys that ask parents if they would send their children to private schools if the state paid the tuition reveal that a much higher proportion of parents would choose private schools for their children.[60] Yet those surveys probably significantly overestimate the number that would actually do so, at least in the early years of any such program. On the other hand, the longer that choice options are available, and the more that choosing a school becomes part of the general culture, the more likely it is that families will act upon the options made available to them.[61] In any event, the design of a broadly expanded school choice plan can greatly influence who, and how many, will take advantage of the scheme. For example, there is likely to be a world of difference between a reform that gives high-value school vouchers to low-income families exclusively and one that gives modest-value school vouchers to all families.

For now, school vouchers play a trivial role in the world of school choice. Charter schools, while expanding rapidly, still account for a very small proportion of America's schoolchildren, and almost three-quarters of the charter schools in operation are located within only seven states.[62] Fascination with these options plainly lies in their potential to transform the sorts of choice arrangement now in place. Families with limited financial means are dependent upon the public education system to start up school choice programs and to include in those programs the types of schools that the families want for their children. Charter schools and school vouchers, by contrast, contain the promise that schools will form wherever there is demand—indeed, that innovators will start new schools that will create demand. It is this prospect—of a possibly enormous expansion in the range of choice that ordinary families will have and will exercise—that excites school choice advocates.

In such a world, families would be expected to pursue choice options in their own self-interest, in most cases in what they see as the best interest of their children. While the aggregate of such decisions might be a great benefit to our nation, many fear that this sort of extensive and intensive pursuit of private interest would not be in the public interest. Again, the design details of any large-scale choice plan could play a critical role in determining the answer to this vital issue (a matter taken up in depth in Frank Kemerer's chapter in this book).

Few suggest that the public school choice that is now in place is bad for society, and many believe that the current level of private school choice, dominated as it is by the religious and nonprofit sector, has its public virtues as well. This leads choice supporters to say the more, the merrier. But a widely expanded choice regime, especially if a significant share of the supply-side is provided by those who are in it for financial profit, could have quite different consequences, both good and bad. For these reasons, it is not surprising that people of good will are divided over whether a much broader system of school choice is a threat or an opportunity.

Notes

1. Paul E. Peterson, "Monopoly and Competition in American Education," in William H. Clune and John F. Witte, eds., *Choice and Control in American Education,* vol. 1 (London: Falmer, 1990). "It is an iron law of organizations that they seek to expand their size, their scope of operation, and their autonomy from external influence," writes Peterson, and "public schools in the United States, although also constrained by competition in many ways, have come closer than most institutions to consolidating a position of monopoly power" (p. 48).

2. Larry Long, "Changing Residence: Comparative Perspectives on Its Relationship to Age, Sex, and Marital Status," *Population Studies,* vol. 46 (1992), pp. 141–58.

3. Carl Sewell, "The Impact of Pupil Mobility on Assessment of Student Achievement and Its Implications for Program Planning" (Brooklyn, N.Y.: Community School District 17, 1982).

4. Bruce C. Straits, "Residence, Migration, and School Progress," *Sociology of Education,*

vol. 60 (January 1987), pp. 34–43.

5. National Center for Education Statistics (NCES), *The Condition of Education, 1997* (U.S. Department of Education, 1997).

6. This number is derived by applying the 50 percent rate only to those families who do not otherwise exercise school choice, public or private.

7. William H. Frey, "Mover Destination Selectivity and the Changing Suburbanization of Metropolitan Whites and Blacks," *Demography*, vol. 22 (May 1985), p. 239.

8. NCES, *The Condition of Education*. How many families exercise public school choice in these many ways? A fairly rough study using 1993 data (NCES, *Use of School Choice* [U.S. Department of Education, 1995]) estimates that about 11 percent of children enrolled in grades three through twelve attend public schools that their families choose for them (other than by choosing where to live). This is about 12 percent of all public school children in those grades, and if this figure is extrapolated to cover all public school children in grades kindergarten through twelve (about 45 million children), it would amount to more than 5 million children. A somewhat more detailed study using different 1993–94 data (NCES, *Public School Choice Programs, 1993–94: Availability and Student Participation* [U.S. Department of Education, 1996]) produced more fine-tuned estimates and a somewhat smaller overall number. It found that nearly 3 million children participate in what it calls intradistrict choice programs. (This includes all children living in those districts that force all families to choose.) Another approximately 1 million children participate in magnet programs, which themselves are generally intradistrict choice schemes but which the survey counted separately. Together, these two categories amount to something over 8 percent of all public school children.

9. NCES, *Public School Choice Programs*.

10. Vernon H. Smith, *Alternative Schools: The Development of Options in Public Education* (Lincoln, Neb.: Professional Educators' Publications, 1974); Mario Fantini, *Public Schools of Choice* (Simon and Schuster, 1973).

11. Lauri Steel and Roger Levine, *Educational Innovation in Multiracial Contexts: The Growth of Magnet Schools in American Education* (U.S. Department of Education, 1994).

12. Amy Stuart Wells, *Time to Choose* (Hill and Wang, 1993), chap. 2.

13. NCES, *Public School Choice Programs*; NCES, *The Condition of Education*.

14. Rolf Blank and others, *Survey of Magnet Schools: Analyzing a Model for Quality Integrated Education* (U.S. Department of Education, 1983); Rolf Blank, Roger Levine, and Lauri Steel, "After 15 Years, Magnet Schools in Urban Education," in Richard Elmore and Bruce Fuller, eds., *Who Chooses? Who Loses? Culture, Institutions, and the Unequal Effects of School Choice* (Teachers College Press, 1996).

15. Adam Gamoran, "Student Achievement in Public Magnet, Public Comprehensive, and Private City High Schools," *Educational Evaluation and Policy Analysis*, vol. 18 (Spring 1996), pp. 1–18. Gamoran finds that fully four of ten central city high school students attend some kind of school of choice: stand-alone magnet (10 percent), school-within-a-school magnet (8 percent), other public specialty or theme school (6 percent), Catholic (11 percent), non-Catholic religious (3 percent), nonreligious (3 percent). This was almost twice the percentage in the nation at large.

16. *Brown v. Board of Education*, 347 U.S. 483 (1954).

17. *Green v. County School Board*, 391 U.S. 430 (1968).

18. Two large districts—Boston and Montgomery County, Maryland—have controlled-choice plans operating in parts of the district. Examples of smaller and newer controlled-choice initiatives include Brockton, Massachusetts, and Lee County, Florida.

19. In addition to the home-grown model in Cambridge, the Massachusetts efforts in this area are attributable to strong support at the state level. The state's Office of Educational Equity, directed during several key years by Charles Glenn (a major proponent of the

controlled-choice approach) played an important role in encouraging the spread of the model. Charles L. Glenn, Kahris McLaughlin, and Laura Salganik, *Parent Information for School Choice: The Case of Massachusetts* (Boston: Center on Families, Communities, Schools, and Children's Learning, 1993). Other Massachusetts examples include Boston, Chelsea, Fall River, Holyoke, Lawrence, Lowell, Northhampton, Salem, and Springfield. Along with Cambridge, these districts in 1993 enrolled more than 145,000 students.

20. Seymour Fliegel, "Parental Choice in East Harlem Schools," in Joe Nathan, ed., *Public Schools by Choice* (Minneapolis: Institute for Learning and Teaching, 1989), pp. 95–112; Seymour Fliegel, *Miracle in East Harlem: The Fight for Choice in Public Education* (Times Books, 1993).

21. Mark Schneider and others, "Institutional Arrangements and the Creation of Social Capital: The Effects of Public School Choice," *American Political Science Review*, vol. 91 (March 1997), p. 85.

22. Division of Student Services, "Summary: Number of Out-of-Boundary Students by Level and Ward" (District of Columbia Public Schools, March 23, 1993).

23. Center for Education Reform, "Choice in Action: What's Working around the Country" (http://edreform.com/pubs/choice1.htm), August 9, 1999.

24. John E. Coons and Stephen D. Sugarman, *Scholarships for Children* (Berkeley, Calif.: Institute of Governmental Studies, 1992).

25. Celia Rouse and M. McLaughlin, "Can the Invisible Hand Improve Education? A Review of Competition and School Efficiency" (Washington, D.C.: National Research Council, 1998).

26. *Milliken v. Bradley*, 418 U.S. 717 (1974).

27. St. Louis in 1983 adopted a substantial interdistrict plan as part of a settlement agreement that evolved out of desegregation litigation. While nominally a voluntary program, the settlement almost certainly would not have occurred without the explicit threat of judicial intervention, and its implementation was overseen by a special master appointed by the U.S. District Court. D. Bruce La Pierre, "Voluntary Interdistrict School Desegregation in St. Louis: The Special Master's Tale," *Wisconsin Law Review*, no. 6 (1987), pp. 971–1040.

28. Center for Education Reform, "Choice in Action."

29. Rouse and McLaughlin, "Can the Invisible Hand Improve Education?"

30. NCES, *Public School Choice Programs.*

31. Statement of Richard J. Wenning, director of Educational Accountability, District of Columbia Schools, to the Subcommittee on the District of Columbia, Committee on Government Reform and Oversight, U.S. House of Representatives, March 13, 1998. (http://www.dcwatch.com/schools/ps980313b.htm), August 4, 1999. Even though many critics of the school system find this estimate unbelievably high, there are many anecdotal reports of parents in cars with out-of-state tags dropping children at District of Columbia schools. The District offers an unusually extensive array of prekindergarten and all-day kindergarten options, which are not generally available in the surrounding jurisdictions. For the 1998–99 school year, officials instituted a strict requirement for proof of residency; about 2,000 students had not complied by the deadline date. Valerie Strauss, "2,000 Pupils Fail to Prove Residency in District: Schools to Send Children Home," *Washington Post*, September 30, 1998.

32. Chartering bodies can be states, school districts, universities, or specially constituted bodies. State laws may allow the conversion to charter school status of existing public or private schools.

33. RPP International and the University of Minnesota, *A Study of Charter Schools: First Year Report, 1997* (U.S. Department of Education, 1997), p. 1.

34. Chester E. Finn and others, *Charter Schools in Action: Final Report*, vol. 1 (Washington, D.C.: Hudson Institute, 1997). See Center for Education Reform, "Choice in Action," for the 200,000 number.

35. Center for Education Reform, *The Charter School Workbook* (Washington, D.C.: 1997), p. 11.

36. See, for example, Charles Leslie Glenn Jr., *The Myth of the Common School* (University of Massachusetts Press, 1988).

37. *Pierce v. Society of Sisters*, 268 U.S. 510 (1925); *Meyer v. Nebraska*, 262 U.S. 390 (1923).

38. *Griffin v. County School Board*, 377 U.S. 218 (1964).

39. *Norwood v. Harrison*, 413 U.S. 455 (1973).

40. *Runyon v. McCrary*, 427 U.S. 160 (1976).

41. *Bob Jones University v. United States*, 461 U.S. 574 (1983).

42. National Center for Education Statistics, *Public and Private Schools: How Do They Differ?* (U.S. Department of Education, 1997); NCES, *Private School Universe Survey, 1995–96* (U.S. Department of Education, 1998).

43. NCES, *Private School Universe*.

44. *Committee for Public Education v. Nyquist*, 413 U.S. 756 (1973).

45. Statistics from NCES, *Private School Universe*.

46. Compare John J. Convey, *Catholic Schools Make a Difference* (National Catholic Education Association, 1992), table 3-6; Maryellen Schaub and David Baker, *Serving American Catholic Children and Youth* (Catholic University of America, Life Cycle Institute, 1993), figure 1.

47. Isabel Lyman, "Homeschooling: Back to the Future?" *Policy Analysis* (Cato Institute), no. 294 (January 7, 1998), pp. 1–20.

48. "Home School Statistics and Reports: How Many Home Schoolers Are There?" (http://www.hslda.org/central/statsandreports/ray1997), August 9, 1999.

49. *New York Times*, February 2, 1997; *Cincinnati Enquirer*, January 18, 1998.

50. Milton Friedman, *Capitalism and Freedom* (University of Chicago Press, 1962).

51. *Jackson v. Benson*, 578 N.W. 2d 602 (Wis. cert denied, 119 S. Ct. 466 [1998]).

52. Dan Murphy, F. Howard Nelson, and Bella Rosenberg, *The Cleveland Voucher Program: Who Chooses? Who Gets Chosen? Who Pays?* (Washington, D.C.: American Federation of Teachers, 1997).

53. "School Voucher Program Becomes Law in Florida," *New York Times*, June 22, 1999.

54. Center for Education Reform, "Selected Education Reforms At-A-Glance," (http://www.edreform.com/pubs/glance.html), August 9, 1999.

55. "Partners Advancing Values in Education," (http://www.pave.org/donors.html), August 9, 1999.

56. Valerie J. Martinez and others, "The Consequences of School Choice: Who Leaves and Who Stays in the Inner City," *Social Science Quarterly*, vol. 76 (September 1995), pp. 485–501; R. Kenneth Godwin, Frank R. Kemerer, and Valerie J. Martinez, "Final Report: San Antonio School Choice Research Project" (University of North Texas, Center for the Study of Education Reform, 1997).

57. Anemona Hartocollis, "Private School Choice Plan Draws a Million Aid-Seekers," *New York Times*, April 21, 1999.

58. These plans do not involve public dollars and, in that sense, might appropriately be regarded as simple extensions of the traditional private school alternative. Yet it seems apparent that many of those funding and promoting these plans view them as stalking horses for public voucher plans.

59. Hamilton Lankford and James Wyckoff, "Primary and Secondary School Choice among Public and Religious Alternatives," *Economics of Education Review*, vol. 11 (1992), pp. 317–37. See also Charles F. Manski, "Education Choice (Vouchers) and Social Mobility," *Economics of Education Review*, vol. 11 (1992), pp. 351–69.

60. Gallup polls in 1996 and 1998 found that 36 percent and 38 percent, respectively, of parents then using the public schools would send their oldest child to a private school if the government paid the tuition. Another 6 to 8 percent would send the child to a different public school, leaving just over half who said they would keep the child in his or her current public school. See "The 30th Annual Phi Delta Kappa/Gallup Poll of the Public's Attitudes toward the Public Schools," (http://www.pdkintl.org/kappan/kp9809-a.htm), August 9, 1999.

61. See Schneider and others, "Institutional Arrangements."

62. Michael Mintrom and Sandra Vergari, "Charter School Laws across the United States: A Policy Report, 1998 Edition" (Michigan State University, Institute for Public Policy and Social Research, 1998), p. 7.

CHAPTER TWO

The Shifting Politics
of School Choice

ROBERT C. BULMAN

DAVID L. KIRP

Few educational reforms in recent decades have gener-ated as much attention and as much controversy as school choice.[1] Passions are aroused whether the specific policy enables students to attend a public school outside their neighborhood or enables them to attend private schools at public expense. Advocates speak of choice as the civil rights issue of our times, while critics deride choice as wors-ening race and class inequities. Debates about choice are as likely to focus on political motivations as to explore the impact of choice on student learning. Evaluations of the relationship between choice and achievement, couched in the nominally objective language of numbers and formulas, have touched off bitter battles over the researchers' alleged biases.[2]

The ideological character of the school choice debate, as well as the per-sisting struggles over the implementation of choice plans, call for an analy-sis rooted both in theory and on-the-ground reality. This chapter undertakes that task. It examines several attempts to introduce public and private school choice plans in the United States during the past thirty years: the federal government's effort to conduct a voucher experiment in Alum Rock, California, in the early 1970s; the emergence of choice within public schools during the 1970s and 1980s, with a focus on the case of Minnesota; the unsuccessful 1993 campaign to secure popular approval, through the ini-tiative, for a private school voucher plan in California; the first publicly funded private school voucher plan in Milwaukee; the failure of vouchers to take root in Jersey City, New Jersey; and the rapid emergence during the past five years of a national movement for charter schools, a public-private hybrid, with attention paid to the experience in Arizona and California.

These cases were selected because each represents a pivotal moment in the evolution of school choice politics from vouchers to charters. The complex politics of school choice today draws upon the lessons of the Alum Rock experiment, the innovative use of public school choice in Minnesota, the failure of Proposition 174 in California, the successful implementation of vouchers in Milwaukee and Cleveland (as well as failed efforts elsewhere, as in Jersey City), and the rapid nationwide development of charter schools. These cases cannot be understood without reference to the others; each political episode of school choice leaves behind a residue of new coalitions, new ideas, and new possibilities.

Additionally, changes in both racial politics and educational politics have opened windows of opportunity for school choice policies.[3] A full-scale voucher system, impossible to institute in Alum Rock in the 1970s, became reality in Milwaukee and Cleveland in the 1990s. In the wake of declining support for attempts to integrate public schools through busing, the continued poor performance of students in inner-city schools, and the successful example of public school choice programs, black activists formed tenuous alliances with conservative politicians, Catholic church leaders, and libertarian foundations to advance the cause of vouchers for urban children.

Meanwhile, the voucher wars have opened up political opportunities for charter schools, which have proliferated in recent years. Charter school legislation, first passed in Minnesota in 1991 and California a year later, is now on the books in thirty-six states and the District of Columbia, and the number of charter schools has increased exponentially, from a single school in 1992 to over 800 in 1998.[4] In one form or other, school choice is here to stay.

Explaining the Political Dynamics of School Choice

The diverse history of school choice has been examined through a variety of lenses. Competing explanations proliferate concerning the emergence and evolution of the phenomenon; they provide a useful starting point for a discussion of the politics of choice.

In *School Choice: The Struggle for the Soul of American Education*, Peter Cookson locates the origins of support for choice in the breakdown of the half-century-old consensus concerning the value of public institutions and in an alternative, market-centered paradigm.[5] As the public schools began, during the 1960s and 1970s, to struggle with the conflicting demands of an increasingly heterogeneous student population, Cookson argues, privileged social groups felt increasingly anxious. During the 1980s, many white middle-class families opted to exit the public schools in favor of private "educational enclaves."[6] At the same time, a group of school choice "revolutionaries" took advantage of the popularly perceived crisis in public education and introduced school choice into public discourse. In the 1980s' political atmosphere of privatization and market competition, school choice resonated with people as they sought to reclaim the private benefits of schooling.

Cookson's analysis, though adding dimension to the explanation of school choice politics, stumbles over the complexities of history. The "consensus breakdown" thesis fails to explain why there continues to be widespread support for the public schools.[7] When asked in 1997 to grade the public school their oldest child attends, 64 percent of a national sample of parents awarded the school a grade of A or B, a figure that has not substantially changed in a generation.[8] And while status anxiety may well be one element in the political equation, Cookson's account glosses over enthusiasm for choice among poor and minority populations. In 1997, 72 percent of African Americans favored the right to choose a private school at "government expense," compared to just 48 percent of the general population.[9]

Kevin Dougherty and Lisabet Sostre, in "Minerva and the Market," frame their argument in terms of state autonomy theory: the state has its own independent interests as well as the power to advance those interests.[10] In the search for politically popular and fiscally affordable education reforms, necessitated by the perceived crisis in public education, governors and legislators seized upon school choice. Choice was their preference, Dougherty and Sostre argue, not because it was regarded as the best among a number of competing options but simply because it happened to be "readily at hand" when a political response was needed.

Undoubtedly, entrepreneurial government officials have had a powerful influence on the direction of the choice movement, but their authority does not offer sufficient explanation for the politics that surround the diverse formulations of choice. Although there is something to be said for the notion that policies arise out of happenstance, that is not the entire story. Over time, wars among politicians and among interest groups have moved the issue on and off the policy agenda.

In *Rethinking School Choice*, Jeffrey Henig offers the most fully developed and persuasive account of the evolution of school choice. It is at once an intellectual and political history, which links "a thread of ideas and theories" with "a thread of practice and adjustment."[11] When the first modern-day voucher plan, a pure market scheme, was propounded by Milton Friedman more than forty years ago, it had little impact on educational policy.[12] At that time, public schools were generally well regarded, and Friedman's proposal was dismissed as ultraconservative. Not until the 1970s, when choice became disentangled from free market ideology, did the idea start to catch on politically. Public school educators began to make use of choice. Magnet schools combined pedagogical excitement and racial integration; alternative schools promised new ways of reaching turned-off students. Those developments partially decoupled choice from conservative ideology, since it was now plain that choice could be used in the service of other agendas.

To deflect attention from controversial voucher plans that subsidized private and parochial schools, conservatives also began to emphasize public school choice. The Reagan administration, which initially sought federal funding for vouchers, later focused its energies on public school choice plans such as the East Harlem program.[13] For a time, private school vouchers were off the political table. But, Henig suggests, shifting the debate away from vouchers and toward public school choice gave new political legitimacy to the notion of choice in general—and in turn, this intellectual shift made possible a return to the kind of market-based plans advanced by Friedman decades earlier. A policy window had been opened, as this repackaging of choice made the concept more generally palatable, and choice became a more feasible policy concept.[14] As reconfigured, choice appealed not only to market-oriented conservatives but also to diverse constituencies interested in pedagogical innovation and equity.

This debate about ideas, Henig contends, set the agenda for school choice politics. In practice, choice has been relied on mostly by public officials, who have used it to muddle their way through an assortment of policy dilemmas.[15] Controversies about racial justice have shaped choice in practice, from the sham freedom of choice strategies that southern school officials devised to resist desegregation in the post–*Brown* v. *Board of Education* South to the design of magnet schools and open-enrollment programs in order to boost integration. Voucher advocates sought to recast these experiences as evidence of the virtues of the free market. In so doing, they have "reshaped the political landscape" of choice. The popularity of school choice in the 1990s, Henig concludes, is due less to shifts in political power among interest groups than to the repackaging of theories about school choice.

The persistence of school choice cannot be explained simply as the embodiment of the will of a powerful interest group or a coterie of state actors; nor does it reflect a breakdown in political consensus. Moreover, the political history of choice is not just a tale about how to spin a policy concept. As an idea, school choice is hardly new; it has been debated for almost half a century. When, where, and how choice has taken root has as much to do with the particulars of the political setting as with the merits or the packaging of the concept. The politics of choice thus needs to be grounded in these messy specifics, not just in theory. John Kingdon's theoretical framework, put forward in *Agendas, Alternatives, and Public Policies*, is particularly useful in this project.[16] In response to a defined problem, different policy alternatives compete for attention in ever changing political contexts. Changes in the political context (electoral shifts, new coalitions, changes in the government) open up policy windows that, with effective entrepreneurship, make policy initiatives possible.

The concept of choice represents an amalgam of policies, linked to a large and ever changing political cast. Over time, the rhetoric has shifted, as has the balance of political power. A critical factor is the extent to which the specific policy proposal is market based or equity based.[17] These terms represent real, not rhetorical, policy differences. Market-based plans rely on competition to determine what students attend which schools, while equity-based plans are designed to benefit poor or minority students.[18] As proponents of market-based schemes have suffered repeated political reverses, advocates of equity-based plans have been able to forge broad and sometimes successful coalitions. Public school choice and charter schools, backed by different coalitions, have been even more successful. This complex politics has been evident since the truncated federal experiment with vouchers more than a quarter of a century ago.

The Alum Rock Experiment: Whatever Happened to Vouchers?

The voucher experiment in Alum Rock, California, is noteworthy not only because it was the first significant, widely publicized choice plan to be implemented but also because its political history says much about the dynamic tension between market-based and equity-based school choice plans. Many of the issues that surfaced in Alum Rock remain central in the political contests over choice.

The Office of Economic Opportunity was the moving force behind the experiment. While OEO had been launched in 1964 as part of Lyndon Johnson's war on poverty, under Richard Nixon the agency was turned into a research entity, the R&D office for federal social programs.[19] The voucher project was one of OEO's undertakings, but not for the market-oriented reasons advanced earlier by Milton Friedman. The hope was that vouchers would give greater voice to economically disadvantaged families and make schools more responsive to their needs. OEO commissioned the Center for the Study of Public Policy, based at Harvard, to devise an experimental design.[20] Christopher Jencks, who wrote the innovative report, recommended an experiment that was equity-based—a "regulated compensatory" plan, not the unregulated market-based plan earlier propounded by Milton Friedman.[21]

Jencks proposed giving vouchers to the parents of public school students. The vouchers could be redeemed at any school, public or private, that participated in the experiment. Poor children would receive vouchers worth additional dollars as a way of encouraging schools to accept these students and providing those schools with the extra funds needed to educate them. Schools that opted to join this experiment would be required to accept the voucher as full payment. If there were more applications than a school could accommodate, it could admit up to half of its students using its own selection criteria, but the remaining slots would be filled by lottery. As a way of aiding parents to make informed choices, participating private schools would be required to publicize the school's programs and its students' academic performance.

The intention behind the voucher idea, Jencks pointed out in testimony to the Senate Committee on Equal Educational Opportunity, was to blur the line between public and private schools.[22] Although the OEO embraced the Jencks plan, the plan met with a chorus of opposition. The fact that it enabled students to attend nonpublic schools aroused the suspicions of teachers' unions, school boards, and civil liberties groups—an alliance that has been maintained in subsequent fights over vouchers. At a moment when racial integration was a major national concern, the emphasis on parental choice worried groups like the National Association for the Advancement of Colored People (NAACP), which feared desegregation would be undermined.

The national teachers' unions were the most ardent opponents. OEO's proposal had no safeguards against the closing of unpopular public schools.

More generally, it was seen as threatening teachers' livelihoods. Representatives of the American Federation of Teachers and the National Education Association testified against the plan before the House Committee on Education and Labor. Uniquely among teachers' union leaders, AFT president Albert Shanker voiced his admiration for Jencks's proposal. Nonetheless, Shanker opposed OEO's experiment because he feared that it would become more market based and "conservative" as it was processed by the political machinery.

> There is no legislature in the nation that will enact a voucher plan that will give substantially more money to each poor child and bar private schools from freely selecting the students they want and rejecting those they don't want. By the time the Jencks model goes through the political-legislative wringer, it will become the conservative model that its author himself opposes.[23]

Such opposition discouraged school districts from participating.[24] In the end, despite the promise of federal funding, only a single district, Alum Rock, signed on. That relatively small district—twenty-five elementary and middle schools, enrolling 15,000 students, situated on the east side of San Jose—served a poor and racially diverse student body. Its superintendent, William Jefferds, had earned community support by securing federal grants and decentralizing school governance. He regarded the voucher demonstration as a way to raise yet more funds for the district and promote decentralization. A feasibility study reported that 40 percent of parents, 53 percent of teachers, and 69 percent of Alum Rock administrators wanted to participate in the demonstration. However, only a few nonpublic schools were interested; most were wary. In particular, religious and private academies feared that their participation would require loss of control over admissions and curriculum decisions.[25] Still, enough private schools expressed interest to make the experiment appear feasible.

The voucher plan eventually implemented in Alum Rock differed significantly from Christopher Jencks's proposal but not in the ways the AFT's Albert Shanker had predicted. Instead, it was far less market oriented; indeed, it was not really much of a voucher plan. Private schools were not permitted to participate, because the state legislature balked at passing the needed legislation.[26] Still, the OEO, which by then was desperate for a site in which to conduct even this weak variant of its experiment, accepted this constraint. Local interest groups further watered down the design. Principals wanted to maintain administrative autonomy. Parents wanted to maintain the right to send their children to the local neighborhood school. Teachers and their unions wanted to ensure that no public school instructors would lose their jobs. Teachers also wanted to limit competition with private schools and encourage teacher autonomy in the classroom.[27] They all got their wish. All that remained of the grand idea of vouchers were minischools, operating within each participating public school, forming a "relatively decentralized, open-enrollment system of alternative programs."[28] In effect, Superintendent Jefferds had secured federal funding for the decentralization he really desired.

The demonstration began in the fall of 1972, with six schools participating. That number later increased, to fourteen, and the number of minischools, which were free to budget and run their programs, eventually reached forty-five. Federal funding for the experiment ran out five years later, and with little local support, the program itself disappeared.[29] By then, the OEO had been abolished and the National Institute of Education was the agency responsible for overseeing educational demonstrations. The NIE made a stab at implementing a purely market-based voucher plan in New Hampshire, but even there, a state known for its suspicion of publicly run endeavors, school districts were able to kill the proposal.[30]

The Shift to Public School Choice

While the Alum Rock experiment ultimately had little to do with vouchers, the idea of school choice did not die with its demise. During the 1970s and 1980s, there was a dramatic growth of alternative public schools, and their history is an important chapter in the politics of choice. Many of the new entities were magnet schools. These academies offered specialized themes or programs—a concentration in the arts or science, Montessori technique, or back-to-basics—which were intended to draw students away from their neighborhood schools and so to promote integration. Alternative public schools, which were often run along communitarian lines, attracted students for whom the regular program was, for one reason or another, unsatisfactory.[31]

These new options did not satisfy those who were ideologically committed to choice. By the end of the 1970s, Milton Friedman had again written on the subject.[32] Two Berkeley professors who had long been involved in school finance equity litigation, John Coons and Stephen Sugarman, set out their own equity-based voucher plan. Yet as with Friedman's earlier foray, these proposals failed to capture the public's interest. In 1979 Coons and Sugarman sought to place a voucher initiative on the California ballot, but the petition drive fell well short of the half-million signatures required to qualify for the ballot. While voucher initiatives did appear on the ballot in Michigan in 1978 and in Washington, D.C., in 1981, in each case they were defeated.[33]

Not even master politician Ronald Reagan could sell a market-based voucher plan. After Congress twice rejected an ambitious scheme, Reagan offered a more modest proposal, which contemplated letting districts use some of their federal aid to supply vouchers to poor children in need of remedial education. When even this scaled-back, equity-oriented voucher plan failed, Reagan abandoned the pursuit. Instead, he embraced public school choice and magnet schools, and this policy direction was maintained in the Bush administration.[34] In opting for public school choice rather than vouchers, the Reagan and Bush administrations favored what by then had become an educational commonplace. An idea that first took root in the beleaguered New York City school district of East Harlem in 1974 was subsequently implemented in hundreds, eventually thousands, of districts across the country.[35] The 1983 publication of A Nation at Risk had alerted the republic to the sorry state of its public schools. Soon thereafter, an array of reforms were proposed to save the schools from themselves.[36] Public choice, although little discussed, turned out to be one of the most significant of these innovations, the quiet revolution in American education.[37]

Minnesota's statewide public school choice plan was the best known. That state had earlier adopted legislation that permitted families to deduct some educational expenses, including private (though not parochial) school tuition, from their state taxes.[38] In 1983, a policy research group, the Citizens League, tried to build on this base, proposing an equity-based voucher plan that would have enabled poor families to attend private schools. However, when faced with resistance from teachers' unions and other education groups, the Citizens League lacked the political strength to see its voucher proposal through. Its campaign failed, but not before it had placed choice and vouchers on the political agenda.

A year later, when the Minnesota Business Partnership, a lobbying organization representing Minnesota's largest corporations, issued its own recommendations for educational reform, stipends for eleventh and twelfth graders—vouchers by another name—were among the suggestions. Republican governor Rudy Perpich, who had opposed the earlier voucher initiative, endorsed parts of this plan, although not the stipends. A firm believer in public education who had grown increasingly frustrated with the rigidity of the state's school systems, Perpich began campaigning aggressively for his own proposal, which emphasized statewide public school open enrollment.[39]

Perpich's crusade shifted the focus of the debate from vouchers to public school choice. It also reconfigured the alignment of provoucher and antivoucher forces, as antivoucher groups like the Parent Teacher Association joined provoucher groups like the Citizens League in supporting open enrollment.[40] When first put to a vote in the legislature, in 1985, open enrollment was narrowly defeated. In 1987 Perpich orchestrated the efforts of all the interest groups and won the lawmakers' approval. This legislation gives students the right to enroll in any public school in the state, with state dollars following the students. High school students may take college courses at state expense, and at-risk students may attend the educational program of their choice.[41] (In school districts under court order to desegregate, reassignment cannot exacerbate patterns of segregation.)

The implementation of public school choice plans in Minnesota and elsewhere paved the way for charter schools. In 1993 Minnesota became the first state to pass charter school legislation. It also prompted renewed attempts to win state backing for vouchers. The successful example of public school choice opened a political window of opportunity for voucher advocates. Instead of opposing or ignoring public school choice, they wisely used this policy history as an inspiration for their own renewed, and somewhat more successful, efforts. While market-based voucher proposals once again failed, equity-based voucher plans experienced some success.

Voucher Plans Redux: Renewed Interest, Problematic Politics

Even as a well-known academic, Milton Friedman, had introduced the concept of a market-based system of educational choice to policymakers nearly four decades earlier, two members of the academy, John Chubb and Terry Moe, refocused attention on this policy option in *Politics, Markets, and America's Schools*.[42] Their voucher scheme essentially restated Friedman's proposal. Although Milton Friedman's plan had received little policy attention, the reaction to *Politics, Markets, and America's Schools* was overwhelming.

Times had changed and so had the tactics of artful suasion. Chubb and Moe were able to capitalize on a moment when *choice* was the mantra; they also drew upon empirically based analysis to support their policy preferences. Friedman had applied a classic welfare economics model to education. Chubb and Moe added a data-driven defense, deploying interpretations of national test scores to buttress their contention that students from similar socioeconomic backgrounds do better in schools organized by the market rather than the state. It mattered little to political partisans in the choice debate that these claims were contested by other scholars, who pointed out flaws in Chubb and Moe's methodology that called into question their anti–public school conclusions.[43] In a policy world captivated by the seeming neutrality of regression analyses, *Politics, Markets, and America's Schools* offered valuable cover for what otherwise could be dismissed as an ideologically rooted preference for the market.

At a time when other efforts to reform public education were being criticized as too little and too late, Chubb and Moe's more sweeping critique found a receptive audience. A growing number of policymakers, impatient with costly public school reform that seemed incapable of producing dramatic results, preferred radical surgery. They wanted to invent a new system—to construct the educational counterpart to the interstate highway system. Chubb and Moe obligingly, and explicitly, promised that choice represented the sought-after panacea.[44]

The Failure of Market-Based Vouchers in California

Intellectual excitement did not necessarily translate into political triumph. Despite this renewed attention, efforts to pass voucher legislation failed in Oregon in 1990 and in Colorado in 1992.[45] A 1993 California initiative, Proposition 174, would have provided a voucher, worth about half the average per pupil public school expenditure in California, to all families with children in private schools.[46] That measure failed for politically instructive reasons. Initial drafts of the initiative drew heavily on an equity-based voucher plan developed by Berkeley professors John Coons and Stephen Sugarman in *Scholarships for Children*.[47] As consultants to the sponsoring organization, Excellence for Choice in Education League (EXCEL), they proposed a plan that primarily benefited poor students.[48] But EXCEL's financial backers opted instead for a market-based plan more philosophically attuned to Milton Friedman's nostrums.

After failing to qualify for the 1992 ballot, the proposition appeared on a special election ballot one year later. The campaign pitted the wealthy and conservative southern Californians of EXCEL against the teachers' unions.[49] The California Teachers Association (CTA) vowed to do "whatever it took" to defeat the proposition.[50] The union's passion and dollars prevailed. Opponents outspent proponents by a ten-to-one margin, with the CTA alone spending an unprecedented $13 million.[51] "The business community wimped out," complained Ken Kachigian, the campaign manager for Proposition 174, by not delivering comparable sums to the effort, but money was not the only reason for the outcome of the campaign.[52] Political support was also lacking. Pro-initiative forces were startled when, shortly before the election, Governor Pete Wilson announced his opposition to the measure, ostensibly because of concerns about its fiscal impact.

Some commentators argued that the measure failed because suburbanites were satisfied with their schools and did not want public money drained from them to support private education.[53] A poll taken two months before the election, however, suggests otherwise: the real problem resided in the particulars of the voucher plan, not in the attitudes of the citizenry. Hefty majorities—62 percent of urban residents and 64 percent of suburban residents; 64 percent of blacks and 60 percent of whites—were for vouchers in principle.[54] Californians were suspicious of Proposition 174 in particular, not vouchers in general. Widely aired fears that this plan would mainly benefit the wealthy, drain public schools of needed funds, and publicly support bizarre private schools—a witches' coven school became the favorite nonhypothetical example—killed the measure.

Concerns about inequities and the lack of meaningful state regulation led to the defeat of market-based voucher plans such as California's. By contrast, carefully regulated equity-based plans were considerably more successful.

The Modest Success of Equity-Based Voucher Plans

By the 1990s, the social and political climate had sufficiently changed so that private school vouchers, which could muster almost no political support a generation earlier, had become a political reality in two heavily African American cities, Milwaukee and Cleveland, as well as in the state of Florida. The equity and regulatory components of those reforms gave them political feasibility.

AN ODD ALLIANCE IN MILWAUKEE. The Milwaukee Parental Choice Program, launched in 1990, was the first to provide public funds for private schooling, offering poor inner-city students an opportunity to attend private schools at public expense. Its success marks a significant shift in racial politics and shows a greater willingness of conservative groups to support equity-based school choice.

The political history of vouchers in Milwaukee has its start in the long struggle over desegregation. A lawsuit alleging deliberate segregation by the city's schools was filed in 1965; eleven years and countless hearings later, the district was required fully to desegregate. In an effort to encourage the transfer of white students from suburban to city schools, and black students from Milwaukee to suburban schools, Wisconsin implemented a voluntary desegregation program. As a result of enrollment shifts, several public schools in Milwaukee's black neighborhoods were either closed or converted to magnet schools, but the plan neither fully integrated the schools nor significantly boosted the achievement of black students. By 1991 slightly over one-quarter of the 99,000 students in the Milwaukee public schools were white and nearly 60 percent were black. Only 4,000 African American pupils (7 percent of the entire black student population) took advantage of the opportunity to transfer to suburban schools. Just 873 students, about 3 percent of the total white student body in Milwaukee, transferred into city schools.[55]

Black parents who had earlier backed the desegregation lawsuit became angry that their local public schools had closed, that their children bore the primary burden of busing, that the suburban districts had creamed off the best students, and that the educational performance of their children had not improved.[56] Their frustration prompted them to search for new answers. Among the possibilities were all-black schools, locally controlled schools, and parental choice.[57] Annette "Polly" Williams, an African American Wisconsin state representative, summarized the feelings of many black Milwaukee parents:

> The only kids who are benefactors of this whole system [desegregation] are the White students. . . . We don't want this desegregation. Desegregation in the city of Milwaukee is terrible, and I'd like to see it abolished and go back to educating our children in our neighborhoods regardless of color. And it doesn't matter if they're all Black schools. I think Black kids can learn in an all-Black situation.[58]

Unhappy with the public schools, many African American families who could afford to do so enrolled their children in private schools. Some of these schools were formerly Catholic schools that had been transformed into nonsectarian community schools serving mainly black and Latino students. These schools had long been engaged in a struggle for public funds. Initially, they hoped to affiliate with the Milwaukee school district, receiving public funding while maintaining administrative autonomy, but when these efforts failed, the community schools urged that their students receive vouchers. Although the district opposed the idea, it had in effect set a precedent by having contracted with these very schools to educate a small number of at-risk students.[59] Meanwhile, African American activists led by Polly Williams proposed the creation of an autonomous district in a nearly all-black part of the city.[60] Within this new district, teachers and administrators would have control over the schools, and parents would have the freedom to choose among them. The teachers' union, the school board, and the NAACP were arrayed in opposition.

The Republican governor of Wisconsin, Tommy Thompson, took no position on this proposal. Thompson was a national pioneer in efforts to reduce government provision of social services generally. He had promoted welfare reform and twice previously, in 1988 and 1989, had put forward private school voucher schemes. Williams had supported Thompson's voucher plans, but her priority was the creation of the inner-city district. Although the legislature approved neither the new school district nor Governor Thompson's voucher scheme, some change in school governance seemed imminent. These pressures prompted Milwaukee to suggest a controlled public school choice plan, then to propose expanding the at-risk voucher plan. Williams regarded this latter idea as a strategy for dumping problem youngsters onto private schools.[61]

Together with other community activists, Williams made a counterproposal. The state, not the school district, would administer the voucher plan; and poor families generally, not just those with at-risk children, would be eligible to participate. The black community in Milwaukee rallied behind Williams's plan; Governor Thompson embraced it as a way to advance the cause of school vouchers; and soon this local controversy became a topic of national interest. President George Bush supported the proposal, and so did other influential conservatives, including Michael Joyce, president of the Milwaukee-based Bradley Foundation.[62] The Catholic Church in Milwaukee gave its blessing to a plan that it regarded as a step toward public financial support for the schools it ran. The Milwaukee voucher plan was promoted by an unusual political coalition, which included both liberal black Democrats and conservative white Republicans. Although the state's education department and the teachers' unions maintained their historic posture of resistance, the liberal-labor political coalition that had traditionally opposed school vouchers was fatally split.[63]

The Milwaukee parental choice plan became law in 1990. It gives vouchers to children of families whose incomes do not exceed 1.75 times the poverty level. Participating schools cannot charge more than the voucher; if oversubscribed, those schools must use a lottery to admit students. Initially, no more than 1.5 percent of the Milwaukee student population could participate in the voucher program, and no more than 65 percent of the students in any private school could receive vouchers.[64] The program survived a series of court challenges, with the Bradley Foundation, a frequent supporter of conservative causes, paying the bulk of the legal costs.

In 1995, the Wisconsin state legislature, newly controlled by Republicans, broadened the Milwaukee voucher plan. The new law expanded eligibility to include students already attending private schools; increased the number of students allowed to participate to 15,000; and allowed all students in a private school to receive vouchers. Most significantly, it authorized religious schools to participate—a provision upheld in a landmark 1998 Wisconsin Supreme Court ruling.[65] These changes troubled some members of the coalition whose backing had been vital to winning passage of the earlier voucher statute.[66] Polly Williams was interested in strengthening the equity-based elements of the choice program, not expanding it to parochial schools. "Right now," Williams says, "I'm one of the only ones talking about preserving the Milwaukee public schools system. Things like choice always used to be about improving the public schools."[67] This split illustrates a deeper division among the provoucher forces. To many market-oriented conservatives, equity-based choice is a politically expedient way to promote broader, market-based choice. To the black activists who embraced vouchers, choice itself is essentially a means to an end—promoting equity. The future of school choice, in Wisconsin and elsewhere, will depend on the strength and character of the political coalition that promotes it.

NO VOUCHERS FOR JERSEY CITY. An equity-based voucher plan similar to Milwaukee's is operating in Cleveland. In 1999, Florida became the first state to adopt a statewide voucher scheme. That legislation (which has been challenged in the courts) provides vouchers worth $4,000 to students who attend the state's worst-performing public schools; vouchers may be redeemed at any school—public, private, or parochial—that accepts them.[68] While these cases represent noteworthy developments and suggest that the voucher movement has some steam, they remain the exception. Most equity-based voucher proposals have been political nonstarters. In Jersey City, New Jersey, for instance, equity-based vouchers in an urban area with a large minority population failed to materialize, despite backing from a Republican governor and a Republican mayor with a passion for vouchers. In 1993 Bret Schundler became the first Republican to be elected as Jersey City's mayor in three-quarters of a century. Campaigning on a platform that prominently featured vouchers, he won 69 percent of the vote.[69] Republican Christine Whitman was elected governor of New Jersey the following year. Schundler endorsed Whitman, with the expectation that she would push for a voucher plan in Jersey City. Although Whitman stated in her campaign that she was "constitutionally a little bit uncomfortable with vouchers," once elected, she appointed a provoucher education commissioner, Leo Klagholz, and praised vouchers in her inaugural address.[70]

When unveiled, though, the state's voucher proposal was surprisingly vague. The plan for a five-year experiment did not specify the size of the voucher, but it was plainly modest: estimates hovered around $1,000. Vouchers would be granted to economically disadvantaged students, but only those then enrolled in the first and ninth grades, and could be redeemed at parochial schools. The announcement of a new voucher system launched a flurry of political activity. Polly Williams traveled from Milwaukee to New Jersey to generate support. The New Jersey Catholic Conference lobbied heavily for it, even passing out provoucher literature in masses held across the state. The New Jersey Educational Association pledged to oppose it and earmarked $10 million for the campaign. At one point tensions became so heated that, at a rally, the debate degenerated into a brawl.[71]

The state legislature was not especially keen on the idea, with most Democrats and many Republicans arrayed against it. The Republican chair of the senate education committee feared that the plan would harm public schools. Another GOP lawmaker worried that government funds would compromise the integrity of private schools. Still other Republicans were unhappy because the proposal was too modest. For her part, Governor Whitman did not want vouchers to undermine the tax reduction initiatives that were her top priority.[72] Perhaps the most worrisome factor, for Republicans and Democrats alike, was the small fortune that the teachers' union was prepared to spend to fight the measure. In the months leading up to the 1995 legislative elections, the union made it clear that it would treat vouchers as a litmus test for its support. By the end of 1994, voucher legislation had not even been introduced.

When Mayor Schundler grumbled that Whitman had not fought hard enough for the plan, the governor agreed to raise the issue again in the new legislative term. Rather than putting forward another bill, she bought time by appointing a commission to study the issue.[73] Sentiment in the legislature did not change with the elections. Without a charismatic advocate like Polly Williams, without the attentive and unambiguous support of a governor like Tommy Thompson, without grassroots support, and with the solid opposition of a strong teachers' union, the idea of vouchers quietly faded away. In 1996, New Jersey did pass new school choice legislation, with bipartisan support. This time, though, choice assumed a different form—not vouchers but charter schools.[74] The new law proved particularly popular in Jersey City, where Mayor Schundler himself proposed to run a charter school. Schundler's gesture led those skeptical about choice to conclude that this innovation might simply represent vouchers under another name.[75]

Charter Schools: A Public Choice or a Private Market?

For the first several decades of the debate over choice in education, the concept signified one of two things: either the elaboration of a system of options entirely within the public system or the expansion of options, through vouchers, to encompass private schools. The Alum Rock experiment attempted, but ultimately failed, to find a middle ground. Today, charter schools, an idea barely a decade old, do represent a middle ground—schools that are privately run but publicly regulated and financed, a system of governance intended to promote both autonomy and accountability. Part public school and part private school, they challenge the public-private paradigm that defines so much of the politics of school choice.

Origins

Unlike vouchers, there was no grand theory to support charter schools; no Milton Friedman or Christopher Jencks to give them intellectual respectability; no shift in the rhetorical ground to accompany their emergence; and no empirically based discussion to justify them. If charter schools have less dramatic origins than vouchers, however, they have also had a much greater impact on education.

The beginnings of the charter school movement date to a 1988 conference on public school reform, held in Minneapolis, which drew together many of the key participants in the Minnesota public school choice movement.[76] Albert Shanker, head of the American Federation of Teachers, who fifteen years earlier had embraced the concept of Christopher Jencks's voucher model, delivered the key speech. Shanker praised a concept—charter schools—that he had come across in *Education by Charter: Restructuring School Districts*, a report by the former schoolteacher and administrator Ray Budde. The AFT president gave this obscure report credibility, not only at the Minneapolis conference but also in a speech at the National Press Club and in his weekly *New York Times* advertisement cum opinion piece.[77] While Shanker and Budde had in mind a reform that would enable teachers, with the approval of their union, to develop new programs within existing schools—something not so different from the Alum Rock experiment—the concept and the term *charter school* were now available for policy entrepreneurs to tinker with.

Tinker they did. Two tireless advocates, Joe Nathan, a former schoolteacher and now a researcher at the Hubert Humphrey Public Policy Institute at the University of Minnesota, and Ted Kolderie, the former executive director of the Citizens League, played key roles in shaping the charter school concept, first in Minnesota and then elsewhere. They drew for inspiration upon Shanker's remarks as well as on a variety of existing initiatives, including alternative public schools, site-based management, and British grant-maintained schools.[78] The choice-promoting measures that Minnesota had recently implemented were themselves an inspiration for charter schools. As Kolderie noted in a widely circulated report, while those earlier reforms formally opened up choice to parents, they did nothing to create any additional *school* choices. Charter legislation encouraged the creation of new schools—not schools within schools, as Shanker envisioned, but "new public schools" that exist outside the "exclusive franchise" of the public school district—to meet the new demand.[79] A 1988 Citizens League report, *Chartered Schools = Choices for Educators + Quality for All Students*, drew together the many strands of the charter concept. Enabling legislation was introduced by the same state senator who had carried the public school choice bill and, three years later, the first charter schools in the nation were authorized.[80]

The concept has proved astonishingly popular. Since Minnesota acted, in 1991, thirty-six states and the District of Columbia have authorized this new kind of institution, and with each legislative term that number grows. The Clinton administration, which initially limited its involvement with charter schools to providing modest subsidies for new schools and supporting a national evaluation, is contemplating a substantial increase in direct federal aid.[81] As with vouchers, where Milton Friedman–inspired market plans vie with Christopher Jencks–influenced equity plans, charter schools have come to mean very different things in different states. Indeed, charter regimes are as different from one another as vouchers in Alum Rock and Milwaukee. Those differences reflect distinct philosophies underlying the legislation. In some states, charter schools have been promoted as a way to manage discontent by offering an outlet for students unhappy with the public schools. Elsewhere, they are regarded as a way of educating the hardest to educate, those at-risk students on whom the Milwaukee voucher plan initially focused. Charter schools are sometimes viewed as incubators for new ideas that can be adapted by the public schools. In other places, they are seen as the entering wedge in a war on publicly run schools, a way to demonstrate that the market can replace the bureaucracy.

The history of charter school legislation in two states, California and Arizona, suggests how these variations play out in the field.

Charter Schools in California

California was the second state to adopt charter school legislation. As in Minnesota, the 1992 law had bipartisan support in the legislature and the backing of a Republican governor. There, however, the political similarities end.

The political history of charter schools in California is intertwined with the politics of vouchers. Democrats supported charter schools in hopes that this variant of choice would diminish support for Proposition 174, the voucher measure that was about to be put to the voters.[82] The author of the legislation, Democratic state senator Gary Hart, sought a way to achieve greater choice that, while responsive to the frustrations of voucher supporters, was less threatening to the public schools. That balancing act was critical to securing the support, or at least not arousing the potent opposition, of the teachers' unions. As Hart later observed,

> It seemed possible to us to craft a legislative proposal that did not sacrifice the attractive features of the voucher movement—namely, choice of schools, local control, and responsiveness to clients—while still preserving the basic principles of public education: that it be free, nonsectarian, and nondiscriminatory.[83]

The 1992 California law reflected this mix of hopes and suspicions. It permitted the creation of no more than a hundred charter schools. These schools could be either new start-ups or public school conversions. At least 10 percent of the teachers in a district, or half of the teachers in any one school, were required to endorse the proposed school.[84]

Six years later, California significantly liberalized its charter school law. The legislation expands the number of charter schools, to 250, and authorizes an additional 100 charter schools in each subsequent year. It also makes obtaining a charter much easier. The reason for this legislative shift has less to do with pedagogy than with politics, especially teacher union politics. When the possibility of liberalizing the charter school regime was first broached, in 1997, the California Teachers Assocation, which had demonstrated its political muscle in the voucher wars, was opposed. The union was prompted to reconsider its position, though, when a group of Silicon Valley businessmen, hostile to the public system, gathered enough signatures to demonstrate that it could place an even more open-ended charter school initiative on the November 1998 ballot. That initiative allowed an unlimited number of charter schools, removed the proviso that teachers approve the conversion of a public school to a charter school, and eliminated the requirement that charter school teachers be certified.[85]

This was bad news from the union's perspective, but another measure that had already qualified for the June 1998 ballot posed a far greater threat. Proposition 226, widely regarded as payback for the teacher union's earlier antivoucher campaigns, was designed to prevent unions from spending their members' dues on political activities without the written consent of each member. Had this measure passed, it would effectively have killed unions as a political force in the state. In the spring of 1998, as the legislative deal on charters was being negotiated, polls showed that Proposition 226 was likely to pass. The CTA, which spent more than $20 million in the ultimately successful effort to defeat it, lacked the resources to mount a second costly campaign. For that reason, the union agreed to work with the legislature on a new charter law if the sponsors of the initiative would agree, as they did, to withdraw their ballot measure.[86]

In the ensuing negotiations, both sides gave ground. The new law permits a substantial increase in charter schools and loosens the system of public regulatory controls. For example, a school district cannot turn down a charter application unless it is prepared to show that the proposed venture is educationally unsound, a very hard burden to meet.[87] But the CTA's influence is felt in provisions that fix a limit on the total number of charter schools, require that charter school teachers have some form of state certification, and mandate that half of all permanent teachers in a public school approve its conversion to a charter school. Nevertheless, the expanded charter school legislation confirms a fact on the ground: charter schools in California are a significant presence. As one exultant charter advocate proclaimed: "These schools are the ram's horn of Joshua that will one day bring the walls of Jericho tumbling down."[88]

A Market of Charter Schools in Arizona

While charter schools in California have been touted as alternatives to vouchers, elsewhere they have taken on the complexion of vouchers, for the state has effectively abdicated its regulatory role. Charter schools in Arizona exemplify this possibility. Arizona's charter school law, passed in 1994 and liberalized in 1996, is without question the broadest, most charter-promoting statute in the nation.[89] It establishes multiple routes for the granting of charters and, unlike almost all other states, does not limit the total number of charters that may be granted. There is no requirement that teachers be certified by the state, and, with the exception of auditing standards, participation in a statewide testing regime, and antidiscrimination requirements, the regulations that govern public schools are waived. Thus once a charter is granted in Arizona—for a period of fifteen years, by far the longest in the nation—a school is effectively subject only to the discipline of the market. "Charters have already closed their doors; that is the genius of this plan," says the Republican speaker of the house, one of its initial backers. Schools are left to sink or swim in an educational environment characterized by ever increasing competition, not only from other charter schools but also from private schools and newly market-conscious public school districts.

In Arizona as in California, charter schools were initially regarded as a way to forestall vouchers. In the early 1990s a statewide task force of business and education leaders proposed an array of public school reforms, including statewide open enrollment, site-based management, and school "report cards." The task force also urged stronger statewide academic standards as well as the development of a test that would assess students' ability to meet those standards. Many Arizona conservatives, including Governor Fife Symington, regarded such reforms as inadequate. The replacement of bureaucratic accountability with outcome accountability, as the task force was urging, was insufficient; the surest form of accountability, they argued, was market accountability. In their view, the real problem lay with public education itself, which needed to be subjected to competition, not simply mended.

Taking their cues partly from the Goldwater Institute, a conservative local think tank, Governor Symington and others, among them house education committee chair Lisa Graham, framed their arguments for more fundamental change not in educationese but in the language of welfare economics. Public schools, like other monopolies, were naturally unresponsive to consumer (that is, parent) demand; only the introduction of choice would pry open this market, enabling parents to obtain an education for their children that they regarded as responsive to their needs.

The preferred strategy for introducing competition into the Arizona education market was vouchers. Over a three-year period beginning in 1992,

voucher legislation passed the state house of representatives, only to be bot-
tled up in the senate. In 1994, with the election of a GOP Senate majority
coupled with strong gubernatorial support, voucher advocates were confident that they would finally prevail. Leading conservative figures, among
them William Bennett, Pat Robertson, and Jack Kemp, were flown into the
state to stump for vouchers (by many accounts, the tactic backfired, as the
outsiders' perceived arrogance turned off the lawmakers). Although earlier
voucher statutes were sweeping in scope, the 1995 measure, modeled on
Wisconsin's legislation, provided vouchers to 10,000 low-income children
from the primarily black South Phoenix area. That bill was regarded by its
proponents as a first step toward a statewide voucher plan.

After passing the house, the bill was put to a vote in the senate, where
it came tantalizingly close to passing. Backers hoped that a deal could be
cut with one or two conservative Democrats; opponents feared that the bill
might squeak through. Confronted with this perceived deadlock, as well as
mounting public demands that the state do something about the issue, Lisa
Graham and Beverly Harmon, the respective chairs of the senate and house
education committees, opted for compromise, and some Democrats went
along. In a special legislative session called to address this single issue, the
voucher bill was shelved, and in its place a charter school law was approved.
Passage came swiftly, with broad bipartisan support and almost no debate.
The Teachers Association (teachers' unions are not permitted in Arizona)
and the School Boards Association, natural opponents of the measure, had
little input. Most Arizona lawmakers ignored the details, concentrating
instead on the concept, but those details have proved crucial. Not only has
this measure led to a proliferation of charter schools—more than anyplace
else in the nation—it has also changed the nature of political debate over
public education in the state.

Charter supporters were determined that these new schools have an
immediate and visible presence. In a matter of months, the state gave charters to scores of schools. As one legislator observed, "anyone who could
stand up and breathe got a charter." In order to protect the charter school
concept from the local school boards and state board of education, both
regarded as hostile to the innovation, the legislation created a new entity,
the Charter School Board, whose sole mission was issuing charters and promoting charter schools. The Charter School Board was authorized to issue
up to twenty-five charters each year. Thus if school districts turned down
charters and the state board of education balked, a significant number of
new schools would still be launched. In addition, school districts were

authorized to issue charters to schools anywhere in the state. As a consequence, a market for charters has sprung up, with districts charging upward
of $20,000 to would-be school operators.

Charter schools have become a fixture in Arizona's educational landscape. In 1998, 266 such schools operated under 166 charters granted by
state and local educational agencies; they serve some 35,000 students, nearly
3 percent of the school-age population. These schools are freed from most
of the nearly 800 pages of regulations that govern public schools. Back-to-
basics schools, often with strong religious ties, have flourished in the suburbs, while in Phoenix, new schools have sprung up for hard-to-educate
youngsters and school dropouts. Some are "chain" schools, which package the same educational approach in several sites. For-profit educational
organizations regard Arizona as a promising new market.

Charter schools, not vouchers, are the vehicle for educational choice in
the state. Since the passage of the charter school law, there has been little
pressure to revisit the voucher issue, a result that was not anticipated when
the charter school law was passed.[90] Nor is this the only unanticipated development. Instead of the state providing vouchers for 15,000 poor children—
the measure that failed because of liberals' qualms—Arizona underwrites
the education of a potentially unlimited number of youngsters in essentially
unregulated schools. Conservatives are as surprised as liberals by these
developments and what they suggest about the pent-up demand for choice.
"The charter school movement took off far more rapidly than any of us
imagined," says the head of the Goldwater Institute, which earlier had been
unsuccessful in pushing the concept of market-oriented vouchers.

Charters and the Future of Public Education

In theory, public accountability—that is, the satisfaction of public values as well as family preferences—distinguishes charter schools from vouchers, where accountability is supposed to flow entirely from family
sovereignty. In practice, however, the two choice models blur the boundary between accountability and sovereignty. The laws governing the Milwaukee and Cleveland voucher plans prohibit the use of such admission
criteria as prior academic achievement; require that the voucher cover all
regular school costs; and determine who is eligible, based on their family
income. In these respects, the voucher schemes are more attentive to equity
concerns than the Arizona charter school law.

The philosophy of regulation that prevails in Arizona is that parents are
the real regulators and that the state's role should essentially be limited to

financial oversight. Schools that are chartered by districts hundreds of miles away are even less subject to monitoring, since the chartering districts lack the resources, the personnel, and the inclination. Thus while oversight is in theory a way to ensure public accountability, the practice in Arizona is otherwise. The department of education, acknowledges the state superintendent of public instruction Lisa Graham Keegan (formerly Lisa Graham; the provoucher legislator was elected state superintendent in 1995), is advocate, licenser, and reviewer for charter schools. "There is no separation of powers." Nor is there any interest on the state's part in closing bad schools. "These are small businesses, which live or die by the market," says the bureaucrat with responsibility for regulating them. Superintendent Keegan is entirely unapologetic. "In Arizona, charter schools are effectively group vouchers."[91]

In Arizona as in California, there is widespread popular acceptance of charter schools. Even among those who were initially resistant, there is growing acknowledgment that, because of their small size and focused curricula, these institutions can help students who would likely fare poorly in more impersonal public institutions. The Arizona Education Association, the statewide teachers' group, is designing its own charter school plan, and even the state School Boards Association, the most vehement opponent, concedes that charter schools have become a fixture. Superintendent Keegan, borrowing President Clinton's welfare rhetoric, wants to "change the face of public education as we know it." In 1998 Keegan introduced a school financing plan that could do just that, further blurring the line between ordinary public schools, charter schools, and vouchers. Arizona currently provides school districts with per pupil allocations. Dollars follow a student across district lines; thus pupils who take advantage of open enrollment to attend schools outside their community of residence bring their allocation to their new districts. Charter school funds, by contrast, are given directly to the school. In effect, each school is its own school district.

It is this model that Keegan wants to apply to public education. If her proposal becomes law, dollars would be distributed not to school districts but directly to individual public schools, thus giving real teeth to the concept of site-based management.[92] A public school, like a charter school, would depend for its survival on the number of students it attracted. It would be free, within the broad constraints of state law, to shape its own curriculum; it would be free as well to draw students from outside its historic attendance boundaries. If this plan passes, the typical Arizona public school would look not so very different from the "public school conversion" charter schools that elsewhere in the nation represent a substantial proportion of all charter schools.

Conclusion: The Transformed Politics of School Choice

Political support for school choice has mushroomed in a quarter of a century. In 1972 the federally sponsored Alum Rock voucher experiment had to drop private schools from its design; even its public school choice plan was initially controversial and ultimately insignificant. By 1999 two voucher programs were operating in urban school districts, and one statewide program had been launched; public school choice was commonplace across the country; and most states had initiated a new public-private hybrid, charter schools.

The growing importance of choice in educational policy is partly explained by the ways advocates have been able to characterize their ideas, creating a more sympathetic picture by shifting the conversation away from an emphasis on market-based choice and toward an emphasis on equity-based choice. This transformation set the stage for charter schools, equity-based voucher programs, and public school choice plans; and these in turn have kept less regulated, market-based plans under consideration. The primacy of choice is attributable to more than a new political vocabulary, however. In Cleveland and East Harlem, Phoenix and Milwaukee, diverse coalitions of special interest groups have struggled to shape and implement a variety of school choice plans. The details of those plans, hammered out through bargaining, have proved at least as important as the concept and the rhetoric. Altered political contexts have opened new windows of opportunity to implement school choice policies, and able entrepreneurs have taken advantage of these situations.

The federal government's efforts to launch a voucher experiment in the 1970s failed because of a hesitancy to alienate the teachers' unions, concerns about undermining school desegregation efforts, a reluctance of private schools to subject themselves to state regulation and a lack of grassroots political support. By the early 1990s, however, public school choice had become commonplace, and educational and racial politics had begun to shift. Vouchers, in turn, became a viable political possibility. In Milwaukee and Cleveland, anger at failed desegregation policies and poorly performing public schools led some blacks to split from the traditional liberal-labor coalition that had previously blocked any voucher plan. The cultivation of private schools eager for public funding added an element that was missing from the Alum Rock equation. Renewed efforts among conservative politicians and foundations to support school voucher reforms, including support for equity-based plans, produced much needed funding as well as ideological support. Vouchers, however, have yet to take off, for reasons suggested in the New Jersey story: the traditional antivoucher coalition— teachers' unions, civil rights organizations, civil libertarians—has generally stayed united and potent in its opposition.

While only two cities and one state have implemented voucher plans to date, the voucher wars boosted the fledgling charter school movement. Opponents of vouchers pin their hopes on charter schools as the public alternative to private school aid, even as voucher advocates support charters as a foot in the door of the public school monopoly.[93]

What is the political future of school choice? The historic capacity of public school bureaucracies and their political supporters to resist the best efforts of reformers suggests that the safest prediction is that little will ultimately happen—that choice will remain a marginal phenomenon in education, functioning as a regulated safety valve for unhappy parents, students, and professionals.[94] Among the structural reforms currently receiving serious attention, systemic change of public schooling notable among them, choice seems the likeliest to survive.[95] It has become institutionalized in recent years through open enrollment, alternative schools, and especially charter schools, and this makes it hard to dislodge it from the system. Each new site where choice exists brings new constituents into the movement.

New equity-based voucher plans are most likely to emerge in urban school districts where black activists and conservative politicians and foundations forge an alliance that contests the traditional liberal-labor coalition. Whether vouchers will eventually have wider appeal, though, remains uncertain. Insisting on an equity component in a voucher plan risks losing the support of existing private schools and middle-class parents, who may well find the new charter school regime a better bet. On the other hand, market-based plans are unlikely to get very far. The absence of equity strings and accountability-promoting regulation makes them threatening, not only to the politically powerful teachers' unions and civil rights groups but also to the majority of families who report that they are happy with their local public schools and do not want public dollars siphoned off to private schools. For these groups as well, charter schools may be more attractive precisely because of their public-private character.

The wild card in these political projections is the judiciary. If the U.S. Supreme Court reverses nearly forty years of precedent and permits the expenditure of public funds for parochial school tuition, the political fortunes for vouchers will dramatically improve.[96] The Catholic Church will renew its push for vouchers. Parents who send their children to parochial schools, including a sizable number of non-Catholic, inner-city parents, will support that effort as well, thus further splintering the old antivoucher coalition. The fastest growing segment of the private school sector, fundamentalist Christian schools, will also back vouchers as long as restrictions on admissions and curriculum are not perceived as undermining their mission.

Whether the new political dynamic set in motion by a changed constitutional standard actually leads to voucher legislation may turn on whether support can be generated in suburban districts, where support for vouchers has so far been weakest and charter schools are beginning to be a presence. If the next generation of voucher proposals includes religious schools as an option, if voucher-supported private schools can peacefully coexist with a system of quasi-private charter schools, and if elements of equity and regulation are included in the design—that is, if these proposals resemble the original Alum Rock proposal outlined nearly three decades ago by Christopher Jencks—then once again the politics of choice will shift dramatically.

Notes

1. School choice may occur exclusively within the public sector through open enrollment, magnet schools, controlled public choice, or charter schools. Choice policies that provide public support for private schools include plans that grant tuition vouchers to parents, tax credits to parents, or vouchers given directly to the chosen school by the state. In each case, the amount of the voucher, the administration of the voucher, and the eligibility for the voucher (that is, whether it is given directly to the parent or to the school) can vary. (This chapter does not discuss in detail privately funded, private school choice programs.)

2. Jay Greene and others, "The Effectiveness of School Choice in Milwaukee: A Secondary Analysis of Data from the Program's Evaluation," paper prepared for the American Political Science Association annual meeting, 1996; John F. Witte, "Politics: Who Benefits from the Milwaukee Choice Program?" in Bruce Fuller and Richard Elmore, eds., *Who Chooses? Who Loses? Culture, Institutions, and the Unequal Effects of School Choice* (Teachers College Press, 1996); Bob Davis, "Class Warfare: Dueling Professors Have Milwaukee Dazed over School Vouchers," *Wall Street Journal*, October 11, 1996.

3. John W. Kingdon, *Agendas, Alternatives, and Public Policies* (Harper/Collins, 1995).

4. Joe Nathan, *Charter Schools: Creating Hope and Opportunity for American Education* (San Francisco: Jossey-Bass, 1996); Joe Nathan, interview by author, June 29, 1998.

5. Peter W. Cookson Jr., *School Choice: The Struggle for the Soul of American Education* (Yale University Press, 1994).

6. Also see Albert O. Hirschman, *Exit, Voice, and Loyalty* (Harvard University Press, 1970).

7. Robert C. Bulman, "School Choice Stories: Unraveling the Dynamics of High School Selection," Ph.D. diss., University of California, Berkeley, 1999.

8. Lowell C. Rose and others, "The Twenty-Ninth Annual Phi Delta Kappa/Gallup Poll of the Public's Attitudes toward the Public Schools," *Phi Delta Kappan* (September 1997), pp. 41–56.

9. Ibid.

10. Kevin Dougherty and Lisabet Sostre, "Minerva and the Market," *Educational Policy*, vol. 6, no. 2 (1992), pp. 160–79.

11. Jeffrey R. Henig, *Rethinking School Choice* (Princeton University Press, 1994).

12. Milton Friedman, "The Role of Government in Education," in Robert A. Solo, ed., *Economics and the Public Interest* (Rutgers University Press, 1955); Milton Friedman, *Capitalism and Freedom* (University of Chicago Press, 1962). Friedman argued that as a public monopoly the public schools restricted the freedom of parents, prevented competition between schools, undermined efficiency, and depressed educational achievement. He was among the first to suggest that state-issued vouchers be used by consumers to purchase an education in a market of public and private schools. Friedman's publications restated an idea propounded by John Stuart Mill a century earlier in *On Liberty* (London: 1859).

13. David L. Kirp, "What School Choice Really Means," *Atlantic Monthly* (November 1992), pp. 119–29.

14. Kingdon, *Agendas, Alternatives, and Public Policies.*

15. Robert Behn, "Management by Groping Along," *Journal of Policy Analysis and Management*, vol. 7, no. 4 (1988), pp. 643–63.

16. Kingdon, *Agendas, Alternatives, and Public Policies.*

17. Peter W. Cookson Jr., "Redesigning the Financing of American Education to Raise Productivity: The Case for a Just Voucher," in Simon Hakim and others, eds., *Privatizing Education and Educational Choice: Concepts, Plans, and Experiences* (Praeger, 1994).

18. The distinction between market-based and equity-based voucher plans is similar to the distinction that Coons and Sugarman make between universal plans and focused plans. John E. Coons and Stephen D. Sugarman, *Scholarships for Children* (Berkeley, Calif.: Institute of Governmental Studies Press, 1992).

19. George R. LaNoue, introduction to George R. La Noue, ed., *Educational Vouchers: Concepts and Controversies* (Teachers College Press, 1972).

20. During his tenure at Harvard, Daniel P. Moynihan, counselor to President Nixon and his chief adviser on social policy issues, had been associated with the Center for the Study of Public Policy.

21. Christopher Jencks, "Education Vouchers: A Report on Financing Education by Payments to Parents" (Cambridge, Mass., Center for the Study of Public Policy, 1970). By the early 1970s several social scientists were proposing school choice policies of one sort or another. In addition to Friedman and Jencks, see Henry M. Levin, "The Failure of the Public Schools and the Free Market Remedy," *Urban Review*, vol. 32 (June 1968), pp. 32–37; Theodore Sizer and Phillip Whitten, "A Proposal for a Poor Children's Bill of Rights," *Psychology Today*, vol. 2, no. 3 (1968), pp. 58–71; John E. Coons and Stephen D. Sugarman, "Family Choice in Education: A Model State System for Vouchers," *California Law Review*, vol. 59, no. 2 (1971), pp. 321–438.

22. Statement of Christopher Jencks, U.S. Senate Select Committee on Equal Educational Opportunity, 1971.

23. Albert Shanker, "The Educational Voucher Idea: A Present Danger," in *A Voucher Reader: A Selection of 'Where We Stand' Columns from 1971 to 1993* (Washington, D.C.: American Federation of Teachers, 1993).

24. David K. Cohen and Eleanor Farrar, "Power to the Parents? The Story of Education Vouchers," *Public Interest*, vol. 48 (Summer 1977), pp. 72–97; Eliot Levinson, "The Alum Rock Voucher Demonstration: Three Years of Implementation," Series P-5631 (Santa Mon-

ica, Calif.: RAND, 1976); Evan Jenkins, "A School Voucher Experiment Rates an 'A' in Coast District," *New York Times*, May 29, 1973; Daniel Weiler, "A Public School Voucher Demonstration: The First Year at Alum Rock" (Santa Monica, Calif.: RAND, 1974).

25. Sanford J. Glovinsky, "Final Report: Alum Rock Union Elementary School District Voucher Feasibility Study," in James A. Mecklenburger and Richard W. Hostrop, eds., *Education Vouchers: From Theory to Alum Rock* (Homewood, Ill.: ETC, 1972).

26. Enabling legislation was finally passed in the fall of 1973. However, the conditions for private school participation were so restrictive that no existing private school chose to participate. One private school was created to take advantage of the new legislation, but no children ever enrolled. See Cohen and Farrar, "Power to the Parents?"

27. Weiler, "A Public School Voucher Demonstration."

28. Levinson, "The Alum Rock Voucher Demonstration," p. 34.

29. David W. Kirkpatrick, *Choice in Schooling: A Case for Tuition Vouchers* (Loyola University Press, 1990).

30. Cohen and Farrar, "Power to the Parents?"

31. Ann Swidler, *Organization without Authority: Dilemmas of Social Control in Free Schools* (Harvard University Press, 1979).

32. Milton Friedman and Rose Friedman, *Free to Choose: A Personal Statement* (Harcourt Brace Jovanovich, 1980).

33. John E. Coons and Stephen D. Sugarman, *Education by Choice: The Case for Family Control* (University of California Press, 1978); Coons and Sugarman, *Scholarships for Children*. See also James S. Catterall, *Education Vouchers* (Bloomington, Ind.: Phi Delta Kappa, Education Foundation, 1984).

34. Henig, *Rethinking School Choice*, p. 72.

35. Kirp, "What School Choice Really Means."

36. National Commission on Excellence in Education, *A Nation at Risk* (Government Printing Office, 1983).

37. Allyson M. Tucker and William F. Lauber, *School Choice Programs: What's Happening in the States* (Washington, D.C.: Heritage Foundation, 1994).

38. Tim L. Mazzoni, "The Politics of Educational Choice in Minnesota," in William L. Boyd and Charles T. Kerchner, eds., *The Politics of Excellence and Choice in Education* (New York: Falmer, 1987).

39. Minnesota Department of Education, "Access to Excellence: Education in Minnesota" (St. Paul: 1988).

40. Tim L. Mazzoni and Barry Sullivan, "Legislating Educational Choices in Minnesota: Politics and Prospects," in William Boyd and Herbert Walberg, eds., *Choice in Education: Potential and Problems* (Berkeley, Calif.: McCutchan, 1990); Mazzoni, "The Politics of Educational Choice in Minnesota."

41. Minnesota Department of Education, "Access to Excellence."

42. John E. Chubb and Terry M. Moe, *Politics, Markets, and America's Schools* (Brookings, 1990).

43. For example, John Witte, "Public Subsidies for Private Schools: What We Know and How to Proceed," *Educational Policy*, vol. 6, no. 2 (1992), pp. 206–27.

44. John E. Chubb and Terry M. Moe, "America's Public Schools: Choice Is a Panacea," *Brookings Review*, vol. 8, no. 3 (1990), pp. 4–13.

45. William Celis III, "Oregon Considers Tax Credits to Aid Private Schooling," *New York Times*, August 22, 1990; Jean Merl, "Colorado Is Battle Ground for School Voucher System," *Los Angeles Times*, October 26, 1992; Amy Stuart Wells, *Time to Choose: America at the Crossroads of School Choice Policy* (Hill and Wang, 1993). Measure 11, the market-based education choice initiative in Oregon, would have amended the state constitution to allow a

tax credit of $2,500 to any family with children in private schools, in religious schools, or in home schooling. It also would have introduced open enrollment to all of Oregon's public schools. It failed by a margin of two to one. The Colorado initiative in 1992 was similar to the Oregon initiative. It would have provided a $2,500 voucher to parents in private schools but not to home schoolers. It also failed by a two-to-one margin.

46. Coons and Sugarman, *Education by Choice.*

47. Coons and Sugarman, *Scholarships for Children.*

48. Stephen Sugarman, interview by author, March 25, 1998; William Trombley, "Major Fight Looms over Initiative on Vouchers," *Los Angeles Times,* December 15, 1991.

49. John Jacobs, "Funding the Voucher Battle," *Sacramento Bee,* August 12, 1993.

50. Michael Granberry, "School Voucher Plan Qualifies for June 1994 Ballot," *Los Angeles Times,* August 21, 1992.

51. Dan Walters, "Big Ballot War Ahead," *Sacramento Bee,* December 29, 1997.

52. Robert D. Novak, "Halfhearted Fight for Choice," *Washington Post,* October 18, 1993.

53. John J. Miller, "Why School Choice Lost," *Wall St. Journal,* November 4, 1993.

54. Policy Analysis for California Education, "Californians' Attitudes toward Education and School Vouchers" (Berkeley, Calif.: PACE, 1993).

55. James L. Baughman, *Impact of School Desegregation in Milwaukee Public Schools on Quality of Education for Minorities: Fifteen Years Later* (U.S. Commission on Civil Rights, Wisconsin Advisory Committee, 1992).

56. Ibid.; Jim Carl, "Unusual Allies: Elite and Grass-Roots Origins of Parental Choice in Milwaukee," *Teachers College Record,* vol. 98, no. 2 (1996), pp. 266–85.

57. Baughman, *Impact of School Desegregation in Milwaukee*; Daniel McGroarty, *Break These Chains: The Battle for School Choice* (Rocklin, Calif.: Forum, 1996); David Nicholson, "Schools in Transition: Milwaukee Implements School Choice Program," *Washington Post,* August 5, 1990.

58. Cited in Baughman, *Impact of School Desegregation in Milwaukee,* p. 11.

59. McGroarty, *Break These Chains*; Robert S. Peterkin, "What's Happening in Milwaukee?" *Educational Leadership,* vol. 48 (December–January, 1990–91), pp. 50–52.

60. Carl, "Unusual Allies"; Dan Wycliff, "Right to Choose Schools Gains in Debate on Bias," *New York Times,* June 10, 1990.

61. Carl, "Unusual Allies."

62. Carl notes that the cause of school vouchers in Milwaukee had been given publicity and legitimation through a number of studies, critical of the Milwaukee public schools and supportive of school vouchers, that had been conducted by the Bradley-funded Wisconsin Policy Research Institute in the late 1980s.

63. For example, Eric Harrison, "Milwaukee School Choice Proposal Ignites Bitter Racial, Political Battles," *Los Angeles Times,* August 3, 1990.

64. Witte, "Who Benefits from the Milwaukee Choice Program?"

65. *Jackson v. Benson,* 578 N.W.2d 602 (Wis., 1998).

66. Alex Molnar, "The Real Lessons of Milwaukee's Voucher Experiment," *Education Week,* August 6, 1997.

67. Joe Williams, "Williams Wants Limits on School Choice," *Milwaukee Journal Sentinel,* February 10, 1998.

68. The Cleveland voucher program, initiated in 1995, is the first to provide vouchers for students who attend religious schools. As in Milwaukee, the Cleveland plan has its roots in a mainly black city's decades-long desegregation struggle. The measure was also backed by conservative leadership. The opposition cast was familiar: teachers' unions, the American Civil Liberties Union, the National Association for the Advancement of Colored People, and the

Parent Teacher Association. Even as the constitutionality of the plan is being tested in court, the voucher plan continues to operate, and church-run schools have received state aid. Rene Sanchez, "Cleveland Charts New Educational Course," *Washington Post*, September 10, 1996; Dan Murphy and others, *The Cleveland Voucher Program: Who Chooses? Who Gets Chosen? Who Pays?* (Washington, D.C.: American Federation of Teachers, 1997); Rick Bragg, "Florida Will Award Vouchers for Pupils Whose Schools Fail," *New York Times*, April 28, 1999.

69. Tom Topousis, "Green Light for School Vouchers," *Record*, January 19, 1994.

70. Eugene Kiely, "Whitman Backs Trial Program for Private-School Vouchers," *Record*, March 26, 1993; Topousis, "Green Light for School Vouchers."

71. Kimberly J. McLarin, "Voucher Plan Is Unveiled for Schools in Jersey City," *New York Times*, October 6, 1994; Robert J. Braun, "School Voucher Tryout Proposed for Jersey City," *Star-Ledger*, October 5, 1994; Steve Marlowe, "Fists Fly at School-Voucher Rally," *Record*, October 17, 1994.

72. Robert Schwaneberg and Ron Marsico, "GOP Senator Assails School Voucher Plan," *Star-Ledger*, October 19, 1994; Kimberly J. McLarin, "Support for New Jersey School Vouchers Falters," *New York Times*, December 22, 1994.

73. Mark Walsh, "N.J. Governor Agrees to Delay School Voucher Legislation," *Education Week*, January 18, 1995.

74. Charter school legislation was introduced in New Jersey by Governor James Florio in 1992. Jerry Gray, "Florio Aproves Chartering of Parent-Teacher Schools," *New York Times*, October 9, 1992.

75. Jennifer Preston, "Trenton Senate Votes to Subsidize Charter Schools," *New York Times*, December 12, 1995; Neil MacFarquhar, "Public, but Independent, Schools Are Inspiring Hope and Hostility," *New York Times*, December 27, 1996.

76. Joe Nathan, interview.

77. Albert Shanker, "National Press Club Speech," March 31, 1988; Shanker, "Convention Plots New Course—A Charter for Change," *New York Times*, July 10, 1988; also see Ray Budde, *Education by Charter: Restructuring School Districts* (Andover, Mass.: Regional Laboratory for Educational Improvement of the Northeast and Islands, 1988).

78. Nathan, *Charter Schools*; Gary K. Hart and Sue Burr, "The Story of California's Charter School Legislation," *Phi Delta Kappan* (December 1996), pp. 37–40.

79. Ted Kolderie, *Beyond Choice to New Public Schools: Withdrawing the Exclusive Franchise in Public Education* (Washington, D.C.: Progressive Policy Institute, 1990).

80. Kolderie claims that charter schools had a quiet beginning because a number of distinct and diverse tributaries of influence converged slowly to create a new and larger river; interview by author, June 8, 1998; Nathan, interview.

81. David Kirp is coprincipal investigator in this national evaluation, which is being carried out by RPP International under contract with the U.S. Department of Education.

82. In response to the threat of vouchers the California legislature also passed a pair of public school choice bills in 1994 patterned after the Minnesota open-enrollment legislation. One bill (AB 19) authorized school districts to allow interdistrict transfers provided that classroom space is available and the transfer does not disturb the racial balance of the schools. The other bill (AB 1114) requires school districts to allow intradistrict school transfers provided that there is space in the desired school.

83. Hart and Burr, "The Story of California's Charter School Legislation."

84. An earlier charter school proposal had been vetoed by Governor Pete Wilson because it gave too much power to the teachers to reject a charter school application; ibid.

85. Zachary Coile, "Fear of Initiative Spurs Charter School Bill in Legislature," *San Francisco Examiner*, May 1, 1998.

86. Eric Premack, codirector of the Charter School Development Center at the Institute for Education Reform at California State University at Sacramento, interview by author, June 3, 1998. The Silicon Valley group was also more than happy to make a few concessions in order to forgo a costly campaign in the fall (ibid.).

87. Sue Burr, president of the Network for Education Charters in California, interview by author, June 2, 1998; see also Phil Garcia, "Legislative Panel OKs Bill Bolstering Charter Schools," *Sacramento Bee*, April 29, 1998. With the support of the CTA, newly elected Democratic governor Gray Davis signed legislation in July 1999 that slightly scaled back this charter school legislation. Specifically, the legislation that Davis signed ensures that charter school students receive the same amount of instructional time as regular public school students, requires that charter school students take statewide tests, and limits the amount of non-classroom-based distance learning that charter schools can conduct; "New Restrictions for Charter Schools," *Sacramento Bee*, July 24, 1999.

88. Alan Bonsteel, "The Proposition 174 Story," in Alan Bonsteel and Carlos Bonilla, eds., *A Choice for Our Children* (San Francisco: ICS, 1997).

89. David L. Kirp, "The Law-Policy System for Charter Schools in Arizona" (Emeryville, Calif.: RPP International, 1998). This section is an abridged version of that report.

90. A measure authorizing taxpayers to earmark up to $500 in state tax credits for contributions to scholarship programs that pay for tuition at private schools (including religious schools) was upheld by the Arizona Supreme Court early in 1999. *Kotterman v. Killian*, 972 P.2d 606 (Az), cert. denied, 1999 WL 278906 (1999). A companion measure, authorizing a similar earmarking of $200 for pupils attending public schools, is also in effect.

91. Lisa Graham Keegan, interview by author, March 1998.

92. See generally Anthony S. Bryk and others, *Charting Chicago School Reform: Democratic Localism as a Lever for Change* (Boulder, Colo.: Westview, 1998).

93. Sometimes, as in Arizona, the unintended consequence of charter school legislation is to open up a new market of quasi-private schools operated at public expense, with charters doing the work of vouchers.

94. David Tyack and Larry Cuban, *Tinkering toward Utopia* (Harvard University Press, 1995); Jeffrey Henig, *Rethinking School Choice*.

95. Jennifer O'Day and Marshall Smith, "Systemic Reform and Educational Opportunity," in Susan Fuhrman, ed., *Designing Coherent Educational Policy* (San Francisco: Jossey-Bass, 1993).

96. In fall 1998, the U.S. Supreme Court declined to hear the Wisconsin case, postponing the day of legal reckoning.

CHAPTER THREE

School Choice Outcomes

JEFFREY R. HENIG

Innovative policy ideas present prudent people and pragmatic societies with a dilemma. On the one hand, the tragedy and waste occasioned by some long-standing social problems virtually demand that we shift gears and try something daring and new. Our political system is abundant with institutional biases toward the status quo. The checks and balances among branches of the government, federalism and governmental fragmentation, a multiplicity of veto points, and the privileged position of a bureaucracy vested in established routines combine to make incrementalism the rule, even when conditions and conscience call for more drastic reactions. On the other hand, history provides many examples of governmental overreaction. The authoritative use of public authority can do damage, even when well intentioned. Prudence may require that we test new ideas before we commit to them. Pragmatism may require that we guide our actions by evidence, not by abstract theory. Innovative policy ideas come to us untested and with little empirical evidence to back up their claims.

For Americans grappling with the need for school reform, school choice proposals have presented this dilemma for over forty years. Milton Friedman's early formulation of a school voucher proposal was rooted in microeconomic theory.[1] While the idea stirred some excitement in intellectual circles, efforts to translate it into practice proved frustrating. Federal officials, anxious to develop empirical evidence about the consequences of vouchers, worked hard in the early 1970s to institute true voucher experiments. Only one local school district—Alum Rock, California—ultimately proved willing to risk engaging in such an uncertain venture, and proponents of Friedman's model argued that the conditions that state and local officials placed on the experiment watered it down so much that it was not a legitimate test of his ideas at all.[2] While there are multiple reasons for Friedman's voucher ideas not catching on, certainly one facet was Americans' reluctance to gamble on a seemingly risky and untested idea.[3]

By the mid-1980s, when school choice began percolating its way back into the attention of policymakers and the attentive public, those inclined to seek guidance from social science found the cupboards rather bare. Although many families were indeed exercising forms of school choice—via residential location, private education, magnet schools, or liberal transfer policies—these activities appeared too disparate and too far removed from contemporary policy debates to warrant much attention from serious researchers within the social science community. Grand claims, ideologically grounded predictions, partisan maneuvering, and anecdotal accounts predictably filled the resulting vacuum.

During the 1990s, however, several factors have converged to generate a much richer pool of empirical evidence about whether school choice works. First, there is more school choice going on for researchers to study (see chapter 1, this volume). A number of states and local districts have launched new school reform initiatives, which, while almost never involving vouchers, nonetheless are built around the concept of parental choice and a rejection of the conventional notion of a mandatory attendance zone. The enactment of these programs gave scholars already interested in school choice something to study, rather than simply something to think about and argue about. Second, a broader range of scholars is interested in studying school choice. As choice began to move up the policy agenda, scholars began to more fully develop intellectual linkages between this technical tool for initiating school reform and some very broad theoretical questions about the nature of and relationships among markets, bureaucracies, social capital, and democratic institutions. These linkages added momentum to the collective enterprise of school choice scholarship by drawing into the debate social scientists and funding sources that did not specialize in education issues.

Third, and perhaps the most important because it helped set the stage for these other changes, was a broad redefinition of school choice to encompass a range of programs and conditions that were already in place. At least symbolically, this redefinition can be dated to January 1988, when President Ronald Reagan chose a public magnet school in Prince George's County, Maryland, as the setting for a major speech on the benefits of school choice. "Previously, choice proposals had been associated with private schools and market principles; previously, magnet schools had been associated with authoritative government action to bring about racial integration rather than educational quality."[4] Linking the idea of vouchers to the existing practice of choice within the public system permitted market proponents to argue that school choice was demonstrably feasible and compatible with societal values such as racial integration. It also made available for empirical analysis a wide range of manifestations of school choice that previously had been overlooked as a relevant data source.

Learning from Experience

The market model, which is closely tied to arguments in favor of school choice, makes predictions about how consumers and suppliers will behave and about the ways that demand and supply will intersect to generate more efficient and effective outcomes. Critics of the market model as applied to education raise questions about the empirical validity of its key assumptions about parent-consumers (demand-side), schools (supply-side), and the products that a market in education would generate. Figure 3-1 offers a stripped-down representation of the basic model and summarizes some of the important research questions about the demand-side, the supply-side, and the educational outcomes of school choice.

This section reviews some of the relevant evidence that social scientists have garnered via empirical analysis of choice in all of its guises. The review provides some encouragement for those who retain hope that a serious research enterprise can lead to more informed debate. Just as significant as the increased number of studies is the fact that many of them are thoughtfully conceived, well designed, and competently executed. Many studies of five or more years ago were impressionistic and anecdotal, and even some of the more sophisticated analyses were plagued by inadequate measures and lack of more than rudimentary controls.[5] While there is still a need for more and better studies, the ratio of good studies to poor studies is now much more favorable, and major studies in place will generate important findings over the next several years. Findings from these studies appear to be somewhat stable and consistent across different forms of school choice and in different kinds of settings.

Figure 3-1. *The Market Model Applied to Choice Schools*

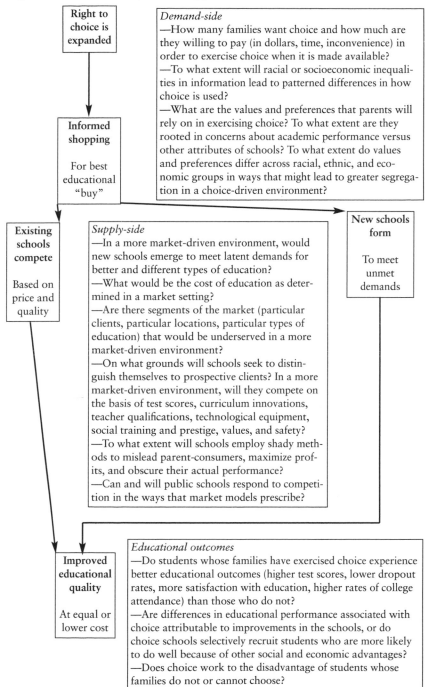

Right to choice is expanded

Demand-side
—How many families want choice and how much are they willing to pay (in dollars, time, inconvenience) in order to exercise choice when it is made available?
—To what extent will racial or socioeconomic inequalities in information lead to patterned differences in how choice is used?
—What are the values and preferences that parents will rely on in exercising choice? To what extent are they rooted in concerns about academic performance versus other attributes of schools? To what extent do values and preferences differ across racial, ethnic, and economic groups in ways that might lead to greater segregation in a choice-driven environment?

Informed shopping

For best educational "buy"

Existing schools compete

Based on price and quality

Supply-side
—In a more market-driven environment, would new schools emerge to meet latent demands for better and different types of education?
—What would be the cost of education as determined in a market setting?
—Are there segments of the market (particular clients, particular locations, particular types of education) that would be underserved in a more market-driven environment?
—On what grounds will schools seek to distinguish themselves to prospective clients? In a more market-driven environment, will they compete on the basis of test scores, curriculum innovations, teacher qualifications, technological equipment, social training and prestige, values, and safety?
—To what extent will schools employ shady methods to mislead parent-consumers, maximize profits, and obscure their actual performance?
—Can and will public schools respond to competition in the ways that market models prescribe?

New schools form

To meet unmet demands

Improved educational quality

At equal or lower cost

Educational outcomes
—Do students whose families have exercised choice experience better educational outcomes (higher test scores, lower dropout rates, more satisfaction with education, higher rates of college attendance) than those who do not?
—Are differences in educational performance associated with choice attributable to improvements in the schools, or do choice schools selectively recruit students who are more likely to do well because of other social and economic advantages?
—Does choice work to the disadvantage of students whose families do not or cannot choose?

Although this broad overview of the evidence about demand, supply, and outcomes emphasizes agreement on some basic evidence, there is an area in which there is much less agreement: what to *make* of the evidence that is accumulating. The weight of the accumulating evidence suggests that the hysteria that marks the dire predictions on both sides is misplaced, even though this has not translated into a new consensus nor even a more civil and thoughtful public debate.

The Demand-Side

Framed in the abstract, the debate between choice proponents and choice critics offers sharply contrasting predictions about the way parents can be expected to behave in a more market-driven system. Market theories predict that well-informed parents, dissatisfied with their assigned public schools, would actively explore alternatives and would do so primarily based upon the quality of the education they provide. Critics predict that information about schools will be incomplete, misleading, and unequally distributed. They predict that direct racial, religious, and class biases—as well as more subtle intergroup differences in culture and values—will lead choice to create a more segregated and fragmented society. And they caution that if parents care about matters other than educational outcomes—protecting their children from threatening ideas, building their children's self-confidence, giving their children the chance to become friendly with children from wealthier or more influential families, saving money, minimizing inconvenience, maximizing safety, getting good grades—schools may emphasize and compete on the basis of those outcomes instead of learning. While some of these nonacademic outcomes may be valuable to the broader society as well as the families that pursue them, in other instances giving greater rein to individual family desires risks redirecting public schools away from collectively defined efforts that are central to maintaining a healthy democratic society.

What does the evidence from the various forms of school choice tell us about the validity of these premises about parental demands? Here, as with most interesting research questions, the empirical literature is not uniform in its findings, but the following eight generally accepted claims seem to be emerging. They point to a more complex situation than either set of abstract arguments would lead one to expect. The first three claims address the question of whether there is a powerful latent demand for school choice based on deep dissatisfaction with assigned public schools.

1. *Choice programs, when in place and publicized, may take a bit of time to build a clientele, but demand appears more likely to grow than to recede.*

This appears to be true of choice in many of its forms. For example, in addition to the roughly 1.2 million children already attending magnet schools, estimates are that more than 123,000 are on waiting lists in various districts.[6] In Minnesota, participation in the open-enrollment program initially was quite small, but it grew steadily. About 8,500 students were using the open-enrollment option in 1991–92, only about 1 percent of the students in the state, but an increase of 46 percent over the prior year.[7] Milwaukee's voucher program initially set a cap of about 1,000 students (later raised to about 1,500). While some individual schools and grade levels had more applicants than they could accommodate, during the first five years the total number of participating families failed to reach that cap. It did, however, increase steadily and in 1996 reached the maximum figure allowed. In at least some cases, the demand for charter schools has been heavy from the outset. Massachusetts opened fifteen charters in 1995 and an additional seven in 1996; by the second year those twenty-two schools enrolled 5,400 students, with about 4,000 more on waiting lists.[8]

2. *Given the opportunity to select their children's school, parents tend to be pleased with the results.*

Parents of students in private schools express higher levels of satisfaction with teachers, academic standards, discipline policy, and the overall school experience than do parents of students in public schools. Parents who indicate that they chose their child's public school are more satisfied than those who sent their child to an assigned school (table 3-1). Similar findings emerge from studies of the voucher programs in Milwaukee, Cleveland, and San Antonio. In the fifth year of the Milwaukee experiment, more than three-quarters of choice parents gave their child's school a "grade" of A or B, and fewer than 5 percent gave it a grade of D or F.[9]

An assessment of Cleveland's program after its first year concluded that two-thirds of parents who used the vouchers to move to choice schools were "very satisfied" with the academic quality of their school, compared to only 30 percent of parents in the public schools. Choice parents also were significantly more likely to be very satisfied with a range of other school attributes, including safety, discipline, personal attention to their child, and the teaching of moral values.[10] In San Antonio, families that moved from public to private schools also showed much greater satisfaction than they

Table 3-1. *Percent of Parents Very Satisfied with Aspects of Their Child's School, 1993, Grades Three through Twelve*

School attended	Teachers	Academic standards	Discipline policy	School overall
Private	75	83	84	83
Chosen public	62	63	63	61
Assigned public	56	55	55	52

Source: National Center for Education Statistics, *The Condition of Education, 1997* (U.S. Department of Education, 1997), pp. 12–16.

had in their previous setting, although there was some indication that satisfaction might have diminished a little in the third year. Parents choosing a special multilingual public school program showed comparable degrees of satisfaction. Interestingly, parents who were eligible for the public choice program but were not admitted showed a steep drop in satisfaction and a decline in involvement in their child's education at home and at school.[11]

3. Concerns about insufficient and unequal access to information have some empirical grounding.

Economic models tend to assume that consumers are well informed about the options available to them, but in the real world we know that information can be scarce, costly, and unevenly distributed. In a 1978 article, Gary Bridge raised the question of whether information imperfections might be the Achilles' heel of voucher systems:

> If socially disadvantaged target groups lack the information to make informed decisions, they will make choices based on educationally irrelevant grounds (for example, emotional responses to hucksters' advertising), and the social equity objectives of the program will be missed.[12]

Data from Alum Rock show that awareness of the voucher program was lower among Mexican Americans, parents with less formal education, and those who had lower expectations for their children's educational attainment.[13]

A survey of parents in Montgomery County, Maryland, found that, even among parents whose children attended schools with magnet programs, many indicated they had never heard the terms *magnet school* or *magnet program* and that this lack of even the most basic information was more apparent among minorities, especially Hispanics.[14] In a survey of parents in two of the districts with the most extensive public school choice arrangements—New York City's District 4 and Montclair, New Jersey—as well as two matched districts without well-developed choice programs, parents were asked to estimate standardized test scores, incidents of violence and disorder, and racial-ethnic diversity at the schools their children attended. These estimates were compared to objective indicators. Researchers found that "the average distance between the percent of students reading at grade level estimated by parents and the actual performance is 25 points," and "parents were 'off' an average of more than 15 percent in their estimate of the racial composition of their child's school."[15] In another study, the same researchers found that minorities and less-well-educated parents depend on information networks of poorer quality: they talk to fewer people about schools, and those they talk to are more likely to be relatives and less likely to have a college education.[16]

Information about choice options is not the same thing as actual utilization, of course. Some choice proponents argue that market forces, while not immune to racial and class biases, will generate less racial and class segregation than a public system that allows more privileged groups to sort themselves into suburban enclaves and use local control over housing, land use, and taxation to bar the door to minorities and the poor. Some critics argue that the costs of exercising school choice—costs associated with tuition and fees, transportation, inconvenience—would lead to limited utilization among minorities and the poor even in the context of relatively high and equal levels of information. The next five accepted claims address the question of whether there are patterned differences in who actually takes advantage of the choice options that currently exist.

4. *Private school choice remains disproportionately the province of children from a higher socioeconomic class. But many minority and lower-income parents also have sought out private schools, and the racial gap between public and private schools is narrowing.*

In 1993, 15.6 percent of children from families earning over $50,000 per year attended private schools, compared to less than 5 percent of those from families earning $30,000 or less; 16.9 percent of children whose parents have a graduate or professional school degree went to private schools, compared to just 2.3 percent of those whose parents failed to earn a high school degree. There is a racial pattern also, but it is smaller and shrinking. In 1993, 16.7 percent of private school students in grades one through twelve were either black or Hispanic, compared to 28.4 percent in public schools. But this ratio (0.59:1) was substantially higher than it had been in 1983

(0.43:1).[17] There is also some evidence that, under certain circumstances, information and participation levels can be raised and gaps can be narrowed.

5. *When public policy has intentionally and aggressively set out to do so, racial and class biases associated with unfettered choice have been reduced or even reversed.*

The evidence from Alum Rock, for example, suggests that information levels among lower-income and minority parents improved over time. In Massachusetts, where parent information centers are part of the standard controlled-choice package, minority parents have done as well as white parents in getting their children into their first-choice schools. But the "'invisible hand' is not enough"; choice requires "effective outreach and individual counseling to assure that as high a proportion as possible make conscious, informed decisions."[18]

Other researchers raise the possibility that, once in place, formal institutions of choice might stimulate the development of informal, self-sustaining processes that would reduce racial and class-based gaps in information and access. They suggest that the institution of formal choice programs may set into motion a process through which low-income neighborhoods develop richer informal networks that work to narrow information gaps over time.[19] Other evidence, however, suggests that neither the existence of options nor the passage of time in and of themselves is sufficient to ensure that parents will have sufficient or accurate information. In Alum Rock, information levels increased until the program structure was altered, and then information dropped precipitously.[20] The low level of awareness about magnet schools in Montgomery County was not due simply to the fact that some magnets had been in place only a couple of years at the time the survey was undertaken. To the contrary, awareness of the term *magnets* was slightly higher among parents whose children attended the schools with more recently inaugurated programs.[21] Overall, the range of public school choice options appears to have counterbalanced some of the biases in the private sphere.

6. *Black and Hispanic children are more likely than white children to attend public schools of choice.*

According to parent surveys, 8 percent of white children attend public schools of choice, compared to 19 percent of black children and 14 percent of Hispanic children. Others, using a different database, examined class and racial patterns of enrollment in public high schools while taking into account whether or not a public school choice option was available to them in their school district. They conclude that disadvantaged families, "whether disadvantaged by reasons of race, ethnicity, or education," exercise choice when selecting a public high school and "do so to a greater degree than do Whites or families with higher education."[22] Minority use of Minnesota's open-enrollment program, while low in total numbers, was at least as high as the participation of white students in the same districts.[23]

7. Nonetheless, some racial and class biases in access are quite persistent, appearing, albeit in a truncated form, even in the context of sharply progressive institutional designs.

Partly due to their historical link to desegregation efforts, public school choice options such as magnet schools and controlled choice are much more common in large, central cities with high minority (especially black) populations. Thus it is not surprising to find that more minorities than whites may have the chance to exercise public school choice. While minorities may exercise public school choice more often than whites overall, within some districts that offer magnet schools white families appear to be the more direct beneficiaries.[24] It is certainly true, as choice proponents emphasize, that even very low-income and relatively uneducated parents are taking advantage of choice options in places like New York City's District 4, Milwaukee, and San Antonio. Yet even in Milwaukee, where the program design mandates that all participants will be poor, the evidence suggests that there may be a class bias in participation. Fifty-six percent of mothers participating in the Milwaukee voucher program reported some college education, compared with 40 percent for all Milwaukee public school mothers and 30 percent of mothers in the city's low-income neighborhoods.[25] In San Antonio, where the private scholarship program is limited to those who qualify for federal free or reduced-price lunches, parents taking advantage of the program are more educated, have fewer children, are more likely to be part of a two-parent household, and are more likely to be white than are nonchoosers in the public schools.[26]

Some critics of school choice have suggested that, even in a world of perfect information and unbiased access, market forces might not improve education and might exacerbate racial and class segregation as a result of the particular values and preferences that parents rely upon. In a perfectly functioning market, suppliers will offer those products that consumers are most anxious to receive. How high does educational quality stand in the preference ordering that parents actually bring to bear?

8. *Factors other than educational quality play a role in structuring school choice, and some of those factors may lead freely choosing families to segregate further by race and by class.*

A Carnegie Foundation review of school choice programs concludes that "many parents base their school choice decision on factors that have nothing to do with the quality of education," among them being day care availability, convenience, social factors, and the range and quality of interscholastic sports.[27] In Massachusetts, children tend to transfer to districts with higher incomes, spending, and test scores than in their home districts.[28] On the other hand, a review of choice plans in five jurisdictions concludes that "when researchers asked parents in the five programs to rate their motives for choosing, parents overwhelmingly picked educational quality or learning climate as their number-one reason."[29] Even when parents really are thinking mostly about educational quality, what remains unclear is the basis on which they make judgments about school performance. Lacking clear and objective indicators about what goes on in the classrooms, parents reasonably enough may rely on aggregate test scores or the socioeconomic characteristics of those already attending the schools as proxy indicators. Reliance on either of these proxies would tend to reinforce differentiation based on class.

Some analysts have concluded that the racial and class composition of schools will not be an important factor in directing school choices, based upon the racially mixed student bodies found in many magnet schools or on surveys of parents who say that race is not a factor that concerns them. But the existing composition of magnet schools is only partially a reflection of parent choices; clear regulations regarding racial balance rule out transfer requests that would lead to racial imbalance. And parents may be reticent about admitting that race plays a factor in their decisions, preferring to emphasize more socially acceptable criteria like educational quality or the existence of special programs. A study of school choice in Montgomery County magnet schools examined racial patterns of transfer requests to determine whether officials charged with maintaining racial balance ultimately approved the moves. The evidence shows that both whites and minorities were directing their choices toward schools in which their children would be less likely to be racially or socioeconomically isolated. This criterion pointed them in different directions, however. White families were most likely to request transfer into schools with low proportions of minorities (which also were those located in higher-income neighborhoods); minority families were more likely to opt for schools in low-income neighborhoods (which also tended to be schools with higher proportions of minority students).[30]

Working directly with a wider range of individual-level data, rather than making inferences about individuals based on aggregate patterns, another study modeled families' choice of a school in Minneapolis—which, under state provisions, has offered open enrollment since 1989. Parent choice in Minneapolis is not unconstrained. Under the state's programs, five districts, including Minneapolis, that operate under court-ordered desegregation plans may reserve the right to deny transfer applications when racial balance would be disturbed.[31] As in the Montgomery County study, then, requests for schools provide a better indicator of market demand than do actual transfers. The study of choice in Minneapolis used four explanatory variables: costs, information, school attributes, and peer attributes. It found that most families returning their preference cards before the filing deadline did take advantage of the choice option; only one in four selected the school that was nearest their home.

Based on the actual preferences of 881 children who were enrolling in kindergarten in the fall of 1993, there was evidence for an "own-group preference" among minorities, a strong peer group socioeconomic status effect, and a tendency for parents to select schools with higher test scores.[32] The racial effect was especially strong when choosers faced the prospect of their child being in a small minority (less than 10 percent). The study acknowledges the possibility that a more competitive, market-based system might alter the incentives and information available to consumers in ways that would make choice more responsive to academic performance. Based on the kind of controlled-choice system in place in Minneapolis, however, "increasing consumer choice in education would likely only result in higher consumer satisfaction at the cost of some segregation by race and class. For school improvement in traditional academic areas, 'a little consumer choice' is not sufficient."[33]

Would it necessarily be a bad thing if school choice exacerbated segregation? From a legal standpoint, it makes a great deal of difference whether segregation is self-selected or imposed by one group upon another, especially if the dominant group is using the power and authority of the government to achieve its exclusionary ends. In the aftermath of the *Brown* v. *Board of Education* decision, some states and school districts resorted to freedom-of-choice policies, including school vouchers, in a deliberate effort to maintain racial segregation. The Supreme Court considered that unconstitutional, and it is likely that most contemporary proponents of choice accept the legitimacy of that ruling. There is considerable disagreement, however, about whether increased segregation is acceptable when it is the unintended consequence of policies designed to promote other social values; thus some choice proponents argue that segregation is an acceptable price to pay for a more effective and responsive educational system. There is considerable disagreement, too, over how one can judge when choices are truly free. Thus some choice opponents argue that an inclination by black parents to send their children to schools with black majorities or an Afrocentric curriculum results from utter frustration with the failure of the current system to deliver high-quality integrated education—and that choices made in such a context of inadequate and restricted options provide a distorted image of underlying preferences. Some of these disagreements rest on differing beliefs about what is happening, or is likely to happen, on the supply-side of the equation.[34]

The Supply-Side

Framed in the abstract, the debate between choice proponents and choice critics also offers sharply contrasting predictions about the way schools can be expected to behave in a more market-driven system. Economic theory predicts that well-functioning markets will tend to bring supply into line with demand. If more families are given the means to exercise choice, existing schools should find themselves competing more aggressively to serve their customers' needs, and sharp entrepreneurs should be ready to fill the gap if the schools fail to do so or charge too high a cost for the product they provide. Critics warn that markets less easily digest some types of goods than others do and that economic theories depend upon a range of assumptions that are never fully realized in real situations. For some types of service, for some types of consumers, and under some settings, suppliers' efforts to maximize their own return may generate profiteering, discrimination, pandering to the rich, fraud, and deception instead of responsiveness and efficiency. Research into the supply-side consequences of school choice is not yet as rich and developed as that on the demand-side of the equation. But evidence is accumulating, and nine preliminary conclusions can be drawn.

1. *Choice systems that incorporate private schools have the potential to reduce the unit cost of education.*
An argument has been made that vouchers worth $3,000, less than half of the average per pupil expenditure in the nation's public elementary and

secondary schools, are sufficient to enable most Americans to purchase a high-quality education in "all types of American cities—high-cost cities, middle-income cities, and comparatively poor cities."[35] This claim is backed by the results of a survey of all private schools in four cities: Jersey City, Atlanta, Indianapolis, and San Francisco. At the elementary school level, the median tuition charged by private schools in the four areas ranged from 21 percent to 57 percent of the average public per pupil expenditure. The cost differences were less pronounced at the high school level. Private high school tuition exceeded overall per pupil public school spending in one area (San Francisco); in two of the areas (Indianapolis and Jersey City) it was less than half. These figures are broadly in keeping with national estimates. Nationwide, the average private school tuition was $3,116 in 1993–94, compared to an average public school per pupil expenditure of about $6,500.[36]

2. *Predictions of large savings rest almost entirely on the inclusion of religious private schools, institutions that are fundamentally not market actors. Nonsectarian private schools charge tuition that is much higher, and private firms that have begun competing nationally to manage public and charter schools do not pretend that they can greatly reduce costs.*

Nationwide, tuition at nonsectarian private schools averaged $6,631 for the 1993–94 school year, about three times that at Catholic ($2,178) and other religious ($2,195) schools and almost exactly the same as the average per pupil expenditure in U.S. public schools.[37] A reanalysis of the four-city study reveals a similar pattern.[38] Based on the names of the schools, it is apparent that about three of every four of the private schools identified in that study are religious schools. Focusing only on those schools whose names do not indicate a religious affiliation, one finds a much different picture than reported. The average tuition at these nonsectarian schools is thousands of dollars higher than the median private school figures noted. Except for Jersey City, where the public school expenditure is unusually high and where only four of the fifty-four private schools surveyed did not have religious affiliations, about half of all private elementary schools and about nine of ten private secondary schools actually charge more than the per pupil expenditure for the district.[39]

Predicting whether choice will lower the cost of delivering a quality education is more complicated than simply comparing private tuition to public expenditures. For instance, public schools disproportionately serve some classes of students whose attributes make them especially costly to educate.

Students eligible for special education services often require special accommodations that can double or triple the cost per student. Many private schools admit that they cannot meet the needs of many of these students and direct the parents toward the public schools. According to one study, special education's share of public school expenditures rose from 4 percent in 1967 to 17 percent in 1991.[40]

A comparison of public to private schools indicates that public schools are about four times as likely to offer bilingual or English as a second language classes, more than three and a half times as likely to offer services to the disabled, about twice as likely to offer diagnostic services, and considerably more likely to provide medical, drug, and substance abuse counseling.[41] If students requiring or desiring such cost-intensive programs were evenly distributed between the public and private sectors, the cost differences would shrink substantially. Also complicating the assessment of relative costs is the fact that many religious private schools are heavily subsidized by the religious institutions that sponsor them and that some of the transportation, text, and supplies costs for private schools are underwritten by the public budget.[42] According to one estimate, tuition covers only about half of the actual cost of educating an elementary school child in the Catholic schools, with 33 percent of the costs supported by the parish and 15 percent coming from other sources, including fund-raising.[43]

For a sense of what the private sector would charge to provide an education comparable to that offered in the public schools, the more appropriate indicator might be the pricing strategies of the several private for-profit firms that have begun competing for contracts to manage public schools, run charters, and tutor segments of the public school population. Even here, direct comparisons are tricky. Major firms like the Edison Project and the Tesseract Group Inc. (formerly Educational Alternatives Inc., or EAI) may subsidize early projects in order to build credibility and expand their base; this means that the amount they charge may be below that which they could sustain on an ongoing basis. Some figures presented for charter schools count only operating expenditures; they do not include the costs of buildings, which in some instances have been donated and in other instances have yet to be found. In addition, figuring out how much of public spending supports necessary central office and special education expenditures (which presumably ought not to be counted when calculating the school-level expenditure against which the private firm's charge should be compared) turns out to raise a complex and highly politicized set of questions.[44]

Although firms like Tesseract and Edison claim they can deliver a better education at about the same cost of regular public schools, they do not claim that they can deliver a comparable education at a sufficiently lower cost. To the contrary. Edison Project, for example, has decided that the average per pupil expenditure in many U.S. districts simply is too low for them to even consider bidding for management contracts. It focuses almost exclusively on lower grade levels, in recognition of the fact that pupil expenditures would be considerably higher at the secondary school level.[45] An independent analysis, in addition, has calculated that expenditures in the nine Baltimore schools that EAI managed were about 12 percent higher than those of comparable schools in the rest of the system.[46] Based on a financial simulation model, one economist concludes that there is room for a private firm to profitably offer educational services if compensated by the equivalent of current public spending per pupil, provided that it generates a large volume of business. He admits, however, that "in actual implementation" the theoretical possibilities of financial viability and high quality "both have yet to be witnessed."[47]

What about competition on dimensions other than cost? In a more competitive environment, would public and private schools focus their competitive strategies on educational quality? Or might they compete on other bases, with less socially desirable results? Politically, the argument that competition would lead public schools to improve is useful to choice proponents, since it allows them to deflect charges that their proposals will lead to the erosion of the public system. To date, however, this claim has been buttressed more by anecdote than by solid research. The picture that is beginning to emerge is still murky and incomplete.

3. There are some indications that expanding choice options might spark greater innovation among public schools.

In a number of districts with magnet schools, parents at nonmagnet schools have pressed for the same types of programs and strategies. An analysis of Minnesota's open-enrollment program found evidence that administrators in districts losing students via open enrollment were expanding course offerings (58 percent), making special transportation arrangements (42 percent), improving the physical plant (42 percent), and increasing extracurricular offers (33 percent), although it is not certain that the open-enrollment option prompted these changes.[48] Charter school proponents credit their efforts with stimulating public authorities in Boston and Houston to launch plans to make existing schools more innovative and flexible.[49]

4. *Some of these very same competitive responses can have undesired consequences.*

In Montgomery County, public officials have had a difficult time resisting pressure from nonmagnet school parents to incorporate special themes and programs into their schools as well. While this can be seen as support for the claim that choice sparks more general innovation, it also has an ironic underside. Regular schools' mimicking of successful magnet programs undermines the basic logic behind magnet schools, which was to use special programs as an incentive for voluntary integration. If the same programs are available closer to home and in more homogeneous racial and economic settings, the prospects that magnets can continue to attract voluntary transfers that promote racial integration are dimmed.[50]

In some of the Minnesota districts losing students under the open-enrollment option, the consequent loss of revenue forced layoffs of teachers (26 percent) or the canceling of some academic courses (16 percent). This could mean that those unable or unwilling to move were left with fewer options than before.[51] An analysis of sixty-four Florida public school districts concludes that greater competition from private schools may simply result in cream skimming: smarter and more advantaged children siphoned off to the private schools, to the detriment of those left behind.[52] Public school systems that respond to such market signals, moreover, may be forced to focus on the educational needs of those most likely to leave rather than on the less mobile, harder-to-educate group that may represent their core constituency.

5. *Comparisons of public schools to private schools suggest that private schools do not, by and large, compete by offering better-trained teachers, innovative teaching methods, or more up-to-date technology.*

National statistics show that public school teachers have higher levels of education than their private school counterparts. Forty-seven percent have at least a master's degree, versus 34 percent in private schools; 7 percent of private school teachers have not even earned a bachelor's degree, compared to 1 percent in public schools. Further, secondary public school students in English, math, and foreign languages are more likely than private school students to be taught by teachers who majored or minored in the subject.[53] Of course, it is possible that private school teachers make up for their lack of formal education with greater pedagogical flexibility and creativity, but there is little evidence that this is the case. One analysis of the difference between public and Catholic schools, including extensive classroom observation, although it supports the claim that Catholic schools provide a better education for most children, concludes that "the character of instruction in Catholic high schools appears quite traditional in format, setting, use of materials, and pedagogy."[54]

If technology is the wave of the future, moreover, public schools seem to be quicker to catch that wave. Public school libraries are substantially better equipped technologically—34 percent of public school media centers had computers with modems in 1993–94, compared to 20 percent in private schools, for example—although private school libraries average more books per pupil. In general, public school teachers were more likely "to work with small groups of students and to demonstrate concepts using a computer, videotape, or other electronic medium, while private school teachers were more likely than public school teachers to lecture to their students."[55]

6. *What private schools do seem to emphasize is a greater sense of community, smaller size of schools and classes, a safer and more orderly environment, and a more consistent policy of encouraging all students to take advanced academic courses.*

Public schools are on average at least twice the size of private schools. Average class size also is larger, although the difference is not so great. In the 1993–94 school year, the average class size in private elementary schools was twenty-two, compared to twenty-four in public elementary schools; in private secondary schools the average class had nineteen students, compared to twenty-four in their public sector counterparts.[56] A nationwide survey of charter schools in January 1996 found that 62 percent had fewer than 200 students; in the ten states that contained most of those charter schools, the comparable figure for the public schools was only 16 percent.[57] Based on reports from teachers at the secondary school level, private schools are much less likely to experience serious problems with alcohol or drug abuse, and based on surveys of sixth to twelfth graders, private school students are much less likely to have been exposed to robbery, bullying, or physical attacks at school.[58]

Higher percentages of private high schools students take advanced math and science courses, although the gap has narrowed somewhat recently. In 1982, private school students were 3.2 times as likely to have taken a course in calculus, for example, and 1.8 times as likely to have taken a year each of biology, chemistry, and physics. Twelve years later, the private school edge was still substantial—but had shrunk substantially as well. In 1994, private school students were 1.6 times as likely to have taken calculus and 1.5 times as likely to have enrolled in the three science courses.[59]

What about concerns that, under more marketlike arrangements, schools will selectively recruit students from higher socioeconomic status families and actively seek to avoid serving racial minorities, students with disabilities, and those with behavioral problems? As noted, private schools do serve a more advantaged group of students, although they are by no means the exclusive preserve of a white elite. Some or all of the racial and class differences distinguishing public and private schools may be due to demand factors. Do schools impose additional screens to ensure that they fill their seats with those who are easier and less costly to educate, thereby increasing the gap between the haves and have-nots? Here, as elsewhere, the supply-side questions have received less attention from researchers than have their demand-side counterparts. And here, as elsewhere, the answers are more complex and contingent than choice proponents or choice opponents typically admit.

7. *Under certain institutional arrangements, school choice can certainly be made to accommodate the needs and interests of "tough case" students, including the disabled, troubled, and the urban poor.*

When public officials have committed themselves to the task, they have proven they can design and implement magnet schools and controlled-choice programs that serve the neediest neighborhoods and facilitate integration. In the private sector, some schools specialize in serving the physically or emotionally less able students, sometimes under contract with public authorities. Of the 252 charter schools in operation by January 1996, 13 percent indicated they were founded "to serve a special population of students, including 'at-risk,' language minority, disabled, or ethnic and racial minorities."[60] Milwaukee's voucher program serves a predominantly minority population (74 percent black, 19 percent Hispanic) that is very poor (60 percent on aid to families with dependent children).[61]

8. *Such progressive arrangements seem, however, to require firm regulations and aggressive enforcement and may be politically vulnerable unless backed by the authority of the courts.*

When not demanded by program design or judicial ruling, many schools exhibit a reluctance to admit students who are seen as expensive to serve or a likely cause of disruption. Voucher schools in Milwaukee, for example, have successfully fought off efforts to make them comply with the Wisconsin All Handicapped Students Act. During the first year of Cleveland's voucher program, students who had ever received special education services related to a disability or learning problem and those who had ever been suspended for disciplinary reasons were much less likely to find placement in a private school. Of those who failed to find placement, 25 percent had received special services, compared to only 11 percent of those who succeeded in getting access to a private school. Of those who failed to find placement, 13 percent had been suspended, compared to 7 percent of those who were admitted to a private school.[62] Although the Cleveland program in principle allowed participants to apply their vouchers toward nonresident tuition in suburban public schools, the suburban districts elected not to participate; as a result, none of the almost 2,000 students who found placements did so in the suburban public schools.[63]

Even including schools that specialize in serving special populations, the national survey of charter schools found that charter schools seem to underserve students with disabilities and limited English proficiency (LEP), although they serve roughly proportionate numbers of children who are poor. Based on reports from the schools, 7 percent of the students in the nation's charter schools had received special services under the Individuals with Disabilities Education Act before their enrollment in the charter, compared to 10 percent of students nationwide. Of the ten states with substantial numbers of operating charters, in only two (Minnesota and Wisconsin) did charter schools serve a proportionate number of disabled students. Only Minnesota and Massachusetts enroll a larger proportion of LEP students than the average of other schools in their states.[64] Significantly, these three states (Minnesota, Wisconsin, and Massachusetts) have long and well-established traditions of progressive politics and good government. In spite of the fact that charters so far seem to be bearing less than their full share of such children, one procharter analysis notes that "charter directors live in fear of a 'fifty thousand dollar kid' rolling in the door, complete with an Individual Education Plan that calls for a full-time attendant to be paid from the school's budget."[65] In just its second year of operation, the Edison Project's Boston Renaissance Charter School was found by the Department of Education's Office of Civil Rights to have been in violation of the federal Rehabilitation Act of 1973, after a family charged that the school had not followed proper procedures in transferring its son to a different classroom setting.[66]

Several public school districts, in the context of choice programs, have attempted to screen out special education students because of the greater costs they are seen to entail.[67] In Chattanooga, for example, the state criteria for admissions into a magnet program included the "capacity to function without special education services other than speech, hearing, and vision services." And a California school district "categorically denied interdistrict transfers to nonresident children because of the expense of educating students with disabilities." In these cases, the federal Office of Civil Rights intervened. This highlights two points. One, unless constrained by legal limitations, unfettered choice systems can encourage selective admissions even within public school systems with traditions and norms supporting broad access. Second, because the existing legal constraints are more extensive for public than private schools, choice systems that incorporate both may exacerbate the filtering process that leaves the public system disproportionately responsible for serving the highest-cost students.[68]

An analysis of the availability of preschools and child care centers provides some indirect evidence about what we might expect from a more market-driven kindergarten through twelfth grade system.[69] Compared to kindergarten through twelfth grade education, the preschool market in the United States has a tradition of private market and nonprofit delivery, with public sector intervention focused primarily on regulation and subsidies. This is the direction that choice proponents would like to see the kindergarten through grade twelve system move toward. The examination of the availability of preschool alternatives across a hundred counties nationwide and of microlevel distribution patterns in Massachusetts, a state with an unusually strong record in using public authority to expand preschool access for low-income communities, found evidence that "counties with higher median incomes and greater concentrations of well-educated, professionally employed parents display more robust preschool markets." In Massachusetts, government efforts seem to have reduced such inequities, primarily by expanding the supply in the lowest-income neighborhoods but at an apparent cost to middle-income and working-class neighborhoods, which are relatively underserved.

The record of private for-profit education among trade schools and correspondence courses should serve as a reminder that private provision sometimes results in fraud and abuse rather than economic efficiency.

9. School choice initiatives have given rise to examples of fraud and corruption, although to date these appear limited and have been quickly discovered and prosecuted.

In June 1996, the founder of one of the Milwaukee private schools participating in the voucher program was charged with defrauding the state by lying about the number of students enrolled.[70] In the District of Columbia, the founder of a private school for emotionally disturbed children that received an $825,000 contract from the local school district in March 1998 was found guilty of bank fraud and ten counts of wire fraud in connection with his running of the school. The U.S. District Court found that he had used about $200,000 of the city's money to pay for luxury cars and other personal expenses.[71] Choice proponents correctly note that fraud and abuse are found in the current public school system as well, and they emphasize that the extent of abuse can be limited through proper monitoring and enforcement. Yet it is not clear that legislators are providing the enforcement mechanisms and necessary funding to ensure that this is the case. The District of Columbia school board, for example, claims it has funds to hire only one person, on a consultant basis, to help it oversee the up to ten schools per year that it is expected to charter under legislation passed by Congress.[72] Evidence from California shows that political pressure reduces the likelihood that public officials will exercise the full range of their formal authority to regulate charter schools.[73]

Educational Achievement

Much of the contemporary debate over school choice emphasizes educational achievement as the bottom line. This is partly attributable to a backlash against some of the educational initiatives of the 1960s and 1970s, which some reformers believe sacrificed educational quality in the pursuit of equity. For some, the most compelling reason for increased reliance on choice is the belief that schools that respond to market signals are more likely to emphasize learning and to succeed in promoting it.

The notion that educational achievement is the ultimate bottom line is not shared by all, even within the prochoice community. Some favor choice because it would reinforce family or religious values, for example, and some might go so far as to publicly align themselves with choice even if they are convinced that it would reduce learning, especially as conventionally measured through standardized achievement tests. Similarly, some opponents of choice base their position on the detrimental consequences they foresee in such areas as interracial relations and economic inequality and might reject choice even if convinced that it could improve educational achievement measured at some aggregate level. The framing of the educational problem that has dominated public debate has been linked to poor test scores, uninformed and unskilled graduates, and fears that the rising generations will not be up to the challenge of maintaining the nation's preeminence in an increasingly competitive global environment. In that context, arguments about school choice frequently center on whether there is evidence that market forces will generate measurable educational gains.

What can be said about the consequences of choice for educational achievement? Efforts to gain empirical leverage on this question have been even more problematic than efforts to get definitive answers to the impacts on demand and supply. One reason, of course, is that the stakes are so high. Another involves measurement ambiguities; there are a wide variety of standardized testing instruments, but none of them has been broadly accepted as an ideal—or even adequate—indicator of the kind of learning that Americans consider important.

The thorniest problem plaguing efforts to empirically determine the educational consequences of school choice, however, concerns selection bias. Most researchers are aware of the extent to which concerns about selection bias have plagued efforts to draw meaningful comparisons between public and private schools, between magnet and "regular" schools, between voucher and nonvoucher students. Those who choose to choose likely differ from those who fail to take advantage of choice opportunities, in such factors as motivation, ambition, and capacity. These factors, rather than choice and its consequences, may account for any higher levels of academic achievement that choice students subsequently reveal, and standard statistical controls for family background may not be sufficient to take this into account. What seems less widely recognized is the extent to which this particular methodological challenge is inherent in the nature of the policy itself. The primary source of selection bias *is* choice. When subjects are in position to determine whether or not they are exposed to a given policy instrument, attributes related to that choice—rather than the policy itself—might account for any difference between them and a comparison group that has not received the policy stimulus. Researchers have turned to a variety of statistical controls and have cleverly sought to take advantage of some natural experiments, but the selection bias threat probably cannot be eliminated without a truly randomized experimental design, and that would require limiting choice to some subjects and schools.

The most fully developed literature relevant to the effect of school choice on educational outcomes involves comparisons between public and private schools. James Coleman and colleagues began the contemporary debate with their analyses of the "high school and beyond" (HSB) data in the early 1980s.[74] Besides combining data on individual family background and test score performance, the HSB data made it possible to trace a panel of students over time. The researchers took advantage of this by operationalizing educational achievement in terms of gains between students' sophomore and senior years. Looking at student gains, rather than absolute test scores, provided an additional control for many of the differences in family background and motivation of students that had plagued cross-sectional comparisons between public and private schools. The study concluded that private school students performed better than public school students in reading, vocabulary, writing, and math even when family background was taken into account. This work was the subject of critical assessments, including charges that the methodology failed to control for the full range of selection biases that were likely to be in effect.[75]

A number of subsequent studies, each offering some innovations in measurement or research design, have supported Coleman's basic finding that private schools produce superior educational outcomes. One study integrated the HSB data with additional information about the characteristics of schools, including teachers' and principals' assessments of the school organization, curriculum requirements, faculty morale, leadership, disciplinary and homework policies, and the like.[76] It found that students perform better when their teachers and principals feel they have the decisionmaking autonomy to enable them to set school direction, and it found such autonomy more likely in private than in public schools. Based on this, it concluded that market forces generate the school conditions most compatible with enhanced learning and that public institutions of majoritarian control are fundamentally incompatible with those conditions. Another study, using both HSB and National Educational Longitudinal Survey (NELS) data sets, found evidence that the performance advantages of Catholic schools are especially concentrated among socioeconomically disadvantaged students. Improving on studies that measure educational benefits exclusively in terms of standardized test scores, these analysts also found evidence that Catholic school students are more likely to attend college after graduating from high school.[77]

Although it is still possible that these differences result from unmeasured selection biases, the major lines of debate have shifted to other grounds.[78] In particular, there are unresolved disagreements about whether the value added by private schools is sufficiently large and assured to warrant radical policy changes, whether observed gains are attributable to market forces or somehow uniquely tied to the religious orientation that characterizes most private schools, and whether the mechanisms that produce the gains are replicable in public schools. A sharp distinction should be made between statistically significant and substantively significant findings. In analyses drawing on large national databases, such as HSB and NELS, very small differences can easily achieve standard thresholds for statistical significance. When policy decisions that could have substantial consequences are under consideration, it is important to consider the size of the impact as well as the statistical likelihood that it is attributable to chance. Based on that criterion, "the size of the differences in achievement are simply so small that we can draw almost no conclusion from them."[79]

Coleman's original analyses emphasized that the private school advantage might be limited to Catholic schools. Non-Catholic private schools "appear not to provide special advantages beyond the public school, except possibly in verbal cognitive skills, a result that is offset by their relatively high drop-out rates and their weakness in mathematics and sciences."[80] Another study concludes that the private school advantage rests on the spiritual and communal elements of the "inspirational ideology" that characterizes Catholic education. "Without commitment to the specific values operative in the Catholic sector, we suspect that neither the quality of internal life found in these [Catholic] schools, nor the more equitable social distribution of achievement, would result."[81]

Although the theoretical underpinnings of the choice movement lie in market models, most of the empirical evidence regarding private school performance is driven by religious schools—especially Catholic schools—which share a private sector location with for-profit private schools but which are adamantly nonmarket actors in many respects. Conventional market models presume that firms are motivated by profit maximization. Religious schools operate in markets, of course, but the core values of their sponsors often place material gain on the periphery; faced with an identical array of market signals, parochial schools and secular schools may apply very different standards in defining and weighing the costs and benefits of different actions.

Most discussions of school choice show little self-consciousness about the manner in which they generalize from one realm to another, and when analysts do make distinctions they often disagree about what forms of generalization are reasonable. For example, a study that generalizes from findings based largely on Catholic schools to the market arena argues emphatically against the possibility that lessons learned from the private arena might be applied by the public schools, at least as long as those authorities are subject to direct democratic control.[82] What makes this analysis so powerful is less the empirical findings about private versus public schools than the strong theoretical claim that public schools, because of their anchor in majoritarian democratic decisionmaking, are fundamentally incapable of replicating the autonomy and flexibility that the authors consider to be the core of the private school advantage. But others see more in common between Catholic schools and public schools, both having core philosophies based on notions of a public interest, than between either of these and purely market-driven schools that may elevate profit over higher values and cater to what individuals want rather than what they need.[83] Those who, on traditional constitutional grounds, oppose voucher plans that include parochial schools see the shared secular traditions of public schools and private nonreligious schools as the overriding factor and reject efforts to generalize from instances in these arenas to proposals that would include religious schools. The problem here is not lack of empirical evidence but lack of theoretical guidance about how to draw inferences from one institutional setting to another.

There is growing evidence that public schools can replicate some of the key elements associated with private school successes—and with similarly positive results. Empirical assessments of the educational consequences of public school choice face some of the same methodological challenges that have complicated the comparison of public and private schools. In particular, families that have the motivation and the capacity to take advantage of choice differ in key respects from those that do not. Evidence that students in choice programs outperform those in traditional public schools accordingly may be more properly attributed to what the children and their classmates bring with them into these schools—differences associated with propensity to learn—than to differences in quality of education.

During the 1980s, some voucher proponents cited public magnet programs as evidence that choice would promote academic excellence. As elaborated elsewhere, most of these claims were based on premature assessments, inadequate measures, and weak research designs. A review of twelve such studies found that only four even made an attempt to control for student background, ability level, or criteria for magnet selection.[84] The study with the strongest design produced mixed findings: magnet students did better than nonmagnet controls on some tests but not others and at some grade levels but not others; students who attended magnet schools by virtue of living in the attendance zone (and whose performance presumably reflected the quality of education provided rather than a higher than normal motivation or parental support) actually fell behind a comparison group of nonmagnet students by the end of third grade.[85]

More recent and more rigorous studies of magnet schools and specialized public schools suggest that they can replicate some of the elements that seem to have been associated with success in Catholic schools. There is evidence that special public school programs for at-risk students created a supportive and more focused setting, allowing students to become more engaged.[86] Another study found that students who got into vocational magnet schools in New York City via lottery did better than a control group of students who lost in the lottery and returned to comprehensive schools.[87] A very recent study presents evidence that public school choice in East Harlem's District 4 led to dramatic initial improvements in test scores and that, even though the scores subsequently leveled off, District 4 elementary students still do significantly better than other New York City students when other factors are taken into account.[88]

Perhaps most interesting are some recent analyses that use the NELS data to incorporate public school choice into a research design that parallels those used in the private-versus-public school comparisons discussed above. One compares test score gains in the first two years of high school for students in public magnet schools, Catholic schools, secular private schools, and public comprehensive schools.[89] The cohort analyzed were sophomores in 1988 and seniors in 1990. Because of the special challenge of educating students in troubled central city schools, the study was limited to about 4,000 students in central city high schools. In raw scores, students in private schools did much better in math, science, reading, and social studies; magnet schools students did better in reading and social studies. When difference in students' background was taken into account, the advantages for nonreligious private schools disappeared in all subject areas, and the Catholic school advantage was maintained only in math. Even controlling for background factors, however, magnet students continued to show greater gains in reading and social studies than did their peers in regular high schools.

While comparisons between public and private schools constitute the most substantial component of the empirical evidence on choice outcomes, without question the most visible and contentious studies of school choice outcomes are those focused on the voucher experiments in Milwaukee and Cleveland. These experiments come closest to implementing the kind of voucher program that Milton Friedman originally envisioned, and as a result the stakes involved in proving their success or failure are very high for those who feel strongly about the promise or threat associated with market-based choice plans.

The debate over the educational outcomes of the Milwaukee voucher program has resulted in heated disagreement. Between 1991 and 1995, John Witte released a series of annual reports analyzing the Milwaukee results, noting high levels of satisfaction among voucher parents, but comparisons of standardized test scores of voucher students failed to show that they were learning more than comparable children in the city's public schools.[90] Jay Greene, Paul Peterson, and Jiangtao Du's critique of these reports, along with their reanalysis of the data using a different research design, appeared to find strong positive effects for those voucher students who remained in the program for at least three or four years.[91] When one works through the tremendous controversy and vastly disparate presentation of findings, it seems possible to draw a tentative conclusion from the Milwaukee evidence. Educational impacts, if genuine, are likely to be limited to those who remain in the choice program for several years; and these impacts are less certain and dramatic than some proponents have claimed.

After all is said and done, the major proponents on both sides of the contemporary debate conclude that we do not yet have very sound evidence about whether vouchers do or do not lead to educational gains. Although the methodological issues surrounding the debate have become complicated, and those complications are further aggravated by the vehemence with which the charges and countercharges have been issued, the central distinction between the two sets of analyses rests on the difference between statistical controls and experimental controls.[92] Witte, for the most part, based his conclusions on comparisons between choice students and a control group of students in the Milwaukee public schools (MPS); because the MPS sample included students with different backgrounds, he used multivariate statistical analyses to control for such potentially relevant background factors as family income; mothers education, employment, and marital status; and parental expectations for their child's educational future. Green, Peterson, and Du observe that this approach may not account for selection biases and suggest that a more appropriate comparison group would comprise students who applied to the program but were randomly rejected due to space constraints. They report that voucher students "in their third and fourth years, scored, on average, from 3 to 5 percentage points higher in reading and 5 to 12 points higher in mathematics" than their control group, an impact they characterize as "extraordinary."[93]

Greene and his colleagues also argue that the lottery mechanism, employed when particular grades at particular choice schools are over-subscribed, provides them with a natural experimental situation that makes their comparison group (students who applied for the voucher program, were rejected by chance, and remained in the Milwaukee public schools) ideal. Yet as their critics have noted, the continued availability of choice may have contaminated both their experimental and control groups. The continued availability of choice allowed some voucher students to opt out of the program; this introduces a bias in favor of the choice schools if those who dropped out would have expressed less satisfaction or performed more poorly on tests than those who remained. Similarly, the continued availability of choice allowed some of those who lost the lottery to escape the Milwaukee public school system in other ways.[94] This introduces a bias in favor of the choice schools if those aggressive or concerned enough to find alternative means of exit would have outperformed those who remained in the Milwaukee public schools and, by virtue of that, remained in the control group. In addition, several of the central findings do not meet standard tests of statistical significance.[95]

In a subsequent reanalysis, which incorporates the "rejects" group, Witte finds no differences in reading scores and only very small differences (in favor of the choice students) in math scores—differences quite likely due to serious problems, including selective attrition, among the reject group.[96] He finds that the magnitude of the gains claimed by Greene and colleagues is extremely fragile, and "the myriad selection problems with both groups indicate the evidence may well be totally spurious." Witte concludes with a call for "caution and modesty" in generalizing the claims. Another researcher found a mixed result when she attempted to replicate both approaches.[97] Math gains were higher among choice students, and there were no consistent differences in reading scores. She concluded with a plea for modesty on the part of evaluators, who should resist the temptation to draw stronger generalizations than their imperfect data and post hoc research designs can legitimately support.

Cleveland's program is of more recent vintage. Enacted by the state of Ohio in March 1995, the Cleveland scholarship and tutoring grant program offered families up to $2,250 toward attending the private school of their choice. The first cohort of nearly 2,000 students began in September 1996, but in May of that academic year a state appeals court ruled that the program as constituted violated federal and state constitutional provisions prohibiting government aid to religion. Nonetheless, in July 1997, the Ohio Supreme Court decided that the program could continue while it reviewed the earlier ruling.[98] As in the case of Milwaukee, this opportunity to garner empirical evidence about the educational consequences of choice has stimulated research but has certainly not quelled the controversy.

An assessment of the educational impact in two of the Cleveland choice schools was based on the performance of students in the Hope Central Academy and Hope Ohio City schools.[99] These were new schools initiated in direct response to the opportunity provided by the new program. Students who were tested in both the fall and spring improved 5 percentile points in reading and 15 percentile points on math concepts. Scores on a language test declined 5 percentile points. Although proponents characterize these as "large gains," they do not have an appropriate control group with which to compare them.[100] They cite estimates that Cleveland public school students' reading scores declined on average 1 or 2 percentile points a year at comparable grade levels. But test score changes from year to year are not directly comparable to changes from fall to spring, since many students—especially those from economically disadvantaged backgrounds—tend to lose considerable ground over the summer. Their ultimate conclusion, that "definitive conclusions about the effects of the scholarship program on academic achievement depend upon the collection of additional data," reflects this limitation and makes it clear that the issues are not yet resolved.[101] As if to underscore this point, an analysis commissioned by the state of Ohio concluded that there were no statistically significant differences in math, reading, or science achievement between Cleveland voucher students and a comparable sample of students attending the city's public schools.[102]

Taking Stock: Knowing More Than Ever, Disagreeing as Much as Ever

The 1990s witnessed a veritable explosion in the number of studies focusing on school choice. Many of these focus on the relatively new forms of school choice—vouchers, interdistrict choice plans, and charter schools—

that have been around for a decade or less. Others focus on choice options with longer pedigrees—magnet schools, special schools, liberal transfer policies, parochial schools—that were not perceived as representing test cases for market theories until the Reagan administration helped to initiate a much broader conceptualization of school choice.

The irony lies in the fact that this growing base of information does not seem to have moved us closer to agreement on policy directions or even to have moderated the harshness and polarization that characterize many public discussions about the risks and benefits of school choice. One possibility is that we need even more and even better studies—and then some time to digest them—before a consensus on policy direction can be forged. Conventional methodological refinements—introducing more and better measures of educational outcomes, independent variables, and intervening factors; augmenting standard quantitative analyses with more qualitative assessments of school- and classroom-level activities; applying more sophisticated analytic techniques—are certainly welcome and needed. As findings accumulate, social scientists might begin to speak more confidently and more uniformly about them; when social scientists emphasize the differences in their findings, they make it easier for policymakers to neutralize them in a game of "you've got your studies, I've got mine."

A second possibility is that ideologies and preconceptions are so ingrained that there is no prospect that empirical research can have any substantial impact on the level or quality of debate. Flawless studies are a fantasy, and ideologically motivated opponents can always find some methodological soft point to exploit as a reason for disregarding studies with which they disagree. The quality of the research being undertaken in the area of school choice may once have fallen below the threshold of scholarly credibility, but that is no longer the case. If the studies reviewed here have not led to more solid common ground, some might reasonably argue that there is not much reason to expect that conventional methodological refinements will suffice to turn that around.

I suggest a third possibility: at least as important as more and better studies is the need for a more sophisticated theoretical framework through which to interpret the evidence as it comes in. The multiplication of choice options and the expansion of the definitional umbrella of what constitutes school choice are double-edged swords. While they are responsible for the sharp increase in the sheer amount of empirical grist for the debate mill, which has brought some abstract arguments down to earth, they have also introduced new ambiguities about how to apply findings drawn from one arena of choice to choice as it might play out in different forms and different settings. Rather than the internal validity of existing studies of separate forms and manifestations of school choice, the source of the major conflicts and confusions today derives from the absence of clear guidance about how to move from findings specific to one manifestation of choice to more general conclusions. Unless we pay as much attention to developing new and more sophisticated theories as we have to unearthing facts, the accumulating evidence threatens to outrun our capacity to make sense of it all.

In at least two ways, the theoretical tools currently available leave us intellectually underequipped to draw strong and clear lessons for public policy. First, the dominance of the market metaphor has obscured the fact that most of the available evidence about school choice may have very little to say about markets at all. Most of what we have learned about school choice is based on evidence drawn from two sectors—religious institutions and public education—in which the key actors and decision criteria are distinctly not market driven in the conventional sense. Existing theories tell us little about what those findings imply about how profit-oriented schools will perform in a less-structured market setting.

The strongest findings about private schools' educational advantages rest heavily on the inclusion of religious schools; the same can be said about the findings related to private schools' willingness to serve minorities and the poor and their ability to keep the costs of education low. While they are certainly not impervious to market forces, religious schools are hardly prototypical market actors. Subsidies from religious institutions, the willingness of teachers and administrators to work for less because of a sense of mission, the added sense of community and solidarity that binds the school and parents, a powerful moral commitment to do good even when that is not profitable, all these are central to the identity of religious schools, all are powerful rival explanations for why those schools perform as they do, and all are distinctly out of line with conventional microeconomic assumptions about self-interested, materialistically motivated behavior by individuals and firms.

That most of the remaining evidence has been drawn from examples of public school choice—the effectiveness of magnets in bringing about integrated schools and more demanding curricula, the apparent successes in New York's District 4 in improving parent information networks and school performance in a low-income community—has been more widely recognized but not, I think, appropriately understood. That these programs incorporate some element of parental choice has been taken to mean that they are analogous to markets in important respects, and their successes have been taken to mean that market mechanisms for control work better than mechanisms defined by democratic processes and public authority. But the fact that one facet of such public programs is analogous to one facet of market processes does not mean that they are like markets in all, or even in most, important respects.[103] To the extent that these examples of public school choice have succeeded, it primarily has been due to parents, citizens, educators, and politicians crafting workable designs, monitoring progress, making corrections, and sustaining interest over time. If principals and teachers have been more innovative and responsive, it is attributable to signals delivered through public institutions, not private bargains, and it is the design and health of those institutions to which we must attend.

This leads us to the second sense in which existing theories leave us underequipped. Market theory provides a well-defined framework for making predictions about the future actions of market actors. But to the extent that the successes of school choice will depend upon the actions of religious institutions, nonprofit organizations, democratic decisionmaking, and the politics of regulatory control, we are on much less certain ground. While many researchers have come to agree that institutional designs matter and that governmental regimes of redistribution, regulation, and oversight are required, we have given relatively little systematic attention to what determines which institutional designs and governance regimes are politically sustainable.

Rather than narrow disagreements about research methodologies, I suspect that the real source of policy stalemate is fundamentally contrasting expectations about how political institutions and governance regimes will respond to and mold choice over time. Choice proponents dismiss concerns that market systems will spawn schools run by profiteers, bigots, and close-minded zealots, partially based on the premise that governmental oversight and regulation will be sufficient to identify and weed out the bad apples. Choice opponents worry that such operators will use their political resources, along with the ideological appeal of privatization and religious freedom, to ensure that oversight is limited and regulations not enforced. Choice proponents dismiss concerns about racial and economic stratification partially based on the premise that legal protections against discrimination are firmly entrenched and that the commitment to progressive provisions (such as larger vouchers for the disadvantaged) can be taken for granted. Choice opponents see judicial protection of civil rights and the political constituency for equalization to be fragile and insecure.

What, if anything, has relevance to policymaking today? I see in the emerging evidence the outlines of a pragmatic orientation toward school choice. Choice can be made to work. In at least some forms and institutional settings, choice can help stimulate needed change. In at least some forms and institutional settings, choice need not exacerbate racial segregation, social fragmentation, or economic stratification. Those who get to exercise school choice believe that it is helping them, and there is some evidence that this may be true. At the same time, there is little evidence that it is individual decisions and market forces, as distinct from democracy, community, and governance, that account for those successes. Public schools have been open to choice and pedagogical innovation. Many of them have proven able to adopt and implement the specific practices on which private schools base their claimed advantages (more demanding curriculum, high standards for all, even school uniforms).

This is not to say that all public school systems have the will and the capacity to reform themselves. To the contrary. Many school districts—especially those mired in the economic and political morass that characterizes many older, central cities—face daunting obstacles that can be overcome only by mounting the kind of broad-based, sustained efforts that so far have proven easier to imagine than to put into place and maintain.[104] But the claims that market-based choice will accomplish more at a much lower cost are almost certainly exaggerated. Choice proponents are correct when they insist that the current system is failing in many respects, but they are almost certainly wrong when they claim that the precipitous introduction of large-scale choice programs could not make anything worse. It could. Choice proponents are correct when they assert that conventional democratic institutions have failed to give school reform the sustained attention it deserves, but they are wrong when they imply that market institutions and individual choice allow us to bypass the challenge of making those democratic institutions work. To avoid the risks of greater segregation, fragmentation, and stratification that unregulated choice brings into play, we would have to ensure that choice programs are fundamentally fair and are embedded in an institutional context that provides oversight and accountability to democratic values.

This suggests the wisdom of a policy approach that is unhurried, reasonably cautious, and tied to specific circumstances and that pays attention to articulating the public interest in supporting education and building healthy institutions of governance.

Notes

1. Friedman's earliest published formulation was "The Role of Government in Education," in Robert A. Solo, ed., *Economics and the Public Interest* (Rutgers University Press, 1955). His more famous presentation is found in his *Capitalism and Freedom* (University of Chicago Press, 1962), chap. 6.

2. James A. Mecklenburger and Richard W. Hostrop, eds., *Education Vouchers: From Theory to Alum Rock* (Homewood, Ill.: ETC, 1972); David K. Cohen and Eleanor Farrar, "Power to the Parents? The Story of Education Vouchers," *Public Interest*, vol. 48 (Summer 1977), pp. 72–97; Laura Hersh Salganik, "The Fall and Rise of Education Vouchers," *Teachers College Record*, vol. 83, no. 2 (1981), pp. 263–83.

3. For a fuller discussion of the resistance to, and subsequent revival of interest in, the voucher notion, see Jeffrey R. Henig, *Rethinking School Choice: Limits of the Market Metaphor* (Princeton University Press, 1994).

4. Ibid., p. 78.

5. Ibid., p. 145.

6. Rolf K. Blank, Roger E. Levine, and Lauri Steel, "After 15 Years, Magnet Schools in Urban Education," in Richard Elmore and Bruce Fuller, eds., *Who Chooses? Who Loses? Culture, Institutions, and the Unequal Effects of School Choice* (Teachers College Press, 1996), pp. 154–72.

7. Kelly W. Colopy and Hope C. Tarr, *Minnesota's Public School Choice Options* (U.S. Department of Education, 1994), p. 11.

8. Massachusetts Department of Education, "Massachusetts Charter School Initiative" (http://www.doe.mass.edu//cs.www/cs.over.html), August 4, 1999.

9. John F. Witte, Troy D. Sterr, and Christopher A. Thorn, *Fifth-Year Report: Milwaukee Parental Program* (University of Wisconsin—Madison, Robert La Follette Institute of Public Affairs, 1995), table 7.

10. Jay P. Greene, William G. Howell, and Paul E. Peterson, *An Evaluation of the Cleveland Scholarship Program* (Harvard University, Taubman Center for State and Local Government and Center for American Political Studies, 1997), table 1-8.

11. R. Kenneth Godwin, Frank R. Kemerer, and Valerie J. Martinez, *Final Report: San Antonio School Choice Research Project* (University of North Texas, Center for the Study of Education Reform, 1997), pp. 9–11.

12. Gary Bridge, "Information Imperfections: The Achilles Heel of Entitlement Plans," *School Review* (May 1978), p. 512.

13. Ibid., p. 514.

14. Jeffrey R. Henig, "The Local Dynamics of Choice: Ethnic Preferences and Institutional Responses," in Elmore and Fuller, *Who Chooses? Who Loses?*

15. Mark Schneider and others, "Shopping for Schools: In the Land of the Blind the One-Eyed Parent May Be Enough," *American Journal of Political Science*, vol. 42 (1998), pp. 769–93.

16. Mark Schneider and others, "Networks to Nowhere: Segregation and Stratification in Networks of Information about Schools," *American Journal of Political Science*, vol. 41 (1997), p. 40.

17. National Center for Education Statistics (NCES), *Public and Private Schools: How Do They Differ?* (U.S. Department of Education, 1997), table 12-8.

18. Charles L. Glenn, Kahris McLaughlin, and Laura Salganik, *Parent Information for School Choice: The Case of Massachusetts* (Boston: Center on Families, Communities, Schools, and Children's Learning, 1993), p. 13.

19. Mark Schneider and others, "Institutional Arrangements and the Creation of Social

Capital," *American Political Science Review*, vol. 91 (March 1997), pp. 82–93.

20. Bridge, "Information Imperfections," table 4.

21. Henig, "The Local Dynamics of Choice."

22. Barbara Schneider, Kathryn S. Schiller, and James S. Coleman, "Public School Choice: Some Evidence from the National Educational Longitudinal Study of 1988," *Educational Evaluation and Policy Analysis*, vol. 18 (Spring 1996), p. 27.

23. Colopy and Tarr, *Minnesota's Public School Choice Options*, pp. 21–25.

24. Susan E. Eaton, "Slipping toward Segregation: Local Control and Eroding Desegregation in Montgomery County," in Gary Orfield, Susan E. Eaton, and the Harvard Project on School Desegregation, eds., *Dismantling Desegregation: The Quiet Reversal of Brown v. Board of Education* (New York: New Press, 1996), pp. 207–40.

25. Witte, Sterr, and Thorn, *Fifth-Year Report*, p. 5.

26. Godwin, Kemerer, and Martinez, *Final Report*, table 1.

27. Carnegie Foundation for the Advancement of Teaching, *School Choice* (Princeton, N.J.: 1992), pp. 50–55.

28. Richard Fossey, "Open Enrollment in Massachusetts: Why Families Choose," *Educational Evaluation and Policy Analysis*, vol. 16, no. 3 (1994), pp. 320–34.

29. Valerie Martinez, Kay Thomas, and Frank Kemerer, "Who Chooses and Why: A Look at Five School Choice Plans," *Phi Delta Kappan* (May 1994), p. 680.

30. Henig, "The Local Dynamics of Choice."

31. Steven Glazerman, "A Conditional Logit Model of Elementary School Choice: What Do Parents Value?" (University of Chicago, Harris School of Public Policy, November 3, 1997); Colopy and Tarr, *Minnesota's Public School Choice Options*, p. 5.

32. In addition to average test scores, an estimate of value added is included; this also had no significant impact on parental choice. Glazerman, "A Conditional Logit Model of Elementary School Choice."

33. Ibid., p. 38.

34. My own view is that racial and economic segregation is a legitimate issue for public concern (although not necessarily public action), even when it is freely chosen. I consider it a matter of public concern because racial, ethnic, and economic segregation create conditions under which resentment, misunderstanding, and hatred are more likely to simmer and, eventually, erupt. Such concern, in and of itself, may not mandate remedial action, however. In that sense, I agree with choice proponents who distinguish chosen segregation from imposed segregation. Whether or not public action is warranted will depend upon a careful weighing of many specifics of the situation, including assessments of how well market-based choice is likely to further other values and how feasible it is that the existing public school system can be improved through existing institutions of democratic reform.

35. David Boaz and R. Morris Barrett, "What Would a School Voucher Buy? The Real Cost of Private Schools," Briefing Paper 25 (Washington, D.C.: Cato Institute, March 26, 1996), p. 9.

36. National Center for Education Statistics, *The Condition of Education, 1997* (U.S. Department of Education), table 12-2.

37. Ibid. Based on the names of the schools, 201 of the 269 could be readily classified as religious. All but three of the others (which had Arabic names that might or might not have indicated a religious affiliation) were classified as nonsectarian for the analysis that follows.

38. The following discussion is based on my reanalysis of the data presented in Boaz and Barrett, "What Would a School Voucher Buy?"

39. New Jersey has the highest school expenditure in the country, and Jersey City has been receiving special attention from the state.

40. Richard Rothstein with Karen Hawley Miles, *Where's the Money Gone?* (Washing-

ton, D.C.: Economic Policy Institute, 1995), p. 8.

41. NCES, *Public and Private Schools*, table 12-28.

42. For discussions of the public versus private cost comparison that make some effort to sort through such issues, see Henry M. Levin, "The Theory of Choice Applied to Education," in William H. Clune and John F. Witte, eds., *Choice and Control in American Education*, vol. 1 (London: Falmer, 1990); Myron Lieberman, *Public Education: An Autopsy* (Harvard University Press, 1993), chap. 6.

43. Joseph Harris, "The Cost of Catholic Parishes and Schools," cited in Dan Murphy, F. Howard Nelson, and Bella Rosenberg, *The Cleveland Voucher Program: Who Chooses? Who Gets Chosen? Who Pays?* (Washington, D.C.: American Federation of Teachers, 1997), p. B5. See also Carrolyn Minter Hoxby, "The Effects of Private Vouchers on Schools and Students," in Helen Ladd, ed., *Holding Schools Accountable: Performance-Based Reform in Education* (Brookings, 1996).

44. Alex Molnar estimates that only about half of Milwaukee's public school expenditures actually go directly to the school. When this adjusted figure is used, he finds that in 1997–98 Milwaukee's kindergarten through grade six public schools received about $3,875 per pupil and kindergarten through grade eight schools received about $4,234. By comparison, the voucher amount available to the twenty-three private schools participating in the Milwaukee program was $4,696. Alex Molnar, *Smaller Classes Not Vouchers Increase Student Achievement* (Harrisburg, Pa.: Keystone Research Center, 1998), p. 13.

45. Comments by Deborah McGriff, an Edison Corporation vice president, at the IDEA Institute conference on choice, charter schools, and privatization, St. Louis, October 24–26, 1996. McGriff mentioned $5,100 per pupil as a bottom line, below which the company felt it could not provide its curriculum. When providing a full high school curriculum, as it was attempting to do in Boston, Edison required about $8,000 per pupil, she indicated. Normal per pupil expenditures in California, for example, were deemed too low for Edison to get involved until the company was given a supplementary $25 million grant from a private foundation. See Somini Sengupta, "Edison Project Gets Aid to Open New Schools," *New York Times*, May 27, 1998.

46. Lois C. Williams and Lawrence E. Leak, *The UMBC Evaluation of the Tesseract Program in Baltimore City* (University of Maryland—Baltimore County, 1995), p. 34.

47. Douglas J. Lamdin, "The Economics of Education Provision by For-Profit Contractors" (University of Maryland—Baltimore County, Department of Economics, January 1998), p. 31.

48. Janie E. Funkouser and Kelly W. Colopy, *Minnesota's Open Enrollment Option: Impacts on School Districts* (U.S. Department of Education, 1994).

49. Angela Dale and Dave DeSchryver, eds., *The Charter School Workbook* (Washington, D.C.: Center for Education Reform, 1997), pp. 153–54.

50. Henig, "The Local Dynamics of Choice."

51. Funkouser and Colopy, *Minnesota's Open Enrollment Option*.

52. Kevin B. Smith and Kenneth J. Meier, *The Case against School Choice* (Armonk, N.Y.: M. E. Sharpe, 1995).

53. NCES, *Public and Private Schools*, table 12-8.

54. Anthony S. Bryk, Valerie E. Lee, and Peter B. Holland, *Catholic Schools and the Common Good* (Harvard University Press, 1993), p. 99.

55. NCES, *The Condition of Education, 1997*, p. 132.

56. NCES, *Public and Private Schools*, pp. 13–14.

57. RPP International, *A Study of Charter Schools: First Year Report, 1997* (U.S. Department of Education, 1997).

58. NCES, *The Condition of Education, 1997*, table 9.

59. NCES, *Public and Private Schools*, p. 27.

60. RPP International, *A Study of Charter Schools*, pp. 31–32.

61. John F. Witte, "Achievement Effects of the Milwaukee Voucher Program," paper prepared for the American Economics Association annual meeting, January 4–6, 1997, p. 4.

62. Green, Howell, and Peterson, *An Evaluation of the Cleveland Scholarship Program*, table 1-3.

63. Murphy, Nelson, and Rosenberg, *The Cleveland Voucher Program*, p. 11.

64. RPP International, *A Study of Charter Schools*, pp. 20–22.

65. Chester E. Finn and others, *The Birth Pains and Life Cycles of Charter Schools* (New York: Hudson Institute, 1997), p. 11. It is not clear whether wariness about taking on such students is attributable to reluctance to do what is necessary to meet their genuine needs or to fear that the attendant federal or state regulations would force the school into unnecessary expenses or modifications of its operations. It is possible that some parents of disabled children would prefer to send their children to private schools because such schools would resist labeling them and resist shuffling them into special classes or curricula. Steve Sugarman has reminded me of the folklore that holds that many Catholic schools have considerable success mainstreaming children with mild disabilities into their regular routine. Even if true, the ability of private schools to sidestep the regulations and expenses that the public schools cannot so readily escape means that simple comparisons between the spending and performance of private and public schools need to be regarded warily.

66. Lynn Schnaiberg, "Disability Provisions Cited at Boston Charter School," *Education Week*, September 1997.

67. Joseph R. McKinney and Julie F. Mead, "Law and Policy in Conflict: Including Students with Disabilities in Parental Choice Programs," *Educational Administration Quarterly*, vol. 32 (February 1996), p. 116.

68. The impact of this disproportionate responsibility depends, of course, upon whether the attendant additional subsidies that accompany disabled and special education students are sufficient to meet these students' greater needs. The avoidance behavior exhibited by many private schools suggests that the market finds the additional funds insufficient, at least for schools that are also attempting to serve a general population. In some metropolitan areas, private schools specializing in dealing with such students have found a viable niche.

69. Bruce Fuller and Xiaoyan Liang, "Market Failure? Estimating Inequality in Preschool Availability," *Educational Evaluation and Policy Analysis*, vol. 18 (spring 1996), pp. 31–49.

70. David Doege, "Fraud Charged in School Choice Case," *Milwaukee Journal*, June 17, 1996.

71. Bill Miller, "Founder of Kedar School Convicted of Wire Fraud," *Washington Post*, March 12, 1998; "Kedar School Founder Guilty of Bank Fraud," *Washington Post*, March 13, 1998.

72. Valerie Strauss and Peter Slevin, "After Garvey Decision, Doubts about Charter Schools," *Washington Post*, May 28, 1998.

73. Amy Stuart Wells, *Beyond the Rhetoric of Charter School Reform: A Study of Ten California School Districts* (University of California Press, 1998).

74. James S. Coleman, Thomas Hoffer, and Sally Kilgore, *High School Achievement* (Basic Books, 1982); James S. Coleman and Thomas Hoffer, *Public and Private High Schools* (Basic Books, 1987).

75. See, for example, Karl L. Alexander and Aaron M. Pallas, "Private Schools and Public Policy: New Evidence on Cognitive Achievement in Public and Private Schools," *Sociology of Education*, vol. 56 (October 1983), pp. 170–82; Glen G. Cain and Arthur S. Goldberger, "Public and Private Schools Revisited," *Sociology of Education*, vol. 56 (October 1983), pp. 208–18; William R. Morgan, "Learning and Student Life Quality of Public and Private School

Youth," *Sociology of Education*, vol. 56 (October 1983), pp. 187–202; John F. Witte, "Understanding High School Achievement: After a Decade of Research, Do We Have Any Confident Policy Recommendations?" paper prepared for the American Political Science Association annual meeting, San Francisco, August 30–September 2, 1997.

76. John E. Chubb and Terry M. Moe, *Politics, Markets, and America's Schools* (Brookings, 1990).

77. William N. Evans and Robert M. Schwab, "Who Benefits from Private Education: Evidence from Quantile Regressions" (University of Maryland, Department of Economics, 1993); William N. Evans and Robert M. Schwab, "Finishing High School and Starting College: Do Catholic Schools Make a Difference?" *Quarterly Journal of Economics* (November 1995).

78. For a review, see John F. Witte, "Private School versus Public School Achievement: Are There Findings That Should Affect the Educational Choice Debate?" *Economics of Education Review*, vol. 11, no. 4 (1992), pp. 371–94.

79. Ibid., p. 388.

80. Coleman, Hoffer, and Kilgore, *High School Achievement*, p. 242; Chubb and Moe, *Politics, Markets, and America's Schools*, take for granted that market forces account for the differences.

81. Bryk, Lee, and Holland, *Catholic Schools and the Common Good*, pp. 315–16.

82. Chubb and Moe, *Politics, Markets, and America's Schools*, argue that the success of private schools is attributable to the discretion they enjoy to make key decisions at the school level. No matter how much democratically elected officials might wish to recreate this discretion within the public sector, Chubb and Moe believe that they are institutionally incapable of doing so. "The raison d'être of democratic control is to impose higher-order values on schools, and thus to limit their autonomy" (p. 38). The crux of their proposals for choice, accordingly, is their insistence that "direct democratic control of the schools—the very *capacity* for control, not simply its exercise—would essentially be eliminated" (p. 226).

83. Bryk, Lee, and Holland, *Catholic Schools and the Common Good*.

84. Rolf K. Blank, "Educational Effects of Magnet High Schools," in Clune and Witte, *Choice and Control in American Education*, vol. 2, pp. 77–109.

85. John C. Larson and Brenda A. Allen, *A Microscope on Magnet Schools, 1983 to 1986*, vol. 2, *Pupil and Parent Outcomes* (Montgomery County, Maryland, Public Schools, Department of Educational Accountability, 1988).

86. Gary G. Wehlage and G. A. Smith, "Building New Programs for Students at Risk," in F. M. Newmann, ed., *Student Engagement and Achievement in American Secondary Schools* (Teachers College Press, 1992), pp. 92–118.

87. Robert L. Crain, Amy L. Heebner, and Y. P. Si, *The Effectiveness of New York City's Career Magnet Schools: An Evaluation of Ninth-Grade Performance Using an Experimental Design* (Berkeley: National Center for Research in Vocational Education, 1992).

88. Paul Teske and others, "Evaluating the Effects of Public School Choice in District 4" (Manhattan Institute, February 17, 1998).

89. Adam Gamoran, "Student Achievement in Public Magnet, Public Comprehensive, and Private City High Schools," *Educational Evaluation and Policy Analysis*, vol. 18 (Spring 1996), table 4.

90. Witte, Sterr, and Thorn, *Fifth-Year Report*, provide an overview of the earlier studies as well as the final evaluation.

91. Jay P. Greene, Paul E. Peterson, and Jiangtao Du, "The Effectiveness of School Choice in Milwaukee: A Secondary Analysis of Data from the Program's Evaluation" (Harvard University, Program in Education Policy and Governance, August 14, 1996).

92. The exchanges include Jay P. Greene and Paul E. Peterson, "School Choice Data Rescued from Bad Science," *Wall Street Journal*, August 14, 1996; and John F. Witte, "Reply to

Greene, Peterson, and Du," *Wall Street Journal,* August 23, 1996.

93. Greene, Peterson, and Du, "The Effectiveness of School Choice in Milwaukee," p. 27.

94. Molnar, *Smaller Classes Not Vouchers Increase Student Achievement,* points out that the existence of Partners Advancing Values in Education (PAVE), a large private voucher program in Milwaukee, may help to account for the fact that the Greene, Peterson, and Du control group performed so poorly on standardized exams. It is possible that the most motivated of those rejected from the voucher program subsequently used PAVE scholarships to move to private schools, selectively paring down the control group to those less motivated and less likely to perform well.

95. For a recent critique on these grounds, see ibid., pp. 17–19.

96. Witte, "Achievement Effects of the Milwaukee Voucher Program."

97. Cecelia Elena Rouse, "Private School Vouchers and Student Achievement: An Evaluation of the Milwaukee Parental Choice Program," *Quarterly Journal of Economics* (May 1998), pp. 553–602.

98. Beth Reinhard, "Ohio Supreme Court Will Allow Cleveland Voucher Program to Begin Its Second Year," *Education Week,* August 6, 1997. In May 1999 Ohio's Supreme Court struck down the program on technical grounds but indicated in doing so that the general structure of the voucher program was constitutional.

99. Paul E. Peterson, Jay P. Greene, and William G. Howell, "New Findings from the Cleveland Scholarship Program: A Reanalysis of Data from the Indiana University School of Education Evaluation" (Harvard University, Taubman Center on State and Local Government, 1998). Murphy, Nelson, and Rosenburg, *The Cleveland Voucher Program,* report that both schools were launched by David Brennan, an Akron entrepreneur who "was a major campaign contributor not only to Voinovich but also to candidates who would serve as chairs of the Senate and House education committees in the 1995 legislative session. Recently, he was a serious contender for the chairmanship of the Republican National Committee." Peterson, Greene, and Howell suggest that the fact that these were start-up schools that Murphy, Nelson, and Rosenburg considered especially problematic makes the finding of educational successes especially significant.

100. Peterson, Greene, and Howell, "New Findings from the Cleveland Scholarship Program." At least they say this in the executive summary (p. vii). In the body of the report they refer to them as "moderate gains" (p. 39).

101. Ibid., p. 41.

102. Kim K. Metcalf and others, "A Comparative Evaluation of the Cleveland Scholarship and Tutoring Grant Program: Year One, 1996–97" (Indiana University, School of Education, Smith Research Center, 1998). Predictably, this analysis promoted a rebuttal by Peterson, Greene, and Howell, "New Findings from the Cleveland Scholarship Program."

103. See Bryan D. Jones, *Reconceiving Decisionmaking in Democratic Politics* (University of Chicago Press, 1994), for a discussion about how a limited span of attention leads to one-dimensional definitions of public problems.

104. Some of these obstacles are elaborated in Jeffrey R. Henig and others, *The Color of School Reform: Race, Politics, and the Challenge of Urban Education* (Princeton University Press, 1999).

PART TWO

Public Policy Flashpoints

CHAPTER FOUR

School Choice and Public Funding

STEPHEN D. SUGARMAN

M ost of the objections that lawyers and policy analysts have made to the traditional approach to funding public education in America rest on the principle that is it unfair for wealth to make a difference in the public schooling that children obtain. Starting in 1968, they have generated a flood of school finance litigation, which has now reached more than forty states. There is an important, but generally unnoticed, connection between this school finance reform movement and the public school choice movement discussed throughout this book. More precisely, the expansion of public school choice may lead to reforms in school funding that could eliminate many wealth-based inequalities. Furthermore, if private school choice is subsidized in a manner that provides fair opportunities to poor children, this reform may also help to eliminate public school finance inequalities. The movement for subsidized school choice may thus be understood to be part of a larger movement that has sought to reform the financing of elementary and secondary education generally.

The Basics of Public School Finance

If there were no public funding of education, it seems fair to assume that American families would be expected to provide for their children's schooling, just as they are expected to provide for their housing, nutrition, health, and other needs. For two main reasons—children's rights and the common good—the education that many parents would provide on their own could be considered inadequate by society, justifying, indeed requiring, public funding.

The Why of Publicly Funded Education

Although Americans tolerate significant inequalities among adults, certain inequalities among children are widely thought to be inconsistent with our nation's deep commitment to democracy, meritocracy, and capitalism. Most Americans believe that before some adults are to fairly enjoy the advantages, wealth, power, high status, and more, children must have a reasonably fair chance of attaining those advantages. Because education is widely thought to be especially crucial to competing for these advantages, a system that brings children to the brink of adulthood having experienced highly unequal educational opportunities is thought unjust by most.

Leaving education entirely to be provided by parents would surely yield a pattern of highly unequal educational opportunities for children. Many parents are very poor, and they could not afford to provide much education on their own. Private charity would help somewhat—but not enough. In addition, some parents would not sufficiently value the education of their children, perhaps out of ignorance, perhaps out of selfishness. Of course, poor and neglectful parents can fail their children on dimensions besides education; the public funding of education is socially attractive because innocent children are seen to be the central beneficiaries. By contrast, it is much harder to think about offsetting significant other inequalities children face without also directly benefiting their parents, who may or may not be thought deserving of that support. In an imaginary world, children could borrow money to finance their own education, paying it back later when they reap its financial benefits. A significant amount of higher education is funded this way. In the real world, however, this is implausible for young children.

The public funding of education in the name of children's rights (or child welfare) overcomes the shortcomings of leaving the funding of education to the family. It may also be thought of as an institutionalized way of allowing all children to, in effect, borrow now and repay later—as an intergenerational compact in which grateful, financially able adults show their gratitude by funding the schooling of the next generation. Notice how these are also the same two images employed in defense of the social security program, our other very large universal social assistance scheme.

Alternatively, public funding of schooling may be seen as redistributive, as in the welfare model, providing needed assistance when the family is poor or neglectful. Some might believe that this rationale would justify targeting the public funding of schooling to only a small proportion of children. It might be argued in response that, as a practical matter, even those parents we do not consider poor would also often have great difficulties funding their children's education, because the costs of schooling tend to be bunched early in their adult lives. Hence universal public funding of schooling may also be thought of as a way that families can finance their own children's education over the whole of their adult working years.

A second argument for public funding of education is that the education of children benefits the rest of us by forming an informed and participatory electorate, thereby bringing democracy to life and justifying our ideas of self-governance; it provides people with a route to financial and personal contentment and hence works to protect the rest of us from the externalities of crime, unemployment, and the like; and by helping to overcome ignorance, education promotes tolerance, thereby facilitating peaceful coexistence in our highly diverse society. From this common good perspective, society at large has a strong self-interest in collectively paying what is necessary to achieve a widely educated population, at least up to some basic level.

The How of Publicly Funded Education

In the United States, public funding of elementary and secondary education is largely (but not entirely) reserved for the public schools.[1] More than 90 percent of the money for American public education comes from local and state taxes. Although individual states vary enormously in the proportion provided by each source, nationwide the state and local shares today are about equal (and have been relatively equal for more than twenty years).[2] Generally speaking, school taxes that are locally assessed and collected (primarily property taxes) are spent by the local school district.

The proceeds of state taxes, like sales and income taxes, are typically allocated by the state to local school districts in one of two ways. Some funds are provided on an unrestricted basis (general aid). Other funds are given in support of a specific program or for the benefit of specific pupils (categorical aid). State categorical aid funds tend to be aimed at an educational need that has been identified by the state; general aid tends to be aimed at financial need. General aid is typically provided in an amount that is inverse to the capacity of the local community to raise its own money; in other words, more general aid per pupil is provided to school districts with less wealth per pupil, generally measured in terms of the assessed value per pupil of the real estate in the district.

Less than 10 percent of the funding for elementary and secondary education comes from the federal government, and it is almost all categorical aid, primarily for the special needs of children with disabilities or those from low-income families.

Objections to the Present Method of Publicly Funded Education

Since the late 1960s, school finance reform advocates have made several claims about what they see as the unfairness of our conventional public school funding arrangements. The basic objections are inequalities among states, among districts, and within districts. These inequalities rest on the same idea, however: wealth matters too much. Wealth differences among the states importantly contribute to the enormous differences in the resources provided to public education from state to state. Indeed, a 1997 study found that interstate spending differences on public school students are twice as large as intrastate differences.[3] For example, in 1997 per pupil spending was $8,548 in Connecticut, $6,038 in Oregon, and $4,541 in Louisiana.[4] It is not surprising that lawyers have paid little attention to these inequalities. They are not the product of congressional action, and so it is difficult to imagine that they could be legally challenged. It is perhaps surprising that policymakers have devoted so little energy to this issue. The explanation for this inattention apparently lies in their resignation to the fact that the federal government is destined to play a minor role in the financing of elementary and secondary education. As long as the federal government continues to provide less than 10 percent of the funds, not a great deal of interstate equalizing could be achieved, even if that were the goal.

In principle, the federal government could, of course, play a much larger role. In most industrialized societies, after all, the federal government is the primary (often exclusive) source of public school funding. In America, federalism is so entrenched that perhaps our very different pattern goes unnoticed. Moreover, of late our federal government has been trying to shed, not add, major financial commitments. Hence it is probably just wishful thinking that Congress might decide to pay for even one-third of current annual spending in the United States for elementary and secondary education.

This is not to say that fairness requires that spending on education be equal everywhere in the country. First, there are legitimate cost differences from place to place. Second, children have unequal needs, and this implies the desirability of unequal spending per pupil; and to the extent that needier children are not randomly distributed among schools, this also implies the desirability of unequal spending at the school level. There is also the delicate matter of taste or effort. Even if it is unfair if wealth differences (in their family, their community, or their state) yield highly unequal amounts of school spending on children, that does not answer the question of whether it is unfair if spending differences result from a differential willingness to make a (tax) effort for education—whether by the child's state, community, or family.[5]

Within states, the inequalities that have gained the most attention are those among school districts, inequalities that have arisen from the traditional reliance, noted earlier, on local taxes (primarily property taxes) to fund public schooling.[6] Some school districts have a much greater fiscal capacity than others to deal with their educational responsibilities. So even though state aid tends to go in greater amounts to poorer districts, throughout the twentieth century wealthier districts have been able to spend considerably more on their pupils. Using various state constitutional provisions and legal theories, lawyers have tried to get courts to break the connection between local wealth and local spending and, in turn, to force spending to better reflect differential costs and needs.[7] In the 1970s and 1980s, most of these lawsuits were called equity cases, and their focus was on district-to-district input (spending) differences arising directly from district wealth differences. Since 1989 a majority of the lawsuits have been termed adequacy cases, and their focus has shifted toward output (achievement) differences and the unequal spending required on some pupils to bring about adequate outcomes for all. As of the beginning of 1999, supreme courts in at least sixteen states have declared their traditional school finance systems unconstitutional on either equity or adequacy grounds or both. This is only partial success.

The major impact of most of the successful school finance cases to date (whether equity or adequacy claims) has been to cause the state to increase its spending on public education, primarily by boosting the spending levels in the formerly low-spending, low-wealth districts.[8] Nevertheless, across the United States children living in wealthier school districts have access to better-funded public schools; this is true both in most states where courts have not ordered school finance reform and even in many states where courts have ordered reform.[9]

Inequalities within school districts have gained far less attention than have interdistrict inequalities for several reasons. First, these inequalities do not arise from the same structural reasons as do interdistrict inequalities. Second, the official data demonstrating these inequalities are not as readily available. Third, from the perspective of lawyers, it is not clear how these inequalities might be legally attacked. A few cases, directly based on claims of racial discrimination, have been filed over the years, but not a great deal has come of this effort.[10]

From a policy perspective, three sorts of intradistrict inequality have been of greatest concern. One concerns differences in the condition of the schools themselves: some schools are bright, clean, and well equipped; others are woefully dilapidated, a condition that all too often exists in the parts of town where poor families live. A second concerns a common practice in the allocation of teaching resources. In many school districts, individual schools are entitled to receive from the central district a certain number of teacher slots for a certain number of pupils. Whoever is hired to fill the slot has her or his salary paid by the district, regardless of the salary amount. According to the typical teachers' union contract, teachers have seniority rights to available teaching jobs within districts, and it is common that the more senior teachers tend to exercise those rights to avoid the "worst" (or "hardest") schools and to cluster in the "best" (or "easiest") schools. The result is that the schools serving the neediest, poorest, and lowest-achieving pupils often have many fewer dollars per pupil spent on their core teaching force. Although having younger and less experienced teachers can carry some advantages (enthusiasm, more recent training, more openness to new ideas), on balance, it is probably worse for a school to have a lower-paid teacher corps. A third concern has to do with pupil needs. The basic argument is that, even though federal and state categorical aid programs do target extra funds to pupils with extra needs, those unequal needs have not been adequately met, especially the extra needs of pupils from low-income families.

The upshot is that, even in some relatively wealthier urban school districts, the neighborhood public schools that children from low-income families have access to are much less adequately funded to meet their educational needs than are the public schools located in neighborhoods where higher-income families live.

New Remedy, Old Problem

In sum, the children's rights and common good arguments for funding public education have carried only so far. As far as most state legislatures and school district leaders are concerned, children attending public schools are entitled only to some politically determined minimum level of spending. Many observers agree that this minimum is insufficient to serve the common good, and it is surely insufficient to satisfy any meaningful notion of children's rights. In short, equal educational opportunity for all American children remains but an aspiration. As a result, the ongoing battle to achieve real equality of opportunity will no doubt continue in courtrooms and legislatures around the country.

The argument advanced in this chapter depends upon the little-noticed connection between school finance reform efforts and the school choice movement. The drive to expand school choice may itself put considerable pressure on the conventional school finance structure and, if successful, could bring about more equality of educational opportunity than decades of litigation and direct legislative policy reform have achieved.

Public Funding of Public School Choice

Why do we traditionally fund access to only the local public school? Speaking generally, in the school financing system just described each child receives a public subsidy that may be used (almost) exclusively at his or her local public school. Can this be justified? One might argue that, since local people are funding the school, it is only the local school to which a child should have access, but this argument hardly takes us very far. It does not explain why children do not routinely get to choose from among all the schools in their local district; yet intradistrict choice options are far more the exception than the rule. Further, a substantial share of the funding in most states comes from the state itself. Anyway, just because much of the funding has traditionally been local, that does not explain why it should be so.

At one time it might have been argued that many people lived out their lives where they grew up, so that decisions about the common good from education, as well as the contours of a child's educational rights, were aptly made locally. In reality, of course, Americans have long been much on the move, and that is decidedly so today. Hence the country now is clearly not a series of rather isolated communities. In the past it might also have been argued that the public school is a common school in the sense that what goes on in all public schools is pretty much the same, and simple expediency might justify local assignment. If it does not matter where you attend, the easiest thing for the administration is just to send you to your nearest school. Today, however, no one believes that all public schools are the same.

To be sure, assigning neighborhood children to the local public school can bring the added benefit of making the school a community institution in the geographic sense. In fact, many Americans cherish their local public school, often rating it far higher than public education in general. Indeed, a preference for neighborhood schools may lie behind both support for public school decentralization reforms (proposed and adopted) that give more power to the school site and opposition to involuntary busing for purposes of school integration. Nevertheless, Americans are now very much accustomed to being part of communities that are not geographically based. For example, people rarely select a church because it is the closest one to their home. They tend first to pick their religion; even then, they might well select a congregation in their faith that is not nearest to where they live. People belong to the Sierra Club or the National Rifle Association, and some of them may care passionately about the community feeling that such membership brings. These are not geographic communities; they are communities of interest. Many find community in the college or university they attend, but higher education attendance is not based on the neighborhood one lives in.

The reality is that the narrow nature of the public school subsidy that has traditionally been available to the individual child has served to keep some children out of other children's neighborhood public schools, whether they are located elsewhere inside the district or in another district. Put bluntly, it has meant that those communities with means, or access to wealth, have been able to provide greater funding for the public schools that serve their own children.

Most school finance reform efforts aim at equalizing the quality of schools from place to place, a strategy that rests on the assumption that children stay put. A different approach, however, is to permit children to use their public subsidy at public schools other than their local schools. This solution permits them to shift to a better school—which is, of course, exactly what public school choice is designed to achieve. Moreover, permitting children to attend other than their neighborhood public schools threatens to undermine the existing school finance system and may pave the way to eliminating what have been said to be its inequalities.

Intradistrict Choice

About one in ten schoolchildren currently attend magnet, alternative, and other choice schools that are run directly by the districts in which they live. Some other children are permitted to transfer into neighborhood schools that are located in other neighborhoods in the district. A small number of districts have abolished neighborhood schools, thereby forcing all families in the community to make a school choice for their children. The funding for these intradistrict choice arrangements is ordinarily an internal matter for the district to work out from its regular funding sources (local, state, and federal), but the mere existence of intradistrict choice may call into question the way that the district has historically funded its neighborhood schools.

Some families will opt out of the neighborhood public school for reasons of educational program or convenience. This is a central purpose of school choice and implies nothing about the way the district's schools are funded. Other families will opt for a nonneighborhood school because their school of choice is better run (that is, it is more effective). Another main purpose of school choice is to permit selection on this basis, with the additional hope that it will prompt currently inefficient schools to become more productive. Suppose families opt for schools because those schools have more resources available to perform their task. Although school choice facilitates selection on this basis, it has not conventionally been touted as an objective of the choice scheme. To be sure, sometimes local specialty schools may be better funded than the average school in the district precisely because the district has decided to showcase them or because it is eager to attract pupils to them. Ordinarily, however, since all families will not be able to gain entry to the better-funded schools, combining intradistrict inequalities with school choice is a recipe for discontent.

Families that successfully gain entry to the schools with a richer resource mix will not complain; nor will those who run such schools. Unsuccessful aspirants and heads of the resource-poorer schools, however, have good reason to protest. Of course, even without school choice, those attending (and working in) schools with relatively fewer resources to do their jobs may complain. Yet with choice, families are clearly encouraged to think beyond the local school and to make comparisons; in turn, they are more likely to know more about schools other than their local school. School principals who lose families on this basis will have new grounds for protest. This pressure that school choice places on intradistrict inequalities has, of course, existed for as long as these types of intradistrict choice have existed. The charter school movement puts additional pressure on intradistrict inequalities.

Interdistrict Choice

More than a third of the states now permit children to attend public schools located outside their home district without gaining the approval of their home district. Although this option is currently used by relatively few families even in states with active interdistrict transfer schemes, it is a growing form of school choice. When this type of school choice is made, how should the transferring child's education be paid for? There are basically two options available to the states: one is to have the child's district of residence pay tuition to the receiving school district; the other option is to treat children as though they are living in the districts in which they are enrolled (even though their families pay property taxes to the district in which they reside). Either way, interdistrict choice exposes and puts pressure on interdistrict school spending differences.

If the district where the child lives has to pay tuition to the district where the child wishes to attend, the first question becomes how the level of tuition is to be set. If the amount is determined by per pupil spending where the child wishes to attend, and that is a high-spending district, the sending district is bound to complain. Why should it spend more on its resident children it does not educate than on those it does educate? In any event, where will it get the extra money? Suppose the tuition required for interdistrict transfers is set at the spending level of the lower-spending sending district. Then the receiving district may well object and is likely to resist entry of such students (by declaring itself full). This, however, undermines the basic goal of the school choice scheme, the free transfer of children across district lines.

The problems do not go away if the child is instead treated as living in the district of attendance rather than where the child actually lives. The sending district probably is not much affected. Having one less pupil to educate both decreases its costs and increases its wealth per pupil; it probably suffers a reduction in state aid approximately equal to its savings from losing the student (at least over time). A high-spending receiving district, however, will probably be adversely impacted. Having one more pupil to educate increases its costs; and while that also lowers its wealth per pupil, if it is a wealthy district its increase in state aid (if any) is likely to be less than its increased cost (at least over time). Some may conclude that, on moral grounds, one should favor this arrangement, in which transferring pupils are treated as living in the district where they attend, precisely because this solution burdens richer receiving districts (and perhaps even drives down their existing wealth-advantaged per pupil spending). The trouble is that districts like this would have a financial incentive to resist in-transfers, thereby undermining the school choice scheme.

Moreover, although parents who do successfully transfer their children to higher-spending districts are likely to be pleased, those who are left behind are likely to be unhappy at seeing their neighbors' children obtain spending advantages in other districts. Parents are especially likely to be irate if they try to transfer their children but are unable to because of the limited number of open places in the receiving district (or if they are, perhaps because of transportation complications, unable to apply for a transfer to the other district). As with intradistrict transfers, once families are encouraged to make comparisons, school resource differences that, in the past, may have been unknown or rather abstract to them may now be vividly appreciated. As with intradistrict transfers, those principals and superintendents who lose pupils have even more reason to complain (who likes to be unpopular?) about the underlying inequalities.

Plainly, if there is to be more and more interdistrict choice, the underlying inequalities between districts become more and more intolerable. Indeed, the more that interdistrict choice is exercised, the more incoherent it becomes that schools are locally funded in the first place. Why are those families whose children transfer from District A to District B still helping to fund District A's schools? Indeed, why are the residents of District A still paying local property taxes to support the local schools when the pupils attending those schools are less and less from the local community?

Charter Schools

How should charter school funding be arranged? First, assume that a school is chartered by a local school district. In that event, one solution would be to treat the school's pupils as part of the district load and have the school's funding come from the district's overall budget. State funding would be the same as if the students attended traditional neighborhood schools, and the district might try to treat the charter school just as it treats its neighborhood schools.

In many districts, regular public schools have their teacher positions funded, rather than having district-average, per pupil, lump sums paid over to them. Charter schools, however, generally want the flexibility of configuring their staffs in innovative ways, of paying their teachers differently, and so on. This wish makes them push for a lump sum per pupil. How should the district deal with this demand? If it pays the charter school the districtwide average, the district could well find it more expensive to fund a charter school than a comparable school it runs itself—that is, assuming the charter school is a conversion of an existing public school filled with an inexperienced staff. Notice also how a policy of making a per pupil allocation to charter schools might create a strong financial incentive for many existing public schools to convert to charter schools and a disincentive for other existing schools to become charter schools. These complications of charter school funding, even more than conventional intradistrict school choice schemes, will put pressure on districts to eliminate the inequalities that now arise from the funding of teacher positions. If a district abandons funding teacher positions for its charter schools, it may well have to do the same for its ordinary schools.

This is not the end of the story. What if the charter school has (or expects to have) a disproportionate share of the district's high-cost pupils? It would then no longer want from the district a lump sum equal to the district average spending per pupil. Instead it would want a per pupil amount adjusted for the needs of the specific pupils it enrolls (or a categorical lump sum addition for that extra need). Without that, it might be financially foolhardy for certain existing schools to convert to charter schools and very difficult for new charter schools to serve their pupils well. These forces will pressure school districts to take more care than they do now in deciding just how much of their budgets to allocate for special pupil needs, both in charter schools and in regular schools.

In short, the development of district-funded charter schools could lead the way to having districts, on their own, eliminate some of the objectionable features found in the traditional approach to intradistrict school funding. Whether this will actually occur, and when, is another matter. So far, in practice, many of those who have created, or wish to create, charter schools object to local district funding altogether. Some object to the built-in inequalities already noted. Some claim that local funding discourages districts from granting charters in the first place—or at least causes districts to drag their feet in paying to charter schools the sums they are due. There has also been some gamesmanship by districts; for example, some districts push charter schools to take far less money than what the district spends on its own pupils.[11] Hence many charter school supporters push for state, rather than district, funding.

Another factor that encourages state funding of charter schools should be emphasized. Suppose a charter school draws a fair number of pupils from outside the district in which it is located. If it is funded by its local district, this, of course, raises the equity problems of interdistrict choice. But there is more. If a charter school draws pupils living in many districts, the school might be better off obtaining a charter from the local district spending the most per pupil. Of course, for the reasons explained earlier, some wealthier districts may be reluctant to grant charters to schools that will draw in new pupils from outside the district. To the extent that they do, this will probably create a situation that will surely seem unfair to charter school operators. Those charter schools created by higher-spending districts are likely to have more resources with which to compete for pupils than those created by lower-spending districts.

Consider the alternative approach to funding charter schools: having the state directly fund them. This probably strikes many as an especially apt solution for schools that receive their charters from an agency other than a local district, such as the state board of education or a state university (which are chartering bodies in several states). Many claim that all charter schools should be funded in this way. Yet this solution creates other problems and pressures. If a poorer, lower-spending district loses pupils to a charter school and those pupils are no longer counted as part of its enrollment, the result is the same we saw earlier when pupils who transfer out of a district are no longer treated as belonging to the sending district. The district probably comes out financially about even over time. If, however, a wealthy, high-spending district loses pupils to charter schools and those pupils are no longer counted as part of its enrollment, that district enjoys a gain. It in effect becomes even wealthier because its educational burden is lightened and its loss of state aid, if any, is likely to be much less than its cost savings. This not only magnifies existing inequalities but also affects the state's financial obligations.

First, if the state funds charter schools, although it may save considerable sums from a reduction in the state aid it formerly provided to poorer districts for their students who now attend charter schools, the state will likely save little or no money when pupils transfer into charter schools out of higher-spending districts. To the extent that occurs, the state will have to come up with new funding to replace savings enjoyed by already rich districts. Second, and perhaps more fundamentally, at what level should the state fund charter schools? Should it be at the level of lower-spending districts, higher-spending districts, the state average, an "adequate" level, or something else? Whatever sum the state selects raises questions as to the fairness of having quite different sums spent on the schooling of individual pupils depending upon which type of school they choose.

Moreover, if charter schools are generously funded, they might well draw off many more pupils, especially from currently low-spending districts. Those districts would likely adopt one of two very different responses. Some might object that it is unfair that they must remain lower spenders when charter operators get more money; others might take advantage of the state's generosity and convert all of their schools to state-funded charter schools. When the state reckons with this latter possibility, however, it might become reluctant to fund charter schools at generous levels.

Even if charter schools are fully funded by the state at less generous levels, a local community that now spends that sum or less on its public schools might still decide to convert all of its public schools to charter schools. Its citizens might realize that not only would its pupils not suffer reduced spending, its taxpayers would seemingly be completely relieved of paying local property taxes for schools. Widespread reaction of this sort, of course, would put large new financial burdens on the state and could well prompt the state to take over the property tax for its own uses. Once it goes down that road, it is hard to see how the state could tolerate wealthy districts spending as much as they now do per pupil when the state average is considerably lower.

As with local funding of charter schools, if the state fully funds charter schools, there will be pressure on the state to adjust the payment for the nature of the pupils actually enrolled in the charter school (as well as its location in a high- or low-cost part of the state). Indeed, it is especially crucial in the charter school setting that sufficient extra money is provided for high-cost pupils. Otherwise, charter schools will be tempted to discourage, reject, or later exclude those students, thereby denying them the same rights to choose that have been extended to others. In short, once we start thinking about charter schools drawing pupils from many communities and being founded by other than local school districts, it is hard to come up with any fair or coherent funding arrangement that will allow charter schools to thrive and that will also maintain the inequalities of the traditional school finance system. This is why a big expansion in charter schooling may eventually so undermine our old system of financing neighborhood public schools as to require the ending of those inequalities that have for so long been built into the structure of local, wealth-based, public school finance. Although a shift to full state funding of all public schools is not the only possible remedy to the problem, it is the simplest to imagine.

Of course, the scenario sketched here might not transpire. Entrenched interests may force charter school funding to remain at the district level, as though the charter school were just another local school; and in turn charter schools open to outsiders may form primarily in relatively lower-spending districts. Rather than successful school choice reform driving school finance reform, conventional school finance arrangements may strangle efforts to expand choice in the public sector.

Funding Choice in the Private Sector

If the children's rights and common good arguments justify taxpayer support for elementary and secondary education, it is yet not clear why this financial support should go only to those who attend public schools. Note that, in a world of subsidized education, choice is not about the abstract right to select a school for one's child. That right is already guaranteed to parents by the U.S. Constitution. The real issue is whether the family's choice is subsidized.

At one time, in some small communities, there were not enough children to fill more than one school. Such education might be viewed as a natural monopoly. If there is to be but one provider, perhaps it should be the government—although notice that the local school might also be provided by a regulated private provider. In any event, this condition rarely applies now. Even if it is assumed that young children should travel only a short distance from home to school, in most places there are enough children in reasonable range to support more than one school, especially because it is by no means obvious that significant economies of scale are achieved in larger schools for younger children.

If there is a principled defense of the (near) exclusive funding of public education, we should look for it in the underlying reasons for public funding of education at all. Basically, the argument must be that only through public education can society be confident that pupils will be steeped in tolerance and the values of democracy and that the money will be used to bring about their education. By contrast, the strongest fear must be that were nonpublic schools equally subsidized, they might turn out to be subversive, intolerant, or fraudulent, thereby undermining, instead of achieving, children's rights and common good objectives. A more moderate argument for exclusive funding of public education is that private education too much promotes private, rather than public, goals. This outlook is reflected in one conventional understanding of the religion clauses of the First Amendment—that is, while religious exercise must be ensured, it ought not be subsidized.

Supporters of subsidized private school choice, of course, reject the premises of both the stronger and the milder arguments against the funding of nonpublic education. They see private schools as promoting public objectives in the same way that they see private providers as serving the public good in programs like food stamps, medicaid, and section 8 subsidized housing. But in America the political reality from nearly the beginning of our system of public education has been largely to restrict public funding to public schools.

Private School Tuition

The tuition charged by private schools varies enormously. Most private schools are religious schools. Their tuition levels tend to be low—very low indeed at many elementary schools in some parts of the country. This is possible first because religious schools generally make do with rather lower spending per pupil as compared with the public schools. They tend to have lower-paid teachers, tiny administrative staffs, and no frills; many have substantially more pupils per classroom. Second, sometimes these schools benefit from using facilities and other subsidies provided by the church with which they are affiliated, so that their true costs may be substantially greater than the tuition they collect.

Other private schools, especially those aimed at children from well-to-do families, have very high tuition levels. These schools tend to spend more per pupil than is typically spent in public schools, often opting both for smaller classes and more administration, including college and personal counselors, admissions and financial aid directors, fund-raisers, and the like that public schools tend to go without or to spread very thin.

State Aid to Private Schools

In the period between 1875 and World War II, there was widespread political and societal hostility toward private schools, especially Catholic schools. In the late 1800s a majority of states adopted constitutional provisions (generally called Blaine amendments) designed to prevent their legislatures from ever providing any assistance to these schools. Before then, before we had public education in the way we know it today, some states financially supported both Protestant and Catholic schools.[12]

After World War II, this legislative hostility began to thaw, and some states began to pass modest measures especially aimed at assisting pupils enrolled in private schools. Public officials realized that the public schools were getting away with not having to educate pupils who would otherwise be a substantial burden on the public purse; they appreciated the reality that taxpayers had an interest in making sure the private education sector did not collapse financially. Moreover, parents of children attending private schools complained about having to pay twice, and some modest assistance might ameliorate those complaints. The willingness to provide any assistance to private schools also signaled an acknowledgment that these schools were not undermining the collective educational goals for the country's children. But although the U.S. Supreme Court agreed that states could offer religious school users both bus rides and textbooks, in a series of decisions issued during the 1970s, it put substantial roadblocks in the way of further public support of religious schools.[13]

In recent years, the Supreme Court has eased its opposition to certain types of state assistance to pupils attending private schools, including religious schools. Minnesota enacted a law that made a limited amount of private school tuition payment deductible for state tax law purposes, at the same time granting a similar deduction for education costs connected to public schooling. The Supreme Court upheld this measure. The Court also upheld the provision of federal compensatory education services to low-income children attending religious schools.[14]

As a result, in many states private schools benefit from public support in several small ways. The conventional approach remains one of permitting private school students to participate in certain categorical aid programs, most commonly receiving not only free bus rides to school or free textbooks but also a range of targeted, clearly secular, educational services. How much financial aid, if any, is actually provided in any state remains, of course, a matter of state politics, and in some states powerful opposition still exists to assisting private school users. Moreover (as discussed in more detail in Frank Kemerer's chapter in this book), some state constitutions are so restrictive that financial support that would be allowed under the federal constitution is nonetheless forbidden.

Although private nonprofit schools also benefit indirectly from the fact that voluntary charitable contributions to them are typically deductible under state and federal tax laws and from the fact that in some states their property is not subject to property taxes,[15] all of this assistance taken together still constitutes a very small amount of financial support of private schools as compared with public schools.

Experimental Funding Programs for Private Schools

There have been growing calls for much more generous funding of pupils who choose to attend private schools, and recently two communities have experimented with schemes that provide considerably more financial aid. In both plans, public funds are targeted to needy children.

Milwaukee's plan came first and has gained the most attention. By the end of the 1998–99 school year, it provided about 6,000 children from low-income families with scholarships worth about $4,400 a year. Cleveland's plan is newer; as of 1998–99, it had about 3,500 participants, who received scholarships worth up to $2,500 a year.

From the start, the Cleveland plan has permitted families to use the scholarships at religious schools. The Ohio Supreme Court found this aspect of the plan constitutional but concluded that the program ran afoul of technical state rules about legislation.[16] The Ohio legislature repassed the plan in 1999, and opponents shifted their legal attack to federal court. The Milwaukee plan originally applied only to nonreligious private schools, but in 1995 it was extended to cover religious schools. This decision was challenged in court, and in June 1998, the Wisconsin Supreme Court upheld the plan as constitutional under both the Wisconsin and U.S. Constitutions. In late 1998 the U.S. Supreme Court declined to review the case.[17] As Jesse Choper explains in his chapter in this book, it is not certain how the U.S. Supreme Court will rule on these schemes when it eventually confronts the issue.

Other Funding Programs for Private Schools

Although the Milwaukee and Cleveland plans are the most discussed schemes of public funding of private school choice, they are not the only such plans. Vermont has for decades allowed small school districts to be nonoperating. Instead of running schools, they purchase schooling elsewhere for their pupils. In some districts, this has meant that all the children are sent to a neighboring public school. In others, it has meant that all the children are offered places in a specified private school. In still others, the district has been willing to pay for the child's education in a variety of schools, both public and private. It is this latter arrangement—when families have a choice that includes some private school options—that has attracted the greatest attention of advocates of school choice. Eventually, the Vermont scheme was challenged in court, and in 1999 the Vermont Supreme Court held the funding of religious school choice illegal on state constitutional grounds.[18]

Thirty years ago, before there was school litigation on behalf of children with disabilities and before there was federal statutory protection of the education rights of children with disabilities, many public schools refused to educate such children, at least those with the most serious disabilities. In some places, these children were allowed to attend special private schools at public expense. Although the public school treatment of children with disabilities has changed considerably, the tradition of a small wedge of private schools specializing in the education of the disabled continues. Sometimes the public schools eagerly support sending the child to such a school. Sometimes the parents have to fight, perhaps through appeals processes, to win that remedy for their children. Altogether, these specialized private schools now enroll less than 2 percent of all private school pupils (around 90,000 pupils nationwide).[19] Some other children with disabilities attend ordinary private schools, where, as Laura Rothstein explains in her chapter in this book, they are supposed to receive public financing for the special education services to which they are entitled.

In some communities, the local school district has financial arrangements with private school providers to take over the education of small numbers of certain at-risk children who are seen to be poorly served by the public schools (such as children who are chemically dependent, pregnant, or well behind grade level in achievement). In effect, the local public school district contracts out the education of these pupils to specialized private schools if the families of these pupils choose to enroll them in such schools. In the Minneapolis program, the local school district basically puts up the funds that it would otherwise spend on these children, and most of the participating nonprofit schools supplement that money with their own fund-raising efforts so as to provide the extra dollars required to serve this high-cost population.[20]

Charitable Funding of Private Schools

Some years ago a private foundation was formed in Indianapolis that offered to provide small scholarships to enable children from low-income families to attend private schools, usually low-tuition private schools (which were usually religious schools). This type of charitable tuition organization has caught on, and as of the summer of 1999 programs broadly patterned on the Indianapolis model were said to exist in sixty-five cities, serving some 57,000 children.[21] Moreover, two new nationwide programs serving 40,000 additional pupils were announced in 1999 for the 1999–2000 school year. Usually in these programs the foundation pays half of the child's tuition, up to a limited ceiling. These schemes are publicly supported in the sense that contributions to these tuition organizations are themselves tax deductible.

Arizona passed a measure designed to attract far more money on behalf of this approach. Under the law, any Arizona taxpayer may obtain a 100 percent state income tax credit of up to $500 a year by making a contribution of up to $500 to a qualifying tuition organization.[22] Under this measure, contributions are not really charity; the Arizona law, in effect, allows taxpayers to write a check on the state treasury by directing a portion of their tax payments to a tuition organization instead of the government. (Oddly, the Arizona law does not require that the money be paid out by the tuition organization only to low-income families, even though this has been the practice of the organizations in operation to date.) This Arizona measure was challenged in court, but in early 1999 it was upheld by a divided Arizona Supreme Court.[23]

The Future of Public Funding for Private Schools

Increased public funding of public school choice is both a threat and an opportunity to those who favor public funding of private school choice. The threat is that much of the demand for choice will be satisfied, and so there will be little enthusiasm for further expanding subsidized choice. The opportunity comes from the reasons that the society has welcomed public school choice: it could spill over to subsidized choice for all schools.

The Productivity Claim

Some advocates of publicly funded school vouchers valid for use in private schools argue that competition will produce more effective schools. They claim that both children's rights and the common good will be better served by having public and private schools compete for pupils. Public funding of private schools has been seen as the way to bring the power of the market and competition to elementary and secondary education in the way, for example, that Federal Express and United Parcel Service have brought competition to the U.S. Postal Service. Opponents of private schools often talk about the risk of fraud, pointing to arguably analogous fraud problems in medicaid, in private trade schools, and the like. Supporters of wide-open school choice counter that public education in the urban centers is the real fraud.

It is at this moment unclear how expanded public school choice will play out for private school choice supporters on this issue. If most states were to adopt so-called strong charter school laws, permitting easy access to the creation of this form of schooling, opponents of public funding of private schools are sure to argue that the charter schools will provide enough competition. If charter schools also remain relatively unregulated, this argument may well be persuasive, or at least it may make the public want to wait to see how competition in the public sector plays out before expanding subsidized choice to the private sector. The productivity argument for funding private school choice may be especially weakened if charter schools are permitted to contract with private entrepreneurs to deliver significant aspects of their program.

The Pluralism Claim

Other advocates of subsidized private school choice emphasize pluralism. They argue that tolerance would be promoted by trusting parents and by allowing a wide range of family groups with similar values to have their own schools. Rather than undermining our democratic values (as school voucher opponents claim), supporters insist that empowering the ordinary family to take charge of its children's educational goals is fundamental to our democracy. The current scheme, they argue, is designed to socialize the children of the working class and the poor in ways determined by elites, the result of which is interclass resentment. In other words, our commitment to the rights of children and families is incomplete if public subsidy is available only in the public sector.

Yet if strong charter school legislation is widely adopted, it is possible that a charter would be granted to nearly any respectable group that would otherwise have started a private choice school in a regime that gives out vouchers or scholarships. One major exception to this, however, is the religious school, which it is fair to assume will not be able to become a charter school. Although this fact may arouse the passion and political zeal of families seeking religious education for their children, it will also satisfy those who believe in a high wall of separation between church and state, regardless of whether aid to users of religious schools is permitted by the U.S. Constitution. The other side would emphasize fairness to families with religious beliefs: Why should they have to pay twice to get the schooling they want for their children? Moreover, some pragmatists would argue that the religious-based controversies that now haunt public schools—school prayers, the teaching of evolution and sex education, and so on—would largely disappear if those with strong religious beliefs were enabled to form their own schools with public support.

Competing attitudes toward religious schools are not the only issue here. Some would favor stopping with a strong charter school regime just because that approach imposes at least a minimal political filter on who can begin a school.[24] A market filter alone, they worry, will not keep out kooks, hate mongers, and con artists. Private school choice supporters counter that it is preferable to rely on statutory limits to exclude socially unacceptable schools, for example, by requiring disclosure from participating schools and by prohibiting participating schools from teaching racism.

The public stances taken on the issue by leaders of the have-nots could be decisive. In the past, for example, African American leaders have widely opposed school voucher schemes, making it difficult for supporters to convincingly claim that black children would benefit. This near unanimity may be crumbling, as surveys reveal strong support for choice among ordinary African American families, as black families participating in the Cleveland and Milwaukee plans like what their children are getting, as the federal courts are pulling out of the school desegregation business, and as the education achievement of all too many African American children remains too low.[25]

Other Issues in the Funding of Private Schools

Assume that much more generous funding of private school choice occurs. Would this development create additional pressure to eliminate the public school finance inequalities discussed in this chapter? Or might it bring about greater inequality? The answer depends upon the specific way in which private school choice is subsidized.

Milton Friedman, the Nobel laureate economist, has proposed a system of unregulated school vouchers in which all children would receive a subsidy equal to, say, half of what is now spent on average per pupil in the public schools.[26] As Robert Bulman and David Kirp discuss in their chapter in this book, a proposal of this sort was put to the California voters a few years ago and badly defeated. This scheme, I believe, would increase inequality of educational opportunity. Poor families could hardly expect to purchase high-quality schooling with such a sum; nor could they afford to add significantly to it.[27] Rather, these vouchers would be used mostly by well-to-do families, who could add to the public subsidy from their own income. Moreover, economic segregation would increase even further under the Friedman plan, not only because schools could charge as much tuition as they wish but also because they could admit or deny any pupils they wish. In short, the Friedman plan magnifies the traditional inequalities of the public school system, using the government in a way that ensures that the rich are able to provide greater educational opportunities for their children than the poor can provide for theirs.

Yet there are ways of funding private school choice that are friendlier to the poor. For one, the subsidies for private school attendance could be offered exclusively to children from low-income families. That is what the private foundations that have stepped into the field are now doing, and it is what Milwaukee and Cleveland have done. Other variations might target subsidized choice to low-achieving children, students attending low-performing schools, at-risk pupils, and so on.[28] Indeed, Florida passed a "failing school" scheme in 1999.

Alternatively, participating private schools could be funded like charter schools. Were that approach adopted, many would also favor imposing at least two key requirements on participating private schools that parallel requirements often (but not always) imposed on charter schools: the school would be open to all applicants (with excess demand handled by lottery); and no tuition could be charged beyond the public subsidy. If a private school did not comply with these requirements, none of its students could obtain a public subsidy. This regime, which basically mirrors the plan that Sweden has put in place in recent years, would give children of the poor much greater access to private schools of their choice than the Friedman plan does.

Of course, not all supporters of subsidized private school choice support public regulation of admissions and tuition. Some argue that private schools ought to be able to have academic selection criteria if they wish, pointing to public choice schools like Bronx Science. Other people argue that it would be unfair if participating religious schools could not favor children of local parishioners. This issue haunts charter schools too, when founding parents want their children to have preference. In practice, the concern about insiders is not likely to be a serious problem in a regime in which everyone has choice, but the selection issue is a thorny one.

The opportunity to charge extra tuition is often justified by its supporters in the hope that this would facilitate the participation of today's elite private schools, schools that now generally charge considerably more than the public funding would likely be. Because giving schools the right to charge more risks pricing out low-income families, this concern has generated compromise proposals to guarantee the poor fair access to extra-tuition schools. One idea is to require private schools to means test their tuition add-ons and to require them to guarantee low-income families a reasonable share of the school's places (say, 20 percent).[29] Such a regime might not only draw today's elite schools into the subsidized choice plan but also prompt them to recruit talented children from low-income families. It might also be compatible with a scheme that permits selective admission of the other, say 80 percent, of the school's pupils.

In contrast to the Friedman voucher plan, schemes for subsidizing private school choice that are friendly to the poor would put pressure on existing public school funding arrangements. First, assume that districts would have to pay for private school choice for everyone in the community who exercises it. Under this scenario, one might initially imagine that many district leaders would object to picking up the new cost of all the students in the community who already attend private schools. In response to that, some would say that it is only fair that communities that have been getting a free ride are now forced to pay for those students. Both of these viewpoints exaggerate what is at stake. It is important to remember that the poorer districts would gain substantial new state financial support for these extra pupils, not only because they increase the district's average daily attendance but also because they reduce the district's measured wealth per pupil. In poorer school districts, the state would fund these pupils up to approximately the state-guaranteed spending amount anyway.

Even so, if the basic scholarship (or voucher) amount were set somewhere around the state's average spending per pupil, then low-spending districts might actually have to spend more on the pupils who leave them for private schools than they spend on their own pupils. That would certainly be objectionable. Could this problem be fairly solved by having the scholarship amount vary with what the local district now spends? I doubt it. If, on the one hand, this means that students from low-spending districts will have to top up their scholarships to meet their school's regular tuition, that seems unfairly harsh on the poor. On the other hand, it seems zany to force participating private schools to accept in full payment of their tuition whatever value of scholarship the pupil presents, if for no other reason than this would give the schools incentives to avoid pupils with low-value scholarships.

This line of analysis may suggest to some the desirability of full state funding of scholarships that would not vary in amount based on the financial circumstances of the child's home district. For reasons discussed in connection with charter schools, this solution raises other problems. Most important, it is still probably not a stable solution for some children who opt for private choice to get a subsidy that is greater than what their district would have spent on them, while others get less than what would be spent on them if they remained in their neighborhood schools. But that would remain true as long as the traditional, underlying school finance system remains in place.

Conclusion

An expansion of subsidized public school choice and of subsidized private school choice that is friendly to low-income families threatens the linkage between the local tax base and the local public school, which has been the basis for the publicly subsidized U.S. public education system for more than a hundred years. As a result, school choice might pave the way to a reexamination and reform of school funding across the board, an outcome that thirty years of litigation have only partially accomplished.

What might that reformed school finance system look like? The most readily understood solution would be for the state itself simply to take over the full funding of elementary and secondary education, possibly relying on a statewide property tax for a substantial share of the needed revenues. Under this approach, both choice schools and conventional public schools would receive their funding from the state. Indeed, state funding might well flow directly to local schools, bypassing local school districts altogether.

Under this approach, the state would decide how much money to provide to each pupil (whether enrolled in a local public school, charter school, or participating private school). Earlier I mentioned the need for the state to set a basic amount for the typical child, with upward adjustments for children with special needs and those living in higher-cost communities. But if full state funding of education occurs, the state would have to be more precise about it. Moreover, it could now aspire to be more scientific, drawing on the research emerging from the literature on school financing. These studies provide insights into, first, how much money ought to be enough to allow an average school with average children to bring a substantial majority of them (say 80 percent) up to high educational standards (say the top quartile of pupils on similar tests given around the world) and, second, how much extra money should be supplied to schools facing higher costs because of their location or their pupils in order for them to meet the same achievement target.[30] In terms of the arguments for public funding of education made at the start of this chapter, these adequacy goals operationalize what constitute children's rights and the common good.

It is certainly possible to combine full state funding of education with a largely hands-off approach to the regulation of schools that many believe is essential if school choice is to have a chance to succeed in America. Sweden and other countries have so far nicely managed this balancing act; but in other nations, such as the Netherlands, public financial support of private schools has been accompanied by considerable regulatory control.[31] Because of these concerns, some school choice advocates seek to give participating choice schools state constitutional protection from state regulation beyond that currently imposed on the state's private schools; such a provision is a common feature in proposed state constitutional initiatives seeking to establish school choice plans.[32]

Besides the issue of regulatory freedom, there is the issue of spending freedom. In the public school finance field generally, some of those who have fought the interdistrict spending inequalities that arise from local wealth differences nonetheless oppose full state funding as the remedy. They argue that local public school districts still ought to be allowed to spend extra money for their schools, provided it is raised on a wealth-neutral basis. Some favor variety in school spending because they believe, as a practical matter, it helps ensure higher average spending on schooling.[33] Others believe, in principle, that communities may have different tastes for education, which the state ought to accommodate (with wealth removed as an influencing factor, adequacy should be determined locally). To achieve this result, such solutions as "district power equalizing" and "guaranteed yield" are usually proposed. These schemes rely upon a redistributive state aid formula that permits poorer districts to generate as much money per pupil as richer districts with the same local tax effort.[34]

This sentiment toward decentralized funding decisions could be even stronger in a world of widespread charter schools and voucher schools. After all, despite the experience in Sweden and other countries, some may find contradictory the combination of uniform state funding of education and family choice of schools for their children. If so, a variation on district power equalizing—family power equalizing—would permit variety in a school's per child spending without disadvantaging the poor.[35] Under this plan, the state would subsidize a fairly wide range of school costs (tuition obligations), and schools could locate themselves anywhere along this continuum, from say $4,000 to $9,000 a year per child. Families wanting to send their children to charter or voucher schools that are relatively more expensive, or perhaps even to more expensive conventional public schools, would have to make a proportionately larger contribution toward that greater cost from their own income. To use some arbitrary numbers by way of illustration, a family might not be required to pay anything for a $4,000 scholarship but would have to contribute 2 percent of its income for a $6,000 scholarship and 5 percent for a $9,000 scholarship. This would mean that a family with an income of $30,000 would contribute $600 toward the $6,000 scholarship and $1,500 toward the $9,000 scholarship; a family with an income of $10,000 would contribute $200 and $500, respectively; a family with an income of $100,000 would contribute $2,000 and $5,000, respectively. In each case the state would make up the difference. Since a scheme like this is inherently means-tested, it would thereby permit those low-income families who cared to to send their children to more expensive schools pretty much as easily as higher-income families.

One final point. The analysis so far has envisioned that a rapid expansion of school choice will put such pressure on today's basic school finance scheme as to require its reform. It is also possible to imagine the causal connection running the other way. In school finance litigation to date, plaintiffs have sought structural remedies—that is, new systemic arrangements that eliminate the inequalities of the traditional finance system. Suppose instead, however, that aggrieved children sought individual rather than group remedies. More specifically, suppose they asked for individual scholarships of fair value as their damages for the unconstitutional deprivation they have suffered.[36] Were such relief granted, then the school finance reform movement and the school choice movement would be joined in a symbiotic relationship arising from the other direction.

Notes

1. See generally James W. Guthrie, Walter I. Garms, and Lawrence C. Pierce, *School Finance and Education Policy* (Prentice-Hall, 1988); Allan R. Odden and Lawrence O. Picus, *School Finance: A Policy Perspective* (McGraw-Hill, 1992).

2. U.S. Department of Education, *Digest of Education Statistics, 1994.*

3. William Evans, Sheila Murray, and Robert Schwab, "Schoolhouses, Courthouses, and Statehouses after Serrano," *Journal of Policy Analysis and Management*, vol. 16 (1997), pp. 10–31.

4. U.S. Department of Education, *Digest of Education Statistics, 1997.*

5. Stephen D. Sugarman, "Two School-Finance Roles for the Federal Government: Promoting Equity and Choice," *Saint Louis University Public Law Review*, vol. 17 (1998), pp. 1–29.

6. John E. Coons, William H. Clune, and Stephen D. Sugarman, *Private Wealth and Public Education* (Harvard University Press, 1970).

7. For a review of school finance litigation, see Paul Minorini and Stephen Sugarman, "School Finance Litigation in the Name of Educational Equity"; and Paul Minorini and Stephen D. Sugarman, "Educational Adequacy and the Courts: The Promise and Problems of Moving to a New Paradigm," both in Helen Ladd, Rosemary Chalk, and Janet Hansen, eds., *Equity and Adequacy in Education Finance* (National Academy Press, 1999).

8. Evans, Murray, and Schwab, "Schoolhouses, Courthouses, and Statehouses." Whether this change by itself has had a substantial impact on pupil achievement is another matter, although one is entitled to be somewhat skeptical. See also Thomas A. Downes, "The Effect of Serrano v. Priest on the Quality of American Education: What Do We Know? What Do We Need to Know?" in *Proceedings of the Eighty-Ninth Annual Conference on Taxation* (Washington, D.C.: National Tax Association, 1999).

9. U.S. General Accounting Office, *School Finance: State Efforts to Reduce Funding Gaps between Poor and Wealthy Districts* (1997).

10. The most well known is *Hobsen v. Hansen*, 327 F.Supp. 844 (D.D.C. 1971).

11. To be sure, many believe that charter schools ought to be more efficient and so ought to get by on, say, 85 to 90 percent of what regular public schools spend (provided that reasonable funding for the cost of school facilities is also included). A fixed discount could at least guarantee charter schools a clearly defined sum. Yet even this has proved illusory when districts require charter schools to purchase certain services from them and then charge what the charter schools view as excessive sums. This in turn has caused charter schools to seek to buy such services (like purchasing, accounting, maintenance, and insurance) in the private market. For a disheartening story from Arizona about districts selling school charters for a fee, see Steve Stecklow, "Arizona Takes the Lead in Charter Schools: For Better or Worse," *Wall Street Journal*, December 24, 1996.

12. Denis Doyle, "Vouchers for Religious Schools," *Public Interest* (March 1997), pp. 88–95.

13. *Everson v. Board of Education*, 330 U.S. 1 (1947), and *Board of Education v. Allen*, 392 U.S. 236 (1968); *Lemon v. Kurtzman*, 403 U.S. 602 (1971); and *Committee for Public Education v. Nyquist*, 413 U.S. 756 (1973).

14. *Mueller v. Allen*, 463 U.S. 388 (1983); *Agostini v. Felton*, 115 S.Ct. 2510 (1995).

15. *Walz v. Tax Commission*, 397 U.S. 664 (1970).

16. *Simmons-Harris v. Goff*, 711 N.E.2d 203 (Ohio 1999).

17. *Jackson v. Benson*, 578 N.W.2d 602 (Wis. 1998); *Jackson v. Benson*, 578 N.W.2d 602 (Wis.), cert. denied, 119 S.Ct. 466 (1998).

18. *Chittenden Town School District v. Vermont Department of Education*, 1999 Vt. LEXIS 98 (June 11, 1999) (finding that it violates the state constitution's Compelled Support Clause for a district to reimburse tuition paid to a sectarian school when, as in the existing Vermont program, there are no adequate safeguards against the use of such funds for religious worship). Maine, too, has quietly operated a similar plan for quite some time, but for many years its districts refused to support attendance at religious schools because of a legal opinion issued by Maine's attorney general. That restriction was challenged in two similar cases, but in 1999 both the Maine Supreme Court and a federal appeals court ruled that it would be unconstitutional to extend the Maine program to such schools. See *Bagley v. Raymond School Department*, 728 A.2d 127 (Maine 1999), and *Strout v. Albanese*, 178 F.3d 57 (1st Cir. 1999).

19. National Center for Education Statistics, *Private School Universe Survey, 1995–96* (U.S. Department of Education, 1998).

20. John E. Coons and Stephen D. Sugarman, *Scholarships for Children* (Berkeley, Calif.: Institute of Governmental Studies Press, 1992), pp. 69–71.

21. Center for Education Reform (http://edreform.com/pubs/glance.htm), August 9, 1999.

22. A.R.S. Section 43-1089 (1997).

23. *Kotterman v. Killian*, 972 P.2d 606 (Az.), cert. denied, 1999 WL 278906 (1999). In 1998, a bill closely resembling the Arizona plan was introduced in California (AB 2110 Khaloogian).

24. Paul T. Hill, Lawrence Pierce, and James Guthrie, *Reinventing Public Education: How Contracting Can Transform America's Schools* (University of Chicago Press, 1997).

25. "Blacks are the group most likely to support . . . choice, with 59% in favor." "The 30th Annual Phi Delta Kappa/Gallup Poll of the Public's Attitudes toward the Public Schools" (http://www.pdkintl.org/kappan/kp9808-a.htm), August 9, 1999; Paul E. Peterson, Jay P. Greene, and Chad Noyes, "School Choice in Milwaukee," *Public Interest* (Fall 1996); *Board of Education of Oklahoma City v. Dowell*, 498 U.S. 237 (1991); *Freeman v. Pitts*, 503 U.S. 467 (1992); *Missouri v. Jenkins*, 515 U.S. 1139 (1995).

26. Milton Friedman, *Capitalism and Freedom* (University of Chicago Press, 1962).

27. Although poor families could afford to send their children to many existing religious

schools, if there is space, it is hard to see how new good schools could get going on such a limited budget.

28. See generally John E. Coons and Stephen D. Sugarman, *Making Choice Work for All Families* (San Francisco: Pacific Research Institute, 1999).

29. Under the proposal made by Coons and Sugarman, *Scholarships for Children*, children of the poor are guaranteed the places if they apply. Under the Kemerer proposal in this book, the school has to actually enroll a minimum share of low-income pupils for any of its pupils to gain state subsidies.

30. Ladd, Chalk, and Hansen, *Equity and Adequacy in Education Finance*.

31. Peter Mason, *Independent Education in Western Europe* (London: ISIS, 1997).

32. Coons and Sugarman, *Scholarships for Children*, p. 11.

33. For discussion of this issue, see Caroline Hoxby, "All School Finance Equalizations Are Not Created Equal" (Harvard University, March 1996); Evans, Murray, and Schwab, "Schoolhouses, Courthouses, and Statehouses."

34. Coons, Clune, and Sugarman, *Private Wealth and Public Education*.

35. For an early discussion of this idea, see ibid., pp. 256–68.

36. John Coons and I proposed this remedy as amici in the briefs we filed in Los Angeles and Kansas City school segregation cases, but we were ignored by the judges. Even more to the point, Allan Parker of the Texas Justice Foundation in San Antonio sought to intervene on behalf of vouchers for low-income families in the *Edgewood* v. *Meno* school finance litigation on August 13, 1993. After providing an opportunity to amend the petition, the district court dismissed the claims with prejudice, a decision the Texas Supreme Court refused to disturb. Said the latter, "We do not prescribe the structure for 'an efficient system of public free schools.' The duty to establish and provide for such a system is committed by the Constitution to the Legislature. Our role is only to determine whether the Legislature has complied with the Constitution. The Gutierrez appellants now ask the Court to go beyond this role, and to prescribe the structure of this state's public school system. For the reasons stated in our prior opinions, we decline to do so" (citations deleted). *Edgewood I.S.D.* v. *Meno*, 893 S.W.2d 450, 481 (Tex. 1995). See also Michael Heise, "State Constitutional Litigation, Educational Finance, and Legal Impact: An Empirical Analysis," *University of Cincinnati Law Review*, vol. 63 (1995), p. 1735.

CHAPTER FIVE

The Supply-Side of School Choice

PAUL T. HILL

No educational proposal excites as much hope and fear as school choice for kindergarten through grade twelve. Opponents fear that universal school choice can reverse progress toward desegregation and accelerate the class stratification of society. Supporters hope that choice can reconnect families to schools, encourage major improvements in school productivity, and increase low-income children's access to all good schools.

Many of the hopes and fears for choice are stated as expectations for the structure of demand for schools. Opponents fear that many low-income and minority families will not understand the differences between good and bad schools, will not be able to get good information even if they want it, and will neglect to express any preferences, thus putting their children last on any good school's admissions list. Supporters of school choice expect that parents' interest in education will be stimulated by the opportunity to choose, that parents who have never before had choices will soon learn to use published data about schools and find reliable sources of advice, and that, having chosen, parents will pay attention to whether schools perform as promised.

These conflicting hopes and fears about the demand-side of choice are all based on different assumptions about the supply-side, about what kinds of schools will become available if all parents can choose schools. Fears of resegregation and restratification depend on certain assumptions: for example, that there will be very few good schools, that school quality varies on one dimension from high to low, and the real choosers will be the good schools, which will have their pick of students. Hopes for better schools overall, and for disadvantaged children's access to good schools of all kinds, also depend on certain assumptions: for example, that a vigorous supply response to parental choice will produce many good schools; that good schools will vary in many ways, not just on a single dimension of quality; and that competition will raise the quality of schools for all students.

Much of the available research on the effects of choice has been based on situations in which both demand and supply were constrained. In the Alum Rock experiment, for example, parents were allowed to choose among only existing public schools, and the variety of new school options was limited to a few magnet programs. Other voucher experiments have also made only the lowest-income families eligible to choose and have limited choices to a small set of schools. Voucher programs like Cleveland's, which tried to attract large numbers of low-income minority parents and hoped to offer choices of suburban public schools as well as city private schools, were constrained by the refusal of suburban public systems to admit voucher students. Supply limitations reduced demand for vouchers. Parents who learned that suburban schools were closed to them, and that well-known Catholic schools were filled, often refused vouchers rather than seek placements in little-known schools run by less mainstream religious and social groups.

In most recent choice experiments and demonstrations, supply has been the most limiting factor. The Milwaukee voucher program, over whose effects on students John Witte and Paul Peterson have battled so fiercely, limited parents to marginal, low-cost, nonreligious, private schools and cut off access to the larger, more stable, and more capable Catholic schools.[1] Many of the choice programs analyzed by the famed Harvard choice study limited parental choice to small numbers of publicly run magnet or busing programs.[2]

There are strong, if unconscious, biases in any study that tries to project the consequences of a universal choice program from situations in which the supply of schools that can be chosen is strictly limited. The parents who are the most eager to get their children out of their current school placements will be the most alert to the possibilities and will try the hardest to learn to negotiate the steps of whatever admissions process is established. The most sophisticated among the eligible parents are also likely to be the best at working within whatever system is established. Schools that repre-

sent new alternatives will have more suitors than they have seats. They too
have strong incentives to selectively inform and surreptitiously recruit families that they think will fit their programs best.

Thus any choice program that limits choices to a few schools increases the
likelihood that the most advantaged will get the best placements. This is the
case in many urban school systems that offer a few magnet and specialty
schools. These schools are often highly popular and have long waiting lists.
Families play every possible angle, and the most advantaged parents—those
who know the rules, have personal access to decisionmakers, can write strong
and persuasive letters, and will stand in line to get low numbers on admissions lotteries—are the most likely to get their children admitted. Parents who
can capture scarce opportunities have little incentive to make changes in the
rules of access that might eliminate their special advantages or dilute the special characteristics of the schools their children attend. People who fear that
choice will increase inequities often try to limit the number of schools or programs that can be chosen. However, fear of the sorting effects of choice, when
exercised through supply limitation, can be a self-fulfilling prophesy. Limited
supply virtually guarantees inequitable access.

Clearly the ultimate outcomes of any choice program depend on both
demand for schools and supply of options. Just as clearly, demand and supply will interact. If there are strict limits on supply (for example, if parents
are allowed to choose only among schools run by existing public school
systems and if those systems are unable to change the mix of schools they
offer), demand will have little room to operate. If there are strict limits on
demand (for example, if only a few families are allowed to choose schools,
or if school choices are constrained by rigid racial or income quotas), any
supply response will inevitably be muted. Even among those who want to
give the idea of choice a fair shake, inattention to supply-side issues can be
self-defeating. Local school systems that declare universal choice but add
only a few attractive new options normally find that only a few intensely
interested middle-class families avail themselves of the opportunities. Legislators who hope competition from charter schools will stimulate change
in public education are frustrated when the laws they write make it impossible for any but the irrationally dedicated to start a charter school.

Careful regulation of the demand-side will not make school choice truly
equitable and universal and will not provide widespread access to good
schools. Those results depend on the supply-side, that is, on the success of
arrangements that promote the creation of a wide variety of school options,

expose all schools to performance pressures through competition, and permit constant replacement of weak schools by promising new ones.

This chapter aims to put these hopes and fears about choice into perspective and to suggest what must be done if choice is to advance, not threaten, quality public education and equitable access to good schools. It makes four arguments: first, that choice requires schools that are coherent, distinctive, and reliable; second, that existing public school systems are not designed to provide schools with those attributes, other than as relatively rare exceptions; third, that the current charter school movement is unlikely to produce a large supply of coherent, distinctive, and reliable schools, unless state laws greatly clarify charter schools' access to funding and facilities and the grounds on which charter schools will be held accountable for performance; and fourth, that choice-oriented programs must include overt supply-side strategies intended to increase the numbers of independent organizations capable of providing public education.

Sources for the analysis encompass several ongoing research projects, including studies of publicly funded voucher programs, notably Cleveland's; analysis of the experience of private organizations taking contracts to run public schools; analysis of charter school start-up experience; and studies of public agencies' practices in approving charter applications and monitoring charter school operation.[3]

The Kinds of Schools Necessary for Choice

People who think universal choice is desirable assume that all families will be able to choose among schools that are *distinctive, coherent,* and *reliable.* Distinctive schools—schools that differ from one another in ways that parents can readily understand—are important because their existence means that families have real alternatives. Schools might share many attributes, but the fact that families and teachers see differences—as is the case among Catholic schools, which share many values but which differ enough that parents believe their choices matter—is sufficient. Coherent schools—schools in which all teachers and staff members discipline their collaboration via a common set of goals for students and ideas about instruction—are important because they ensure that parents will get what they choose.[4] Reliable schools—schools that are consistent over time—are important because they ensure parents that their children will not be subject to random changes over time in materials presented and methods used and because prospective parents can learn about the school from parents whose children currently attend it.

Once such a supply of schools exists, universal choice will probably maintain it. Competition will favor schools that parents can understand and can judge whether they will fit their children's needs and interests, keep their promises and discipline the work of children and adults to produce measurable results, and are stable enough to build clienteles of satisfied, trusting families.

However—and this is the central proposition of this chapter—demand alone might not create such a supply of schools. Powerful forces—incentives, habits, political pressures—resist the creation of a supply of distinctive, coherent, and reliable schools, whether by transforming existing public schools or creating new ones.

Today's Public School Systems

Public educators argue against charters, contracts, and vouchers by claiming that they are already doing everything necessary and that the current system can produce the supply needed (chapter 1 in this volume identifies the choices now available in large public school systems). However, the choices are limited in three ways: they are limited in size so that the most successful and attractive programs typically have long waiting lists; they are carefully regulated to avoid threatening the enrollments and financial security of regular district-operated schools; and many exist only as long as they maintain majority political support, whether or not they are academically successful.

In general, conventional public school systems lack the flexibility to create a significantly different supply of schools; and public education's habitual approach to low-performing schools—to pour in money and new programs but to leave the schools' core missions and identities alone—cannot change the fundamental character of confused, undisciplined, unreliable schools. In short, the ideologies promoted by public education intellectuals are hostile to distinctive, coherent, and reliable schools.

The Inflexibility of Public School Systems

Many people who like the idea of choice wonder why there is a need for vouchers, charter schools, or public schools run by private contractors. We have a whole government agency dedicated to running schools; why does it not provide the choices? The answer is based on the history, mission, and structure of the traditional public school system. There is no reason that some public agency might not oversee the creation of a supply of diverse schools among which families might choose. The public institutions we do have, however, are not suited to the task.

Until the early 1960s public school systems oversaw systems of relatively independent neighborhood schools. However, efforts to rectify serious social injustices, starting with desegregation and efforts to equalize spending in richer and poorer areas, exposed school systems to pressures and mandates from the political and legal systems. Over time, school systems became formally organized, complex, compliance-oriented government bureaus. These were truly unintended consequences of efforts to solve other problems. During the early struggle for desegregation, school systems came under court orders and government regulations governing the assignment of students to schools and classes and the behavior of teachers toward students. President Lyndon Johnson's aid to education program, known as Title I, introduced a new regime of federal regulation that defined disadvantaged children's access to both regular and federally funded instructional programs. This program also created new classifications of federally paid teachers and governed the ways they and regular classroom teachers could work together.

Throughout the 1970s, Congress and state legislatures created additional funding and regulatory programs, all on the premise that the needs of some group—racial minorities, refugees, limited-English-proficiency children, and many categories of handicapped and gifted children—were not being met. Those programs created new separate categories of funds, new rules on how children with particular characteristics were to be treated, and new regulations on how different groups of teachers could work and with whom.[5] At about the same time many school boards found that they could no longer meet the salary demands of teachers' unions. They started to offer unions concessions on teachers' work rules, on teachers' assignment, on teachers' responsibility outside their classrooms, and on school principals' management discretion.[6] The result was that individual schools became vector sums of the pressures on them, defined by regulations, court orders, and employment contracts. Similarly, the head offices of local school districts became holding companies for compliance officers and others who intervened in schools on behalf of defined, limited objectives.

Over time many Americans have come to accept such a system as the essence of public education, that is, a system defined by rules and constraints laid down by successive eras of interest group bargaining and official resolution. Public educators—loyal and serious public servants—often pride themselves on their willingness to work under difficult and sometimes conflicting rules; many say that there is a reason for every rule. They are right, of course. As the Washington state legislature found when it reviewed the state education code with the object of simplifying it, an interest group somewhere takes pride in and reassurance from every rule that applies to public schools. But studies show that regulation has hobbled public schools and deflected attention from student learning.[7] The point is that public school systems are strongly inclined to maintain the kind of schools they have and, when they have the opportunity to create new schools, to follow the same rules that made existing schools what they are. Even when school systems try to close and reconstitute schools that have failed, most only change leaders and some teachers, and the newcomers typically have the same values and life experiences as those departing.

Not everyone in public education accepts these premises, and many fight to build and maintain schools that are sharply defined and predictable enough to form the basis of a choice system. Despite all the energy that goes into creating them, such schools seldom survive the expiration of the special grant that subsidized the school or the departure of a strong principal. An unpublished gem of a paper by Linda Darling-Hammond, Jacqueline Ancess, and others identifies many of the forces at work against such schools, even when they are part of a large and well-funded new schools development effort.[8] The authors describe how New York City's new coalition campus schools, despite the support of the chancellor, had to fight continually against having their staff and students reassigned, had to contend with different student enrollment rules each year, and were forced to move to a different building each year. They report a

> pattern of isolating the traditional schools from the practices of their "nontraditional" counterparts. It leaves the standard system intact without acknowledging that the regulations warranting exception by alternative schools—exceptions that have allowed these schools to be successful—also strangle traditional schools. . . . Managing alternative schools by exception has mediated the tension between the standardization characterizing the system as a whole and the freedom from regulation required for innovation; however it has also obviated the need for core systemic change. . . . This strategy works well only when innovation is at a low volume.

There are examples of dynamic school system leaders and of school systems that have adopted radical methods of starting and supporting choice schools. School systems that have become suppliers of such alternatives change fundamentally. They eliminate their large central offices, focus the work of the superintendent and other officials on the improvement of individual schools, concentrate funding and spending discretion at the school level, and offer parents choices.[9] Such systems might transform at least some existing public schools into schools of choice. But public school systems that fit this description are extremely rare and are different in kind from the standard bureaucratic systems that, despite the hopes of supporters, cannot supply the well-defined and varied schools that universal family choice requires.

The Futility of Trying to Transform Public Schools

Many supporters of public education object to charters, contracting, and other efforts to create a new supply of schools. They claim that the money can be better spent to improve some key factor present in all schools, for example, teachers' attitudes and knowledge. Major funders of public education typically try to improve public school systems by investing in key parts of their operation. In the past decade or so, the federal government has invested millions of dollars in improved teacher certification and student achievement testing. State governments have invested billions of dollars in new textbooks. California has targeted more than $1 billion annually to reducing class size in city schools. Foundations like Rockefeller and the Lila Wallace Reader's Digest Fund have invested tens of millions of dollars in in-service training of teachers. Businesses have paid to rewire schools and to install new computer systems. The Annenberg Foundation alone has invested more than $400 million in combinations of the above for ten urban school systems. With the exception of extensive—and mutually contradictory—studies on the effects of class size, there is little evidence either way about whether any of these initiatives has had a measurable impact on school quality or student learning.[10]

These investments are examples of a block upgrade philosophy, which posits that a whole school system can be improved by a dramatic investment in one of its key operations or functions. There is nothing wrong with spending more money on public education or trying to ensure that schools have access to well-trained teachers and high-quality materials. However, making investments with a one-size-fits-all philosophy can weaken individual schools and make it less, not more, likely that families will have a supply of well-defined schools from which to choose.

Since the beginning of federal efforts to subsidize kindergarten through grade twelve education, one fact has been known about the effects of major investments in systemwide initiatives or services: they seldom make schools stronger, more focused, or more distinctive. To the contrary, most such investments treat all schools as if they were pretty much alike, assuming that programs addressing systemwide needs are well targeted to the needs of individual schools. However, people working inside schools know that such systemwide initiatives seldom fit particular schools well. It is easy to see how such mismatches occur. Imagine a district in which all of the schools order their areas of greatest need. All might rank mathematics second. If schools differ on what they rank first, some emphasizing reading and others science, mathematics would get the highest average score. A local school system that uses such a process to decide what forms of teacher training or instructional materials to buy could neglect every school's most important need. Any other investment strategy guided by systemwide averages could encounter the same problem.

The costs of misdirected block upgrades can be high. Because teachers and school administrators have only so much time to attend workshops or learn how to use new equipment and materials, one emphasis naturally competes with another. Many schools are therefore forced to shelve their top-priority problem in order to send staff to compulsory training or to install a new curriculum or piece of equipment. If the broader system authoritatively allocates staff time for a particular form of upgrade, there is little time left for other priorities.

Staff training and new materials and equipment are all good things, but everything depends on how and where priorities are set. Schools that lack a clear idea what they should do to improve instruction might not perceive the opportunity costs of block upgrades. Schools that have identified their problems and are struggling to improve can see the costs clearly. Principals and teachers in New York City's coalition campus project report that citywide teacher training priorities—for AIDS education, fire safety, student self-esteem programs, and so on—exhausted the time they had hoped to put aside to make their schools work better. As an official in another city said, "The system puts too much new equipment and technical assistance into schools. It is easy for teachers and principals to fall into a habit of responding to these opportunities rather than figuring out what their school needs." Thus schools struggling to define themselves and hold themselves accountable for performance can be deflected from those tasks toward priorities set for the system as a whole. From this perspective, the power of a block upgrade to dominate how schools use time can be the power to destroy.

Richard Murnane and Frank Levy provide a vivid example of a block expenditure that had nil or negative effects on most schools. Fourteen troubled schools in Austin, Texas, were given $300,000 annually for five years. In twelve of the schools, the funds were used for extra teachers to reduce class size, but they used the same basic instructional methods as before and did nothing to promote collaboration or schoolwide change.

> Like all organizations, schools are places of vested interests and fixed routines. If new resources arrive, the path of least resistance is to spend the resources in ways that change as little as possible. . . . New resources were spent to reduce class size, but little was done to change what happened inside the classes.[11]

The two schools in which the new funds led to measurable results made changes in their instructional programs that directly affected students' exposure to facts and ideas. The difference between these two schools and the others was not created at the district level but within each school: the two successful schools took control of the extra funds and regarded them as opportunities for fundamental rethinking and change. School leaders and staff committed themselves to a comprehensive change in their school's approach to instruction. They "found ways to engage teachers, parents, and students in pursuing" the school's goals. To improve, a school "had to provide teachers with the incentives and the opportunity to improve their teaching. It had to put in place a way of measuring progress. It had to make clearer to students and parents why achievement was so important."

Competition for public funds often drives a school district's leaders to emphasize one specific need, which can be dramatized in terms of the plight of particular children or teachers. Similarly, foundations and business donors like making donations that are easily understood and have apparent systemwide application. Unfortunately, expenditures consistent with the rationale used to raise the funds might be poorly matched to an individual school's needs. Block upgrades are not always harmful, but even the most flexible resource, dollars, can retard development of clearly defined schools of choice if they are spent for systemwide, rather than school, priorities.

The Opposition of Public Education Ideologies to Distinctive Schools

The intellectual leaders of conventional public education have adopted an ideology that is hostile to focused, distinctive schools. The ideology has many sources: modern interpretations of the writings of John Dewey; progressivist thinking about schools as mechanisms for forging a unified community out of diverse groups; and a preference for public negotiation over private initiative as a guide to action. A popularized version of these preferences is evident in a recent newspaper op-ed attack on the idea of charter schools:

> The disadvantaged population that charter schools are meant to help will find it hard to examine all the options, to elude the clever advertising, to shun fads. By putting the selection of schools firmly in parents' hands, you interfere with the way pluralistic public schools traditionally help children escape from a smothering family culture. (Charter schools are family values pushed too hard.)

The piece claims that these schools

> will seek niche-market distinctiveness, which means a schoolwide uniformity in which students have less chance to explore different approaches and social groups. Most teachers want to be free to teach well, not to become overworked educational entrepreneurs.[12]

The key elements of opposition ideologies are

—for the school as common space in which people of unlike backgrounds gather to find a higher conception of their common interest. Public schools should create community by teaching children that issues that divide groups are unimportant and that what matters is joint commitment to the values of liberty, equality, and fraternity.[13]

—against the school as an organization that attracts students and parents because of some distinctive interest in subject matter or teaching method. Schools should aim at creating an adult population whose formative experiences are substantially identical and whose social and emotional relationships transcend color, religion, and social class.

—against teaching students specific value systems or defined ways of thinking, for example, as defined by religions. Schools should liberate students from ways of thinking imposed by religions and other traditional systems of thought, providing students with the basis on which to define themselves as free individuals.[14]

—against competition and the capitalist values of efficiency and acquisitiveness. Schools should prepare students for a future world of real equality—economic, social, and political—and should help them value cooperation, not competition.[15]

Large parts of the U.S. population (including this author) agree with some of these beliefs, and it is not my intention to refute these statements individually. However, taken together, these beliefs are highly inimical to distinctive, coherent, reliable schools. One who thinks schools should always respond to the current state of public deliberation cannot accept the idea that a school will be stabilized by its commitments and respond to the needs of a group of students and parents to whom it is committed rather than to the politically bargained preferences of society as a whole. One who thinks a democratic society must be free of group and class differences cannot accept the possibility that schools might be places where people of like mind gather. One who fears that white parents will always use school choice to escape from people of color is sure that distinctive schools will resegregate America. One who thinks systems of thought and values are socially dangerous is afraid to allow children to be trained in a particular system of thought.

The empirical bases for these fears are very weak. The early experience of charter schools show that these schools of choice enroll, on average, the same proportion of racial and minority and economically disadvantaged students as are served by the surrounding public school districts.[16] Sociologists and political scientists consistently report that adults who attended distinctive private schools are the most likely to participate in civic affairs, respect democratic processes, and endorse socially tolerant values.[17]

For all students, general academic performance, not experience in a diverse school, is most correlated with interest in public affairs and understanding of democratic institutions.[18] Attending distinctive, focused high schools greatly increases minority students' chances of success in college and work.[19] Social trust and community feeling are higher when schools are distinctive and families have choices.[20] In an ongoing study, the author has found that students in schools based on a clear set of common premises are more likely than students in less well-defined schools to engage in vigorous discussion of values and social policy. In schools that throw together students from different races and social classes without creating a common intellectual and values framework, students are likely to resegregate socially and academically along racial and class lines. The extensive research literature on tracking and student ability grouping documents the pressures toward resegregation of schools that serve racially mixed student bodies.[21]

If the findings cited above do not refute the dominant public education philosophy, they surely raise questions about its empirical foundation. However, people who fear the implications of a full system of choice will not be

persuaded by the kinds of evidence cited here. Their fears are not of existing private schools or other isolated exemplars of choice. What they fear is
entering a slippery slope toward universal school distinctiveness, competition, and choice. The essence of a slippery slope argument is that taking a
relatively innocuous action sets one on a road that will inevitably lead to a
harmful conclusion. Like most forms of argument, slippery slope arguments
are sometimes valid and sometimes not. Whether a small step leads inevitably
to a disastrous consequence depends on whether there is an obvious principle that can guide the decision about where to stop. Thus the decision to
drink a glass of wine does not put one on a slippery slope toward alcoholism.
Similarly, the decision to open an all-girls public school does not put a community on a slippery slope to approving schools run by anarchists and religious extremists any more than the decision to open a school for arts or
sciences puts the community on the road to opening schools of the occult.

There are obvious principles governing whether some form of schooling should be accepted as part of a choice plan and others should be avoided.
One such principle is whether there is a recognized need for a particular
kind of school; another is whether a specific school does any direct harm
to others who do not attend it. A school that emphasizes the needs of girls
or of African American boys and helps them get into college is not dangerous just because some other group with a transparently separatist or seg-
regationist agenda might also want its own school. Public officials are
elected to make distinctions between beneficial and harmful actions, and
courts exist to enforce principles of fairness and political equality. There is
no reason to dismiss an educational option because someone sees it as slop-
ing in some direction.

Subscribers to the dominant ideology of public education are not likely
to support a move to choice until long after its beneficial effects are demonstrated to most other people's satisfaction. In the meantime those who
would increase the supply of schools of choice must be prepared to argue
against slippery slope reductionism and to distinguish sharply between
kinds of schools that should and should not receive public support.

The Current Charter Movement

State laws allowing private groups to operate public schools under agreements with local school systems and other state agencies are obviously a
good start on the supply-side of choice. However, there are severe limitations to what the current charter school movement can accomplish. The

most important limitation is on the numbers of charter schools: aside from Arizona, which has no cap on the numbers of new and existing schools that can be chartered, and California, which now allows a hundred new charter schools to open each year, most states have very restrictive caps. Thus the average state with a charter law has less than twenty-five charter schools, and no locality has more than fifteen. For places like New York, Chicago, and Los Angeles (with, respectively, 1,000 public schools, 600 public schools, and 650 public schools), these numbers of charter schools are truly drops in the bucket. Future state laws might remove these limits. However, three other important limitations on the current charter movement's ability to create a large supply of choice schools will remain:

—Charter laws create unreasonably high barriers to entry for new schools.

—Neither government officials nor charter school operators and advocates understand how schools of choice must be held accountable, and charter operators are accepting accountability schemes that will ultimately erode their schools' distinctiveness, coherency, and reliability.

—People starting charter schools are often burdened by the ideology of public education and do not understand the importance of making sure their schools stand for something in particular and make clear promises and demands to parents and teachers.

High Start-up Costs

Charter laws and other publicly funded efforts to create a new supply of schools impose extremely high costs of entry. Many localities are trying to create new schools. For example, the Chicago public school system has started many new small elementary schools through a request for proposals from local educators; it has used the state charter schools law to start a dozen new high schools; and it has closed a number of failing high schools and reconstituted them under new leadership and with some new teachers. Boston has devised its own within-district charter program, called pilot schools. Springfield, Massachusetts, and several California districts have encouraged internal chartering. San Francisco and Seattle have also reconstituted schools. Wichita has contracted directly with Edison for several schools, and several cities, including all of those named above, are considering operating a few schools through contracts with Edison, Sabis, Beacon, and other for-profit school providers.

These cities' arrangements with school providers vary, but many of them create tough barriers to the creation of strong schools. In-district charter programs constrain schools to draw from the existing teacher force and strictly limit schools' options on how money is spent. With few exceptions, local reconstitution efforts amount to tossing one set of teachers out and inviting a new set in, without any explicit commitment to rethinking a school's basic mission, instructional methods, or philosophy of student development.[22] Arrangements with for-profit school providers are exceptions: firms like Sabis have expressly developed educational philosophies and instructional methods and avoid entering contracts with districts that will not guarantee the contractor freedom to implement its instructional program.

Charters, by far the most numerous of the new schools, are also the ones most burdened by laws and policies. Most charter schools receive substantially less than the total state and local per pupil funding available to the local public school system. Depending on state laws, charter schools either get a set percentage of total per pupil expenditure (from 75 to 95 percent) or only that fraction of total per pupil expenditure provided by the state (typically 50 to 80 percent). From these amounts, charter schools must pay for administration and teaching staff, service their debt, obtain insurance and legal representation, pay for any student transportation and ancillary student services they choose to offer, and rent school facilities.[23]

These requirements create financial burdens. There are offsetting advantages in some cases: schools may be able to buy services on the open market for less money than the school system taxes away from regular public schools for the same purposes. Combinations of federal and private foundation funds also help many charter schools defray some of their up-front costs. The one obviously crippling burden on charter schools is the need to find and pay for school facilities. For regular public schools, facilities' costs are not counted as part of average per pupil expenditure; they are carried in separate capital accounts. No such arrangements are made for charter schools: they must pay for facilities out of their basic operating funds. These costs compete directly with teacher salaries and other instructional expenditures and can severely limit charter schools' development as educational institutions.

Financial burdens aside, the growth and development of charter schools are also constrained by the difficulty of gaining access to school buildings. Many school systems, even those in which some public schools are running below capacity, refuse to rent space to charter schools. Others permit charter schools to petition for access to unused space in existing public schools but require the incumbent principal's approval. In a climate in which many school administrators regard charter schools as unfair and unwarranted competition, such approval can be very hard to obtain. Despite the Chicago superintendent's strong support of a district-initiated charter school program, the vast majority of that city's new schools have had to lease or buy and renovate private space.

In many localities, the new supply of public schools created through the chartering mechanism is limited by the number of abandoned Catholic school buildings. These exist in small numbers in cities like Chicago, Boston, and Philadelphia, but they are rare to nonexistent in younger and more rapidly growing cities and in suburban and rural areas. In most localities, people who want to start a charter school, even under a program officially endorsed by their local public school system, face what amounts to a dare: if you can pay start-up costs and operate with less money than neighboring public schools and find and pay for a building despite bureaucratic resistance, you may run a school. These facts can be highly discouraging to visionaries who have a zest for education but no interest or competence in business management.

A lack of reliable access to school space is also a major handicap for programs for new schools, even those that have the strong support of district superintendents. The frequent changes in location forced on them by the New York City central office adversely affected the coalition campus schools in that city:

> The impact of space on the successful launching of a new school is overriding. It impacts budget, the delivery of necessary materials, the quality of education, the morale of the staff, [and] the school's credibility with its parents and students. . . . School directors had to devote considerable attention to site location and design, diverting them from their role of instructional leader. The new schools had to spend money on moving costs, door locks, and items that were lost in delivery.[24]

This is clearly not the approach a community would take toward schools that were seen as possible ways to educate its children (instead of a concession to an intransigent group that just had to be given what they demanded). Most school systems treat charters as exceptions, not new ways of addressing the public's interest.

The existence of more than a thousand charter schools nationwide—and the fact that most states have more applications for charter schools than they have slots available—testify to many parents' and educators' determination to increase the supply of schools of choice. Since many state laws favor applicants who intend to locate in low-income neighborhoods and serve poor and disadvantaged children, charters are likely to continue serving a fair cross section of children.

However, there is reason to think that the charter movement will be limited in size unless charter schools get access both to the full amounts of per pupil funding now spent for public schools and, crucially, to public school buildings. Public school systems as now constituted are not likely to make available existing unused buildings or to press principals who control unnecessarily large buildings to accept rival schools as cotenants. This author has argued elsewhere for a radical re-missioning of public school systems, to require them to contract out for or to charter all schools, to provide every school with the full real-dollar per pupil expenditure for every student enrolled, and to lease out all school buildings on a cost-competitive basis.[25] This would make creation of a new supply of choice schools the fundamental business of local school systems and would counter current incentives to burden new schools.

Confusion about Accountability

In theory, chartering (and public school contracting) should allow schools to exercise considerable autonomy over their instructional programs in return for clear accountability for results. Charter schools should operate without interference, avoiding the eroding effects of successive political mandates, as long as they demonstrate the expected student benefits. However, the vast majority of charter agreements leave accountability—what performance schools must demonstrate and what the school board or other public authority must do if a school meets or fails to meet its student performance goals—essentially undefined. Neither public officials nor charter school operators know whether the schools are obligated only by the specific terms of their charters or whether the schools must also abide by the other rules that apply to other public schools.[26] Consequently, charter schools in many states and localities are in danger of being drawn toward the dominant accountability practices of the public education system.

Ambiguous accountability exposes schools to the very political and administrative arbitrariness that chartering was supposed to eliminate. Charter schools' exposure comes from two sources: a lack of clear signals to mainline school administrators that charter schools are not expected to fill out every report and submit to every compliance inspection expected of regular public schools; and efforts by many charter school advocates to avoid being held accountable through objective measures of student achievement.

LACK OF CLEAR SIGNALS. Few mainline state and local school administrators understand charter schools, or the legal authorities under which they operate, in detail. Though some have the impression that they are to keep hands off charter schools, others assume that charters, like every other public school, must fill out standard financial, attendance, and service reports. Administrators of federal categorical programs assume that charter schools must use funds and deliver services pretty much the way other schools do. In the course of my own studies in Illinois and Massachusetts, researchers were told of civil rights agencies that charged charter schools, whose core instructional strategy was to mainstream all students, with violating the civil rights of disabled students who had previously been assigned to special programs.

Few state laws specify the exact grounds on which charters will be granted, renewed, or canceled, and the vast majority of individual school charter agreements leave accountability processes and criteria to be defined. Charter and contract school operators, for their part, were so convinced that their schools would be effective that they took little care setting clear performance expectations. In the absence of clear outcome goals and measures, the public agencies that authorize schools to receive public funds are free to judge a charter school as they would a regular public school. Is the school popular with parents? Has a school become controversial? Does it measure up well on the issues a political body can easily assess, such as compliance with administrative requirements and use of familiar instructional methods? These mechanisms of accountability are the reason public schools must respond to so many masters.

Some local and state administrators may be deliberately testing charter school operators to see how much of the normal regulatory burden they will accept. Others, for example, advocates of special education, may be trying to preserve a regime of regulation whether or not disabled children and their parents have deliberately chosen the kinds of instructional environments available in charter schools.[27] But most are probably only doing their jobs as they see them, reasoning that if other public schools must submit a particular report or plan, a charter school must be similarly obligated.

AVERSION TO STUDENT TESTING. Many charter school operators dislike standard achievement testing, feeling that it takes time away from instruction, narrows the focus of instruction, and provides discouraging and inappropriately negative feedback to disadvantaged students. Many prefer to measure student learning through essentially subjective judgment of student performance or portfolios.

Unfortunately, these preferred measuring devices lack credibility with public oversight bodies. Such measures are not reliable from student to student or from judge to judge. They are also not highly correlated with the results of the standardized achievement tests that public officials are accustomed to interpreting.[28] Though public officials express their concerns in different words, they are concerned about external validity: standardized achievement tests do a good job on average of predicting school grades, school completion, and college admissions, but student performance and portfolios appear to have little predictive power.

Faced with the alternative between accepting tests they dislike and taking their chances on being able to persuade a public authority to continue their charters even without test-based evidence, many charter operators take the latter course. Many are willing to rely on their ability to win a future political struggle with a school board that is yet to be elected rather than to accept student achievement testing. Some are even willing to accept new mandates not contemplated by their charters as a way of building up political credits. In the future, such charter schools may be judged on the same grounds as regular public schools—on whether they have avoided controversy and satisfied all parties. This represents a Faustian bargain: in order to operate today and to avoid testing students, school operators accept compliance-based accountability. This is not to say that charter supporters should accept just any set of student achievement measures or goals. Charter operators must negotiate realistic goals that make sense in light of their schools' instructional focuses.

A public authorizing agency must also take care in negotiating charter accountability agreements. An agency that requires all schools to meet particular absolute achievement levels could place insupportable burdens on schools that, because of their location in low-income areas or because of their chosen mission, serve educationally disadvantaged children. Such schools might be targeted for penalties or closure even if their students gained at a high rate. Minority and low-income families could find that promising schools are constantly being snatched away from them and replaced by unfamiliar new schools. Those perils are, however, not reasons to avoid achievement testing altogether. For their own protection schools need to tie their accountability to student achievement test results.

Some schools have tried to avoid accountability by suggesting other standards on which public authorities should evaluate them: student creativity, teacher energy, collaboration, imaginativeness, the openness and good cheer of the school climate. Many public education administrators find this prospect attractive, but for reasons inimical to the creation of a diverse supply of coherent schools it can lead to assessment of schools according to whether they fit current professional views of best practice. Complex best practice standards open schools to subjective judgments and to the vagaries of political decisionmaking, which inevitably interferes with schools' ability to pursue coherent and distinctive approaches to instruction.

Publicly funded schools of choice need to regard student achievement test results as the analog of corporate profits: firms must make a profit, but that is not the only reason they exist. Boeing, for example, exists to make airplanes and will do so as long as it can remain profitable. Thus profit is a constraint that Boeing must meet, not its only goal. Any business firm must be profitable in the long run in order to pay its employees and satisfy investors, but it also has commitments to staying in a particular business and to serving particular customers.

Schools need to adopt an analogous approach to student achievement test results. In simple form and related to core student skills, they are constraints that a school must meet if it is to continue operating. The school's deeper goals, which are expressed in terms of its commitments to student service, climate, interpersonal relations, and links to other institutions, can drive its internal accountability and its accountability to parents, colleagues, and the broader teaching profession.[29] Its direct relationships with public authorities, however, should be as simple and predictable as possible. These conclusions will trouble those in the charter movement who understandably fear that public officials will try to control them through setting exhaustive test requirements. There is reason to worry about this: state standards that hold schools accountable for formal tests in certain areas can overconstrain schools. However, state standards in basic skills can be major assets for charter and contract schools, if they represent only core subjects and skills that higher education institutions and employers recognize as minimal attainments.

Squandered Advantages

As discussed, charter and contract school operators can succumb to the temptation to barter their special advantages for short-term support. They can also fail to recognize and use some of their most important intrinsic advantages. In particular, many charter operators are oblivious to the value of providing schools that are distinctive, coherent, and reliable.

On the basis of our observation of early charter school operation, it is clear that many charter schools have unclear commitments and fuzzy profiles. Some charter schools are started by parents or teachers who agree with one another about the failings of the regular public school system but who have not worked out much else about how their schools will operate. Other charter operators positively seek to create schools that evolve continuously through parent-teacher collaboration. Such schools may indeed differ from the public school norm, but they do little to advance the cause of creating a new supply of choice schools.

Many educators avoid associating their schools with labels, specific educational goals, and instructional methods, assuming that such commitments might inhibit creativity and foreclose desirable options. Some even claim that deciding in advance what approach a school will take and attracting teachers and parents on the basis of that commitment is undemocratic and a form of coercion. It is, of course, extremely important that teachers and administrators stay intellectually engaged in their work and accept responsibility for the ways their schools serve children. There are, furthermore, many good schools that are unique results of the work of their teachers, administrators, and parents.

However, the avoidance of any prior structure can be a major problem. Teachers and parents who agree on what their school must *not* be often cannot agree on what it *should* be. Endless efforts to negotiate first principles can cause confusion, low morale, and in some cases, school failure. Teachers' reflection and problem solving are more vigorous and productive in schools with well-defined goals and instructional methods than in less strongly anchored schools.[30] Poorly defined schools are handicapped by lack of internal clarity. Schools that do not have a clear theory of how they will operate, how adults will do their jobs and interact, and how the combined work of adults will help students to learn have little basis on which to organize or judge themselves.

Parents who cannot be sure what a school is offering them have little basis for choice. Schools that cannot say in advance what they will be cannot make promises. Schools that claim that they are always a unique product of the mix of personalities currently present cannot be trusted to be the same year to year. Some parents might be willing to take their chances, reserving the right to participate in deliberations and to complain or leave if they do not like the ways things are going. But they cannot expect the school to do anything in particular.

Poorly defined schools also lose out on important sources of leverage on parental support and student effort. Schools that make definite promises can say what parents must contribute in return, in terms of service to the school and assurance that children will have the time, the place, and the encouragement to study.[31] Similarly, schools lose the leverage over students that comes from a bargain reached in advance about what students will gain from attending the school, what the staff will do to ensure that students learn, how the staff will help struggling students, and what effort, attendance, and deportment the school will demand in return. Such bargains are the core of a coherent, effective school, yet many charter schools eschew making them.

Charter schools and other schools of choice can benefit from the fact that all members of the school community have chosen a situation with known characteristics. Once a school has established an identity it must deliver on its promises well enough to keep current students from transferring out, to create loyalty among families with several children, and to attract enough new families to fill the entering class each year. Teachers in such schools have strong incentives to keep their own work in line with the school's mission, to help one another, to identify weaknesses, and to ensure that variations in teacher performance do not harm the school's ultimate product and reputation.

New schools must work hard to get the full advantages of choice, and many are just waking up to the need to do so. My colleagues and I, in our research on charter schools, enountered many schools that were reluctant to define themselves sharply or to use a strong basic commitment to particular goals and methods as the basis on which to attract (and discourage) teachers and parents. Leaders in poorly defined new schools often find themselves forced to enunciate standards of student attendance and behavior that they had preferred to leave implicit. Students and parents in poorly defined new schools often express shock that school rules are to be taken seriously and that certain actions have, for good or ill, certain consequences.

Parents' attitudes are also often a problem. Parents accustomed to regular public schools often think that school rules are observed only until someone complains and that few administrators will tangle with a determined mother or father. In a school of choice, however, administrators must sometimes choose between offending one parent and breaking faith with many others. Leaders eager to maintain a school's internal coherency and preserve its reputation have strong incentives to make good on both promises and threats. As James Coleman has explained, the authority to uphold internal standards of performance and conduct is a particular advantage of a school of choice.[32] Having made commitments about school methods and climate, and fearing to lose the support of other parents, school leaders will resist individual parents' demands to waive rules or overlook student transgressions. This leads to a high degree of trust (in Coleman's term, social capital) within the school community. On the other hand, leaders of regular public schools, to which students are assigned automatically, have no particular pact with parents. They do, however, have an incentive to avoid controversies that might come to the attention of school system leaders. When individual parents make demands, school leaders have little reason to resist. Over the long term the policy of serial concessions leads to a de facto weakening of standards of performance and behavior, often to a level below that which all parents want for the school as a whole.

The conflict between school leaders' incentives and parents' habits is particularly evident in new charter and contract high schools in inner cities. These schools often aspire to maintaining a higher level of order and attention to work than is common in urban high schools. Parents who clash with school operators on these issues typically resort to complaints to higher authority, expecting the school board or the central office to avert conflict by ordering concessions.

Distinctive, Coherent, Reliable Schools

Some observers recommend supply mechanisms in addition to charter schools and system-initiated new schools, charters, and reconstitutions. Larry Pierce, James Guthrie, and I recommend a system under which school boards would not have the authority to operate schools directly and would supply schools by contracting with independent organizations. Parents would choose schools, and schools would receive the full per pupil expenditure in cash, employ teachers, and manage their own operations. Many writers propose a universal voucher system, under which parents would choose schools, money would follow students, and schools would be run by private organizations. (The difference between the contracting and voucher proposals is on the supply-side: under contracting, public authorities would solicit proposals and be responsible for maintaining a portfolio of schools balanced to meet the needs of all students; under a pure voucher plan, schools would be started and managed entirely at private initiative.)

These are promising alternatives to both the current system and the charter school approach, which leaves the existing bureaucracy intact but allows certain schools to operate outside of it. All of the alternatives would give parents choices and allow money to follow children to the schools their parents choose. That alone is enough to create the demand-side of a new social market for high-quality schools. However, neither chartering nor contracting nor vouchers completely solve all of the supply-side problem. All these proposals leave unresolved the questions, Who will provide schools for parents, especially low-income and minority parents, to choose? And by what mechanisms will those schools become and stay distinctive, coherent, and reliable?

Policy analysts and educators are just coming to terms with the supply problem, and this chapter surely does not solve it.[33] But it is possible to sketch the three basic elements of a solution.

—There must be a concerted effort, including significant private resources, to create large numbers of organizations capable of operating schools or setting up new schools on a turnkey basis.

—There is a need for public-private collaboration on the creation of a supply of independent, fee-based providers of school facilities, technical assistance, teacher recruitment and training, and legal and financial services.

—There is a need for improved measures of school productivity, especially those linked to short-term increases in student learning, so that schools can be held accountable for results rather than for compliance.

The following discussion elaborates on these ideas.

New Organizations to Operate Schools

Today if a major city decided to put all its schools out for contract or to allow an unlimited number of students to carry vouchers to independently run schools, there would be far fewer groups prepared to run schools than there were opportunities. Though many organizations are interested in—and potentially able—to provide schools, few are poised to open new schools with little preparation. In two jurisdictions studied, hundreds of groups requested information, dozens tried to organize to write proposals, but far fewer were prepared to open schools within a few months. In these jurisdictions (in Massachusetts and Chicago), which required new charter operators to meet stringent organizational and financial criteria, the numbers of charters that opened in the first two years were twenty-five and fifteen, respectively.[34]

New organizations cannot form out of thin air: all must be capitalized in some ways, by investments of individuals' time and someone's—whether governments', philanthropists', or investors'—money. Though start-up funds for new schools are not easy to get, they are available from philanthropies like the Challenge Foundation and Charter Friends' networks and from the U.S. Department of Education. In 1999 the federal charter school grant program will provide $100 million in start-up funds for charter schools. At an average of $50,000 a school, this program provides some support for about two hundred new schools each year, or about the number of new charter schools currently starting up. However, a school supply effort large enough to make a visible difference in America's more than 65,000 schools would require a much larger investment. If barriers to entry were lowered, so that school providers could readily gain access to public school funding or get public support to rent commercial space, the numbers of successful applicants would surely rise. Challenges would remain, especially for groups hoping to operate in inner-city neighborhoods and other challenging areas.

Many of the challenges of starting a new school are educational, but at least an equal number are financial and managerial. Further, as government agencies empowered to authorize charter schools learn more about what it takes to start up a school, keep it going, and ensure that students benefit, their demands for track records and demonstrated organizational competence are becoming more stringent. Though newly formed groups will undoubtedly continue to seek charters, the advantage is clearly with established educational and youth service organizations, colleges and universities, professional organizations like teachers' unions, and for-profit contractors. Though there are enough such groups to handle the current demand for contract and charter school operators, their real capacities are small. Even for-profit contractors like Edison, which hopes eventually to operate hundreds of schools, start small and add schools carefully to maintain quality. After five years Edison is still operating fewer than fifty schools, and an increase of more than twenty-five schools a year would certainly overtax the company's staff training and quality control processes. Other for-profit contractors, including Sabis, Voyager Schools, and Tesseract, are not yet organized to operate on as large a scale as Edison.

Some other organizations might respond to a vastly increased demand for new choice-oriented schools, but they would have to adapt carefully and would have limited capacity. The New American Schools (NAS) corporation has assembled eight design teams to create new approaches to instruction and school management. Because NAS has worked for conventional school districts, which want help for existing schools, not providers for new ones, NAS teams are not now prepared to operate schools themselves. However, they could organize to operate schools or to work as turnkey start-up contractors. NAS teams could also work intensively with staffs or existing public schools that want to prepare themselves to operate as independent organizations rather than as dependent parts of the school district.

The new school design efforts supported by the federal government's Porter-Obey bill could increase the numbers of organizations like the NAS design teams. Other organizations—for example, Paideia, the School Excellence Network, the International Baccalaureate, the Coalition of Essential Schools, Stanford University's Accelerated Schools, the University of Virginia's Core Knowledge Network—try to help schools take distinctive approaches to education. None of these organizations is prepared to run schools or to help others start new schools of choice, but their ideas, instructional materials, and teacher training methods are almost certainly adaptable to that task.

Design teams and school providers require intensive development and quality control. Because no one provider is likely to be able to run or even to assist a large number of schools, a large number of providers is necessary. Johns Hopkins University's Success for All is now working in approximately a thousand schools, the most served by any such organization. Actually operating or overseeing the management of that same number of schools would require much more capacity than Success for All now has.

Though several of the school design organizations are dedicated to working in low-income areas, there is an obvious need for additional organizations linked to urban minority community groups, colleges, and churches. Organizations like the National Urban League are moving toward support for new school providers, but many mainstream minority organizations, such as the National Association for the Advancement of Colored People (NAACP), are constrained by their alliances with teachers' unions from supporting new providers for schools of choice. The most concerted efforts to create new providers for inner-city areas come from within the cities themselves; in Detroit, Milwaukee, and Chicago, the new school initiatives have been minority led. Much larger efforts, some drawing on the credibility, competence, and wealth of inner-city churches, are necessary.

Once there are several thousand publicly funded schools of choice in big cities and elsewhere, demand might drive supply. As the publicly funded voucher programs in Milwaukee and Cleveland have shown, low-income parents create information networks about schools of choice; as in other places, schools where children learn and are lovingly treated quickly build waiting lists. If potential school operators know that students come with enough public funds to support a solid instructional program, successful schools can be expanded and imitated. Principals and teachers experienced in running one school can create others on the same model. That is how Catholic religious orders expanded their school systems in the early twentieth century. For the present, however, neither the public nor the private sector in this country is prepared to supply the schools needed by a serious choice system.

How can large numbers of new urban schools be created? This is not a familiar question, and nobody has thought much about it. Organizations capable of supplying schools of choice could be developed, however, through any of the following methods or through several in combination:[35]

—Workshops for new school providers, to give potential school operators opportunities to learn about school start-up and management from leaders of charter schools and independent private schools. Such incubators could also help potential school providers by forming support groups, helping them visit schools they might imitate, and arranging for them to try their instructional methods in friendly schools.

—School development schools in which the staff of a prospective school would train together in an environment they might imitate, allowing them to develop their ideas and to build good staff collaboration.

—School shadowing arrangements in which the key staff of a potential school could work closely with their counterparts in a school whose basic approach they hope to imitate.

—Staff circulation arrangements in which key staff members from a school that another group would like to imitate temporarily join the staff of the new school.

—School pairing, or hiving, in which a new school is established as a branch of an existing one, with key staff members permanently assigned to the new school as leaders, selectors of staff, trainers, and eventually as regular administrators and teachers.

Taken together, these activities could greatly increase the number of organizations that want to run schools of choice and that have well-developed ideas about how they would operate. Although there are hints of each activity in one place or other, no conscious effort has been made to combine them into a broad supply-enhancing strategy. School board and teachers' union interests, and their powerful representation in state capitals and Washington, D.C., make it unlikely that the government will take the necessary initiative. Foundation investment is the best hope for timely preparation in anticipation of demand for schools of choice.

Major national foundations could support new school incubators, which could operate statewide or in big cities to promote the formation of school provider organizations. Some might be dedicated to forming new schools for low-income and minority neighborhoods. Like business incubators, school incubators would provide the kinds of experiences listed above and would help potential school providers find legal, financial, and technical advice.[36] Ideally, foundations would pay the up-front design and salary costs for the development of these incubators and provide salaries or stipends to allow individuals to spend a few months working full time on their plans for school provider organizations.

Private Providers of Assistance and School Space

Because public school systems are not designed to support the distinctive, coherent, and reliable schools needed for a choice system, schools that aspire to these attributes must find the help they need from other sources. They must obtain their own legal help, personnel and payroll services, insurance, and so on. These burdens are the necessary costs of the freedom to operate. Though some charter schools have struggled to find the kinds of assistance they need, the component expertise is not in particularly short supply. In localities with large numbers of charter schools (for example, Mesa, Arizona) private firms and professionals have learned what they must know to sell their services to the schools. Charter schools in the Mesa area can choose to act as their own prime contractors, hiring specific legal, accounting, maintenance, and other help as they need it. Alternatively, they can hire one of several comprehensive service firms that have sprung up to serve the charter school market. Though these firms have come under some criticism on grounds of cost and efficiency, few charter schools have to pay as much for services as is taxed away from regular public schools by district central offices; charter schools also do not need to wait months to get the help.

A similar private services infrastructure is likely to arise in any locality with large numbers of schools of choice. However, there is as yet no organized private response to charter schools' most severe need, which is reliable access to school facilities. Without major political or legal pressures, regular public school systems are unlikely to make school space available to charter schools or schools that arise under a voucher system. School systems seem more predisposed to providing facilities to schools they hire under contract, perhaps because most districts consider contracting only if they have a school building available. Choice schools in localities in which regular public school system authorities are unfriendly, or in which the total school population is growing, will have to find their own buildings. Some schools, as in Chicago, have obtained private grants or low-interest loans to purchase and renovate business buildings. Others have leased space at market rates. These solutions can work, but they burden schools with high payments.

The long-term solution, of course, is for publicly funded schools of choice to have the same access to publicly owned and subsidized space as all other public schools. As discussed above, this is likely only if someone other than a conventional district central office has control of school buildings. This can be accomplished in two ways. The first is to require school boards to enter contracts with all schools, which would include specification of the space to be provided for the school or the amounts the board will provide to help a school lease private space.[37] The second is to create an independent authority that owns, maintains, develops, and rents space to schools.

Such authorities could be created by state legislatures, which would allow new local public school real estate trusts to take control of all local school system property and of capital funds now set aside for school building construction and maintenance. These authorities would also have the authority to float bonds. These authorities could buy, sell, and redevelop land and buildings and could even enter long-term leases to obtain use of privately owned property. Each year the authority would publish a price list showing the square-foot lease costs of available school space and of privately owned space available on the market. Schools could bid on space and enter into long-term leases, with renewal and cost-escalator clauses similar to those used for private space. Schools could also accept private donations of space or funds to buy space. Since all schools in a locality would have nearly identical incomes per student, all schools would have comparable purchasing power. Schools in low-cost neighborhoods—for example, poor inner-city areas—could benefit from relatively lower rents. Because few schools could afford the cost of leasing lavish facilities, the local real estate authority would probably have to rent out swimming pools and large auditoriums on a per-use basis.

This proposal is crude and needs serious analysis. It is, however, a promising way to break the stranglehold on school space that allows existing public school systems to burden and marginalize schools of choice. A major foundation or business coalition could test the concept by entering an agreement with a willing medium-sized school system to form such a trust. The trust would become the owner of all public school buildings and would receive all state and local funds earmarked for school construction and maintenance. The trust would maintain a stock of buildings, which it would make available on a medium-term lease basis to all public schools, including charter and contract schools. It would sell surplus buildings and build or lease new space in areas with too many children for the space available. It would also help schools find space and help schools find sublease tenants for space they no longer need. Urban districts with surplus buildings in one area of town and overcrowding elsewhere might find such an arrangement attractive. So might rapidly growing inner suburbs, many of which face the need to develop new school capacity but do not want to initiate major building programs.

Better Accountability Methods

Choice provides an automatic way for parents to hold schools accountable, but parental preferences and satisfaction alone are not enough to structure the relationship between individual charter or contract schools and the public agencies that authorize them. Authorizing agencies must have good measures of school productivity. Without such measures public agencies inevitably reward and punish schools for whether they follow rules, not whether they work for students.

It is crucial that schools of choice have ways of measuring student learning, ways that are precise enough to gauge individual students' growth over relatively short periods of time (for example, the duration of a school year) and flexible enough to measure how much a student knows regardless of the methods by which he or she has learned. In the absence of such methods, schools of choice risk either being judged inaccurately or being forced to use instructional methods designed in light of the characteristics of a test. Tests that measure individual students well emphasize basic ability rather than period-specific learning, and tests that measure student learning well are most accurate if they are aligned with specific curricula and used to measure average rates of progress among large groups of students. The result is that schools with distinctive curricula or instructional methods must choose between having their effectiveness underestimated or disrupting their regular instructional program to prepare students for particular tests.

Some of the new statewide standards-based tests might eventually prove appropriate for schools of choice. At present, however, these tests are controversial, and many force schools to teach students particular materials at particular times, especially outside the core subjects of reading and mathematics. Stephen Klein and Laura Hamilton of RAND have proposed a promising alternative to existing testing practices.[38] A national, internet-based testing program could maintain a bank of tens of thousands of test items, each related to a specific academic skill and calibrated for level of difficulty. To test an individual student in a particular subject, the program would first administer a few screening items to establish the student's basic level of competency. The program would then generate a randomly chosen set of approximately a hundred questions, all tightly clustered around the skill to be assessed and the student's performance level. The school could get results instantly—within seconds of the time the student finished the test. The resulting score would be a highly accurate assessment of a student's performance. If the same student were to be tested a short time later, the program would draw a different set of questions from its item bank, but the results could be easily, and validly, compared with the first set of scores. The cost of testing an individual child would be relatively small, no greater that the current cost of buying, administering, and scoring a paper and pencil test.

Whether or not this specific approach is the best one, choice definitely requires new thinking about school and student performance measurement.

Conclusion

Many people assume that parents' growing demand for school choice makes it inevitable. Yet in the face of an entrenched system that controls virtually all of the funds and buildings, and whose structure is deeply rooted in state laws as well as habits, the desire for choice does not look like such an irresistible force. A small industry has grown up around identifying the political, legal, and financial changes that must occur if America is to have public education based on parental choice, professional freedom of action, and school accountability for results.[39] As an active member of that industry, I believe its tenets are valuable and important. However, as this chapter shows, the preconditions for choice go beyond the legal and political. Serious efforts are necessary to develop schools that can take full advantage of potential new charter, contracting, and voucher laws. The existing public school system will not make these efforts; worse, it will promise to develop and sustain distinctive, coherent, and reliable schools and then prove unable to do so.

There is an urgent need for investment in the incubation of schools suited to a choice system; for development of other financial arrangements, such as real estate trusts, that can allow such schools to flourish; and for methods of holding schools accountable for performance. The day a major choice-oriented law or court order comes into effect is too late to start on these tasks. The time to start is now.

Notes

1. Paul E. Peterson, Jay P. Greene, and Chad Noyes, "School Choice in Milwaukee," *Public Interest* (Fall 1996), pp. 38–56; John F. Witte, "Politics: Who Benefits from the Milwaukee Choice Program?" in Richard Elmore and Bruce Fuller, eds., *Who Chooses? Who Loses? Culture, Institutions, and the Unequal Effects of School Choice* (Teachers College Press, 1996).

2. Elmore and Fuller, *Who Chooses? Who Loses?*

3. Paul T. Hill and Stephen P. Klein, "Toward an Evaluation Design for the Cleveland Scholarship Program" (Seattle: UW/RAND Center on Reinventing Public Education, 1997); Paul T. Hill, "Contracting in Public Education," in Diane Ravitch and Joseph Viteritti, eds., *New Schools for a New Century* (Yale University Press, 1997); Marc Dean Millot and Robin J. Lake, "Supplying a System of Charter Schools: Observations on Early Implementation of the Massachusetts Statute" (Seattle: UW/RAND Center on Reinventing Public Education, 1997); and three ongoing studies: Dean Millot and Paul Herdman's study on the school start-up process in Massachusetts; Lawrence Pierce and colleagues' study on provider recruitment and school start-up in the Chicago charter schools program; and a national study of charter school accountability led by Pierce and Paul Hill. See also Chester E. Finn, Bruno V. Manno, and Louann Bierlein, *Charter Schools in Action: What Have We Learned?* (Indianapolis: Hudson Institute, 1996).

4. For evidence on how school coherency contributes to effectiveness, see Anthony S. Bryk, *Charting Chicago School Reform: Democratic Localism as a Lever for Change* (Boulder, Colo.: Westview, 1998).

5. For an account of the effects of these programs, see Jackie Kimbrough and Paul T. Hill, "The Aggregate Effects of Federal Education Programs" (Santa Monica, Calif.: RAND, 1980).

6. See Lorraine McDonnell and Anthony Pascal, "Organized Teachers in America's Schools" (Santa Monica, Calif.: RAND, 1979).

7. See John E. Chubb and Terry Moe, *Politics, Markets, and America's Schools* (Brookings, 1990); Deborah Meier, *The Power of Their Ideas: Lessons for America from a Small School in Harlem* (Beacon, 1995); Paul T. Hill, Lawrence Pierce, and James Guthrie, *Reinventing Public Education: How Contracting Can Transform America's Schools* (University of Chicago Press, 1997).

8. Linda Darling-Hammond and others, "The Coalition Campus Project: Inching toward Systemic Reform in New York City" (Columbia Teachers College, 1994).

9. See, for example, Richard F. Elmore and Deanna Burney, "Investing in Teacher Learning, Staff Development, and Instructional Improvement in Community School District #2, New York City, New York" (Philadelphia: Consortium for Policy Research in Education, 1997). See also Seymour Fliegel, *Miracle in East Harlem: The Fight for Choice in Public Education* (Times Books, 1993).

10. For an excellent exchange of views about the effects of small class size, see Eric Hanushek, "The Evidence on Class Size"; and Frederick Mosteller, "How Does Class Size Relate to Achievement in Schools?" both in Susan Mayer and Paul Peterson, eds., *When Schools Make a Difference* (Brookings, 1998).

11. Richard J. Murnane and Frank Levy, "What Money Matters Sometimes: A Two-Part Management Lesson from East Austin, Texas," *Education Week*, September 11, 1996, p. 48.

12. David Brewster, "Saving Public Schools," *Seattle Times*, March 20, 1998.

13. Carl D. Glickman, *Revolutionizing America's Schools* (San Francisco: Jossey-Bass, 1998). See also Benjamin R. Barber, *An Aristocracy of Everyone: The Politics of Education and the Future of America* (Ballantine, 1992).

14. John C. Goodlad, "Democracy, Education, and Community," in Roger Soder, ed., *Democracy, Education, and the Schools* (San Francisco: Jossey-Bass, 1996), p. 92.

15. Donna Kerr, "Democracy, Nurturance, and Community," in Soder, *Democracy, Education, and the Schools*.

16. Finn, Manno, and Bierlein, *Charter Schools in Action*.

17. Andrew M. Greeley, *The Catholic Myth: The Behavior and Beliefs of American Catholics* (Scribner, 1990). See also Christian Smith and David Sikkink, "Is Private School Privatizing?" *First Things*, no. 82 (April 1999), pp. 16–20. Much of the research on this problem has been done in the Netherlands, a religiously divided country in which government funds religious schools. See, for example, A. Need and N. D. Degraaf, "The Changing Electorate of the Confessional Parties: Effects of Socialization and Intragenerational Religious Mobility in the 1956–1991 Elections," *Netherlands Journal of Social Sciences*, vol. 32 (1996), pp. 210–28. See also Karin Wittebrood, *Politieke Socialisatie In Nederland: Een Onderzoek Naar De Verwerving En Ontwikkeling Van Politieke Houdingen Van Havo* (Amsterdam: Thesis, 1995).

18. M. Kent Jennings and Richard G. Niemi, *The Political Character of Adolescence: The Influence of Families and Schools* (Princeton University Press, 1974).

19. Jacqueline Jordan Irvine and Michele Foster, *Growing up African American in Catholic Schools* (Teachers College Press, 1996).

20. Mark Schneider and others, "Institutional Arrangements and the Creation of Social Capital: The Effects of Public School Choice," *American Political Science Review*, vol. 91 (March 1997), pp. 82–93.

21. See, for example, Jeannie Oakes, "Two Cities' Tracking and Within-School Segregation," *Teachers College Record*, vol. 96, no. 4 (1995), pp. 681–90. See also Jeannie Oakes and others, "Multiplying Inequalities: The Effects of Race, Social Class, and Tracking on Opportunities to Learn Mathematics and Science" (Santa Monica, Calif.: RAND, 1990).

22. Jennifer O'Day and Matt Kelemen, "Fixing Failing Schools: Reconstitution and Other High-Stakes Strategies" (Madison: Wisconsin Center for Education Research, 1997).

23. For detailed analyses of these costs, see Marc Dean Millot and Robin J. Lake, "So You Want to Start a Charter School? Strategic Advice for Applicants" (Seattle: UW/RAND Center on Reinventing Public Education, 1996); see also Millot and Lake, "Supplying a System of Charter Schools."

24. Darling-Hammond and others, "The Coalition Campus Project," p. 32.

25. See Hill, Pierce, and Guthrie, *Reinventing Public Education*.

26. Priscilla Wohlstetter and others, "Charter Schools in the United States: The Question of Autonomy," *Educational Policy*, vol. 9 (December 1995), pp. 331–58.

27. Jay P. Heubert, "Schools without Rules: Charter Schools, Federal Disability Law, and the Paradoxes of Deregulation," *Harvard Civil Rights–Civil Liberties Law Review*, vol. 32 (1997), p. 301.

28. Karen Mitchell, "Reforming and Conforming: NASDC Principals Discuss School Accountability Systems" (Santa Monica, Calif.: RAND, 1995). See also the sections on charter school accountability in Greg Vanoureck, Chester E. Finn Jr., and Bruno V. Manno, "Charter Schools as Seen by Those Who Know Them Best: Students, Teachers, and Parents" (Indianapolis: Hudson Institute, 1997).

29. For a discussion of internal versus external accountability, see Fred M. Newmann, Bruce King, and Marc Rigdon, "Accountability and School Performance: Implications from Restructuring Schools," *Harvard Educational Review*, vol. 67, no. 1 (1997), pp. 41–74. For a discussion of the ways schools can be accountable to audiences other than public authori-

ties, see Paul T. Hill, "Accountability under Charters and Other School-Centered Reforms," *Advances in Educational Administration*, vol. 5 (1997), pp. 191–207.

30. Meier, *The Power of Their Ideas*; Theodore R. Sizer, *Horace's Compromise: The Dilemma of the American High School* (Houghton-Mifflin, 1992). These ideas are elaborated further in Paul T. Hill and Lawrence Pierce, "Schools' Integrative Capital" (Seattle: UW/RAND Center on Reinventing Public Education, 1998).

31. For a more complete development of this argument, see Paul T. Hill, "Private Vouchers in New York City: The Student-Sponsor Partnership Program," in Terry M. Moe, ed., *Private Vouchers* (Stanford, Calif.: Hoover Institution Press, 1995).

32. James S. Coleman, *Foundations of Social Theory* (Harvard University Press, 1990), chap. 12.

33. One problem that affects both regular public schools and schools of choice is supply of qualified teachers. Several studies report a shortage of high-ability new entrants to teaching, particularly those qualified to teach mathematics, science, and history. They also note that inner-city schools are especially likely to employ marginally qualified teachers and to lose their better teachers to other schools and to nonteaching opportunities. Schools of choice will suffer from these problems, though possibly less than regular public schools. A study sponsored by the National Education Association shows that charters, which are not constrained to hire all their teachers from within public school system bargaining units, attract teachers from other sources, including experienced teachers who left public schools for other jobs and well-educated individuals who want to enter teaching. For an analysis of the current teacher labor supply, see Linda Darling-Hammond, "What Matters Most: Teaching for America's Future" (Washington, D.C.: National Commission on Teaching and America's Future, 1998); and Kati Haycock, *Education Watch: The Education Trust National Data Book*, vol. 2 (Washington, D.C.: National Education Trust, 1998). On charter school teachers, see Julia E. Koppich, Patricia Holmes, and Margaret L. Plecki, "New Rules, New Roles? The Professional Work Lives of Charter School Teachers" (Washington, D.C.: National Education Association, 1998). For an analysis of possible reserve pools that might compensate for education schools' low rates of production of qualified teachers, see David W. Grissmer and Sheila Nataraj Kirby, "Patterns of Attrition among Indiana Teachers, 1965–1987" (Santa Monica, Calif.: RAND, 1991).

34. Millot and Lake, "So You Want to Start a Charter School?" and Millot and Lake, "Supplying a System of Charter Schools."

35. See Mary Beth Celio, "Building and Maintaining Systems of Schools: Lessons from Religious Order School Networks" (University of Washington, Graduate School of Public Affairs, 1995).

36. As this is written, two school incubators are being formed, one in Seattle, at the University of Washington, and one in Massachusetts, at the Francis B. Parker School. After a brief development phase, these first two incubators will assist with the formation of similar incubators throughout the country.

37. Hill, Pierce, and Guthrie, *Reinventing Public Education*.

38. Stephen P. Klein and Laura S. Hamilton, "Moving toward a National Testing System" (Vanderbilt University, Peabody College, Consortium on Renewing Education [CORE], 1998).

39. See, for example, Hill, Pierce, and Guthrie, *Reinventing Public Education*; Charles T. Kerchner, Julia Koppich, and Joseph G. Weeres, *United Mind Workers: Unions and Teaching in the Knowledge Society* (San Francisco: Jossey-Bass, 1997).

CHAPTER SIX

School Choice Accountability

FRANK R. KEMERER

How can we tell whether choice schools are successful? In what ways should they be held accountable? First, choice schools must be accountable to parents. Parents expect the schools their children attend to be safe, the teachers reputable, and the educational program of high quality. They expect the schools to be governed well. And they expect complaints regarding the education of their children to be resolved equitably. Meaningful information about school options and programs is a critical component of a parent accountability system, for without it, parents are handicapped in making wise decisions about the education of their children. Second, choice schools must be accountable to the state. A state accountability system should encompass financial and enrollment monitoring, assurance of enrollment diversity, promotion of toleration, and performance assessment. Relying on market pressures alone to ensure accountability to parents and the state is unrealistic. It also is politically naive, for the threat as school choice options expand is not too little regulation but too much.

Despite the shift to the more market-based accountability system inherent in school choice, legislators appear reluctant to relax traditional state and school district top-down controls.[1] These include per pupil spending requirements, class size restrictions, and teacher certification. To a large extent, this reluctance reflects the political clout of powerful interest groups with a stake in the existing public school system: school board associations, administrator groups, and teachers' unions. However, an effective account- ability system can be instituted that intrudes minimally on institutional autonomy by abandoning traditional input and process requirements that are weakly, if at all, related to student achievement.[2] Such a system can still ensure that all parents are informed consumers and have an equal oppor- tunity to participate; that schools are efficient, equitable, and competitive; and that the public value of an educated and tolerant citizenry is advanced. While the accountability system discussed in this chapter is tailored to choice schools, elements of it can be applied to traditional public schools as well, thus leveling the competitive playing field for all schools.

The purpose of this chapter is to describe the components of this sim- plified school choice accountability system and to show how it can serve the interests of parents and the state without compromising institutional autonomy. The system is based on empirical findings and on legal and pub- lic policy considerations. Legal considerations cannot be ignored, because as choice options expand, litigation is bound to follow. Indeed, the illus- trations from contemporary case law presented in this chapter reflect this fact. The model statutory provisions advanced here demonstrate how accountability measures can be legislatively addressed.

Accountability to Parents

The three important accountability measures for parents are information preparation and dissemination, governance, and dispute resolution.

The Dissemination and Preparation of Information

Information is central to a market-oriented schooling system. Without good information, parents are constrained in making wise decisions for the education of their children. A mismatch between student and school trig- gers unnecessarily high student attrition. In San Antonio, nearly half of the students who used a privately funded scholarship to transfer from public to private schools and one-third of students enrolled in a districtwide thematic choice program dropped out over a three-year period.[3] While much of this attrition is due to normal mobility among families, a study of attrition in the San Antonio public school choice program suggests that both parents and students would have benefited from having more complete information about the nature of the school, the rigor of the curriculum, and the sacri- fices necessary when students attend schools outside their neighborhood.[4]

What motivates parents to choose schools for their children? Consistently across diverse school choice programs, parents identify educational quality as the most important factor.[5] Discipline and safety also are important, as are location and small size. In the case of choice programs encompassing sectarian private schools, religion is among the top-rated reasons.

While some state laws in recent years have mandated that school districts and individual schools prepare school report cards about schooling performance, school-produced information is often hard to obtain and difficult to understand. Consequently, in many communities parents rely on television, radio, and newspapers for information about choice opportunities.[6] Friends and relatives also are an important source of information about both choice options and individual school programs, as are churches for programs encompassing sectarian private schools. Stories in the media, however, are of questionable value in conveying accurate information important to parents. While a few newspapers, such as the *Philadelphia Inquirer* and the *Seattle Times,* have begun to provide comprehensive reports encompassing statistical and survey data about public and private schools in their regions, most do not.[7] Moreover, social networks composed of friends and relatives are highly segregated by race, income, and education, and the quality of information they provide varies by class. In the context of providing quality information for choosing a school, social networks have been labeled networks to nowhere.[8]

On the other hand, there is empirical evidence that, as school choice becomes part of the culture of a school community, the level of information among all parents improves and the gap between advantaged and disadvantaged parents narrows. In District 4 in New York City, a region known as Spanish Harlem, intradistrict choice has been available for more than twenty years, and institutional structures are in place to disseminate and facilitate the flow of information among parents.[9] Still it cannot be expected that a public school district will be eager to provide parents with information about programs involving out-of-district or private schools. During the first four years of the Milwaukee voucher program, the percentage of parents identifying friends or relatives as their primary source for information was nearly double the percentage for any other source.[10]

To make timely, accurate, and understandable information available to interested parents and students, an accountability system should encompass information preparation and dissemination. The state has an important role to play in making information available to parents about school choice opportunities. The school has a responsibility to provide prospective parents with information about the school's mission, its teachers, and any special programs it offers. Parents also need information from the school about student achievement and retention rates and, for high school, both its graduation rate and its success at college or job placement among its graduates. Direct mail and utilization of nontraditional dissemination channels, such as churches, civic groups, and the media, will help ensure that parents learn about choice opportunities. Where warranted, school choice information must be made available in the native language of non-English-speaking parent populations. These informational outreach efforts will help choice schools avoid replicating the same race and class concentration evident in many segments of the traditional public school system. The goal need not be to provide all possible choosing families with comprehensive information—it appears sufficient for a small subset to be relatively well informed, who will serve as role models for others.[11] A statutory provision covering information preparation and dissemination might be worded as follows:

1. The state education agency shall prepare annually a state school directory to include public school districts and schools, public choice schools within districts, public choice schools serving an interdistrict student population, and accredited private schools. The directory shall include the name of each district and school, their addresses and phone numbers, their supervising administrator, and the grade levels they serve. The directory shall be available to parents in all schools and shall be available at cost from the state education agency. The state education agency shall notify the parents or guardians of all school-age children annually of the availability of the directory.

2. No later than three months before opening, each choice school shall develop an informational brochure to include a description of the school and its mission, its governance structure, its curriculum, the qualifications of its administrators and teachers, students' responsibilities, discipline procedures, admissions requirements and procedures, transportation arrangements, and (if applicable) student fees and graduation requirements.

Following its first year of operation and each year thereafter, the choice school shall incorporate in the brochure student outcomes information, including dropout rates, achievement results, and (if applicable) graduation, college attendance, and employments rates.

The brochure shall be made available in the prevailing languages spoken in the general geographic region the school serves.

Each choice school shall develop a dissemination plan describing how the school will make the information in its brochure widely available to interested parents and students. The plan shall be included with the initial choice school application and updated periodically thereafter, as determined by the [sponsoring agency or state board of education].

3. Before the start of 20xx–20xx school year and each year thereafter, traditional public schools shall comply with the first three paragraphs of section 2.

Because studies reveal that lack of financial resources is the most significant problem that charter school operators face, the state should provide the necessary resources to assist charter school operators with these information-marketing efforts.[12] In addition, since information dissemination is not an activity that educators traditionally do well, assistance should be provided to help build skills in this area to those who seek it, including those in traditional public schools that compete with choice schools for clients.

The Governance Structure

The governance structures of choice schools vary considerably. For example, state law sometimes details the composition and functioning of the governing board of charter schools, following the prevailing practice in corporate governance law. In Minnesota the charter school law requires that the majority of a charter school's board of directors be licensed teachers at the school, describes the election process for board members, and specifies that the board must comply with the state's laws regarding open meetings and collective bargaining.[13] In New Hampshire and Texas, the law simply requires a charter school to describe its governing structure in the application for approval, leaving the internal form of governance to the charter school.[14] The Wisconsin and Ohio voucher laws do not regulate the governing structure of private schools participating in their programs.

Overly restrictive laws intrude on the autonomy of a choice school to choose its own governance system. Overly permissive laws, however, play into the hands of unscrupulous entrepreneurs. The permissive 1994 Arizona charter school law allowed virtually anyone to start a charter school and obtain funding, with little state oversight. Within three years, 285 charter schools sprang up, enrolling more than 30,000 students, each entitled to $4,000 in state funding.[15] According to the *Wall Street Journal*, abuses flourished, the most notorious of which involved Citizen 2000, a Phoenix charter school with a multicultural theme.[16] The school attracted hundreds of students, only to close in November 1996 amid charges of mismanagement, leaving more than 200 students without a school. The school's founder hired herself as principal, several relatives as teachers, and her sister to keep the books. Bankruptcy filings showed the school paid its administrative personnel extravagant salaries and benefits. The Citizen 2000 experience demonstrates how a weak governance system contributes to financial mismanagement.

As part of their information base for making a tutored schooling decision, parents should know what the governance structure of a choice school is and what role parents may play in it. The following accountability provision represents a balance between the right of a choice school to structure itself as it sees fit and the right of both parents and the state to know how the school is managed:

> A choice school must have a formal governance system, including a board of directors that has a fiduciary responsibility for the financial affairs of the school. The process for selecting board members, the length of their terms, and the frequency of board meetings must be specified. A secretary shall be designated as the school's primary contact person to outside persons and agencies. Board meetings of public choice schools must be held in accordance with the state open-meeting law. The board of directors shall develop a set of bylaws and institutional policies that are clearly communicated to parents, students, staff members, and to [the sponsoring agency or state board of education].

(Because charter schools and other forms of public school choice are public entities fully funded by tax dollars, their governing boards, like other political subdivisions of the state, should be required to comply with the state's open-meeting law. For reasons discussed by Robert M. O'Neil in this volume, private schools do not change their character by participating in a publicly funded school choice program. Thus unless the legislature specifies to the contrary, they would be exempt from this requirement.)

The Resolution of Disputes

In the seminal *Goldberg* v. *Kelly* decision, the U.S. Supreme Court set forth the principle that before important government benefits can be taken away, due process must be provided.[17] Education is an important benefit;

indeed, under the compulsory school law, it is considered a Fourteenth Amendment property right at public schools. Consequently, students are entitled to due process procedures before they can be suspended or expelled.[18] Even though being denied the opportunity to have one's child attend a school does not deprive the parent or child of a recognized constitutional right in the same way expulsion from the school does, it is nevertheless a significant deprivation. A parent should be given the opportunity to challenge a choice school's decision not to enroll the parent's child as legally impermissible because allegedly predicated upon, for example, the student's ethnicity or gender, before having to resort to formal action through civil rights agencies or the courts. A parent also should be able to present a grievance to the choice school concerning the education of the child. At the same time, channeling and resolving disputes should not be overly burdensome. The following grievance procedure satisfies these concerns.

A. The board of directors ("board") of a choice school shall establish a grievance procedure under which the board shall address grievances it receives from a parent concerning the alleged illegal denial of admission of the parent's child to the school or, if the child is in attendance at the school, concerning the education of the child at the school or the suspension or dismissal of the child from the school.

B. The decision of the board under section A shall be final and nonappealable unless the parent or student files an exception to the decision with the board as constituting a denial of any right of the parent or child under the United States Constitution or federal laws. If the board does not act on the exception within thirty days or overrules the exception, the parent may appeal the board's decision to the state department of education. An adverse decision by the state department of education may be appealed by either party into state district court. This section does not deprive a parent of any legal remedy.

(Compliance with federal constitutional law is required only at public choice schools. Though private schools participating in a publicly funded choice system probably would not be governed by federal constitutional law, they would continue to be subject to various provisions of federal civil rights legislation. See the chapter by O'Neil, this volume, for a full discussion.)

The three accountability measures discussed here—information preparation, governance, and dispute resolution—do not preclude several other forms of accountability that serve parent interests. Fiscal accountability, important to both parents and the state, is addressed in the next section.

Routinely, states require all public and private schools to comply with health and safety laws. More recently, criminal history checks have been required of public school employees. There appears to be no good reason why schools participating in a publicly funded choice system should not be subject to this requirement, just as they are to health and safety codes.

Accountability to the State

This section addresses the several areas in which choice schools need to be accountable to the state.

Constitutional Considerations

Accompanying the advent of compulsory education laws and the rapid expansion of public schools in the early twentieth century were state constitutional provisions imposing on the legislature the obligation to ensure that all students regardless of residence have access to a uniform system of free public schools. To strengthen the government's role in education and to prevent public dollars from flowing to private religious schools, a number of constitutions were amended to restrict public funding to public schools only. Some protect the authority of the local school board. For example, the Colorado Constitution has a provision stipulating that directors of local boards of education "shall have control of instruction in the public schools of their respective districts."[19] While the Colorado Charter Schools Act gives lip service to the instructional authority of local boards, it also establishes that charter schools are to "encourage diverse approaches to learning and education and the use of different, proven, or innovative teaching methods."[20] Whether the nod in the direction of recognizing the authority of the local school board will suffice under existing Colorado constitutional law is open to question. One commentator concludes that "so long as the local board of education, under the terms of the contract itself, is able to maintain control of instruction in the charter school *at all times*, article IX, section 15 [of the Colorado Constitution] would seem to remain inviolate."[21] Of course, this interpretation would subvert the very purpose of charter schools.

Constitutional provisions like these may frustrate legislative efforts to create a more autonomous, market-driven educational system. Even if future litigation does not bear this out, fear of litigation may be enough to prompt legislators to add undesirable accountability measures to choice programs. While this is less a concern for such traditional forms of school choice as magnet schools and open enrollment, it does pose a threat to the autonomy of charter and voucher schools. Here, we explore the possible implications of state constitutional provisions for both.

PUBLIC SCHOOLS ONLY. Michigan has a state constitutional provision requiring the legislature to establish a public school system and prohibiting it from funding private schools.[22] In 1997 the Michigan Supreme Court became the first court in the nation to uphold a charter school law, rejecting a constitutional challenge and overruling two lower court decisions.[23] At issue, as the court saw it, was whether the charter schools, known in Michigan as public school academies, are sufficiently under the control of the state to be considered public schools.

The Michigan charter school statute allows persons and entities, including private organizations, to operate public school academies on a nonprofit basis.[24] Religious organizations are excluded. The statute specifies the content of the charter application and provides that those granted charters are subject to state and federal law applicable to public school districts. Academies may be authorized by Michigan school boards, community colleges, and state universities. The authorizing body acts as the fiscal agent for the public school academy, monitors compliance with the charter, and has the power to revoke it. If a school district is the authorizing agent, the district's collective bargaining contract applies to the academy's employees. The plaintiffs contended that the scheme violates the state constitution because the public school academies are not controlled by the state and because boards of directors are not publicly elected.

The supreme court found no requirement in the state constitution that the state have exclusive control of the school system or that a board of directors be elected. The court found it sufficient that a public body retain oversight through the charter-granting and monitoring process. For example, the state board of education already had exercised its authority by refusing to approve funding for the Noah Webster Academy because, as a home study school, it did not meet the terms of the statute. Moreover, the justices noted that, after the lower court rulings, the legislature amended the charter school law to require that all academy teachers be state certified and to clarify that the academies are subject to the rule-making authority of the State Board of Education, thus significantly limiting the freedom of the charter schools. Note how legislative concern about complying with the state constitution produced these two measures. Whether either can be justified in terms of improving academy effectiveness is irrelevant. The amendments exist to satisfy constitutional requirements. As dissenting Justice Patricia

Boyle noted, "freedom from regulation is precisely that element of the charter school concept that brings it into potential conflict with the constitution."[25]

Massachusetts has a constitutional provision prohibiting the use of public money for a school "which is not publicly owned and under the exclusive control, order and supervision of public officers or public agents authorized by the commonwealth or federal authority or both."[26] A number of states have similar provisions.[27] The Massachusetts charter school statute allows the state board of education to grant a charter to a board of trustees to create what is called a "commonwealth charter school."[28] The trustees are public agents under the law, and the charter school is deemed a public school. However, there is no statutory restriction on allowing the board of trustees to subcontract with a for-profit corporation to run the school. Thus the for-profit Edison Project is under contract to operate the Seven Hills Charter School in Worcester and the Boston Renaissance Public Charter School, one of the largest charter schools in the nation, with more than 1,200 students. Although there have been no challenges to this practice in Massachusetts, unconstitutional delegation law, discussed later in this chapter, may pose a threat to such creative ways of circumventing restrictive constitutional provisions elsewhere.

THE COMMON SCHOOL REQUIREMENT. Thirteen state constitutions require the establishment of a system of "common schools."[29] The Washington State Constitution, for example, requires the legislature to establish a system of common schools and to dedicate revenue from the common school fund and the state tax for their support.[30] In a 1909 decision, the Washington State Supreme Court defined a common school as "one that is common to all children of proper age and capacity, free, and subject to, and under the control of, the qualified voters of the school district."[31] One commentator concludes that because charter schools are not "under the control" of the local community, the Washington State Constitution would have to be amended to accommodate them.[32]

The absence of applicable case law precludes knowing whether a common school provision constitutes a restraint on the legislature to allow choice schools to be different. The Oregon Supreme Court noted in a school finance decision that the common school provision in the Oregon Constitution does not require uniformity in physical facilities or programs but rather a minimum of educational opportunities in all districts.[33] By contrast, the California Supreme Court has construed the California Constitution's common school provision to mean that "the educational system must be uniform in terms of the prescribed course of study and educational progression from grade to grade."[34] The implications of this statement for charter schools is unknown, however, because so far there has been no litigation on the issue.

The common school provision is most likely to pose problems for choice school autonomy when used in combination with other restrictive provisions. For example, the Idaho Constitution requires the legislature "to establish and maintain a general, uniform and thorough system of public, free common schools."[35] The combination of the terms *general, uniform, thorough, public,* and *common* could result in legislative limitations on the autonomy of choice schools if the matter comes before the Idaho legislature or courts.

PUBLIC FUNDS FOR PUBLIC PURPOSES. Most states have a constitutional provision that public monies must be spent for a public purpose. Typical is Kentucky's constitutional provision section 171 stipulating that "taxes shall be levied and collected for public purposes only." Courts routinely defer to legislative judgment on what the public purpose is. As the Nebraska Supreme Court noted in a decision upholding a state scholarship program for students attending sectarian private colleges, "to justify a court in declaring a statute invalid because its subject is not a public purpose, the absence of public purpose must be so clear and palpable as to be immediately perceptive to the reasonable mind."[36]

In the school choice context, the Wisconsin Supreme Court ruled in 1992 that the original Milwaukee private school voucher program, which provided vouchers to low-income families to enroll their children in nonsectarian private schools, served the judicially developed public purpose doctrine.[37] The court ruled similarly in 1998 after the program was expanded to encompass sectarian private schools.[38] In both decisions, the majority noted sufficient government oversight to ensure that the schools attain the public purpose of improving educational quality. While there are few statutory requirements placed upon participating private schools beyond those required of Wisconsin private schools in general, regulations originally developed by the state superintendent of public instruction were more encompassing. One provision stood out. It required that private schools, like public schools, observe "all federal and state guarantees protecting the rights and liberties of individuals including freedom of religion, expression, association, unreasonable search and seizure, equal protection, and due process."[39] Regardless of its merit, this requirement alone fundamentally alters the relationship between a private school and its patrons and employees. Normally a matter of contract law, the relationship between a private school and both its students and teachers under this regulation becomes to some extent a matter of constitutional law. For example, to terminate a teacher or expel a student, a private school would have to follow the same due process procedures as a public school. By treating private schools as political subdivisions of the state, the measure constituted a significant intrusion on institutional autonomy.

Closely related to the public purpose requirement is the nondelegation of legislative authority doctrine, which restricts the ability of a legislature to turn its responsibilities over to public or private entities. A case in point is a 1976 Rhode Island Supreme Court decision striking down a statute requiring public school districts to bus children residing within their boundaries to private schools.[40] The court found the statute an unconstitutional delegation of legislative authority to private entities because it did not limit the ability of a private school to pass its transportation costs on to public school districts. In effect, the statute allowed private schools to determine not only which townships had to provide busing but also how far students were to be bused. For delegation to be valid, the court set forth two conditions. First, the public policy of the legislation has to be clearly specified. Second, there must be sufficient regulation to prevent private actors from exercising power in their own self-interest. Thereafter, the legislature corrected the problem by establishing the geographic parameters within which transportation services to private schools could be provided. Three years later, the court found the changes acceptable.[41] In the context of school choice, the nondelegation doctrine may restrict a legislature from turning over to private entities its constitutional responsibility to provide public schooling altogether or unless accompanied by sufficient accountablity measures. Much will depend upon the wording of constitutional schooling provisions and upon judicial perspective.

THE UNIFORMITY REQUIREMENT. How much regulation must there be for a choice program to satisfy a constitutional provision requiring a general and uniform system of education? There are fifteen states with such a constitutional provision.[42] To date, the Wisconsin Supreme Court is the only state supreme court to have considered the matter in the context of school choice; once again, it deferred to the judgment of the state legislature. The applicable provision of the Wisconsin Constitution states that "the legislature shall provide by law for the establishment of district schools, which shall be as nearly uniform as practicable."[43] Because the private schools participating in the Milwaukee voucher program are not part of the public school system, yet children participating in the program can always return to the public schools, the court determined that the program met this requirement. Further, the court noted in its 1998 decision that the uniformity provision "provides not a ceiling but a floor upon which the legislature can build additional opportunities for school children in Wisconsin."[44]

On the other hand, the Ohio pilot scholarship program enabling public school students in Cleveland to attend sectarian and nonsectarian private schools fared less well before the state appellate court. In addition to violating the First Amendment Establishment Clause, the program violated a provision of the Ohio Constitution providing that "all laws, of a general nature, shall have a uniform operation throughout the State."[45] Since the program was limited to the city of Cleveland, it could not be considered a uniform school law. The Ohio Supreme Court came to the same conclusion in striking down the voucher program on state constitutional grounds in 1999. However, the Ohio high court noted that the legislature corrected the problem after the appellate court ruling by extending eligibility to any school district in the state that might in the future be under federal court order requiring takeover by the state superintendent. As amended, the voucher program did not violate the uniformity clause.[46]

Uniformity provisions have been involved in school finance litigation. Supreme courts in thirteen states have found the school financing system in their states unconstitutional because substantial interdistrict disparities undermine a uniform system of education.[47] However, several high courts have rejected equality of school finance claims, construing their state constitution's uniformity clause to mean, in the words of the Supreme Court of Idaho, "uniformity in curriculum, not uniformity in funding."[48] If construed strictly (as noted with regard to California), uniformity in curriculum poses as great a threat to choice school diversity as does uniformity in funding and student selection.

In sum, state constitutional provisions pose a potential threat to the autonomy of choice schools because they prod litigation-wary legislators to enact accountability measures in the hopes of staving off lawsuits. While legislatures may attempt to finesse these provisions, state courts will make the final determination. The fact that judges are elected in thirty-eight states bodes well for school choice proponents because elected state jurists may be more attuned to public policy shifts and voter sentiment than their federal counterparts—and thus more willing to interpret constitutional provisions flexibly.[49] Wisconsin Supreme Court Judge Louis Ceci's campaign-like rhetoric in concurring to uphold the original Milwaukee parental choice program affords an illustration:

> Let's give choice a chance. . . . The Wisconsin legislature, attuned and
> attentive to the appalling and seemingly insurmountable problems

confronting socioeconomically deprived children, has attempted to throw a life preserver to those Milwaukee children caught in the cruel riptide of a school system floundering upon the shoals of poverty, status-quo thinking, and despair. . . . Let's give choice a chance.[50]

Monitoring Finances and Attendance

In most states, constitutional or statutory provisions require that the state monitor expenditure of public funds.[51] Early abuses in school choice programs have demonstrated the need to do so. For example, in the first year of the Milwaukee parental choice program, an elementary school withdrew from the program and went bankrupt.[52] In 1995–96, three additional choice schools ran into financial trouble and eventually closed. The director of one of the schools was found guilty of falsifying attendance and employment records to receive an overpayment of $42,000.[53] Since only seventeen schools were participating in the program at the time, this is a relatively high failure rate. These events prompted Polly Williams, author of the Milwaukee choice program, to call for increased financial monitoring.[54] During the first year of the Texas open-enrollment charter school program, one of the schools was given more than $240,000, though it never opened and enrolled no students.[55] In Ohio, audit figures show that the Cleveland voucher program may have misspent $1.9 million in 1997, some $1.5 million of which was used for transporting students to their private schools by taxi because the Cleveland school district did not have sufficient buses and drivers to transport the students.[56]

It is of course in the best interest of choice school operators to avoid scandals that tarnish the choice movement and invite skeptical legislators and state education officials to impose regulations. While the comment is often heard that fiscal problems and outright failures are to be anticipated given the high rate of failure of new businesses in the corporate sector, neither the public nor state officials are likely to tolerate a high rate of school closings. Certainly the state, in combination with professional associations, can help reduce the failure rate by providing business management training for school choice operators. Training, together with due diligence by the state in ascertaining the financial acumen of choice school applicants, independent fiscal monitoring, and annual audits, along with appropriate sanctions, will go a long way to avoid inconvenience to parents and students and to assure taxpayers that state funds are being well spent. For much the same reason, the state has an obligation to monitor student enrollment and to require that schools be in session a minimum number of days.

Sophisticated computer information systems enable the state to undertake such tasks without an intrusive on-site presence.

Diversity in Enrollment

Liberal democracies always have viewed education as the primary mechanism through which the state could reduce inequalities caused by family circumstances.[57] Unless the state addresses the manner in which its school system separates students based on race and class, it is rejecting the basic human equality of those whom such segregation has placed at a disadvantage: African Americans, Hispanics, Native Americans, and the poor. This point was repeatedly made by the Connecticut Supreme Court in its landmark 1996 *Sheff* v. *O'Neill* decision: the court held that the state constitution requires the state, as an affirmative duty, to end racial and ethnic isolation in the Hartford school system, whether caused by the state or not.[58]

The history of school desegregation demonstrates the evils of a de jure racially segregated system. But even a de facto segregated system denies students the opportunity to interact with others different from themselves, a situation that may hamper cognitive learning, since the amount a student learns depends in large part on the background characteristics of the student and the student's classmates.[59] By promoting homogeneous student bodies, de facto segregation hinders the state's ability to promote the civic value of tolerance for individual differences across race and class. Even if there is some benefit to a self-segregated system—for example, fostering cultural identity—the political weakness that accompanies ethnic isolation may lead to discrimination in the provision of resources over time and thus contribute to inferior education.[60] For these reasons, the state's educational policy should foster school integration across race and class.

One-third of American public school students are persons of color, and like public schools, most school choice programs serve sizable minority populations. Table 6-1 displays the racial and ethnic composition in recent years of traditional public and private schools and charter schools in several states. Except in California, charter schools and the Milwaukee voucher program serve a larger proportion of minority students than traditional private schools and public schools in nonurban areas.

The fact that the overall student population of the American public school system is one-third minority does not mean that white and minority students attend school together. In fact, the opposite is true. Two-thirds of all African American and almost three-quarters of all Hispanic public school students attend predominately minority schools as a result of hous-

Table 6-1. *Student Enrollment by Race and Ethnicity*
Percent

School or program	Whites	African American	Hispanic	Other
U.S. public schools[a]	65	17	14	4
Central city public schools[b]	15	47	32	6
U.S. private schools	78	9	8	5
Charter schools in ten-state study[c]	52	14	25	10
Public schools in California	42	9	37	13
Charter schools in California	48	12	32	9
Public schools in Texas	46	14	37	3
Charter schools in Texas[d]	24	29	45	2
Public schools in Minnesota	84	7	2	9
Charter schools in Minnesota[e]	55	25	2	18
Milwaukee public school system	29	55	10	6
Milwaukee voucher program[f]	5	73	21	1

Sources: National Center for Education Statistics, *Digest of Education Statistics, 1997* (U.S. Department of Education, 1997); *Deepening Segregation in American Public Schools* (Harvard Project on School Desegregation, 1997), table 9; National Center for Education Statistics, *Private School Universe Survey, 1993–1994* (U.S. Department of Education, 1996); Office of Research and Improvement, *A Study of Charter Schools: First-Year Report* (U.S. Department of Education, 1997); *Texas Open-Enrollment Charter Schools: Second-Year Evaluation* (Texas Education Agency, 1998); Center for Applied Research and Educational Improvement, *Minnesota Charter Schools Interim Evaluation Report* (University of Minnesota, 1996); John Witte, *Fifth-Year Report: Milwaukee Parental Choice Program* (University of Wisconsin—Madison, Data and Library Services, 1995).

a. Data are for fall 1995.

b. Data are for the ten largest central city districts, 1994–95.

c. These data show the racial composition of the aggregate charter school student bodies in the ten states operating charter schools in 1995–96. More recent data show little change, even though the number of states with charter schools has grown significantly. For example, 1997–98 data show the white, African American, and Hispanic percentages for charter schools in twenty-four states to be 52, 19, and 21, respectively. The earlier data are used here and in table 6-2 because the reporting format and time frame are compatible with other data in these tables.

d. Conducted by a consortium of researchers, this study encompassed nineteen charter schools during their second year of operation in 1997–98.

e. Data show racial composition of students attending sixteen charter schools in ten communities in comparison with their host public school districts for spring 1996. Native Americans account for 10 percent of the 18 percent in the charter school "other" category. Minnesota has operated charter schools since 1991, the longest of any state.

f. Data show racial composition of students in the twelve nonsectarian private schools participating in the voucher program during 1990–94, in comparison with the racial composition of a control group of students enrolled in the Milwaukee public school system in 1991, when the voucher program began.

ing patterns, school district boundaries, and individual school attendance zones.[61] More than a third of these students are in public schools in which more than 90 percent of students are from minority groups. Having many small school districts in a metropolitan area intensifies racial and ethnic segregation. In Illinois, Michigan, New York, and New Jersey, a majority of African American students attend schools in which more than 90 percent of students are from minority ethnic groups. Income and racial segregation are highly related. A student in an intensely segregated minority school is sixteen times as likely to be in a high-poverty school as a student in a school with less than 10 percent African American or Hispanic students. Furthermore, the trend toward racial and economic isolation is increasing, especially among Hispanic students, prompting one researcher

Table 6-2. *Minority Students in Public Schools
and in Selected School Choice Programs*[a]
Percent

School or program	0–20% (mostly whites; few minorities)	> 80–100% (mostly minorities; few whites)	Total, ethnically distinctive schools
U.S. public schools	61	9	70
Charter schools in ten-state study	44	21	65
Public schools in California	17	23	40
Charter schools in California	37	17	54
Public schools in Texas	22	27	49
Charter schools in Texas	5	58	63
Public schools in Minnesota	83	2	85
Charter schools in Minnesota	50	31	81
Public schools in Wisconsin	83	3	86
Milwaukee voucher program	0	42	42

Source: See table 6-1.
a. For Milwaukee, five of the twelve schools participating in the original voucher program were more than 80 percent minority. Four were substantially minority. Data are not available for three of the schools.

to remark that "the bridge from the twentieth century may be heading back into the nineteenth century."[62]

Table 6-2 shows the concentration of minority students in public schools and charter schools during the mid-1990s. More than three of every five public schools were predominately white, while nearly one of every ten was predominately minority. In Minnesota and Wisconsin, public schools were even more predominately white. A higher percentage of charter schools than public schools was predominately minority, and a lower percentage was predominately white, except in California, where the reverse was true. During the second year of charter school operation in Texas, nearly two-thirds of the charter schools served predominately minority students. Four schools enrolled more than three-quarters of all white students; none of the four had an explicit mission to serve former dropouts or students otherwise at risk of school failure. In Minnesota half of the charter schools were more than 80 percent white, while nearly one-third were more than 80 percent minority. In Milwaukee, almost half of the twelve nonsectarian private schools participating in the original voucher program were nearly all one race, with another four serving a high concentration of minority students.

The percentage of schools with either high concentrations of white students or high concentrations of minority students reveals significant ethnic isolation in both traditional public schools and choice schools. Racial and economic distinctiveness in choice schools is attributable to three major factors: the location of the school, its mission and curriculum, and communication networks.

SCHOOL LOCATION. Most charter schools serve an intradistrict school population. Consequently, like any intradistrict choice program, their service area is limited to the school district's boundaries, and they potentially can be only as racially and economically integrated as the district. At present, many of these schools are located in urban areas and serve students who are at risk of dropping out of school. Since most of these students are low income and minority, it is not surprising that the student bodies are racially and economically distinctive, sometimes more so than the public school district within which they are located. Conversely, charter schools located in suburban districts are likely to be largely white. This pattern is apparent in Arizona, where a permissive legal climate has fostered the rapid growth of charter schools. In 1998, Arizona had more charter schools than any other state. A recent study compared the racial and ethnic composition of individual Arizona charter schools with that of regular public schools in the same neighborhoods or attendance zones, rather than with all public schools in the state. The study shows extensive racial clustering, with charter schools typically twenty percentage points higher in white enrollment than regular public schools serving the same area. Charters with a majority of ethnic minority students tended to be either vocational education secondary schools or alternative schools for students expelled from traditional public schools.[63]

Unrestricted interdistrict choice programs are not likely to break down racial and economic barriers now any more than during the white flight days of the 1960s. Experience with open enrollment in Omaha and Des Moines has shown significant underrepresentation of African Americans among students applying to leave districts with desegregation plans.[64] The result is disparities in educational services between separate white school districts and progressively poorer inner-city districts. Open-enrollment programs across districts are unlikely to reduce existing inequalities of opportunity in education to any great extent. While facilitating white departure from inner-city schools, such programs do not alter the desire of many suburban parents to avoid having their children educated with inner-city minority students. These attitudes discourage the out-transfer of minority children.

As for imposing racial balance restraints on such transfers, outside the context of de jure segregation and court-approved school desegregation plans, there is increasing doubt that judges will uphold controlled-choice plans that seek to maintain integrated schools through the use of racial quotas. In the first case of its type, an Ohio federal district court in 1996 struck down a policy developed by the Akron city school district that prohibited white students from transferring out of the school district and taking their state funds with them under the state's newly enacted open-enrollment statute.[65] The school district also had prohibited minority students from transferring into the district. The court found no compelling purpose for the policy in a district that had not engaged in discrimination in the past.

MISSION AND CURRICULUM. Quite naturally, the mission and curriculum of a school may contribute to racial and economic distinctiveness. For example, the Dakota Open Charter School in Minnesota, which has since closed, offered a program geared to the Dakota culture and attracted a Native American student body. In Milwaukee, the mostly one-race Urban Day School and Woodlands School feature an Afrocentrist curriculum, while the Bruce-Guadalupe School caters to Hispanic students. In Texas, the North Hills Charter School, located in North Dallas, offers the challenging international baccalaureate curriculum that attracts few non-Asian minority students.

COMMUNICATION NETWORKS. Studies of school choice programs reveal that communication by word of mouth through family and friends is an important source of information for parents about school choice programs. Word-of-mouth communication networks tend to be homogeneous with respect to race and class.[66] First-come, first-served selection polices also contribute to ethnic distinctiveness. According to the U.S. Department of Education's ten-state charter school study, 74 percent of the surveyed charter schools reported that applications for admission exceeded capacity.[67] Of the schools with excess demand, 41 percent reported using a first-come, first-served admissions policy; another 10 percent reported using a combination of lottery and first come, first served. Unlike a lottery system, first-come, first-served admissions policies tend to accommodate those with greater access to information—persons who in many cases are more likely to be economically better off and white.

Racial distinctiveness in choice schools provides renewed opportunities for legal challenges. These challenges are most likely to be successful in the context of prior de jure discrimination, in which school choice does not have a happy history. In the seminal 1968 *Green* v. *County Board of New Kent County* decision, the U.S. Supreme Court refused to accept freedom of choice as a school desegregation remedy because it did not reduce racial distinctiveness.[68] For school choice to be acceptable in the context of school districts and states under school desegregation court orders, the sponsors bear a heavy burden. Consider Texas's open-enrollment charter school program, which was developed to create new school districts in the form of charter schools serving an interdistrict student population. Most of the state remains under a 1971 school desegregation court order.[69] The legislation provides that the charter submitted to the state board of education for approval must "describe the geographical area served by the program."[70] Charter school applicants generally opt to serve racially concentrated areas, and the state board has not objected. A comparison among the open-enrollment Texas charter schools operating in 1996–97 and the school districts each charter identified as within its service area shows that the majority of the charter schools are more racially distinctive than the districts. If a charter school's geographic service area designation results in the school's fencing out particular ethnic groups because they do not live in the designated service area, the school may be faced with a discrimination challenge under the court order.

Even in the absence of a history of discrimination, a desegregation challenge in federal court likely will be successful if plaintiffs can show an intent to discriminate or if it can be shown that school choice has a disparate impact on minority groups without adequate justification.[71] Both claims were argued in a lawsuit against the Pueblo, Colorado, school district. Plaintiffs claimed that the closing of the elementary schools that their children attended and the opening of an arts and sciences charter school had a racially disparate impact and was racially motivated. In support of the claim, they noted that the closed schools were 75 percent Hispanic, compared with 50 percent for the charter school in its first year of operation. The plaintiffs also argued that students in the closed schools were bused to other predominately minority schools, which were overcrowded. The U.S. Court of Appeals for the Tenth Circuit rejected the lawsuit in 1996, noting that the plaintiffs were unable to show either an intent to discriminate or sufficient disparate impact on a minority group.[72] The court found that the board was motivated to improve the education of at-risk students by opening the innovative charter school and observed that the charter school had the same ethnic makeup as the district as a whole. However, the judges expressed concern about a provision in the Colorado Charter Schools Act defining at-risk students as those "who, because of physical, emotional, socioeconomic, or cultural factors, [are] less likely to succeed in a conventional educational environment." Said the court, "We share the Parent's concern with the practice of drawing classifications based on 'culture,' which might in some circumstances be used as a proxy for ethnicity, race, national origin or some other suspect classification."[73]

The best way for the state to avoid litigation is to afford low-income and minority parents a meaningful opportunity to participate in school choice programs. To promote enrollment diversity, the state must do more than set forth a general nondiscrimination provision that lacks sufficient sanctions and incentives to discourage white or minority flight. On the other hand, the state cannot establish racial quotas outside the context of a court-approved desegregation plan. Nor should it unduly restrain choice schools from selecting their students based on programmatic considerations. The Massachusetts charter school law goes too far when it includes academic achievement as among the impermissible bases for selection because it curtails the ability of the school to tailor its program to a segment of the school population.[74] Academic achievement may be an important consideration for a choice school specializing in the education of at-risk students or offering a rigorous math and science curriculum to high-achieving students.

Two statutory approaches to promote enrollment diversity for choice schools are set forth below. The first, based on the North Carolina charter school law, often is found in charter school legislation.[75] While a step in the right direction, this approach has serious weaknesses. The second combines sanctions and incentives to achieve enrollment diversity. For both approaches, a lottery provision is included to minimize the discriminatory effects of a first-come, first-served admissions policy.

Option 1. A choice school shall be subject to all federal and state laws and constitutional provisions prohibiting discrimination on the basis of race, religion, color, gender, national origin, ancestry, marital status, or need for special education services. Within one year of operation, a choice school must have a student population that reasonably reflects the racial and ethnic composition of the general population residing within the local school administrative unit in which the school is located or the racial and ethnic composition of the special population that the school seeks to serve residing within the local school administrative unit in which the school is located. Each choice school shall establish a uniform admissions date before each semester and, if oversubscribed, shall admit eligible new students by lottery.

Option 2. A choice school shall be subject to all federal and state laws and constitutional provisions prohibiting discrimination on the basis of race, religion, color, gender, national origin, ancestry, marital status, or need for special education services. To continue to receive state funding, a choice school must within three years of its first year of operation enroll a mini-

mum of 20 percent of its student body from families who qualify for federally assisted school lunches. A school that maintains its complement for
a minimum of two years is eligible for a one-year grace period if its enrollment of students whose families qualify for federally assisted school lunches
drops below 15 percent. Each choice school shall establish a uniform admissions date before each semester and, if oversubscribed, shall admit eligible
new students by lottery. The lottery for the 20 percent enrollment set-aside
shall be conducted separately from the lottery for the remainder of the student body.

The first option forces choice schools to broaden their recruitment and
admissions efforts to achieve a racially balanced enrollment in order to avoid
a showing of disparate impact against a minority group, which in itself is
a good thing. However, it does not further integration beyond the boundaries of a specific school district. Thus a thematic or charter school established in a suburban upper-income white school district at best would not
look any different from the school district. Furthermore, while maintaining ethnic balance reflective of the community is certainly important from
both pedagogical and public policy perspectives, it remains uncertain
whether doing so remains sufficiently compelling from a legal perspective
to survive judicial challenge.[76] During the height of U.S. Supreme Court
support for school integration, Chief Justice Warren E. Burger acknowledged that

> school authorities are traditionally charged with broad power to for-
> mulate and implement educational policy and might conclude, for
> example, that in order to prepare students to live in a pluralistic soci-
> ety each school should have a prescribed ratio of Negro to white stu-
> dents reflecting the proportion for the district as a whole. To do this
> as an educational policy is within the broad discretionary powers of
> school authorities.[77]

But more recent developments have cast doubt on the constitutionality
of doing so. For example, in *Adarand Constructors, Inc.* v. *Peña*, a 1995
employment case, the justices backed away from deferring to so-called
benign racial classifications designed to remedy racial imbalance. Instead,
the Court held that "all governmental action based on race . . . should be
subjected to detailed judicial inquiry to ensure that the personal right to
equal protection of the laws has not been infringed."[78]

Assume that a charter school for language-gifted students is located in
a 40 percent non-white district with no history of racial discrimination.

According to option 1, by the end of the first year of operation, the school must reasonably reflect the racial and ethnic makeup of the district. To achieve this, the school's operators reasonably could decide to enroll only minority students after 70 percent of the spaces are taken by whites. In 1996 a federal district court struck down just such a racial balance plan for magnet schools within the Alexandria, Virginia, county school system. The purpose of the plan was to ensure a diverse student body reflective of the overall school system. The court noted that racial balance plans are inherently suspect under the Fourteenth Amendment and that, in the absence of a history of discrimination, they do not serve a compelling purpose. Wrote the judge,

> Although the advantages of composing a student body whose racial makeup mirrors that of the community at large may be real, more is needed than the facile talisman of 'diversity' to justify infringing the constitutional right not to be discriminated against on the basis of race.[79]

In 1998 the U.S. Court of Appeals for the First Circuit reached the same conclusion with regard to a race-conscious admissions policy at the elite public Boston Latin School. Applying the strict scrutiny test from the Supreme Court's decision in *Adarand Constructors, Inc.* v. *Peña*, the appellate court in a two-to-one decision concluded that the admissions policy "is, at bottom, a mechanism for racial balancing—and placing our imprimatur on racial balancing risks setting a precedent that is both dangerous to our democratic ideals and almost always constitutionally forbidden."[80]

Option 2 is similar to the John Coons and Stephen Sugarman proposal to reserve 20 percent of new admissions for applicants from low-income families in choice schools regardless of the school's location and irrespective of a history of racial discrimination.[81] It is different in that Coons and Sugarman do not require schools to seek out students to fill the 20 percent set-aside. If too few students show up to constitute the 20 percent, Coons and Sugarman require the school to admit those students but do not insist that the school find additional students. Under option 2, the school must employ sufficient recruitment strategies to meet the enrollment set-aside. Failure to do so results in the school's ineligibility to receive public funding. This is the sanction that option 2 carries.

Socioeconomic status is not a suspect class under the Fourteenth Amendment; therefore it does not have the same constitutional infirmities facing option 1.[82] Yet because socioeconomic status and race often overlap, option

2 will most likely promote school integration. Admittedly, it constitutes a one-way ratchet, in that urban choice schools by their nature will satisfy the set-aside. This will result in student bodies in some schools that are homogeneous across race and class, thus depriving students of role models conducive to improved learning and socialization. It also may lead to diminished resources made available to minority schools. However, given past state-supported fencing out of minorities and the poor from improved schooling opportunities, the better public policy is to allow it until its outcomes become clearer. Thus low-income groups should be able to start their own schools, provided that state and federal antidiscrimination laws are observed.[83]

If private schools are included in the choice program, the option 2 set-aside provides a large economic incentive for many parents whose children currently attend private schools and for parents who want to send their children to private schools but cannot afford to do so. Many of the latter group will be able to afford the cost of private education if the private school of their choice recruits its complement of low-income children, since all families then will become eligible for a voucher.[84] More advantaged parents will pressure private schools to recruit less-advantaged students. This pressure should increase the efforts of private schools to inform less-advantaged families of the benefits of attending their school, and it will encourage schools to provide transportation and other benefits to low-income families. The result should be greater integration of private schools by class and race. In a recent survey, roughly three-quarters of parents and nonparents alike agreed that private schools participating in a state voucher program should be required to set aside a certain percentage of new spaces every year for low-income students.[85] Among inner-city respondents, more than 85 percent thought so. It is important to point out that no private school should be forced to participate in a choice program. If the school and its patrons are not interested in vouchers and have no desire to meet the set-aside, they continue to operate independently of the voucher program.

Whichever option is used, it must be enforced to be effective. Political realities may militate against doing so. In North Carolina in 1998 one-third of the state's sixty charter schools violated the ethnic diversity provision reflected in option 1 by enrolling a disproportionate percentage of black students. Teachers' unions and some legislators called for their closure, but Republican legislators were opposed.[86] According to a 1998 California study, the racial and ethnic distinctiveness of that state's charter schools is attributable to the state's failure to enforce the requirement that charter schools reflect the racial and ethnic makeup of their districts.[87] In short, failure to follow through with good intentions will worsen race and class segregation of American schools.

The Promotion of Toleration

A central purpose of public schools is the inculcation of fundamental values necessary to the maintenance of a democratic political system. One of the most important is toleration. The sine qua non of democratic liberalism is that individuals tolerate other points of view, even when they do not agree with them. While commentators differ on the extent to which the state should control the curriculum of choice schools (I believe that the state should not specify the curriculum at all and, accordingly, there are no accountability measures addressing curriculum in this chapter), few would oppose having the state prohibit a school from teaching intolerance. The problem is defining intolerance. Certainly the state has an interest in prohibiting violations of the nation's civil rights laws. The state also has an interest in disallowing a school to foment racial hatred or religious strife or to denigrate individuals or groups. However, the state must not be so controlling that it denies choice schools the right to develop their own mission and curriculum. This is particularly true for private schools, which have a right to be free from unreasonable state regulation. The matter is further complicated by the fact that since 1969 students in public schools have a constitutional right to express their views at school as long as their expression does not cause material disruption or substantial interference with the rights of others.[88] Public school teachers in some parts of the country have a right to discuss controversial issues in class, even if school officials do not want them discussed.[89] Thus a restriction on intolerance cannot be so broad that it stifles all unpopular views from being expressed at school.

With these considerations in mind, the accountability requirement should be narrowly tailored to serve the state's interest in promoting a tolerant society without unnecessarily intruding either on the rights of the school to structure its curriculum or on the rights of parents, teachers, and students to free expression. The following accountability provision is designed to serve this end:

> Choice schools, their officers, and employees shall create and maintain a congenial educational environment that is tolerant of individual and group differences. The measures that the school employs to achieve this goal shall be included in the school's informational

brochure and institutional policies. Choice school faculty and staff have an obligation to promote and enhance equality, tolerance, and fairness. Each choice school shall accord parents, students, faculty, and staff the opportunity to utilitize the school's grievance system to seek effective redress for alleged violations of this provision, including, but not limited to, discrimination on the basis of race, color, national origin, ancestry, religion, sex, physical disability, or need for special education services.

The Assessment of Performance

Most new accreditation approaches focus either on state-determined performance standards or on benchmarks of adequate progress.[90] States publicly report district or school test scores along with other outcome measures, such as attendance and dropout rates. The notion is that parents and community members will pressure schools into doing better. A market-based educational system would give parents the oppportunity to find alternatives to poorly performing schools, provided that they have reliable student and school performance data. The problem is that most new accountability systems are flawed. In some states, such as Kentucky, policymakers disagree as to whether the purpose of the system is to improve student achievement or to assess school performance. Disagreement results in the gathering of information that may not be relevant to parents' interests. The design of testing programs often is overly complex. Some tests are designed to assess students or schools using specific criteria of acceptable performance. Others compare student and school performance with a normed group. Few tests are comparable, and the findings are often incomprehensible to the layman.

School choice systems are plagued by these problems too. Until recently, charter schools in Minnesota, the state with the longest-running experience in school choice, used a variety of measures to assess academic achievement and thus could not be compared either with each other or with other public schools. According to the 1996 *Minnesota Charter Schools Evaluation Interim Report*, some schools used norm-referenced tests required by the sponsoring district, some used criterion-referenced tests, and some used multiple measures, including performance assessments and portfolios. The latter are notorious for their subjectivity. A number were just starting the process of documenting student achievement.

While outcomes-based assessment is still in its infancy, this information is essential to meaningful parent participation in a school choice system.

Parents need reliable, comprehensible information about their children's performance, information that can be compared to a set of recognized and accepted national standards.[91] Criterion-referenced tests in such standard areas as math and reading are preferable to norm-referenced tests for this purpose because they assess students against some predetermined standard of performance rather than against the performance of the normed group. Parents also need information about the effectiveness of the school. Is school A as effective as school B in terms of the value added to their child's education? However, unless intervening variables such as the racial and economic composition of the student body are controlled, comparative information may do more harm than good. As one authority points out, "prospective students, both academically advantaged and disadvantaged, could be fooled into abandoning an excellent neighborhood school simply because the school served students that were disproportionately academically disadvantaged."[92] The downside is that a value-added assessment system that controls for intervening variables may be overly complex.

In the discussion above on information preparation and dissemination for parents, a statutory provision is proposed that would require schools to include performance data in their informational brochure. It would be the school's responsibility to describe the overall achievement rates of its students on standardized tests. To make the information meaningful to parents, information should be included showing the performance of students in other schools serving essentially the same clientele. It would be the state's responsibility to designate the standardized tests and to provide comparable school performance data to all schools. It would also be the state's responsibility to identify exemplary and low-performing schools, controlling for student population, and to impose sanctions, including closure, for those schools that cannot or will not improve. A school's performance status could be included as part of a school directory compiled and disseminated by the state education agency. In this way, the state would facilitate the accountability of schools to the consumer and to the general public without undue regulation.

In addition to whatever grading system a school uses, the school must periodically provide parents with individual assessments of their children on standardized tests in such basic areas as reading, writing, mathematics, and science. By giving information to parent consumers in this way and allowing them to choose the schools their children attend, a market-based accountability system would serve the state's interest in securing an educated citizenry.

Accountability and Private Schools

Since more than four-fifths of the nation's private schools are religiously affiliated, would including them in a publicly funded school choice program violate federal and state constitutional law? For a choice program encompassing sectarian private schools to have the best chance of passing muster in states with a supportive state constitutional climate, funding should go to parents and be tailored to the cost of instruction, parents should have a wide choice of public and private schools, the public purpose of the program should be clearly stated, and sufficient accountability measures should be included to demonstrate that the program will achieve its public purpose.[93] The last design feature concerns us in this section.

Even in the absence of state funding, a state can regulate private schools without violating the federal Constitution as long as the regulation is reasonable, a test that is difficult to fail. In upholding the right of private schools to coexist with public schools, Supreme Court Justice James Clark McReynolds wrote in the 1925 *Pierce* v. *Society of Sisters* case,

> No question is raised concerning the power of the State reasonably to regulate all schools, to inspect, supervise and examine them, their teachers and pupils; to require that all children of proper age attend some school, that teachers shall be of good moral character and patriotic disposition, that certain studies plainly essential to good citizenship must be taught, and that nothing be taught which is manifestly inimical to the public welfare.[94]

States have relied on this passage to set standards for private schools encompassing such matters as compliance with health and safety regulations, length of the school year, and enrollment reporting. Less frequently, states have included state certification of teachers and curricular specifications. In 1996 the U.S. Court of Appeals for the Sixth Circuit added state student testing to the list.[95] While there have been challenges to state regulations on the basis of unreasonableness and unconstitutional interference with First Amendment freedoms, especially religious freedom, states generally prevail.[96] For a time in the 1990s, it appeared that enactment of the federal Religious Freedom Restoration Act might restrict the state's ability to regulate sectarian private schools. The law required that whenever a state regulation substantially burdened a person's religion, the government had to show a compelling justification that was the least restrictive way of accomplishing the government's goal. However, the U.S. Supreme Court

declared the law unconstitutional in 1997 in the context of state government action.[97] Thus as long as state regulatory laws are generally applicable and neutral on their face, there is no violation of the First Amendment
Free Exercise Clause.[98]

At first blush, it appears that the case for regulation is strengthened when
taxpayer dollars flow to private schools. People expect that private schools
benefiting from public monies should be accountable in the same way that
traditional public schools are accountable. In a recent national survey, more
than three-quarters of parents and nonparents agree that private schools
participating in a voucher system should be required to hire teachers certified by the state, follow certain curriculum requirements about what courses
to offer and what their contents should be, submit yearly financial statements and undergo public audits, and administer standardized tests to students and publish the results.[99] Despite these expectations, legislators should
resist the imposition of a full complement of regulations on private schools,
for three reasons. First, there is no convincing research showing that regulations such as teacher certification or state curricular control improve student outcomes.[100] In fact, for generations most private schools have
functioned quite well in their absence. Second, intrusive regulations invite
lawsuits over interference with free exercise of religion, intrusion on parental
rights, and unreasonable regulation of private school operation. Third, as
Robert O'Neil discusses later in this book, excessive regulation undermines
the distinctiveness of private schools and, at the extreme, may convert them
to public entities under the U.S. Constitution. In the main, the limited
accountability measures advanced in earlier sections of this chapter should
be sufficient to ensure private school accountability to the public without
excessively intruding on institutional autonomy.

School choice does not alter the status of public schools as political subdivisions of the state. As public entities, these schools must recognize all the
protections of the U.S. Constitution that the federal courts have applied to
public school students and teachers. Subject to some limitations, these protections include the freedoms of speech, religion, and association; the right
to be free from state-supported religious indoctrination; the right to be free
from unreasonable searches and seizure; and the right to due process of law
before expulsion or job loss. Should private schools participating in publicly funded choice programs be required to observe these rights as well?
Recall that the Wisconsin state superintendent of public instruction thought
so and added an accountability provision requiring all private schools participating in the Milwaukee voucher program to recognize students' con-

stitutional rights. There is much to the argument that an educational institution whose mission is to prepare students for living in a democracy ought
to respect individual rights. Students can best learn to tolerate values and
beliefs different from their own in a setting in which free speech flourishes.
The U.S. Supreme Court pointed out in its *Tinker v. Des Moines School
District* ruling in 1969 that, as "persons" under the Constitution, students
"may not be regarded as closed-circuit recipients of only that which the
State chooses to communicate."[101] Free speech is essential for a marketplace of ideas to flourish in school. If there is no marketplace of ideas, then
the school's important role in fostering toleration of differing values and
beliefs is thwarted. The same is true for developing an appreciation of due
process in channeling and resolving disputes. As Harvard Law Professor
Zachariah Chafee said many years ago, "an institution which professes to
prepare youth for life in a democracy might easily give them an example
of fair play when it is conducting its own affairs."[102]

On the other hand, a requirement that private voucher schools recognize all their constituents' constitutional rights represents a significant intrusion into school autonomy and goes a long way to diminish the uniqueness
of the private schooling sector as an alternative to public schools. While
the question is close, perhaps it would not be good public policy to restrict
private schools any further than described in earlier sections of this chapter, as long as parents, students, and employees are fully aware that private
voucher schools do not provide the same panoply of constitutional rights
as public schools (some schools, of course, may find it competitively advantageous to do so).[103] This way, the choice of whether to participate or not
is up to the individual. On the other hand, if privatization of public schooling becomes extensive, the issue should be revisited.

Finally, should the state stipulate that private schools may not charge
more for tuition and fees than the amount of the voucher? As with constitutional rights, such a policy has much to recommend it. If schools can
require add-ons to a state-provided voucher, then lower-income families are
disadvantaged. The drawback of such a system is that it limits institutional
autonomy. A cap on tuition and fees likely will diminish both the variety
and number of schools available to choosing parents. The better public policy is to allow the amount of the voucher to vary inversely with income. A
means-tested voucher in combination with the low-income family set-aside
described earlier will equalize choice opportunities and diversify enrollment
without sacrificing private school autonomy. A 20 percent low-income set-
aside constitutes a powerful incentive to both private schools and their clien-

tele, because all parents become eligible for a tuition voucher if the school achieves the set-aside. Thus participating private schools likely will refrain from imposing add-on fees that make it difficult for low-income families to enroll.

Conclusion

The thrust of this chapter is the development of a choice school accountability system that serves parent and state interests without overly burdening schools. Input and process controls have been limited to those essential for making the market function efficiently and effectively in meeting the needs of parents and the state. Rather than rule accountability, the emphasis has been placed on performance accountability.

Within the parameters of state constitutions, the challenge for state legislatures and administrative agencies is to resist the inclination to regulate. One cannot be optimistic. Legislatures are in the business of legislating, and administrative agencies are in the business of regulating. Over time, there is a real danger that controls will gradually intrude on institutional autonomy. A single, widely reported incident of abuse or malfeasance is likely to set in motion an effort to enact new laws and regulations. It will take a concerted effort by researchers, educators, and public policymakers to see that the potential for school choice to improve American education through innovation and competition is not compromised by unnecessary top-down controls.

Notes

1. Priscilla Wohlstetter and others, "Charter Schools in the United States: A Question of Autonomy," *Education Policy*, vol. 9 (December 1995), p. 345.

2. Eric Hanushek, "Assessing the Effects of School Resources on Student Performance: An Update," *Educational Evaluation and Policy Analysis*, vol. 19 (Summer 1997). Based on his review of nearly 400 studies that update previous summaries, Hanushek concludes that "there is no strong or consistent relationship between school resources and student performance" (p. 148).

3. Center for the Study of Education Reform, "Final Report: San Antonio School Choice Research Project" (University of North Texas, 1997).

4. Kay Thomas, "Who Leaves and Why: An Examination of Attrition from a Public School Choice Program," *ERS Spectrum*, vol. 15 (Spring 1997).

5. Valerie Martinez and others, "Who Chooses and Why: A Look at Five School Choice Plans," *Phi Delta Kappan* (May 1994).

6. Ibid.

7. The *Seattle Times*, for example, publishes a 256-page book that includes statistics on more than 530 public and private schools. The *Philadelphia Inquirer* had sixty-eight people

working on its 1998 school report cards for New Jersey and Pennsylvania. Lynn Olson, "A New Accountability Player: The Local Newspaper," *Education Week*, June 17, 1998.

8. Mark Schneider and others, "Networks to Nowhere: Segregation and Stratification in Networks of Information about Schools," *American Journal of Political Science*, vol. 41 (October 1997).

9. Melissa Marschall, "The Role of Information and Institutions in Stemming the Stratifying Effects of School Choice," paper prepared for the Midwest Political Science Association meeting, April 1996.

10. John Witte and others, "Fifth-Year Report: Milwaukee Parental Choice Program" (University of Wisconsin—Madison, Department of Political Science and the Robert M. LaFollette Institute of Public Affairs, December 1995). (http://dpls.dacc.wisc.edu/choice/choice_rep95txt.html), August 5, 1999.

11. Mark Schneider and others, "Shopping for Schools: In the Land of the Blind, the One-Eyed Parent May Be Enough," *American Journal of Political Science*, vol. 42 (July 1998).

12. See, for example, Office of Research and Improvement, *A Study of Charter Schools: Third-Year Report* (U.S. Department of Education, 1999).

13. Minn. Statutes Ann., § 1240, 10 Subd.4(c) and Subd.21 (West 1999).

14. New Hampshire Revised Statutes Ann., §§ 194-B:3 II(b) and 194-B:13 II (1999); Texas Education Code Ann., § 12.111(8) (West 1999).

15. Hilary Martin, "Best and Worst of Charter Schools," *Rocky Mountain News*, November 23, 1997.

16. Steve Stecklow, "Start-Up Lessons: Arizona Takes the Lead in Charter Schools—For Better or Worse," *Wall Street Journal*, December 24, 1996.

17. *Goldberg* v. *Kelly*, 397 U.S. 254 (1970) (state welfare benefits constitute a property right under the Fourteenth Amendment and cannot be terminated without a due process hearing).

18. *Goss* v. *Lopez*, 419 U.S. 565 (1975).

19. Colo Const, Art IX, § 15. In early decisions, the Colorado Supreme Court appeared to read the provision strictly.

20. Colo. Revised Statutes, § 22-30.5-102(2)(c) (1999).

21. Peter Perla, "The Colorado Charter Schools Act and the Potential for Unconstitutional Applications under Article IX, Section 15 of the State Constitution," *University of Colorado Law Review*, vol. 67 (1996), p. 193. Emphasis in original.

22. Mich Const, Art VIII, § 2. While a number of state constitutions have similar provisions, the Michigan Constitution is unique in specifically prohibiting tuition vouchers. For a detailed discussion, including interpretive law and citations, see Frank Kemerer, "State Constitutions and School Vouchers," *West's Education Law Reporter*, October 2, 1997, pp. 1–42.

23. *Council of Orgs. and Others for Educ. about Parochiaid, Inc.* v. *Governor*, 566 N.W.2d 208 (Mich. 1997).

24. Mich. Comp. Laws Ann., § 380.501 and the following (West 1997).

25. *Council of Orgs.*, 566 N.W.2d at 224.

26. Mass Const, Art XVIII. In two decisions, the Supreme Judicial Court of Massachusetts unanimously advised that channeling money to students to pay for private schooling would violate this provision. *Opinion of the Justices to the House of Representatives*, 259 N.E.2d 564 (Mass. 1970); *Opinion of the Justices to the Senate*, 514 N.E.2d 353 (Mass. 1987).

27. Other state constitutional provisions limiting public funding to public schools include Cal Const, Art IX, § 8; Colo Const, Art V, § 34; Neb Const, Art VII, § 11; NM Const, Art IV, § 31; Wyo Const, Art III, § 36, and Art VII, §§ 4, 7. Alabama and Pennsylvania's similar constitutional provisions can be overridden by a two-thirds vote of the legislature. Ala Const, Art IV, § 73; Pa Const, Art III, § 30. Virginia's constitution allows funding for educational purposes at nonsectarian private schools. Va Const, Art VIII, § 10. Kentucky's constitution allows voters to decide the matter. Ky Const, § 184. In Connecticut, Delaware, Rhode Island,

and Texas, constitutional provisions restricting funding to public schools are limited to certain sources of funding, like the public school fund, thus arguably allowing the use of other public monies for private school funding. For a full discussion, including interpretive law and citations, see Frank R. Kemerer, "State Constitutions and School Vouchers," *West's Education Law Reporter* (October 2, 1997).

28. Mass. Gen. Laws Ann., chap. 71, section 89 (a) (West 1999).

29. See Ariz Const, Art XI, § 6; Calif Const, Art IX, § 5; Idaho Const, Art IX, § 1; Ind Const, Art VIII, § 1; Ky Const, § 183; Miss Const, Art VIII, § 206; Nebr Const, Art VII, § 1; Nev Const, Art XI, § 2; NY Const, Art XI, § 1; Ohio Const, Art VI, § 2; Ore Const, Art VIII, § 3; SDak Const, Art VIII, § 15; Wash Const, Art IX, § 2. In some cases, case law uses the term *common school* in referring to state public schooling constitutional provisions, which themselves do not employ the term. *Wilson v. Stanford*, 66 S.E. 258 (Ga. 1909).

30. Wash Const, Art IX, § 2.

31. *School Dist. No. 20 v. Bryan*, 99 P. 28, 30 (Wash. 1909).

32. L. K. Beale, "Charter Schools, Common Schools, and the Washington State Constitution," *Washington Law Review*, vol. 72 (1997).

33. *Olsen v. State ex rel. Johnson*, 554 P.2d 139, 147–48 (Or. 1979).

34. *Serrano v. Priest*, 487 P.2d 1241, 1249 (Cal. 1971).

35. Idaho Const, Art IX, § 1.

36. *Lenstrom v. Thone*, 311 N.W.2d 884, 888 (Neb. 1981). There are exceptions to general legislative deference. For example, the Kentucky Supreme Court struck down a textbook loan program for students in private schools as not serving a public purpose, contrary to section 171 of the Kentucky Constitution. That provision requires that "taxes shall be levied and collected for public purposes only." The court observed, "Nonpublic schools are open to selected people in the state, as contrasted with public schools which are open to 'all people in the state.'" Unless the question is approved by the voters in a special election as required by the state constitution, such use of tax monies is unconstitutional. *Fannin v. Williams*, 655 S.W.2d 480, 482 (Ky. 1983). The court concluded by observing, "We cannot sell the people of Kentucky a mule and call it a horse, even if we believe the public needs a mule" (p. 484).

37. *Davis v. Grover*, 480 N.W.2d 460 (Wis. 1992).

38. *Jackson v. Benson*, 578 N.W.2d 602 (Wis.), cert. denied, 119 S. Ct. 466 (1998). While the expanded program eliminated annual evaluation reports to the legislature and performance audits conducted by the state superintendent of instruction, the justices noted that sufficient accountability measures still exist to satisfy the public purpose test. These include an annual financial audit conducted by the state superintendent and a performance and financial audit conducted by the Legislative Audit Bureau for reporting to the legislature in the year 2000. Quoting from its earlier *Davis* decision, the Court noted that accountability also is inherent in the choice process: "If the private school does not meet the parents' expectations, the parents may remove the child from the school and go elsewhere." *Jackson*, 578 N.W.2d at 630.

39. Milwaukee Parental Choice Program Notice of School's Intent to Participate (1991). In 1998, after the voucher program was modified by the legislature and upheld by the Wisconsin Supreme Court, the constitutional rights provision was made essentially advisory. (Interview with Charlie Toulmin, Wisconsin Department of Public Instruction, September 27, 1999.)

40. *Jennings v. Exeter-West Greenwich Reg. Sch. Dists. Com.*, 352 A.2d 634 (R.I. 1976).

41. *Jamestown Sch. Comm. v. Schmidt*, 405 A.2d 16 (R.I. 1979).

42. Ariz Const, Art XI, § 1; Colo Const, Art IX, § 2; Fla Const, Art IX, § 1; Idaho Const, Art IX, § 1; Ind Const, Art VIII, § 1; Minn Const, Art XIII, § 1; Nev Const, Art XI, § 2; NMex Const, Art XII, § 1; NC Const, Art IX, § 2; NDak Const, Art VIII, § 2; Ore Const, Art VIII, § 2; SDak Const, Art VIII, § 1; Wash Const, Art IX, § 2; Wis Const, Art X, § 3; Wyo Const, Art VII, § 1.

43. Wis Const, Art X, § 3.

44. *Jackson* v. *Benson*, 578 N.W. 2d 602, 628 (Wis. 1998). The U.S. Supreme Court refused to hear the case in the fall of 1998. 119 S. Ct. 466. Thus vouchers are constitutional in Wisconsin under the ruling of the Wisconsin Supreme Court. The fact that the U.S. Supreme Court did not hear the case conveys no impression one way or the other of the high court's views on the subject.

45. Ohio Const, Art II, § 26.

46. *Simmons-Harris* v. *Goff*, 711 N.E.2d 203 (Ohio 1999). While the Ohio Supreme Court did not find the voucher program to violate either the federal or Ohio constitutions against government aid to religion, it did find that enactment of the legislation violated a state constitutional provision prohibiting bills from containing more than one subject. The legislature subsequently reenacted the program in conformity with the provision.

47. See Comment, "The Limits of Choice: School Choice Reform and State Constitutional Guarantees of Educational Quality," *Harvard Law Review*, vol. 109 (1996).

48. *Idaho Schs. for Equal Educ. Opportunity* v. *Evans*, 850 P.2d 724, 730 (Idaho 1993).

49. Stephen Croley, "The Majoritarian Difficulty: Elective Judiciaries and the Rule of Law," *University of Chicago Law Review*, vol. 62 (1995). Croley notes that state judges are chosen by legislative or executive appointment in only twelve states.

50. *Davis* v. *Grover*, 480 N.W.2d 460, 477–78 (Wis. 1992).

51. Frank Kemerer and others, "Vouchers and Private School Autonomy," *Journal of Law and Education*, vol. 21 (1992), pp. 606–09.

52. John Witte, "First-Year Report: Milwaukee Parental Choice Program" (University of Wisconsin—Madison, Robert M. La Follette Institute of Public Affairs, 1991).

53. David Doege, "Exito School Founder Sent to Prison," *Milwaukee Journal Sentinel*, August 28, 1997, p. 3.

54. Curtis Lawrence, "Choice Schools Take Double Hit," *Milwaukee Journal Sentinel*, January 27, 1996; Curtis Lawrence, "Choice School, Seen as Success, Plans to Close," *Milwaukee Journal Sentinel*, August 8, 1996.

55. *Texas Open-Enrollment Charter Schools: Year-One Evaluation* (Texas Education Agency, 1997), p. 27. For a scathing attack on charter school mismanagement in Texas, see Stuart Eskanazi, "Flunking Out," *Dallas Observer*, July 22–28, 1999.

56. Mark Walsh, "Audit Criticizes Cleveland Voucher Program," *Education Week*, April 15, 1998. The cost of taxis ranged from $15 to $18 a day, compared with $3.33 a day for buses. For a comprehensive discussion of start-up problems experienced by the Cleveland voucher program, see Jeff Archer, "Obstacle Course," *Education Week*, June 6, 1999.

57. The points set forth here are discussed in depth in Kenneth Godwin and others, "Liberal Equity in Education: A Comparison of School Choice Options," *Social Science Quarterly*, vol. 79 (September 1998).

58. *Sheff* v. *O'Neill*, 678 A.2d 1267 (Conn. 1996). See note 69.

59. See, for example, James Coleman and others, *High School Achievement: Public, Catholic, and Private Schools Compared* (Basic Books, 1982); Anthony Bryk and others, *Catholic Schools and the Common Good* (Harvard University Press, 1993); Lawrence Steinberg and others, *Beyond the Classroom* (Simon and Schuster, 1996); Daniel Goldhaber, "Public and Private High Schools: Is School Choice an Answer to the Productivity Problem?" *Economics of Education Review*, vol. 15 (April 1996); Adam Gamoran, "Student Achievement in Public Magnet, Public Comprehensive, and Private City High Schools," *Educational Evaluation and Policy Analysis*, vol. 18 (1996); Derek Neal, "The Effects of Catholic Secondary Schooling on Educational Attainment," *Journal of Labor Economics*, vol. 15 (January 1997). For a general discussion, see Kenneth Godwin and others, "Comparing Public Choice and Private Voucher Programs in San Antonio," in Paul Peterson and Brian Hassel, eds., *Learn-

ing from School Choice (Brookings, 1998). See also William Bowen and Derek Bok, *The Shape of the River* (Princeton University Press, 1997), regarding the payoff of diversity in the nation's select colleges and universities.

60. See Stephen Eisdorfer, "Public School Choice and Racial Integration," *Seton Hall Law Review*, vol. 24 (1993).

61. Gary Orfield, "Deepening Segregation in American Schools" (Harvard Project on School Desegregation, 1997), table 4.

62. Ibid., p. 41. Orfield faults the U.S. Supreme Court for the movement away from a commitment to school integration, citing *Board of Educ. of Okla. City v. Dowell*, 498 U.S. 237 (1990) (once vestiges of de jure segregation have been eliminated, federal court supervision may end, even if one-race schools emerge); *Freeman v. Pitts*, 503 U.S. 467 (1992) (courts can relinquish supervision of those areas of school operation that have become unitary even if the full desegregation order has not been implemented); and *Missouri v. Jenkins*, 515 U.S. 1139 (1995) (federal judge exceeded his powers in ordering adoption of a magnet school plan to attract white students from the suburbs). As a result of these decisions, Orfield observes, "desegregation was redefined from the goal of ending schools defined by race to a temporary and limited process that created no lasting rights and need not overcome the inequities growing out of a segregated history." Orfield, "Deepening Segration in American Schools," pp. 7–8. For a full discussion, see Gary Orfield and Susan Eaton, *Dismantling Desegregation* (New Press, 1996).

63. Casey D. Cobb and Gene V. Glass, "Ethnic Segregation in Arizona Charter Schools," *Education Policy Analysis Archives*, vol. 7 (1999). (http://epaa.asu.edu/epaa/v7n1/).

64. Joseph R. McKinney, "Public School Choice and Desegregation: A Reality Check," *Journal of Law and Education*, vol. 25 (1995), p. 657.

65. *Equal Open Enrollment Ass'n. v. Bd. of Educ. of Akron City Sch. Dist.*, 937 F. Supp. 700 (N.D. Ohio, 1996).

66. Schneider and others, "Networks to Nowhere."

67. Office of Research and Improvement, "A Study of Charter Schools: First-Year Report," (U.S. Department of Education, 1996).

68. *Green v. County Sch. Bd. of New Kent County*, 391 U.S. 430 (1968).

69. *United States v. Texas*, 330 F. Supp. 235 (E.D. Tex.), aff'd in part, 447 F.2d 441 (5th Cir. 1971).

70. Texas Education Code Ann., section 12.111 (13) (West 1999).

71. Proof of discriminatory intent is required to establish a violation of the Fourteenth Amendment Equal Protection Clause under *Washington v. Davis*, 426 U.S. 229 (1976). While Title VI of the 1964 Civil Rights Act, which prohibits racial discrimination in any federally assisted program, also is triggered by an intent to discriminate following the U.S. Supreme Court ruling in *Washington* and in *Univ. of Calif. Bd. of Regents v. Bakke*, 438 U.S. 265 (1978), disparate impact on a minority group continues to be sufficient under implementing federal regulations to constitute a violation of the statute. *Guardians Ass'n v. Civil Serv. Comm'n*, 463 U.S. 582 (1983). Once disparate impact is shown, the defendant has the burden to prove that the challenged practice was required by employment or educational necessity. *Larry P. v. Riles*, 793 F.2d 969, 982 (9th Cir. 1984) (use of IQ tests resulting in disproportionate placement of black students in classes for the educable mentally retarded not justified by education necessity); but compare *Georgia State Conference of Branches of NAACP v. State of Georgia*, 775 F.2d 1403, 1417 (11th Cir. 1985) (achievement grouping and placement of black students in special education programs justified by education necessity even though evidence conflicting). In *Elston v. Talladega Cnty. Bd. of Educ.*, 997 F.2d 1394 (1993), the U.S. Court of Appeals for the Eleventh Circuit observed that "the Title VI regulations education cases tend not to explain explicitly what it means to show that a challenged practice has a 'mani-

fest relationship to classroom education.' However, from consulting the way in which these cases analyze the 'education necessity' issue, it becomes clear that what the cases are essentially requiring is that defendants show that the challenged course of action is demonstrably necessary to meeting an important education goal" (p. 1412). The appeals court found sufficient justification for locating a new school in a largely white area. One significant development in this area is *Sheff* v. *O'Neill*, 678 A.2d 1267 (Conn. 1996), wherein the Supreme Court of Connecticut ruled that Art I, § 20, of the state constitution requires the state to dismantle racial and ethnic isolation in Hartford, even though it does not result from any prior intentional segregation by public officials. The high court noted that Connecticut is one of three states—the others being Hawaii and New Jersey—that have constitutions specifically prohibiting segregation. Construing segregation to encompass both de jure and de facto causes, the justices ruled that the state has "an affirmative obligation to respond" (p. 1285). In pressing the need to find a way to "cross the racial and ethnic divide," the justices directed the legislature and the executive branch "to put the search for appropriate remedial measures at the top of their respective agendas" (p. 1290).

72. *Villaneuva* v. *Carere*, 85 F.3d 481 (10th Cir. 1996).

73. Ibid., p. 488.

74. Massachusetts General Laws Ann., chap. 71, § 89 (l) (West 1999).

75. North Carolina General Statutes, section 115C-238.29F (g)(5) (1997).

76. See note 59. Since the 1970s, research has shown that school integration has no significant impact on the achievement levels of whites but does produce gains in achievement levels among minorities. The achievement levels of minorities in integrated schools surpass those of minorities attending largely one-race schools. Robert L. Crain and Rita E. Mahard, "Minority Achievement: Policy Implications of Research," in Willis Hawley, ed., *Effective School Desegregation* (Russell Sage, 1982).

77. *Swann* v. *Charlotte-Mecklenburg Board of Education*, 402 U.S. 1, 16 (1971).

78. *Adarand Constructors, Inc.* v. *Peña*, 515 U.S. 200, 227 (1995).

79. *Tito* v. *Arlington County Sch. Bd.*, 1997 U.S. Dist. LEXIS 7932, at *15 (E.D. Va., May 13, 1997). Later, the same judge rejected the Arlington County School Board's plan to factor in family income and first language in a weighted lottery system as an impermissible means to the same end. *Tuttle* v. *Arlington County School Board*, 1998 U.S. Dist. LEXIS 19788 (April 23, 1998). See also *Hopwood* v. *Texas*, 78 F.3d 932 (5th Cir.), cert. denied, 518 U.S. 1033 (1996) (affirmative action program that favored African Americans and Hispanics at the University of Texas School of Law struck down as not serving a compelling government purpose under the Fourteenth Amendment Equal Protection Clause in the absence of a recent history of racial discrimination by the law school).

80. *Wessman* v. *Gittens*, 160 F.3d 790, 799 (lst Cir. 1998). The admissions policy specified that half of the seats for the entering class were to be allocated strictly on the basis of performance on a standardized test. The other half were allocated on the basis of five different ethnic categories: white, black, Hispanic, Asian, and Native American. Each category was allocated a specific number of places as determined by its percentage of the remaining applicant pool. Thus for the 1997 ninth-grade entering class, the racial-ethnic composition of the remaining applicant pool was 27.83 percent black, 40.41 percent white, 19.21 percent Asian, 11.64 percent Hispanic, and 0.31 percent Native American. This translated to thirteen seats for blacks, eighteen for whites, nine for Asians, and five for Hispanics. As a result, Sarah Wessman and ten other white students were displaced by black and Hispanic students with lower composite test score rankings. The majority concluded that the policy was not justified by acts of prior discrimination and that it was not tailored to serve a compelling government interest. For example, an admissions policy based solely on test scores would not result in an all-white student body. Further, benefited groups included those who had never been victims of

discrimination by the Boston public school system in the past. These included Asians and minority students who had attended private schools. In a lengthy opinion, the dissenting judge argued that the Boston School Committee had presented evidence to justify the policy and that the policy was narrowly tailored to serve this end. He noted that without the policy, enrollment in the ninth-grade entering class at Boston Latin would have dropped from 21 to 14 percent among African Americans and from 10 to 7 percent among Hispanics. He noted that the composition of the Boston school system as a whole is 74 percent African American and Hispanic.

For a general discussion of racial balancing law, see John Dayton, "An Analysis of Judicial Opinions Concerning the Legal Status of Racial Diversity Programs in Educational Institutions," *West's Education Law Reporter*, May 27, 1999, pp. 297–327. Dayton notes that the federal courts of appeals for the First, Third, Fourth, Fifth, Seventh, and D.C. Circuits have issued decisions contrary to nonremedial racial diversity programs in either the education or noneducation contexts, with no recent contrary decisions. At the same time, federal district courts are split on the legality of racial balance measures in schools. Compare, for example, *Hunter* v. *Regents of the University of California*, 971 F. Supp. 1316 (C.D. Cal. 1997) (university interest in operating a laboratory elementary school is sufficiently compelling to permit use of race-based admissions criteria), and *Eisenberg* v. *Montgomery County Public Schools*, 19 F. Supp.2d 449 (D. Md. 1998) (promotion of a diverse student population is sufficiently compelling to allow a race-based transfer policy), with *Equal Open Enrollment Association* v. *Board of Education of Akron City School District*, 937 F. Supp. 700 (N.D. Ohio, 1996) (prevention of racial segregation is not sufficiently compelling to justify policy prohibiting white students from transferring out of an urban school district), and *Brewer* v. *West Irondequoit Central School District*, 32 F. Supp.2d 619 (W.D. N.Y. 1999) (same). Of course, the U.S. Supreme Court will have the last word.

81. See John E. Coons and Stephen D. Sugarman, *Scholarships for Children* (Berkeley, Calif.: Institute of Governmental Studies Press, 1992), pp. 25–26.

82. In *Hopwood* v. *Texas*, 78 F.3d 932 (1996), the Fifth Circuit observed that use of other admissions criteria that may correlate with race and ethnicity would be permissible: "This correlation . . . will not render the use of the factor unconstitutional if it is not adopted for the purpose of discriminating on the basis of race" (p. 947, n. 31). Thus the law school could consider such factors as the applicant's residence, parents' education, and economic and social background.

83. For a detailed discussion, see Godwin and others, "Liberal Equity in Education." See also Kenneth Godwin and Frank Kemerer, *School Choice Tradeoffs* (University of Texas Press, forthcoming).

84. A flat voucher of, say, $4,000 serves as a large incentive for middle- and high-income families to see that the school meets the 20 percent enrollment set-aside. However, a means-tested voucher that can range as high as $8,000 constitutes a powerful incentive for low-income families and families with special-needs children to seek out choice opportunities that may be beyond their reach with a flat voucher. Although a means-tested voucher constitutes less of an incentive to middle- and high-income families because they may not qualify for a substantial voucher, it eases the burden on private schools to fill the 20 percent set-aside. From an equity standpoint, then, a means-tested voucher is preferable to a flat voucher.

85. Terry Moe, *Schools, Vouchers, and the American Public* (Brookings, forthcoming).

86. David J. Dent, "Diversity Rules Threaten North Carolina Charter Schools That Aid Blacks," *New York Times*, December 23, 1998.

87. Amy Stuart Wells and others, "Beyond the Rhetoric of Charter School Reform" (University of California—Los Angeles, Department of Education and Information Studies, 1998), p. 47.

88. *Tinker* v. *Des Moines Sch. Dist.*, 393 U.S. 503 (1969). In a later decision, the U.S. Supreme Court limited this decision to interstudent communication by holding that, through its control of the curriculum, the school can regulate the contents of a school-sponsored student newspaper and other channels of communication controlled by the school. *Hazelwood School District* v. *Kuhlmeier*, 484 U.S. 260 (1988).

89. *Kingsville I.S.D.* v. *Cooper*, 611 F.2d 1109 (5th Cir. 1980) (teacher has a First Amendment academic freedom right to lead classroom discussion on controversial issues and cannot be terminated unless the discussion clearly overbalances the teacher's effectiveness).

90. Richard Elmore and others, "The New Accountability in State Education Reform: From Process to Performance," in Helen Ladd, ed., *Holding Schools Accountable* (Brookings, 1996), pp. 66–67.

91. A national criterion-referenced test is preferable to state-based tests, which vary from state to state. At present, the National Assessment Governing Board (NAGB) has been established by Congress to study President Clinton's proposed national testing program. NAGB is wrestling with problems including linkage of the new testing program to the reputable National Assessment of Educational Progress (NAEP), given by the U.S. Department of Education since 1969. NAEP does not yield results on individual students. Millicent Lawton, "Assessment Board Wrestles with Test Mandate," *Education Week*, December 3, 1997, pp. 22, 26. See also David Hoff, "Panel Assails Assessment Calculations: Calls for Changing NAEP Processes," *Education Week*, September 30, 1998, pp. 1, 23.

92. Robert Meyer, "Comments on Chapters Two, Three, and Four," in Ladd, *Holding Schools Accountable*, p. 139.

93. For a comprehensive discussion of state constitutional law in this context, see Kemerer, "State Constitutions and School Vouchers"; Frank Kemerer, "The Constitutional Dimension of School Vouchers," *Texas Forum on Civil Liberties and Civil Rights*, vol. 3 (1998); Jesse Choper, this volume.

94. *Pierce* v. *Society of Sisters*, 268 U.S. 510, 534 (1925).

95. *Ohio Ass'n of Independent Schs.* v. *Goff*, 92 F.3d 419 (6th Cir. 1996).

96. See the list of decisions in *New Life Baptist Church Academy* v. *East Longmeadow*, 885 F.2d 940, 950–51 (lst Cir. 1989). The most notable exception to general judicial deference to the state is a 1976 Ohio Supreme Court ruling, *State* v. *Whisner*, 351 N.E.2d 750 (Ohio 1976) (state board's minimum regulations for private elementary schools were so intrusive as to violate parents' right to freedom of religion and their right to control their children's upbringing).

97. *City of Boerne* v. *Flores*, 521 U.S. 507 (1997).

98. With the invalidation of the Religious Freedom Restoration Act, *Employment Division, Dep't of Human Servs. of Oregon* v. *Smith*, 494 U.S. 872 (1990), remains the law in this area (providing that as long as government is neutral in treating religion and nonreligion alike, there is no violation of the First Amendment Free Exercise Clause).

99. Moe, *Schools, Vouchers, and the American Public*. See also Lynn Schnaiberg, "Voucher Study Finds Support for Accountability," *Education Week*, February 18, 1998. Schnaiberg discusses a survey of taxpayers, parents, and educators in Wisconsin and Ohio that showed strong support for increased accountability measures for private schools participating in the voucher programs in these states.

100. Hanushek, "Assessing the Effects of School Resources on Student Performance."

101. *Tinker* v. *Des Moines Sch. Dist.*, 393 U.S. 503, 511 (1969).

102. Zachariah Chafee, "The Internal Affairs of Associations Not for Profit," *Harvard Law Review*, vol. 43 (1930), p. 1027.

103. See Frank Kemerer and Kenneth Deutsch, *Constitutional Rights and Student Life* (St. Paul, Minn.: West, 1979).

PART THREE

Legal Constraints

CHAPTER SEVEN

School Choice
and State Action

ROBERT M. O'NEIL

The issue of this chapter may be simply stated: When, if ever, does the existence or the exercise of school choice impose constitutional obligations on an otherwise private educational institution? A cursory review of the case law and scanty scholarship might yield an equally succinct answer: never. Yet such simple responses seldom find favor with legal scholars, especially those of us who focus on individual rights and liberties under the Constitution. The question is in fact an intriguing and difficult one, both in law and in public policy. It deserves far more extensive discussion than it has received, whatever may be the eventual disposition.

The issue is important for several reasons. The extent to which (if at all) a particular type of school must respect the rights and duties that derive from the United States Constitution depends upon whether it is engaged in state action. If on one hand a school is a purely private entity, it may well be subject to statutory or administrative regulation designed to ensure individual rights, but that is wholly a legislative judgment. If on the other hand that school is sufficiently imbued with a government quality or nexus, then certain obligations and liberties apply directly by force of the Bill of Rights. Thus the state-action issue is crucial both to the legal nature of the institution and to its relationship with students, teachers, and community.

We begin by revisiting familiar principles of state action, under which otherwise private conduct may be subject to constitutional constraints. We turn next to several easy choice cases at the extremes, situations in which the conduct is either clearly governmental or clearly beyond reach of the Constitution. We then focus on the difficult situations in between: several educational choice settings to which the application of constitutional rights and remedies may be problematic. We conclude with a few cautions about the handling of such issues in future litigation.

A Primer on State Action

Before revisiting familiar principles of state action, it might be helpful to posit a prototype case to which such analysis might have value. Suppose a teacher has been dismissed by a nominally private choice school for reasons that would warrant constitutional protection within a public school setting (for example, a responsible but unwelcome critique of administrative policy).[1] Should that teacher seek redress in a federal court, the school would presumably insist that, as a private entity, it may hire and fire teachers for any reason that is not forbidden by federal or state law. Since no statute would protect a teacher's speech, that might be the end of the case, unless something in the relationship between the school and the government served to make it amenable to suit in federal court and subject to obligations imposed by the Constitution on how government agencies deal with their employees.

While the school's legally private status would create a strong presumption against such a finding, we know that many private entities have been held subject to constitutional obligations and remedies. Thus it becomes imperative to review briefly the several familiar settings in which state action occurs. The inquiry begins with section 1983 of the original civil rights legislation, which provides redress in federal court for any person who has been deprived of federal constitutional rights or liberties "under color of any statute, ordinance, regulation, custom or usage of any State or Territory."[2]

The Delegation or Exercise of Government Power or Authority

A steady volume of litigation, mainly in the last half century, has given meaning (if not perfect clarity) to this provision. Perhaps the most obvious targets for finding state action are those ostensibly private entities that operate as or for public entities, performing a full range of government functions and services, such as the all-white party preprimaries in the old South or the company town that exercised all municipal powers under formally private ownership.[3]

That doctrine later became the vehicle for extending First Amendment rights to large privately owned malls and shopping centers, though so broad a definition of state action was soon qualified and eventually rescinded, leaving little such private property other than the rare company town subject on this basis to constitutional obligations.[4] Yet the basic concept remains vital, perhaps the clearest case for finding state action: where the government either delegates its power to a private entity, or where, as with the company town, the private entity assumes and exercises power that would elsewhere be governmental, the Constitution follows that power into the private realm.

A Symbiotic Relationship between the Government and a Private Entity

A second rationale for finding state action is the presence of a symbiotic relationship between the government and an otherwise private actor. The early and still prime example is that of a private coffee shop that had leased space from a building owned and managed by a municipal entity.[5] The two entities had become not only operationally and physically but also financially interdependent in ways that had constitutional import. That Supreme Court judgment in the early 1960s, well before the enactment of federal protection for equal rights in places of public accommodation, had been anticipated by a federal appeals court judgment imposing constitutional duties on private lessees of space in public buildings.[6] This important rationale has produced numerous variants and qualifications but remains a durable element of the fabric of state action.

Symbiosis of a different sort produced a finding of state action in *Evans v. Newton.*[7] Property had been devised to a city for use as a park for whites only. In the 1950s, the city desegregated the park. Later the park's managers sued to remove the city as trustee and to substitute private trustees who would enforce the racial restriction. The state courts permitted the substitution, but the Supreme Court ruled that the government had become too deeply involved in administering the park, and for too long a period, to permit the resumption of racial segregation by reassigning the property to private ownership.

Government Endorsement or Validation of Private Action

The third strand of state action involves state encouragement or empowerment of private acts that would be reachable by federal courts if they had been committed directly by a public entity. That theory traces to the restrictive covenant doctrine in *Shelley* v. *Kraemer*, reinforced a few years later by *Barrows* v. *Jackson*.[8] Direct judicial enforcement marks the easiest case, although it is worth noting that two federal courts have declined to find First Amendment violations, on the *Shelley-Barrows* theory, in suits by internet service providers who seek to enforce restrictions against "spamming," or commercial junk e-mail, by users of their systems.[9] The encouragement-empowerment rationale has also been applied to reach government-sanctioned or government-endorsed racial segregation in public facilities and, most visibly, to strike down California's 1964 constitutional condonation of racial discrimination in the sale and rental of real property.[10]

While other cases may lead to findings of state action, these are the major prototypes. Equally important, and analytically more troubling, are many situations in which a lay observer might well believe private action had been taken under color of state law but in which the courts have held otherwise. For starters, recall the Supreme Court's reversal on extending the company town doctrine to large malls and shopping centers that may be nearly as influential in the lives of customers and employees as is the literal company town. Equally puzzling to many observers is the effect of extensive public regulation of a vital activity. The classic case, in which state action was not found, involved the termination of essential utility service to private consumers without the safeguards or procedure that due process would compel in the case of a public provider of such service. Despite the extensive government regulation of the utility, its monopoly position, and the indispensable character of the energy it furnished to its customers, the Supreme Court declined to find the utility engaged in state action.[11]

Closely akin to the regulation cases are those involving government licensing, an empowerment without which private activity could often not take place but the presence of which has not been sufficient to create state action. Though Justice William O. Douglas argued vigorously that licensing alone might impose constitutional duties on a private entity, he was often alone and seldom joined by more than two other members of the Court.[12] Neither a liquor license nor the exclusive right to use the word *Olympic* for commercial and other purposes has been found sufficient to constitute color of state law.[13] The Supreme Court, while seldom unanimous and often sharply divided, has unequivocally rejected government licensing, as well as extensive regulation, as a possible basis for finding state action.

Finally, there is the troubling and obviously relevant issue of government funding and financial support. The Supreme Court many years ago declined to review a case in which the Fourth Circuit found receipt of substantial public funding a sufficient basis for state action in a racial discrimination case.[14] Later, however, the Court was to suggest in several cases that funding alone would not warrant imposing constitutional duties on an otherwise private entity.[15] Such recipients of public funds, said the majority in the later cases, were constitutionally no different from a host of government contractors who did not become subject to suit in federal court on civil rights and liberties claims solely by reason of doing extensive business with the government.

Before concluding this brief review, one other line of cases should be noted. Though they do not directly implicate state action, they have obvious and substantial bearing on the issue before us here. The Supreme Court has stressed that the government may not, consistent with the Fourteenth Amendment, permit private parties to use public facilities or resources in ways that discriminate on racial or other grounds forbidden to the government. Thus in *Gilmore* v. *Montgomery*, the Court held that a city could not grant exclusive use of a public recreational facility to a racially segregated private user group.[16] A year earlier, the justices had ruled that Mississippi could not lend textbooks to students attending racially segregated private schools, even though the Court had earlier validated on Establishment Clause grounds the lending of secular texts to parochial school students.[17] As the concurring justices observed in the recreational facilities case, "the question is not whether there is state action, but whether the conceded action by the city, and hence by the State, is such that the State must be deemed to have denied the equal protection of the laws."[18] Nonetheless, despite the very different posture of such cases as these, their relevance to the subject at hand should be obvious.

The field of state action remains one of substantial uncertainty. A few familiar situations support a ready finding of state action: those that involve a direct delegation, or private exercise, of important government power; those in which a court imposes sanctions for violation of a racially restrictive agreement; those in which public authority has empowered or strongly encouraged private action that the government could not take on its own; and perhaps a few others less readily classified. There are also a few situations in which courts have been reluctant to find state action: licensing alone, regulation alone (even if extensive), and public funding alone. Even so, the results may be complicated by such factors as the particular individual right being asserted, the remedy being sought, and the potential impact of granting or denying relief under the conditions of the case. We return to some of these issues in the particular context of choice schools and public law.

Two Easy Cases: Charter Schools and Home Schooling

It may be helpful to start our analysis at opposite ends of the spectrum of school choice. Take charter schools as a major item on the school choice menu. There appear to be substantial early differences among state structures for the creation, governance, and support of charter schools. Some arrangements appear to grant charter school administrators a substantially greater degree of autonomy than others. Some would rely on state licensing, others on contracts between state or local school officials and private groups. Some systems involve separate charter school boards, while others entrust governance to the local school board. The funding mechanisms also appear to vary among the dozen or so states that have created charter school systems.[19] There has been significant litigation under state law over the validity of structures that place substantial authority over charter schools beyond the direct power of local school boards.[20] While such challenges seem not to have succeeded, it is possible that a charter school structure may yet be ruled to be in violation of state constitutions or school laws.[21]

Whatever the variations, it seems most unlikely that the actions of a charter school would ever be held *not to be* under color of state law. If therefore a charter school teacher, under any of the currently contemplated arrangements, were to be fired for speaking out on a matter of public importance and were to seek redress in a federal court, the case should proceed just as though the action had been taken by a public school, even though members of a private board might well be named among the defendants.[22] Such a case would be governed by the most familiar of state-action principles: the entire authority of such a board or administration has been delegated directly by a government agency or has been empowered by a contract with a public entity. Not only is the charter school substantially (in fact most often fully) funded by the government; it is in every sense a part of the public school system of the state, whatever the degree of autonomy and whatever latitude it may have in framing and enforcing certain of its own rules.

Thus there seems little doubt about the applicability of federal standards and remedies to charter schools built upon any of the current models. A fascinating question lies, however, just beyond the horizon: Might a state create a charter school structure so attenuated from the public school system that its actions might not be deemed under color of state law?[23] The short answer is that such an entity would really no longer be a charter school but would rather be a state-licensed private school of the type to which we turn major attention in the next section. But suppose a state decided to create a unique institution that enjoyed maximal autonomy while remaining loosely affiliated with the public school system. Could such a school be called a charter school but nonetheless be legally free to admit or expel students, hire and fire teachers, and engage in other practices that would be actionable in federal court if carried out by a public school or by a conventional charter school?

While this response may seem tautological, such an entity would not be a charter school as that term is currently understood. Indeed, if it were so attenuated in governance and accountability as to create even the possibility of exemption from Fourteenth Amendment standards, that very attenuation would require a different label—or surely a different concept. It might well partake some of the qualities of a charter school but would be in fact (whatever the terminology) a state-licensed, state-regulated, and possibly state-funded private school.

If the charter school is unmistakably covered, what of the opposite end of the choice spectrum? It is not easy to imagine a state-action issue over home schooling. But let us suppose, following a divorce, that one parent instructs at home the child of whom he has custody. Let us further suppose that the other parent fervently wishes that the child of whom she has custody share in that educational experience. The home-schooling parent, however, flatly refuses—in fact, refuses solely and vocally because of the different race of that child, who is the only adoptee in the family. The divorce decree and custody agreement are completely silent. Nothing in state law resolves the issue. The aggrieved parent considers going to court. She makes two claims: first, that the home-schooling option (affording as it does a unique dispensation from the compulsory attendance and truancy laws) serves to delegate the state's educational power to a private actor; and second, that the exclusion of the child for whose education she is responsible is a blatant act of racial discrimination. Could a federal court ever entertain such a claim? Intriguing as the case may be, a negative answer seems as clear here as the positive view we take of charter school coverage.

Courts have, of course, passed on home-schooling issues, with divergent results. Here, as with most other educational issues likely to reach the courts, there are wide differences among the states. Most interesting among recent litigation may be that in Michigan upholding in general the requirement that home schoolers provide state-certified instructors, though refusing to apply that constraint to home-schooling families whose religious beliefs would be abridged.[24] The parental claim we posit would be most nearly justiciable in a state like Michigan, where regulation of home schooling is extensive. If the state requires that home schoolers provide state-certified instruction, the argument would run, then why could not an aggrieved parent sue at least to prevent the other parent from engaging in state-sanctioned racial discrimination? Or to raise the stakes further, suppose the home-schooling parent flatly refused to hire an otherwise qualified and certified instructor solely because that person was Jewish? We now have two potential plaintiffs, both clearly aggrieved by private action pursuant to a state-sanctioned educational alternative.

However appealing these claims may seem, it is still unlikely that a federal court would intervene. Apart from the unsavory prospect of intruding in what is basically an intrafamily dispute, no essential ingredient of state action seems present here. It is true that the home-schooling parent could be jailed for keeping his children out of school—but for the option that state law expressly provides to such a family. Thus the state has, in a sense, delegated its educational role to the home-schooling family. It is also true that, absent a religiously based objection, the home-schooling parent in places like Michigan must provide state-certified instruction. Yet even these cogent factors do not seem enough to invoke a federal court's jurisdiction, at least when the consequences of intervention are so grave. The very factors that have led lawmakers to sanction, and courts to validate, home schooling in the first place should militate strongly against adjudicating such claims, much less applying Fourteenth Amendment standards to education that occurs in the living room or study of the private home.

Thus we begin with two fairly clear extremes. Charter schools, whatever the model or structure, seem to be acting under color of state law. Home schoolers, with comparable clarity, seem not to be engaged in state action. The hard cases—especially the knotty question of whether state action is ever created by the type of nexus that voucher and similar programs create between the government and otherwise private schools—lie between these two poles. It is to those fascinating issues we now turn.

The Hard Case: State Action and the Public Funding of Private Schools

If charter schools represent the easy case at one end and home schooling the easy case on the other end, the issues created by public funding pose the difficult intermediate cases. Such public funding comes in many forms, several of which have long been held valid for sectarian and secular private schools equally: reimbursing parental costs for transporting students to and from school, lending secular textbooks to individual students, reimbursing schools for the costs of administering diagnostic and therapeutic services and standardized tests, allowing parents a tax deduction for educational expenses, providing interpreters for hearing-impaired students, and most recently furnishing certain remedial education services on private school premises.[25] Perhaps, for the sake of completeness, one should also include in this list of public benefits the exemption from real property taxes, which private schools share with a host of other nonprofit organizations.[26]

Such indirect, albeit important, public benefits have never been thought by themselves to impose constitutional duties on otherwise private schools. It is, however, the prospect of substantial (sometimes nearly total) government funding—of the kind already provided by several pilot voucher programs—that reopens the state-action issue. Whether such payments can be arranged in ways that are consistent with basic principles of separation of church and state is an issue of great difficulty, fully discussed elsewhere.[27] For purposes of the discussion that follows, I assume the validity under the Establishment Clause of some form of voucher payment. That assumption enables us to address the full range of state-action-related issues.

Some observers would argue that the central issue has already been foreclosed. The Supreme Court did assess the constitutional significance of public payments to private schools in a secular context in *Rendell-Baker* v. *Kohn* and seemingly foreclosed a finding of state action.[28] The case involved the claims of two teachers that their free speech had been abridged because a state-assisted private school dismissed them for speaking out against school policy. The school was clearly private in its origin and governance, yet it received at least 90 percent (and in one year 99 percent) of its operating budget from local public school payments for the education of students with special learning needs. Each such student was the object of an individualized instruction plan developed by the referring public school and accepted by the private school. The employment of teachers for the private school had to be approved by the state criminal justice agency. Along with other private educational institutions, the school was also extensively regulated in ways relevant to accreditation, safety, health, and the like.

The discharged teachers sought relief from federal court, claiming that the school's action was clearly under color of state law. Two district judges, before whom initially separate suits were argued, diverged on that issue. The court of appeals combined the cases and ruled that state action did not exist, despite the school's nearly total dependence on public subvention.[29] The Supreme Court affirmed, with two dissents, reaching on the same day an identical result with regard to a private nursing home that received the bulk of its support from public payments.[30] The *Rendell-Baker* majority recognized the constitutional importance of massive public funding but found none of the vital indicia of state action in the case. By contracting with the government to educate students with special needs, this school seemed to the Court "not fundamentally different from many private corporations whose business depends primarily on contracts to build roads, bridges, dams, ships or submarines for the government."[31] While the school was extensively regulated by the state, both in its general role and by reason of its special mission, the specific actions targeted by the teachers' lawsuits were "not compelled or even influenced by any state regulation."

Moreover, the undoubted performance of a public function through education did not constitute state action. It was not the sort of function "traditionally the exclusive prerogative of the State" that had subjected other private entities to civil rights claims. Indeed the lower courts stressed the recency with which the state had undertaken to specifically serve the needs of troubled students who did not fit well in the public schools. Thus whatever might be said in general of education as a public function, the type of education provided by this private school was too recent and too supplemental in nature even to demand such analysis.

The majority also rejected the teachers' suggestion of a symbiotic relationship between the government and the school. Unlike the *Burton* case and others in which symbiosis served to impose public duties on otherwise private actors, the Court found dependence only on one side and not the degree of interdependence that might carry constitutional rights into a private realm. Finally, the Court added in a footnote, there was no evidence here of any "sham arrangement" to avoid constitutional obligations by outsourcing a public activity to a private entity.[32]

Justices Brennan and Marshall dissented on the state-action issue. They agreed with one of the two district judges that "the state has delegated [to the private school] its statutory duty to educate children with special needs."[33] There was extensive evidence here, they felt, of the very symbiosis that had triggered state-action findings in other contexts: comprehensive regulation and supervision, development of individual instruction plans for each student, conferral of diplomas by the public schools, imposition of detailed personnel policies and guidelines, and of course the fact that the private school "receives virtually all of its funds from state sources." The dissenters also stressed that "the school is providing a substitute for public education," a form of delegation that would normally impose on a private actor the full range of the government's duties toward citizens. Finally, Justices Brennan and Marshall observed that even the majority would probably have found state action if the actions challenged in federal court (instead of being the firing of outspoken teachers) had directly affected the students, since the private school fulfilled a statutory duty of public education officials. This last comment suggests the perfect prototype case, the ideal situation for that finding of state action that *Rendell-Baker* might seem to foreclose.

Suppose that under a voucher program of the type being piloted in Cleveland and Milwaukee a single private school enrolls substantial numbers of voucher-assisted students. Suppose also that the school is extensively regulated by the state in myriad other ways: accreditation, curriculum, teacher competence, health, safety, and the like. And now suppose, to present the most appealing case, the school consistently and openly (indeed proudly and aggressively) refuses to accept any nonwhite students, under conditions that neither federal nor state law forbids. (This last assumption, as we see below, needs to be questioned, but let us make it for now in order to frame the most compelling test case.) Must we conclude that, given *Rendell-Baker*, a rejected racial minority student would have no legal recourse whatever? If that conclusion follows inexorably, then this type of choice school would lie beyond the reach of federal courts and the Constitution, however blatant its practices.

Several possibly distinguishing features of *Rendell-Baker* deserve closer scrutiny. Both the nature of the claim and the identity of the claimants (discharged teachers) may be substantially less compelling than our prototype case. A free speech claim surely did not provide the optimal test case. On the facts, there was some doubt whether such claims would have prevailed even against a public school. The speech of people who work for the government in any capacity has received substantial First Amendment protection from the courts, though such expression is less fully protected than is the speech of citizens who are not public workers.[34] If, but only if, a court were to conclude that the teachers' statements raised matters of public concern—not private grievances, even with potential public importance and interest—would the plaintiffs be entitled to relief after being discharged by a public school system for speaking out.[35]

Moreover, there is a vital difference that the Court had no occasion to consider but that we need to recognize: telling a private school it may not regulate the speech of its teachers—that a religious school, for example, is powerless to constrain sacrilege or blasphemy on the part of its faculty because the public schools may not do so—would intrude dramatically into the character or privacy of the private school. Thus the claim presented in *Rendell-Baker* is not only far less clear in public sector terms than many other claims would have been, it is also a type of claim that may seem especially troubling to the very nature and reason for being of nonpublic schools. Conversely, when the basis of the claim is racial discrimination and the claimants are the very students whom the government program is designed to support, the situation would be different and, arguably, much closer to traditional state-action desiderata. This claim is closer to the core of Fourteenth Amendment concern. At the same time, telling a private school that it may not bar students solely because of their race—especially if their tuition is to be paid by the government—is far less threatening to the character and mission of a private educational institution. Reflecting that distinction, and the great strength of the government's interest in eradicating racial discrimination, the Supreme Court has sustained denial of tax-exempt status to private church-related colleges and universities that impose racial barriers.[36] Moreover, the Court has made clear that the post–Civil War civil rights remedies do reach racial discrimination practiced by otherwise private elementary and secondary schools.[37]

The nature of the school and its function may also help to distance or limit *Rendell-Baker*. The private school in that case was a special-purpose institution, fulfilling a mission that the lower courts found to be of rather recent origin among the range of public educational concerns. Further, the nexus between school and state was described as one of "contract," a term likely to create a sense of distance and autonomy as well as to evoke fears of extending state action to every private company dependent on major government contracts. In short, the one precedent that appears to free private schools of all constitutional obligations is far less representative than a quick reading might suggest. The infinite extrapolation of that precedent to the world of private education requires caution.

There are other good reasons for proceeding with caution. The *Rendell-Baker* dissenters argued that the majority had overlooked, or minimized, the very nature of education as a "public function."[38] The point was forcefully stated some years ago by Jesse Choper:

It is clear that the operation of elementary and secondary schools is not an enterprise that is "traditionally and exclusively reserved to the State." But a comprehensive survey of school districts in the United States would surely show that virtually all maintained at least one public elementary and secondary school unless, because of some peculiar development, the educational needs of the community's children were historically met by a privately funded school. Such a school— or at least one of such schools if there are several in the hypothetical community . . . is, in effect, serving as a substitute for the conventional public school that the school district would otherwise provide. In this sense, it is performing a function "traditionally and exclusively reserved to the State."[39]

Apart from the inherent logic of the public function concept, there is a strong case to be made that the Supreme Court has increasingly characterized private education in this way. The process traces back at least to Justice Harlan's troubling dissent in *Evans* v. *Newton*, the case involving municipal administration of a once private and racially segregated park. When the majority ruled that the city could not avoid the obligations of equality by transferring management back to private trustees, Justices Harlan and Stewart objected both to the majority rationale and to its portent for other sectors, most notably that of education:

> Its failing as a principle of decision in the realm of Fourteenth Amendment concerns can be shown by comparing—among other examples that might be drawn from the still unfolding sweep of government functions—the "public function" of privately established schools with that of privately owned parks. Like parks, the purpose schools serve is important to the public. Like parks, private control exists, but there is also a very strong tradition of public control in this field. Like parks, schools may be available to almost anyone of one race or religion but to no others. Like parks, there are normally alternatives for those shut out, but there may also be inconveniences and disadvantages caused by the restriction. Like parks, the extent of school intimacy varies greatly depending on the size and character of the institution. . . . . While this process of analogy might be spun out to reach [other private activities], the example of schools is, I think, sufficient to indicate the pervasive potentialities of this "public function" theory of state action.[40]

The *Evans* dissenters were, of course, seeking not to extend state action to private schools but rather to indict the majority's metamorphosis of private parks. Yet the warning was clear—and seems germane here. While the majority assumed that its judgment would go little further than parks, Justices Harlan and Stewart found it "difficult to avoid the conclusion that this decision . . . jeopardizes the existence of denominationally restricted schools while making of every college entrance rejection letter a potential Fourteenth Amendment question."[41] Such fears of course proved groundless. State action did not move in so bold a direction. By the time of the *Rendell-Baker* case a decade and a half later, the Court's reassurance that private schools were not inherently state actors seemed almost unnecessary.

Nearly two decades have now passed. In this later period, the Supreme Court's own view of the role and function of private education seems to have changed in ways that have clear portent for the issue. Of course, the justices have always viewed education as a profoundly important activity (as far back as 1925), far too important to permit the government to preempt a parent's right to choose a nonpublic school as an alternative.[42] More recently, the recognition of the constitutional role of private education has proceeded apace.

In sustaining Minnesota's tax deduction for private school expenses as applied to parochial school costs, which dominated the use of the deduction, the majority had this to say about the role of the schools that benefited from such indirect subvention:

> Minnesota, like other states, could conclude that there is a strong public interest in assuring the continued financial health of private schools, both sectarian and nonsectarian. By educating a substantial number of students such schools relieve public schools of a correspondingly greater burden—to the benefit of all taxpayers. In addition, private schools may serve as a benchmark for public schools, in a manner analogous to the 'TVA yardstick' for private power companies.[43]

In support, the majority recalled Justice Powell's earlier comment, that

> parochial schools, apart from their sectarian purpose, have provided an educational alternative for millions of young Americans; they often afford wholesome competition with our public schools; and in some states they relieve substantially the tax burden incident to the operation of public schools.

These comments do not, of course, a case for state action make. Even Justices Brennan and Marshall, dissenting in *Rendell-Baker* because they believed state action existed, did not rely exclusively on the vital civic role performed by the defendant school. They conceded that executing a public function creates state action only when that function has traditionally been the exclusive domain of the government, something that could not be said of private education. Yet the growing recognition by the Court of the value and mission of private schools serves to advance beyond *Rendell-Baker*'s grudging concession of one central element in that equation: the public function view of education.

There is more to the equation, which might help tip the balance in the most appealing of cases. If the claimants were voucher-eligible students, then the case would seem stronger than that of the discharged teachers who were the *Rendell-Baker* plaintiffs. The majority was careful to restrict its holding to the claims of teachers. The dissenters argued that students' constitutional claims would have to fare better; the majority "apparently concede that actions directly affecting the students could be treated as under color of state law since the school is fulfilling the state's obligation to those children under [the applicable statutory provision]." Thus the systematic refusal of a private school to enroll some of the very voucher-eligible students for whom the program was designed, while continuing to benefit by enrolling other voucher-eligible students of its own choosing, would surely pose a more compelling case than did *Rendell-Baker*. Now we add to the mix one other volatile ingredient—unabashed racial bias as the basis for the exclusionary actions. The state-action cases leave little doubt that, while deprivation of any federally protected right may be redressed through section 1983, claims of racial discrimination have special appeal to courts facing close questions of whether private action is under color of state law. It is possible that, even in *Rendell-Baker*, the Court would have viewed differently the school's refusal to hire minority teachers had that been the basis of the suit.

There is one more antidote to the conventional analysis: especially in a situation of the kind we have before us, the whole seems more than the sum of unconnected parts. What the Court has often done on the way to rejecting state-action claims is to disaggregate various probative elements, in contrast to the aggregation or fusion that typically occurs in support of a state-action finding. Granting that performing a public function alone, or massive state funding or extensive government regulation alone, or some evidence of a symbiotic relationship by itself would not transform private conduct into state action, there are times when several such elements may blend in probative fashion. Thus it seems appropriate here not only to assess the separate import of each of these elements but also to consider the total impact of such factors on the legal status of a private school. Analyzed in this way, the case for a finding of state action may become more plausible and persuasive.

If therefore we change two key elements—the identity of the plaintiffs and the basis of their grievance—and revisit the public function concept of private action on the basis of post–*Rendell-Baker* jurisprudence, we are not ensured of a federal forum for the redress of civil rights. We are, however, substantially closer than might have seemed the case at the outset. A private school that may, with impunity, discharge teachers for reasons a public school could not invoke, should find a federal court far less sympathetic to its claimed right to practice racial bias in rejecting voucher-assisted students. (As the concluding section notes, alternative grounds for judicial intervention may be less appealing or compelling than racial bias but need also to be considered within a balance or equation somewhat more open than that of *Rendell-Baker*.)

We now return to a premise we earlier put aside: the assumption that so biased a private school admission policy could be challenged only by making the school a state actor for Fourteenth Amendment purposes. That assumption now needs to be tested, though doing so does not directly alter the state-action analysis. One could well argue that the government may not constitutionally provide public funds in any form, direct or indirect, to a private school that practices racial discrimination. Such a constraint would reflect the Supreme Court's judgment in *Norwood* v. *Harrison* that states may not lend textbooks to racially segregated private schools, even under a program that might, as an Establishment Clause matter, include students attending pervasively sectarian schools.[44] Voucher assistance would seem a fortiori from the lending of textbooks and teaching materials. Should such a ruling result, the race-based claim would become essentially moot. It would matter little whether the school could be sued for racial bias in federal court if the source of public funding could be ordered to remove that school from its eligible list. Even so, the race-based claim remains by far the most appealing paradigm for state-action purposes. And once the case has been established for federal intervention in this most compelling of situations, the extension of the rationale to less urgent or appealing cases seems only a matter of degree.

The issue could be made essentially moot in a different way. States might choose to regulate the policies of publicly aided private schools in certain ways that the Constitution requires them to operate their public schools. Thus the voucher-assisted private schools in the Milwaukee program were required, as a condition of eligibility, to observe many conditions that the Bill of Rights imposed on the city's public schools. Thoughtful proposals for government subvention, notably those of John Coons and Stephen Sugarman, also envision imposing conditions on private school participation: nondiscrimination in admissions, a measure of due process in student suspension or expulsion, and safeguards against potentially abhorrent compelled religious activities or ceremonies.[45] Such proposals have the immense virtue of extending certain constitutional rights to private schools without the need to pursue uncertain and costly federal court remedies.

In most states, however, litigation may remain the only viable option, to which we must return. Despite the hazards of ranking in order of legal or policy priority the various interests that might claim the courts' attention in this area, a few general observations may be helpful. Racial nondiscrimination, not only in admission of students and hiring of faculty but in all facets of school life, seems an easy starting point for reasons already explored. Equality of access and opportunity on grounds other than race, especially those grounds, such as gender and nationality, that are constitutionally guaranteed in the public sector, also seem compelling candidates. Nondiscrimination on the basis of sexual orientation surely deserves attention on such a roster, though it is still less fully developed in the public sector and may raise more substantial concerns among religious schools than would the banning of other forms of bias. Freedom of faculty and student speech (the very issue involved in *Rendell-Baker*) also seems an appealing candidate for eventual recognition in government-assisted private education. Finally, while the contours of constitutional protection may be less clear in public schools, minimal guarantees of due process in the termination of teachers or the suspension or expulsion of students might well extend to private schools that receive substantial public subvention. Accordingly, it seems hard to avoid this conclusion: Had the state-action issue first reached the Supreme Court in a case brought by students who had been rejected on racial grounds, and not by teachers discharged for speaking out against school policy, the whole course of litigation might have been profoundly different.

There is a final and perplexing question of policy: If we could persuade federal courts to grant such relief against private schools, would the potential risks outweigh the benefits? From *Pierce* to the present, the whole concept of school choice has been only as meaningful and as valuable as the differences between public schools and increasingly regulated private schools. To take the most extreme case: if the government so extensively prescribes the curriculum of private religious schools that insufficient time remains in the school day for the study of religion or scripture, then choice has little value. There would in practice be little left to choose, even though in theory every parent would still have the right of choice. Thus state regulation that severely constrains meaningful choice should be vulnerable on *Pierce* grounds, if nothing else.

Much the same could be said of litigation: if the result of imposing Fourteenth Amendment obligations on private schools were to destroy their distinctive character, and thus to undermine the value of choice, even the staunchest advocate of justice and equity should be alarmed. We ought to be concerned about either regulation or litigation, however appealing its premises, that would effectively nullify or undermine meaningful school choice. This factor, once again, reflects differences among grounds for intervention. The risks of barring racial discrimination in admissions seem less grave than the risks of interfering with a school's choice of teachers or its control over the activities (including the public statements) of those teachers. Between these two relatively clear extremes are other possible grounds for intervention, the effects of which on the character of a private school, and the value of a family's opportunity to choose that school, will vary substantially as well.

Notes

1. *Pickering* v. *Board of Educ.*, 391 U.S. 578 (1968). The term *choice school* has several possible meanings here. As other chapters in this volume make clear, a wide array of educational arrangements may fall under this rubric: magnet schools and others that would be clearly a part of the public school system, purely private schools that may be the beneficiaries of choice options provided by government at the other end of the scale, and various intermediate options, such as charter schools and the like.

2. 42 U.S.C. § 1983.

3. *Smith* v. *Allwright*, 321 U.S. 649 (1944); *Marsh* v. *Alabama*, 326 U.S. 501 (1946).

4. *Amalgamated Food Employees* v. *Logan Valley Plaza*, 391 U.S. 308 (1968); *Lloyd Corp.* v. *Tanner*, 407 U.S. 551 (1972); *Hudgens* v. *NLRB*, 424 U.S. 507 (1976).

5. *Burton* v. *Wilmington Parking Authority*, 365 U.S. 715 (1961).

6. *Derrington* v. *Plummer*, 240 F.2d 922 (5th Cir. 1956).

7. *Evans* v. *Newton*, 382 U.S. 296 (1966).

8. *Shelley* v. *Kraemer*, 334 U.S. 1 (1948); *Barrows* v. *Jackson*, 346 U.S. 249 (1953).

9. *Cyber Promotions, Inc.* v. *America Online*, 948 F. Supp. 456 (E.D. Pa.); *CompuServe, Inc.* v. *Cyber Promotions, Inc.*, 962 F. Supp. 1015 (S.D. Ohio 1997).

10. *Lombard* v. *Louisiana*, 373 U.S. 267 (1963); *Robinson* v. *Florida*, 378 U.S. 153 (1964); *Reitman* v. *Mulkey*, 387 U.S. 369 (1967).

11. *Jackson* v. *Metropolitan Edison Co.*, 419 U.S. 345 (1974).

12. *Columbia Broadcasting System* v. *Democratic National Committee*, 412 U.S. 94 (1973); *Garner* v. *Louisiana*, 368 U.S. 157, 183–85 (1961).

13. *Moose Lodge* v. *Irvis*, 407 U.S. 163 (1972); *San Francisco Art and Athletics, Inc.* v. *United States Olympic Comm.*, 483 U.S. 522 (1987).

14. *Simkins* v. *Moses H. Cone Memorial Hospital*, 323 F.2d 959 (4th Cir.), cert. denied, 376 U.S. 938 (1964).

15. *Rendell-Baker* v. *Kohn*, 457 U.S. 830 (1982); *Blum* v. *Yaretsky*, 457 U.S. 991 (1982).

16. *Gilmore* v. *Montgomery*, 417 U.S. 556 (1974).

17. *Norwood* v. *Harrison*, 413 U.S. 455 (1973); *Board of Educ.* v. *Allen*, 392 U.S. 236 (1968).

18. *Gilmore* v. *Montgomery*, 417 U.S. 556, 581 (1974) (White, J., concurring).

19. See L. K. Beale, "Charter Schools, Common Schools, and the Washington State Constitution," *Washington Law Review*, vol. 72 (1997), p. 535, n. 6; Robin D. Barnes, "Black America and School Choice," *Yale Law Journal*, vol. 106 (1997), pp. 2375, 2404–05; Karla A. Turekian, "Traversing the Minefields of Educational Reform: The Legality of Charter Schools," *Connecticut Law Review*, vol. 29 (1997), p. 1365.

20. *Council of Organizations* v. *Governor*, 455 Mich. 557, 566 N.W.2d 208 (1997).

21. See Beale, "Charter Schools, Common Schools, and the Washington State Constitution," for a well-developed argument that charter schools, under any of the current models, would fail to meet Washington State's constitutional constraint that the state may fund only "common schools" within a general and uniform system.

22. See Valerie Strauss, "Firing of Charter School Principal Upheld in Court," *Washington Post*, January 16, 1998, for a remarkably analogous case. The principal of one of Washington, D.C.'s first charter schools was suspended for several acts of alleged mismanagement. A group of parents sought her reinstatement in a suit against the charter school board in D.C. Superior Court. The suit was dismissed for lack of standing, as well as on the merits, with no suggestion that the court lacked jurisdiction over the board.

23. If, for example (as several states have envisioned), a public school system contracted with a private group or entity to manage a publicly funded school, the concept of charter school might not fit comfortably. Nonetheless, the same constitutional principles would seem applicable, up to the point at which the school could no longer meaningfully be seen as part of the public school system.

24. *People* v. *Bennett*, 442 Mich. 316, 501 N.W. 2d 106 (1993); *People* v. *DeJonge*, 442 Mich. 266, 501 N.W. 2d 127 (1993).

25. *Everson* v. *Board of Educ.*, 330 U.S. 1 (1947); *Board of Educ.* v. *Allen*, 392 U.S. 236 (1968); *Wolman* v. *Walter*, 433 U.S. 229 (1977); *Mueller* v. *Allen*, 463 U.S. 388 (1983); *Zobrest* v. *Catalina Foothills School Dist.*, 113 S.Ct. 2462 (1993); *Agostini* v. *Felton*, 117 S.Ct. 1997 (1997).

26. *Walz* v. *Tax Comm'n.*, 397 U.S. 664 (1970).

27. See Jesse Choper's chapter, this volume, for a fuller discussion of these issues.

28. *Rendell-Baker* v. *Kohn*, 457 U.S. 830 (1982).

29. *Rendell-Baker* v. *Kohn*, 641 F. 2d 14 (1st Cir. 1981).

30. *Blum* v. *Yaretsky*, 457 U.S. 991 (1982).

31. *Rendell-Baker* v. *Kohn*, 457 U.S. at 840–41.

32. Ibid., p. 842, n. 7.

33. Ibid., p. 843.

34. *Pickering* v. *Board of Educ.*, 391 U.S. 563 (1968).

35. See, for example, *Connick* v. *Myers*, 461 U.S. 138 (1983).

36. *Bob Jones Univ.* v. *United States*, 461 U.S. 574 (1983).

37. *Runyon* v. *McCrary*, 427 U.S. 160 (1976). Further, the Civil Rights Act of 1991 would appear to provide a remedy against racial discrimination imposed upon a student already admitted to an otherwise private school.

38. *Rendell-Baker* v. *Kohn*, 457 U.S. at 848.

39. Jesse H. Choper, "Thoughts on State Action," *Washington University Law Quarterly*, vol. 1979 (1979), pp. 757, 778.

40. *Evans* v. *Newton*, 382 U.S. 296, 321–22 (1966) (Harlan, J., dissenting).

41. Ibid., p. 322.

42. *Pierce* v. *Society of Sisters*, 268 U.S. 510 (1925).

43. *Mueller* v. *Allen*, 463 U.S. 388, 395 (1983).

44. *Norwood* v. *Harrison*, 413 U.S. 455 (1973); *Board of Educ.* v. *Allen*, 392 U.S. 236 (1968).

45. See John E. Coons and Stephen D. Sugarman, *Scholarships for Children* (Berkeley, Calif.: Institute of Governmental Studies Press, 1992).

CHAPTER EIGHT

Federal Constitutional Issues

JESSE H. CHOPER

The subject of school choice is a fruitful source of constitutional problems. It may be that, ultimately, the determinative issues will be those arising under state constitutional provisions. This chapter does not explore that set of principles. Rather, it discusses a series of challenging and unresolved questions presented mainly by five clauses of our national Constitution: the Establishment, Free Exercise, and Free Speech provisions of the First Amendment and the Due Process and State Action requirements of the Fourteenth Amendment.

The Establishment Clause as a Bar to Public Financial Assistance to Sectarian Schools

In 1968, when I wrote "The Establishment Clause and Aid to Parochial Schools," there had been only one significant Supreme Court decision dealing with the subject, the 1947 ruling in *Everson* v. *Board of Education*, which upheld a New Jersey township's payment of the cost of bus transportation for children going to and from all nonprofit schools, including those that were church related.[1] Beginning in 1968, however, numerous high

This chapter could not have been completed without the exceptionally able assistance of Eric B. Wolff, Boalt Hall Class of 1998. I am also grateful to Frank R. Kemerer, Robert C. Post, Stephen D. Sugarman, and John C. Yoo for helpful comments. Research for this work was provided by the Max Weingarten Fund.

court pronouncements and voluminous works of scholarship have considered Establishment Clause barriers to public financial assistance to parochial schools, and for some time, a single justice has effectively dictated the Court's results on the issue.[2]

The Court's two most recent decisions, *Rosenberger* v. *University of Virginia* and *Agostini* v. *Felton,* have led several commentators to suggest that the matter has been resolved: many programs of aid to private schools, and particularly voucher programs that include parochial schools, are now constitutionally permissible.[3] While this may be true, considerable doubt remains, with Justice O'Connor as the swing vote. Below I sketch a brief history of the case law over the last three decades and then focus on *Rosenberger* and *Agostini* and why I believe that they should be read narrowly, reserving decision on the critical questions regarding voucher programs and other forms of aid to parochial schools.

The Lemon Test and Its Application in the 1970s and 1980s

In 1971 the Burger Court used the case of *Lemon* v. *Kurtzman*—for the first time invalidating a program of aid to parochial schools—to articulate its now famous (and highly criticized) three-part test for judging alleged violations of the Establishment Clause.[4] The Court reviewed statutes from Pennsylvania and Rhode Island that provided for payment, either to nonpublic schools or directly to their instructors, of salary supplements for teachers of secular subjects. For example, the Rhode Island law authorized state augmentations of up to 15 percent of the salaries of private school teachers of subjects such as mathematics, physical science, modern foreign languages, and physical education. Chief Justice Burger wrote the opinion for a near-unanimous Court. Justice White, who consistently voted to uphold aid to parochial schools, was the lone dissenter.

The Court found that the statutes in *Lemon* had a secular, as opposed to a religious, purpose, thus satisfying the first element of its three-part test. Seeking to improve the quality of secular education received by children who attend nonpublic schools, including those that are church related, has routinely been held by the justices to be a satisfactory nonreligious purpose. The second and third prongs of the *Lemon* test are that the challenged program must have a primary effect that does not advance religion and must not result in excessive entanglement between church and state. In *Lemon*, the Court hung the states (and the recipient parochial schools) on the horns of a dilemma with respect to these latter two aspects of the test. The Court began with a critical premise: the mission of church-related elementary and secondary schools is to teach religion, and all subjects either are, or carry the potential of being, permeated with sectarian ideology.[5] Therefore, if the government were to help fund any subjects in these schools, the effect would be to aid religion, unless public officials monitored the situation to see to it that the courses being assisted with public money were not infused with religious doctrine. But if public officials did engage in adequate surveillance—this is the other horn of the dilemma—there would be excessive entanglement between the government and religion, the image being state "spies" regularly or periodically sitting in many or all classes conducted in parochial schools.

It is fair to say that application of the *Lemon* test has produced a conceptual disaster area, generating ad hoc judgments that are incapable of being reconciled on any principled basis. For example, a provision for therapeutic and diagnostic health services to parochial school pupils by public employees was held invalid if provided in the parochial school but not if offered at a neutral site, even a mobile unit immediately adjacent to the parochial school.[6] Reimbursement to parochial schools for the expense of administering teacher-prepared tests required by state law was held invalid, but the state could compensate parochial schools for the expense of administering state-prepared tests.[7] The government could lend textbooks to parochial school pupils because, the Court explained, the books can be checked in advance for religious content and are "self-policing," but the government could not lend other seemingly self-policing instructional items, such as tape recorders, films, movie projectors, laboratory equipment, and maps.[8] The public could underwrite the cost of bus transportation *to* parochial schools, which the Court has ruled are permeated with religion, but the public was forbidden to pay for transportation for field trips *from* these schools "to governmental, industrial, cultural, and scientific centers designed to enrich the secular studies of students."[9] Indeed, in an unusually candid dictum, the Court once forthrightly conceded that its approach in this area "sacrifices clarity and predictability for flexibility," a euphemism for expressly admitting the absence of any principled rationale for its product.[10]

The Court first considered a broad-based program of aid to all nonpublic schools during the mid-1970s, in *Committee for Public Education* v. *Nyquist.*[11] New York gave a partial tuition tax credit to parents who sent their children to private schools, including those that were church related. For those parents too poor to be liable for income taxes and therefore unable to benefit from a tax credit, New York gave an outright grant of up to 50 percent of tuition. The Court, speaking through Justice Powell, held this program invalid under the second prong of the *Lemon* test: even though the benefit was awarded to the parents, its primary effect was to aid religion. The rationale, which is realistic enough, was that the program would eventually result in money being funneled to the parochial school.

A decade later, however, in *Mueller* v. *Allen*, the Court upheld a quite similar tax benefit plan.[12] Minnesota gave parents who sent their children to any nonprofit school (public, private, or church related) a tax deduction (rather than a tax credit, as in *Nyquist*) for any school-connected expenditures they made for transportation and tuition and for the costs of textbooks, instructional materials, and equipment, as long as these were not used to teach religion. Even though a footnote in Justice Powell's opinion in *Nyquist* left unresolved the validity of an aid program whose "class of beneficiaries included *all* school children, those in public as well as those in private schools," most observers felt that there was no constitutional distinction between this Minnesota tax deduction program and the New York tax credit scheme of ten years earlier.[13] But with the five votes of Justice Rehnquist, Chief Justice Burger, Justice White, Justice O'Connor, and Justice Powell (who was the only member of the Court voting with the majority in both *Nyquist* and *Mueller*), the Court upheld Minnesota's tax deduction plan. Although Justice Rehnquist's majority opinion found *Nyquist* "difficult to distinguish," his primary distinction was that the Minnesota statute was facially neutral.[14] Unlike the New York statute, Minnesota's deduction plan aided all parents of schoolchildren, whether they sent their children to public schools or private schools of either a secular or sectarian character. Justice Rehnquist drew upon Justice Powell's opinion in *Widmar* v. *Vincent* and reasoned that when the government assists a broad class of beneficiaries, the effect is not primarily to advance religion.[15]

Mueller opened a potentially large window for aid to parochial schools. After *Lemon* and its progeny, especially *Nyquist*, the government had only narrow opportunities for providing financial assistance to church-related schools. After *Mueller*, the issue seemingly became a matter of form, particularly by using programs of aid that went to parents (or children) rather than to the schools themselves. For example, what New York should have done in *Nyquist* to broaden its recipient class was to simply provide tax credits to parents who sent their children to public schools as well as to parents who sent their children to all private schools (including parochial schools).[16]

Plans that pay aid directly to all schools, including parochial schools, remain more doubtful. In *Aguilar* v. *Felton* and *School District of Grand Rapids* v. *Ball*, the Court reviewed programs in which public employees provided "auxiliary services" (remedial and enrichment courses in such areas as mathematics, reading, art, music, and physical education) on the premises of parochial schools.[17] In *Aguilar*, the program was pursuant to Title I of the federal Elementary and Secondary Education Act of 1965, and the enrichment courses were available in public schools as well as private schools. Thus Title I was facially neutral, as in *Mueller*. Even so, the Court held that public employees providing Title I courses on the premises of parochial schools violated the Establishment Clause because of the third prong of the *Lemon* test: "excessive entanglement of church and state," specifically with respect to a monitoring program whereby a public field adviser would make monthly unannounced visits to ensure that no public employees were inculcating religion.[18] In *Ball*, Michigan provided funds for shared time, a program offering "remedial" and "enrichment" courses supplementing the "core curriculum" embodied in state accreditation standards. Although quite similar to New York City's implementation of Title I, the Michigan plan had no provision for monitoring. The Court still struck it down, in this instance under *Lemon*'s "effect" prong, because the publicly paid teachers in parochial schools were at risk of inculcating religion, a "symbolic link" between church and state was created, and religious indoctrination was "impermissibly" subsidized.[19] Considered together, the 1985 rulings in *Ball* and *Aguilar* sharply illustrate the continued vitality of the dilemma posed in *Lemon* for programs that provided aid directly to parochial schools.

A year later, in *Witters* v. *Washington Department of Services for the Blind*, the Court returned to the form of aid that involved payment to the individual rather than to the church-related schools.[20] The case concerned a state grant to a student for attending a religious school for religious purposes and seemed to produce a majority of justices signaling that school voucher programs that included parochial schools would be constitutionally permissible. A Washington plan provided vocational educational assistance to the visually handicapped. Blind persons could get a voucher (although it was not called that) and use it at an educational institution that prepared them for work. The recipient was studying at a Christian college "in order to equip himself for a career as a pastor, missionary or youth director."[21] The Court plainly assumed that he was studying religion; but a unanimous decision written by Justice Marshall—one of the strictest separationists then on the Court—held that there was no violation of the Establishment Clause.

The concurrences, however, addressed the much broader question regarding the permissibility of vouchers. Justice Powell, joined by Chief Justice Burger and Justice Rehnquist, concurred separately, expressing concern that the opinion for the Court did not rely more specifically on *Mueller*, the tax deduction case.[22] Justice Powell then emphasized that the Washington program did not have a primary effect that advanced religion because, quoting from *Mueller*, "state programs that are wholly neutral in offering educational assistance to a class defined without reference to religion do not violate the second part of the *Lemon* v. *Kurtzman* test, because any aid to religion results from the private choices of individual beneficiaries."[23] Justice White and Justice O'Connor wrote separate opinions agreeing with Justice Powell with respect to the significance of *Mueller*. These five justices (who composed the majority in *Mueller*) clearly described a situation that includes many proposed voucher plans: the aid goes to all parents who have children in school, public, private, and parochial; redeeming the vouchers at parochial schools is the product of private choice.

More than a decade ago, I read *Witters* as resolving the federal constitutional issue: "Vouchers are now valid but, on the other hand, if aid is provided directly to the schools, it will usually be held invalid. That is where the law stands."[24] I have become less confident of that conclusion, based not so much on changes in the Court's personnel as on Justice O'Connor's further articulation of her position. Apart from the fact that *Witters* involved higher education, not elementary or secondary schools, and that the Court has drawn a sharp distinction between these different types of recipient of public aid, Justice O'Connor's posture in several recent decisions suggests real uncertainty on her part.[25] Further, she is the needed fifth vote, along with Chief Justice Rehnquist and Justices Scalia, Kennedy, and Thomas, for upholding a voucher program, as well as most other forms of public aid that benefit church-related schools.

Developments in the 1990s

In *Zobrest* v. *Catalina Foothills School District*, the Court upheld the state's payment of a sign language interpreter for a deaf student, pursuant to a program of general assistance to persons with disabilities, even though the student attended a Catholic high school.[26] Relying mainly on *Mueller* and *Witters*, the Court reasoned, inter alia, that payment of government funds to a state employee is distinguishable from payment of public money directly to a parochial school, again emphasizing this formal distinction in respect to the recipient of the aid.

Justice O'Connor dissented in *Zobrest*, although not on the merits, possibly suggesting some reluctance on her part to follow the full distance of the course of reasoning in the earlier opinions that she had joined. Such hesitation was subsequently confirmed, first by her concurrence in *Rosenberger* v. *Rector of the University of Virginia* and more recently in *Agostini* v. *Felton*, overturning *Aguilar* v. *Felton* by a five-to-four margin.[27] It is fair to speculate that when Justice O'Connor was assigned to write the opinion in *Agostini*, it was because hers was the narrowest position in the majority, and thus her vote was particularly needed to reach the majority's conclusion.

In *Rosenberger*, the Court held, five to four, that the University of Virginia had engaged in viewpoint-based discrimination (which is virtually always forbidden) and thus violated First Amendment freedom of speech when it used student fees to support printing newspapers of nonreligious student groups but withheld such funding from religious student newspapers.[28] Wide Awake Productions was a student publication denied an appropriation—because of its "Christian viewpoint"—from the university's student activities fund, monies collected from a mandatory student fee.[29] In rejecting the university's contention that its subsidization of this kind of newspaper would violate the First Amendment separation of church and state, the Court held that a principle of neutrality applied: "official censorship would be far more inconsistent with the Establishment Clause's dictates than would governmental provision of secular printing services on a religion-blind basis."[30]

It has been strongly urged that *Rosenberger* stands for a broad proposition regarding equal access to public benefits for religious educational institutions, making it "abundantly clear" that "inclusion of religious schools in voucher plans is . . . constitutionally permissible."[31] There are two problems with such a broad interpretation of *Rosenberger*: it disregards the narrowness of Justice Kennedy's majority opinion as well as Justice O'Connor's concurrence, and it contradicts many common intuitions regarding the Establishment Clause. I read *Rosenberger* as endorsing only a very limited right of equal access to public funds for religious institutions, which at the very least ends where Establishment Clause violations begin, which is probably wherever Justice O'Connor chooses to find them.

Justice Kennedy placed two clear and important restrictions on the scope of the Court's ruling in *Rosenberger*. First, he emphasized that the university was not transferring money directly to Wide Awake. Rather, the check was drawn to the printer of the newspaper with which the religious student organization contracted to produce it.[32] While this distinction, once again invoking the significance of the aid's recipient, may not be persuasive, it plainly indicates the majority's discomfort in recognizing a general right of equal access to public educational funds by religious institutions. Second, Justice Kennedy pointed out that the case did not involve general support for the activities of a religious institution but was confined to financial aid for newspapers.[33] If the University of Virginia were barred from funding religious newspapers, the Court reasoned, some university administrator would have to review student publications to determine whether they were religious or not. This raises the spectre of classic censorship and the consequent chilling effect on the freedoms of speech and press.

Justice Kennedy's second argument is plainly more appealing than his first distinction. More important for our purpose, however, is that this point underlines the narrowness of the Court's decision, confining its rationale to government funding of newspapers published by religious organizations—and nothing else. Church-related schools can only find solace from an equal access rationale in *Rosenberger* for their inclusion in a voucher program by ignoring this limitation.

Probably the most critical restricting distinction came in the concurrence written by Justice O'Connor.[34] (That it was a separate opinion does not diminish its importance, because Justice O'Connor was one of the five members of the Court that made up the majority.) She stressed that the money for the university of Virginia's student activities fund came from student fees, not from the university's general account. Justice O'Connor opined that any students who object to the way such money is spent may have a right under the First Amendment to opt out and get a refund.[35] This is a far-reaching circumscription of the *Rosenberger* holding. Taxpayers have no constitutional right to opt out if they do not like the way the government spends compulsorily raised tax funds. Thus virtually all other government expenditure programs would be distinguishable from the one in *Rosenberger*, in particular, any tax-funded voucher program or other plan of public assistance that provided benefits to parochial schools.

Apart from the narrowness of the majority's approach in *Rosenberger*, the policies and values that underlie the Establishment Clause would stand in the way of an equal access principle broad enough to reach a voucher program that would fund all costs of a sectarian education, including its acknowledged religious component. For example, suppose that the state were to appropriate money to all voluntary organizations to buy insignias for their members. Public funds would be used to purchase the Chamber of Commerce symbol for one group and the United Way symbol for another. I find it contrary to Establishment Clause principles, however, for public funds to be used to buy Catholic crucifixes and Stars of David for religious organizations. Or suppose that the government decided to construct new buildings for all voluntary associations. Once again, the broad equal access principle ascribed to *Rosenberger* would result in the government erecting a new building not only for the United Way and the Chamber of Commerce but also for the Roman Catholic Church, the Episcopalian Church, and various Jewish religious denominations.

More realistically, suppose that the federal government appropriated funds to public or private organizations for education advocacy programs to prevent teenage pregnancy. This, of course, was true of an actual case: *Bowen* v. *Kendrick*, involving the Adolescent Family Life Act of 1981.[36] Suppose that one of the grantees were the Roman Catholic Church, which proves to be very effective in teaching and advocating abstinence as the way to avoid pregnancy, employing as its primary vehicle of persuasion the inculcation of fundamental Roman Catholic doctrine. Can the government pay for that? Under the broad neutrality principle that commentators find in *Rosenberger*, there would be no violation of the Establishment Clause. Yet I seriously doubt that all five justices that composed the majority in *Rosenberger* would go that far. At the least, Justice O'Connor would appear to have serious reservations regarding such public funding that would pay for religious indoctrination, buildings, and insignias. Her separate opinion in *Rosenberger* strongly hints as much, and her opinion for the Court in *Agostini* is deliberately narrow regarding such questions.

In *Agostini* v. *Felton*, Justice O'Connor emphasized key facts about the Title I program at issue that place extensive limits on the reach of her opinion for the Court.[37] *Agostini* v. *Felton* involved the same parties and facts as *Aguilar* v. *Felton*. They returned to court claiming that "decisional law had changed to make legal what the injunction was designed to prevent," pointing in particular to the statements of five justices in *Board of Education of Kiryas Joel Village School District* v. *Grumet* calling for the reexamination or overruling of *Aguilar*.[38] In *Agostini*, those five members of the Court, agreeing that subsequent decisions had departed from the assumptions of *Ball*, overturned *Aguilar*.

Justice O'Connor, writing for the five-member majority, stressed that the Title I services were "supplemental to the regular curricula" and did not "relieve sectarian schools of costs they otherwise would have borne in educating their students."[39] Strengthening this point, she added that Title I services are only available to eligible recipients.[40] Second, she underlined that "no Title I funds ever reach the coffers of religious schools."[41] Third, her description of the plan before the Court carefully emphasized that assignment of instructors and counselors to private schools

> were made on a voluntary basis and without regard to the religious affiliation of the employee or the wishes of the private school. . . . A large majority of Title I teachers worked in nonpublic schools with religious affiliations different from their own [and] moved among the private schools, spending fewer than five days a week at the same school. . . . All religious symbols were to be removed from classrooms used for Title I services. . . . The rules acknowledged that it might be necessary for Title I teachers to consult with a student's regular classroom teacher to assess the student's particular needs and progress, but admonished instructors to limit those consultations to mutual professional concerns regarding the student's education. . . . To ensure compliance with these rules, a publicly employed field supervisor was to attempt to make at least one unannounced visit to each teacher's classroom every month.[42]

Justice O'Connor's highly fact-specific approach supported her characterization of recent rulings as merely abandoning the presumption that "the placement of public employees on parochial school grounds inevitably results in the impermissible effect of state-supported indoctrination or constitutes a symbolic union between government and religion" and confirmed her exceedingly narrow statement of the holding in the present case.[43] Consequently, it seems that the Court's holding is too narrow and its majority too fragile to support bold claims about a green light for voucher programs or other substantial public aid to parochial schools, as some have suggested.[44]

Justice O'Connor's earlier position in *Ball*, the companion case to *Aguilar*, may be especially instructive regarding where she stands on aid to parochial schools.[45] She dissented from that part of the judgment that struck down the shared time program mentioned earlier, essentially a Michigan-sponsored equivalent of Title I, albeit without a monitoring system. This aspect of Justice O'Connor's opinion in *Ball* became prevailing doctrine in *Agostini*. However, Justice O'Connor concurred in that part of the judgment in *Ball* invalidating a publicly funded program called community education, which offered general academic and hobby courses to children and adults at nonpublic schools:

> The record indicates that Community Education courses in the parochial schools are overwhelmingly taught by instructors who are current full-time employees of the parochial school. The teachers offer secular subjects to the same parochial school students who attend their regular parochial school classes. In addition, the supervisors of the Community Education program in the parochial schools are by and large the principals of the very schools where the classes are offered. *When full-time parochial school teachers receive public funds to teach secular courses to their parochial school students under parochial school supervision, I agree that the program has the perceived and actual effect of advancing the religious aims of the church-related schools.* This is particularly the case where, as here, religion pervades the curriculum and the teachers are accustomed to bring religion to play in everything they teach.[46]

As the only available fifth vote to sustain voucher plans, or most other significant government assistance programs that include religious schools, Justice O'Connor calls the tune. Her views in *Ball* and the narrow and fact-based nature of her opinions in *Agostini* and *Rosenberger* seriously caution against confidently counting on her support for any broad program of aid to parochial schools that she believes a "reasonable observer" (or an "objective observer") would perceive as a government endorsement of religion.[47] On the one hand, Justice O'Connor has been willing to uphold the aid in *Rosenberger* (as well as in *Witters*) despite the resulting "direct funding of core religious activities by an arm of the State."[48] On the other hand, she disapproved of the program in *Ball*, which involved support by the state of only secular courses. Hence it may well be that she will be more inclined to permit voucher programs (and other aid to parents, as in *Mueller*) regardless of the use to which they are put by the ultimate recipient, rather than forms of assistance that go directly to the schools themselves (or to their teachers, as in *Ball*), even when spent for purely nonreligious purposes. This possible outcome illustrates a critical difference between Justice O'Connor's "endorsement" approach (which appears to command the support of five justices) and my own analysis.[49] The test I propose would bar "government aid to church-related schools [that] would inevitably be used for religious ends" but would uphold it when "the state receives full secular value for its money regardless of any [ultimate] benefit to religion."[50]

The Exclusion of Religious Schools from Government Education Funding Programs

Significant doctrinal questions arise under both the Religion Clauses and the Free Speech Clause in respect to two types of education finance plans, one wholly conventional and the other a voucher program or other form of state aid to nonpublic schools. In the first, the state decides only to assist public schools, leaving all private schools (secular and sectarian) without government funding. In the second, under which the state supports nonpublic schools as well, we assume that including parochial schools is constitutionally permissible but that a state implements a system that excludes religious schools from the plan.

The Public-Nonpublic Distinction

Given the long history in this country of funding only public schools, it would surely seem quixotic to challenge the constitutionality of this practice. But a broad reading of the *Rosenberger* decision or *Church of Lukumi Babalu Aye, Inc.* v. *City of Hialeah* presents potential free speech and free exercise problems.[51]

In *Hialeah*, the Court held that "at a minimum, the protections of the Free Exercise Clause pertain if the law at issue discriminates against some or all religious beliefs or regulates or prohibits conduct because it is undertaken for religious reasons."[52] Does the state discriminate against religion when it funds only public schools? After all, most nonpublic schools will be church related.[53] The obvious counterargument is that the state is not discriminating against religion as such but rather against all nonpublic schools. Although determining precisely what constitutes discrimination often presents exceedingly difficult questions, it would likely be concluded that the public-nonpublic distinction has too loose a fit to be considered discrimination against religion. Rather, the state program would likely be characterized as neutral and generally applicable, such that any incidental burden on religion would not have constitutional significance.[54]

Even if funding only public schools does not discriminate against religion under *Hialeah*, it may very well discriminate against certain viewpoints, which as we have seen is particularly disfavored under the Free Speech Clause. All schools teach values of many kinds. Indeed, many believe schools are not doing enough to teach certain values. Moreover,

> the idea that individuals should choose values according to "rational" criteria [as is taught in various public and nonsectarian private

schools] operates conceptually as the ultimate value position of secular humanism, just as the idea that individuals should choose values
on the basis of religious criteria operates conceptually as the ultimate
value in religious education.[55]

Of course, we need not look to "ultimate values" to witness value education in most public schools. Simple messages regarding honesty, equality, abstention from drugs, and respect for parents and elders amount to
the inculcation of values (with many having religious roots). Especially if
"the justification for exclusive funding of public education . . . must be that
through public education society can be more confident that pupils will be
steeped in tolerance and the values of democracy," then a strong application of *Rosenberger*'s free speech principle regarding viewpoint discrimination could raise a serious constitutional question respecting the
conventional practice of states funding only public schools.[56]

The Court is well aware of the tension between its virtually unqualified
stand against viewpoint discrimination and common practices of the government that deliberately influence the thoughts, beliefs, and values of its
citizens and people throughout the world. For example, an uncompromis-
ing prohibition on government viewpoint discrimination would mean that
a student in a public law school, who contends that the federal government
has no power to tax, could not be downgraded in his constitutional law
course for stating a plainly inaccurate position.[57] Or as the Court has
pointed out, an unbending principle of government viewpoint neutrality
would forbid the National Endowment for Democracy from promoting
democracy worldwide unless it also encouraged "competing lines of political philosophy such as communism and fascism."[58] Accordingly, the Court
has recognized that since "Congress has wide latitude to set spending priorities," it "may allocate . . . funding according to criteria that would be
impermissible were direct regulation of speech or a criminal penalty at
stake."[59] Moreover, although the Court has never explicitly conceded that
the government may engage in viewpoint discrimination when exercising
its spending powers, and indeed has hinted strongly that it may not do so,
nonetheless the justices have fashioned the concept of the government as
speaker, a doctrine whose implications would appear to allow the state to
fund only public schools and engage in at least some content and viewpoint
discrimination in their administration.[60]

In *Rosenberger*, the Court explained the "perplexing territory" of the
government as a speaker as follows:

When the State is the speaker, it may make content-based choices. When the [state] University determines the content of the education it provides, it is the University speaking, and we have permitted the government to regulate the content of what is or is not expressed when it is the speaker or when it enlists private entities to convey its own message. In the same vein, in *Rust* v. *Sullivan*, we recognized that when the government appropriates public funds to promote a particular policy of its own it is entitled to say what it wishes.[61]

The Court went on to distinguish the use of the student fees in *Rosenberger*, finding that this was not a situation of the government as speaker but rather the state university's expending funds to indiscriminately "encourage a diversity of views from *private* speakers."[62] At the edges, the line between the government speaking through public schools and the government encouraging diversity by funding student speech at those public schools is complex and blurry.[63] However, when the state is simply determining the content of its education (and not all other forms of education or value lessons that children may receive) through funding only public schools, this presents a fairly clear example of permissible content or viewpoint discrimination by the government as a speaker.

However, even though the Free Speech Clause does not in fact forbid certain viewpoint discrimination when the government speaks, it does not exclude the force of other constitutional provisions in this context. Thus the Establishment Clause forbids the government from engaging in religious speech and from discriminating among religions when speaking.[64] While the government may adopt viewpoints that some or all religious groups favor, such as promoting sexual abstinence, if it does so for secular reasons, it may not, even merely as speaker, choose to promote the viewpoint of Catholicism over Protestantism or Judaism.[65] Still, since under present constitutional doctrine there is no establishment of speech clause, the state may "establish speech" by funding only public schools or by promoting democracy throughout the world, even if some of that speech appears much like a secular religion, as long as the government has secular justifications for doing so.[66]

The Religious-Nonreligious Distinction

While the traditional exclusive funding of public education may survive constitutional challenge under *Hialeah* and *Rosenberger*, if a state were to craft a voucher program that excluded religious schools but included other nonreligious private schools, the program might well run afoul of both free speech and free exercise precepts. First, such a program would plainly discriminate on its face against "some or all religious beliefs," violating the basic protections of the Free Exercise Clause, unless justified after strict scrutiny (that is, unless the exclusion of parochial schools is shown to be necessary to a compelling government interest).[67] Second, since all schools teach values, the state could be fairly seen as discriminating against religious viewpoints, much as the University of Virginia had done in *Rosenberger*, and would also be subject to strict scrutiny under the Free Speech Clause. Unless Establishment Clause concerns with providing support to parochial schools are found to present a compelling government interest— and I am assuming otherwise in this discussion—both *Hialeah* and *Rosenberger* would appear to compel the inclusion of religious schools in any voucher program or other plan of aid to education that included nonreligious private schools.

Moreover, as a consequence of this analysis, states would likely be forbidden to turn to their own constitutions to prohibit any public funding of parochial schools that would be permissible under the federal Constitution. The subsequent history of *Witters* illustrates this point. After the U.S. Supreme Court rejected the Establishment Clause challenge to the voucher for the blind student that would be spent at a religious college, the Washington Supreme Court on remand, interpreting the Washington State Constitution, held that the tuition assistance at issue violated its state constitution, which like a number of others has been interpreted to erect higher barriers to aid or support of sectarian schools than those of the Establishment Clause.[68] Under *Hialeah* and *Rosenberger*, this reading of a state constitution could very well constitute impermissible discrimination against religious schools and the viewpoints they espouse and thus violate the First Amendment.[69] A state might support funding all except religious schools by relying on its power as "speaker" to discriminate against viewpoints. This argument highlights the blurry distinction between the government speaking through schools and the government encouraging diversity of viewpoints at schools. Indeed, with the recent phenomenon of charter schools, states are funding a plethora of new schools, creating a much more diverse patchwork of "public" schools than ever before. On the one hand, if the government were to fund traditional public schools, charter schools, and nonreligious private schools but not parochial schools—the dividing line being whether or not the school is church related—the scheme might well be seen (as suggested above) as directly analogous to *Rosenberger*.

There, the Court found that the use of mandatory student fees to support student publications was an attempt by the university to "encourage a diversity of views from private speakers," and it ruled that excluding religious student publications from this scheme violated free speech.[70] When policymakers speak of vouchers or other forms of government funding of traditionally nonpublic schools, the operative term is always *school choice*, a significant aspect of which concerns the diversity of values provided by participating schools. If the state's goal is seen as encouraging such diversity, then excluding religious schools is impermissible viewpoint discrimination under *Rosenberger*.

On the other hand, the state may contend that it has merely enlisted "private speakers to transmit specific information pertaining to [the government's] own program" or to "convey [the government's] message."[71] By this characterization, the state would seek to be perceived as merely speaking through nonpublic entities, with religious schools communicating a message that the state permissibly chooses not to impart. Such an argument would draw heavily on *Rust* v. *Sullivan*, involving Title X of the federal Public Health Service Act, which subsidized family planning clinics but stated that no money could be used in programs "where abortion is a method of family planning."[72] The Department of Health and Human Services issued regulations implementing the act, which forbade Title X clinic employees from "counseling concerning the use of abortion as a method of family planning or provid[ing] referral for abortion as a method of family planning" and "engaging in activities that 'encourage, promote or advocate abortion as a method of family planning.'" The Court, in a five-to-four decision, upheld the regulations as a permissible instance of the government "selectively fund[ing] a program to encourage certain activities it believes to be in the public interest, without at the same time funding an alternative program which seeks to deal with the problem in another way." The Court found that the regulations did not represent impermissible "viewpoint discrimination" but merely the government's choice "to fund one activity to the exclusion of the other." In subsequently describing *Rust*, the *Rosenberger* Court implied that *Rust* illustrates the principle that when the government is the speaker, viewpoint discrimination does not violate the Free Speech Clause of the First Amendment. Indeed, "when the government disburses public funds to private entities to convey a governmental message, it may take legitimate and appropriate steps to ensure that its message is neither garbled nor distorted by the grantee."[73]

It would follow, the state would reason, that its funding all but religious schools was merely protecting its educational messages from views it considered to be inappropriate or undesirable, a situation not governed by *Rosenberger*, in which the state's purpose (at least according to the Court) was to "indiscriminately encourage a diversity of views from private speakers."[74] Nor is *Rust*'s applicability to an all-but-religious-schools funding program rebutted by the contention that a major reason for the state's support of a diverse array of schools is to encourage teaching programs that will be different in content and values from traditional public schools. The state policy to promote educational diversity and choice, but to exclude only church-related providers, may look very much like what was held unconstitutional in *Rosenberger*. It may also be seen as little different from what was upheld in *Rust*, wherein the government funded a "broad range" of family planning programs, barring only abortion.[75] In sum, it is difficult to predict whether the *Rosenberger* or *Rust* precedent would govern and whether, if *Rust* were to prevail, it would also overcome *Hialeah*'s Free Exercise Clause objection to a state's supporting all schools except those that are church related.[76]

Religious Restrictions by Sectarian Schools in Admissions, Employment, and Other Programs

If parochial schools participate in state-funded school choice plans, may they discriminate on the basis of religion in their admissions and hiring decisions or require students and faculty to participate in religious activities? The Constitution requires strict scrutiny of state action that disadvantages or discriminates against individuals on the basis of religion.[77] Because the recipient schools will receive substantial public funds and probably be subject to significant public regulation, the first issue is whether these schools may be held to the constitutional obligations of the state. Under current state action doctrine, religious-based conduct by parochial schools in voucher programs would not be subject to the Fourteenth Amendment except in the unlikely event that the state compelled such action. On the other hand, it is not unlikely that at least some states (or cities) might apply a general nondiscrimination policy to private nonsectarian and parochial schools in voucher (or other public aid) programs, along with public schools generally. Sectarian schools may argue that such prohibitions against the use of religious criteria in admissions or hiring, or the scheduling of compulsory religious programs, abridge their free exercise of religion. While current constitutional doctrine would not entitle parochial schools to an exemption under the Free Exercise Clause from such neutral, generally applicable laws, a 1925 decision of the Supreme Court, establishing a constitutional right of parents to direct their children's education, may afford some relief. Finally, the state may contend that, regardless of any constitutional rights that church-related schools may have to follow their religious dictates, the acceptance of public financial assistance alters the result.

State Action

Although the subject of school choice and state action is thoroughly covered elsewhere in this book, a brief treatment may be helpful here as well.[78]

Regardless of its receipt of vouchers or other government assistance, it is highly doubtful that a parochial school would be deemed a state actor under the present state of the law if its religious discrimination in admissions or hiring or compelled religious devotion were challenged. The key decisions are *Rendell-Baker* v. *Kohn* and *Blum* v. *Yaretsky*.[79] In *Rendell-Baker*, the case most analogous to the voucher program context, a privately operated school for maladjusted high school students received 90 to 99 percent of its operating budget from public sources. Plaintiff was a vocational counselor at the school who supported a contentious proposal giving greater responsibilities to a student-staff council. When discharged, she brought a federal civil rights (section 1983) action against the school, alleging deprivation of procedural due process as well as violation of her First Amendment rights.[80] The Court, noting that the state action inquiry for Fourteenth Amendment purposes is the same as the "under color of state law" inquiry for purposes of section 1983, held that the private school was not a state actor and thus could not be subject to suit under section 1983. In *Blum*, a procedural due process challenge was brought against several nursing homes, primarily for patient transfer decisions made by nursing home physicians and administrators. The state subsidized the operating and capital costs of the nursing homes and paid the medical expenses of more than 90 percent of the patients.

The Court in *Rendell-Baker* (and *Blum*) applied a four-factor test to determine state action. First, the Court considered public funding. Although the school in *Rendell-Baker* was at least 90 percent publicly funded, the Court ruled that "the school's receipt of public funds" did not make "the discharge decisions acts of the State."[81] Second, the Court surveyed the extensive state regulation of the school but found that "the decisions to discharge the petitioners were not compelled or even influenced by any state regulation."[82] Third, the Court inquired whether the school performed a "public function," defined as an activity that has been "traditionally the exclusive prerogative of the State," and concluded that since the state had only recently undertaken responsibility for educating maladjusted students, the function was hardly an exclusively public prerogative.[83] Finally, the Court rejected any "symbiotic relationship" between the school and the state, characterizing the relationship as "not different from that of many contractors performing services for the government."[84]

The *Rendell-Baker* analysis seemingly would apply to any parochial school that participates in a voucher program or other plan of public assistance. Private schools could select students and staff on the basis of religion and could sponsor compulsory religious rituals and not be state actors under the Fourteenth Amendment, except in the extremely unlikely scenario in which the state compelled such conduct. Under the existing decisions, neither public funding nor the functions performed by parochial schools would render them state actors, and they would have a relationship much like a contractor performing services for the government.[85]

Finally, it should be noted that there are Supreme Court decisions concerning racial segregation in public schools that, if taken literally, would present serious constitutional difficulties for the inclusion of parochial schools in voucher programs. In *Norwood* v. *Harrison*, Mississippi loaned textbooks to students in racially segregated private schools.[86] In holding this to be in violation of the Equal Protection Clause, the Court reasoned that "a State's constitutional obligation requires it to steer clear, not only of operating the old dual system of racially segregated schools, *but also of giving significant aid to institutions that practice racial or other invidious discrimination*": a "State may not grant the type of tangible financial aid here involved if that aid has a significant tendency to facilitate, reinforce, and support private discrimination." Of direct relevance to the question of vouchers, the Court even likened the provision of textbooks to "tuition grants." In dictum, *Norwood* referred to the question of aid to sectarian schools engaging in religious discrimination by saying that such aid could be "properly confined to the secular functions of sectarian schools." Such would not necessarily be the case with vouchers. However, *Norwood* does not involve the question of whether religious discrimination by a sectarian school in a voucher program makes the school a state actor. *Norwood* simply invalidates funding *by* a state. Finally, there is every reason to believe that *Norwood* is sui generis—in particular, to attempts by southern states to evade school desegregation.

Nondiscrimination Laws

In 1990, *Employment Division, Department of Human Resources of Oregon* v. *Smith* held that "the right of free exercise [of religion] does not relieve an individual of the obligation to comply with a valid and neutral law of general applicability on the ground that the law proscribes (or prescribes) conduct that his religion prescribes (or proscribes)."[87] Before *Smith*, parochial schools might well have been able to successfully claim a free exercise right to an exemption from statutory bars on religious discrimination in hiring or admissions, based on the burdensome effect they might have on religion.[88] After *Smith*, however, it would seem that a state could constitutionally put restrictions on the admissions, hiring, and proselytizing practices of parochial schools in school choice programs as long as the regulations are neutral laws of general applicability. Such laws might provide that no accredited school shall engage in religious discrimination in hiring or admissions, nor shall any school require any affirmance of religious belief or prayer by students or staff.[89]

A close reading of *Smith*, however, discloses that the Court may have left room for a substantive due process challenge to state school regulations of this nature. Justice Scalia's opinion for the majority in *Smith* stated that certain "hybrid" situations, involving free exercise claims combined with other constitutional rights, had led the Court to apply a test of strict scrutiny and to invalidate certain neutral state laws burdening religion.[90] Justice Scalia read *Wisconsin* v. *Yoder*, rejecting compulsory school attendance laws as applied to Amish parents who refused on religious grounds to send their children to school, as such a hybrid situation involving both a free exercise right and the substantive due process right of "parents to direct the education of their children," as recognized in the landmark decision of *Pierce* v. *Society of Sisters*.[91]

It should be noted that this characterization of *Yoder* as somehow relying on hybrid rights misreads that decision. Chief Justice Burger's opinion for the Court in *Yoder* did emphasize the religious aspect of *Pierce*, thus bolstering the free exercise ground for *Yoder*. For example, Chief Justice Burger stated in *Yoder* (and Justice Scalia quoted it in *Smith*) that *Pierce* "stands as a charter of the rights of parents to direct the religious upbringing of their children." But although *Pierce* did involve a religious school, its holding was hardly limited to parental control of a child's religious upbringing. As the Court in *Pierce* put it: "We think it entirely plain that the Act of 1922 unreasonably interferes with the liberty of parents and guardians to direct the *upbringing and education* of children under their control."[92] Moreover, Chief Justice Burger ultimately acknowledged the different rationale of *Yoder*. His opinion "expressly stated that parents do *not* have the right to violate the compulsory education laws for nonreligious reasons."[93]

Despite Justice Scalia's effort in *Smith* to make *Yoder* less of a free exercise case than *Yoder* actually was, the final result is that to the extent that *Yoder* was really only a free exercise case, *Smith* overrules it. However, to the extent that *Pierce* has continuing validity, and there is good reason to believe that it does, it will substitute as a rationale for the result in *Yoder* so as to permit parents and religious schools (as well as nonsectarian private schools) to challenge state regulations of school choice programs.[94] The strength of such claims is by no means unlimited, however, because *Pierce* allowed for substantial state regulation.[95] In addition, *Pierce* may not rest favorably with those members of the Court who continue to subscribe to *Smith* or with justices who are generally ill disposed toward substantive due process rights.

Yet the resilience of *Pierce* and Justice Scalia's explicit preservation of *Yoder* in *Smith* raise serious constitutional questions concerning how far a state might permissibly regulate the practices of parochial (and other private) schools through neutral laws of general applicability. For example, the parents who choose to spend vouchers on parochial schools may consider it to be critically important to have their children attend an institution where all students are of the same faith, where all teachers are devout, where worship is a mandatory part of the school day, and where children are expected to be part of proselytizing endeavors. To restrict the ability of the school to discriminate on the basis of religion in hiring and admissions, or to put limits on the religious practices of the school, may well be held to interfere unreasonably with the liberty of the parents to control the upbringing of their children.

The Effect of Public Assistance on Parochial School Autonomy

It has long been argued that increased state financial aid to parochial schools will bring additional state supervision because it is "discriminatory . . . to allow public funds to be spent by private schools without public control and yet insist on such public control for public schools."[96] This may be true as a realistic political matter. On the other hand, the government might believe that many state regulations are unnecessary or undesirable, and funds conditioned on controls thought unsatisfactory by the recipient may be refused. In any event, as a constitutional matter, the state's power to regulate nonpublic schools is largely independent of any allocation of public funds—but as already explained that authority is not unlimited. Thus public aid or not, the Constitution would probably forbid restriction of religious instruction by sectarian schools and would plainly bar dissolution of the parochial school system.

Once again, *Pierce* v. *Society of Sisters,* invalidating a state requirement of compulsory public school education and ruling that due process of law forbids unreasonable state interference with parents' liberty to direct their children's education, establishes two basic points.[97] First, as we explore in detail shortly, the parental right being grounded in the Constitution, state authority to meaningfully curtail it would not appear to be augmented by the grant of government funds. To do so would run contrary to the prohibition of unconstitutional conditions—the principle that the government may not grant a privilege in exchange for the recipient's relinquishment of a constitutional right.[98]

Second, *Pierce* also recognized state authority "reasonably to regulate all schools, to inspect, supervise and examine them, their teachers and pupils; to require . . . that certain studies plainly essential to good citizenship must be taught, and that nothing be taught which is manifestly inimical to the public welfare."[99] Consequently, those whose conscientious scruples constitutionally entitle them to attend a church-related school plainly have no absolute right, under *Pierce* (or under the Free Exercise Clause even before *Smith*), to maintain those schools free of all state regulation, whether or not they receive public financial support. Although the state may have no right "to standardize its children by forcing them to accept instruction from public teachers only," it clearly may impose neutral, generally applicable controls, even when they conflict with action demanded by religion or conscience.[100] While the Free Exercise and Due Process Clauses may ensure private or sectarian schools the liberty "to inculcate whatever values they wish," and thus to engage in virtually any religious instruction they desire, those clauses do not hamper the state's power reasonably to promote children's welfare through requiring certain basic secular education.[101]

To return to the initial point affirmed in *Pierce,* the extent to which a state may impose restrictions as a condition of its financial support will seemingly depend on a variety of circumstances. For example, if a full-blown, voucher-type system (or other kind of comprehensive public program) were enacted, with the (unlikely) consequence that removal of state support for schools would lead to their closing because of financial inability to continue, then any conditions placed upon recipient schools would be essentially as coercive as an outright regulation.[102] So if the state were to say that "schools receiving vouchers" cannot deny the correctness of Darwinism, it would be little different from the state imposing the same condition on "schools whose access leads from public streets" or from the state adopting a general rule forbidding any school from contradicting the theory of evolution. Realistically, the option for the schools in these instances would be either to adhere to the state's message or to shut down.[103] Because of this pervasively coercive effect of the state's funding condition, akin to a "direct regulation," it would in all likelihood be held to violate the constitutional right recognized in *Pierce* (as well as the freedom of speech).[104] Indeed, it might also be treated as "calculated to drive 'certain ideas or viewpoints' from the marketplace," although this characterization would appear to depend more on the lawmaking body's motivation than on the effect of the government action.[105] In a world in which all schools need vouchers to survive, the same analysis would apply to a condition barring prayer exercises and religious discrimination in hiring or admissions (assuming these practices were otherwise protected, that is, in the absence of state financial support).

The Court has not articulated a clear standard of when conditions on government spending in less extreme situations nonetheless become so coercive as to be scrutinized like general regulations. The Court has stressed the importance of recipients of funds being able to comply with the condition by segregating funds and activities and thereby avoiding being penalized for the exercise of a constitutional right through overly broad disqualifications from funding. Thus in *Rust* the Court stated that the

> "unconstitutional conditions" cases involve situations in which the Government has placed a condition on the recipient of the subsidy rather than on a particular program or service, thus effectively prohibiting the recipient from engaging in the protected conduct outside the scope of the [government] funded program.[106]

The Court held that *Rust* was not such a case because the recipient clinics could still provide the prohibited services "through programs that are separate and independent from the project that receives Title X funds."[107] In *Rust* the Court interpreted F.C.C. v. *League of Women Voters* as a case where government funds and conditions impermissibly permeated all aspects of a recipient's speech activities.[108] In *League of Women Voters*, the Court struck down a condition that prohibited editorializing by noncommercial television and radio stations that received federal funds. The *Rust* Court distinguished *League of Women Voters* as resting on the inability of a station "to segregate its activities according to the source of its funding" and as "limiting the use of federal funds to *all* noneditorializing activities."[109] By analogy, in the school choice context, if a state were to condition all funding on the recipient school's not discriminating on the basis of religion in admissions or hiring, or on having no religious ceremonies as part of its educational program, this would appear impermissible under both *League of Women Voters* and *Rust*. It would leave the recipient school no way to separate its funding so as to avoid the condition, in contrast to a permissible condition, for example, requiring that no voucher money be spent on religious ceremonies.

The decisions permitting the government to restrict use of medicaid funds for abortions similarly illustrate the point. In *Maher* v. *Roe*, the Court stated in dictum that "strict scrutiny might be the proper approach" if a state denied "general welfare benefits to all women who had obtained abortions," because this would be more a penalty, akin to a criminal law, than a mere decision not to fund certain activity.[110] In *Harris* v. *McRae*, upholding federal Medicaid limits, the Court acknowledged that "a substantial constitutional question would arise if Congress had attempted to withhold all Medicaid benefits from an otherwise eligible candidate simply because that candidate had exercised her constitutionally protected freedom to terminate her pregnancy by abortion."[111]

Finally, it is important to distinguish the application of a *Rosenberger* free speech analysis and a *Hialeah* free exercise analysis from an unconstitutional conditions analysis based on *Pierce*. First, if state vouchers (or other types of school choice funding) are characterized as seeking to encourage a diversity of views from private speakers, under *Rosenberger* any conditions on spending against religious viewpoints would appear to violate the Free Speech Clause. Second, if the regulation of religious discrimination or religious ceremony was not viewed as a generally applicable law but rather as singling out religion for adverse treatment, a forceful Free Exercise Clause objection could be raised. Finally, even if *Smith*, rather than *Hialeah*, controls the free exercise consideration of such regulations of conduct, still fundamental rights protected by *Pierce* would seem to be implicated, and the unconstitutional conditions analysis from *League of Women Voters*, *Rust*, and the abortion funding cases would apply. They require that the conditions not effectively prohibit protected conduct, that recipients must be able to separate government-funded activity from independently funded activity, and that the conditions cannot be an overly broad penalty for the exercise of the right of parents to direct the education of their children.

Answers to the set of federal constitutional issues presented by school choice programs that include church-related schools cannot be stated or predicted with any real certainty. Whether the present Supreme Court would find that the Establishment Clause forbids the participation of parochial schools appears to depend on the vote of Justice O'Connor, who may well be influenced by the specific details of the challenged system. While it appears that current constitutional doctrine permits confinement of public financing to public schools only, serious constitutional questions, under both the Free Speech Clause and the Free Exercise Clause, are presented if only parochial schools are excluded. These would seem to turn on whether the Court perceives the state's new education subsidies as intended to "encourage a diversity of views" or, instead, as representing the "government as speaker." Existing constitutional principles about "state action" under the Fourteenth Amendment would lead to the conclusion that participation by sectarian schools in state-funded plans would not result in their being forbidden from discriminating on the basis of religion in admission and hiring decisions or from requiring that students and faculty participate in religious activities. Whether a new school finance system would so drastically alter the factual state of affairs as to call for a different result in regard to the state action issue is unknown (and probably unknowable).

On the other hand, if government entities sought to apply general policies forbidding religious discrimination or sectarian rituals by parochial schools, the Free Exercise Clause would probably not demand any exemption for them. It is possible, however, that the constitutional right of parents to direct their children's education recognized in the *Pierce* case might afford some relief. Finally, while ambiguity exists on whether government assistance to church schools could be conditioned on their forgoing practices commanded by their faith, potentially effective constitutional arguments could be made on their behalf under the Free Speech Clause, the Free Exercise Clause, and the *Pierce* principle.

Notes

1. Jesse H. Choper, "The Establishment Clause and Aid to Parochial Schools," *California Law Review*, vol. 56 (1968), p. 260; *Everson v. Board of Education*, 330 U.S. 1 (1947).

2. See Jesse H. Choper, "Dangers to Religious Liberty from Neutral Government Programs,"

U.C. Davis Law Review, vol. 29 (1996), pp. 719, 723 (noting Justice O'Connor as a swing vote in aid to parochial schools cases); Jesse H. Choper, "The Establishment Clause and Aid to Parochial Schools—An Update," *California Law Review*, vol. 75 (1987), pp. 5, 11 (noting Justice Powell as a swing vote in aid to parochial schools cases). The Religion Clauses of the First Amendment provide that "Congress shall make no law respecting an establishment of religion, or prohibiting the free exercise thereof." Both the Establishment Clause and the Free Exercise Clause have been held to apply to the states (as well as the national government) by virtue of the Fourteenth Amendment.

3. *Rosenberger* v. *University of Virginia*, (hereafter *Rosenberger*) 515 U.S. 819 (1995); *Agostini* v. *Felton*, 521 U.S. 203 (1997). See for example Note, "The Supreme Court's Shifting Tolerance for Public Aid to Parochial Schools and the Implications for Educational Choice," *Harvard Journal of Law and Public Policy*, vol. 21 (1998), p. 861; Michael Stokes Paulsen, "A Funny Thing Happened on the Way to the Limited Public Forum: Unconstitutional Conditions on 'Equal Access' for Religious Speakers and Groups," *U.C. Davis Law Review*, vol. 29 (1996), p. 653; Peter Applebome, "Parochial Schools Ruling Heartens Voucher Backers," *New York Times*, June 25, 1997; Douglas Kmiec, "School Choice: Why Hasn't Its Time Come?" *Chicago Tribune*, August 25, 1997.

4. *Lemon* v. *Kurtzman*, 392 U.S. 236 (1968). See for example *Lamb's Chapel* v. *Center Moriches Union Free School Dist.*, 508 U.S. 384 (1993) (Scalia, J., concurring in the judgment) ("Like some ghoul in a late-night horror movie that repeatedly sits up in its grave and shuffles abroad, after being repeatedly killed and buried, *Lemon* stalks our Establishment Clause jurisprudence once again, frightening the little children and school attorneys of Center Moriches Union Free School District").

5. The Court has made the opposite assumption for church-related colleges and universities. See *Tilton* v. *Richardson*, 403 U.S. 672 (1971), decided the same day as *Lemon*.

6. The two cases are *Meek* v. *Pittenger*, 421 U.S. 349 (1975); *Wolman* v. *Walter*, 433 U.S. 229 (1977).

7. The two cases are *Levitt* v. *Committee for Public Education*, 413 U.S. 472 (1973); *Committee for Public Education* v. *Regan*, 444 U.S. 646 (1980).

8. *Board of Education* v. *Allen*, 392 U.S. 236 (1968); *Meek* v. *Pittenger*, p. 365.

9. *Everson* v. *Board of Education*, 330 U.S. 1 (1947); *Wolman* v. *Walter*, p. 252.

10. *Committee for Public Education* v. *Regan*, p. 662.

11. *Public Education* v. *Nyquist*, 413 U.S. 756 (1973).

12. *Mueller* v. *Allen*, 463 U.S. 388 (1983).

13. *Public Education* v. *Nyquist*, p. 782, n. 38.

14. *Mueller* v. *Allen*, p. 396, n. 6.

15. *Widmar* v. *Vincent*, 454 U.S. 263 (1981) (no Establishment Clause violation when state university forum that is open to all kinds of speech includes religious speech). This rationale was hardly persuasive: 96 percent of the Minnesota tax deductions for tuition were taken by parents who sent their children to parochial schools.

16. In *Mueller* v. *Allen*, Justice Rehnquist also distinguished *Nyquist* on the ground that there was a genuine tax deduction in *Mueller*, whereas in *Nyquist* there was a tax credit and an outright grant. Of course, there is a difference between a tax deduction and a tax credit, depending especially upon your income bracket. Both are different from a direct grant, particularly for people who do not have enough net income to take advantage of a tax credit or a tax deduction. Nonetheless, it is difficult to dispute the point made in the dissent of Justice Marshall, joined by Justices Brennan, Blackmun, and Stevens, that in realistic economic terms this is a "formalistic distinction" (p. 411). Indeed, Justice Rehnquist himself acknowledged that "the economic consequences of the program in *Nyquist* and that in this case may be difficult to distinguish" (p. 396, n. 6).

17. *Aguilar* v. *Felton,* 473 U.S. 402 (1985); *School District of Grand Rapids* v. *Ball,* 473 U.S. 373 (1985).

18. *Aguilar* v. *Felton*, pp. 413–14.

19. *School District of Grand Rapids* v. *Ball,* p. 385.

20. *Witters* v. *Washington Department of Services for the Blind,* 474 U.S. 481 (1986).

21. Ibid., p. 483.

22. Justice Marshall's slighting of *Mueller* is not surprising since he dissented in that case.

23. *Witters* v. *Washington Department of Services for the Blind*, pp. 490–91 (footnote omitted).

24. Choper, "Dangers to Religious Liberty," p. 13.

25. Compare *Lemon* v. *Kurtzman,* 403 U.S. 602 (1971), with *Tilton* v. *Richardson.* See also *Roemer* v. *Board of Public Works,* 426 U.S. 736 (1976); *Hunt* v. *McNair,* 413 U.S. 734 (1973).

26. *Zobrest* v. *Catalina Foothills School District,* 509 U.S. 1 (1993).

27. *Rosenberger* v. *Rector of the University of Virginia; Agostini* v. *Felton.*

28. Justice Kennedy wrote for the majority, joined by Chief Justice Rehnquist and Justices O'Connor, Scalia, and Thomas. Justice Souter dissented, joined by Justices Stevens, Ginsburg, and Breyer.

29. *Rosenberger*, pp. 823–27.

30. Ibid., p. 845.

31. Paulsen, "A Funny Thing Happened," pp. 711–13.

32. *Rosenberger*, p. 844.

33. Ibid., p. 840.

34. Ibid., p. 846.

35. In support of this possible right, Justice O'Connor cited *Keller* v. *State Bar of California,* 496 U.S. 1 (1990) (compulsory state bar dues), and *Abood* v. *Detroit Board of Educ.,* 431 U.S. 209 (1977) (mandatory service charges to union members as condition of employment).

36. *Bowen* v. *Kendrick,* 487 U.S. 589 (1988).

37. *Agostini* v. *Felton.*

38. Ibid., p. 214; *Board of Education of Kiryas Joel Village School District* v. *Grumet,* 512 U.S. 687 (1994), p. 718 (O'Connor, J., concurring in part and concurring in judgment); p. 731 (Kennedy, J., concurring in judgment); p. 750 (Scalia, J., dissenting, joined by Rehnquist, C.J., and Thomas, J.).

39. *Agostini* v. *Felton*, p. 228 (quoting partially *Zobrest*, p. 12).

40. Ibid.

41. Ibid.

42. Ibid., pp. 211–12.

43. Ibid., p. 223. On pages 234–35, she adds, "We therefore hold that a federally funded program providing supplemental, remedial instruction to disadvantaged children on a neutral basis is not invalid under the Establishment Clause when such instruction is given on the premises of sectarian schools by government employees *pursuant to a program containing safeguards such as those present here*" (emphasis added).

44. See authorities cited in note 3.

45. *School District of Grand Rapids* v. *Ball*, pp. 376–77.

46. Ibid., pp. 399–400 (O'Connor, J., concurring in the judgment in part and dissenting in part; emphasis added).

47. See *Capitol Square Review and Advisory Board* v. *Pinette,* 515 U.S. 753, 778–82 (1995) (O'Connor, J., concurring in part). Only one case involving a voucher program including sectarian schools has been decided on federal constitutional grounds since *Agostini.* In 1998, the

Wisconsin Supreme Court upheld Milwaukee's school choice plan, which by 1995 had expanded its scope to include pupils attending sectarian schools; at the end of 1998, the U.S. Supreme Court declined to review the Milwaukee case. See *Jackson* v. *Benson*, 218 Wis. 2d 835, 578 N.W. 2d 602, cert. denied, 119 S.Ct. 466 (1998). Just before the *Agostini* ruling, an Ohio intermediate appellate court struck down a Cleveland school district voucher program that included parochial schools. See *Simons-Harris* v. *Goff*, 1997 WL 217583 (Ct. App. Ohio 1997). See generally Margaret A. Nero, "The Cleveland Scholarship and Tutoring Program: Why Voucher Programs Do Not Violate the Establishment Clause," *Ohio State Law Journal*, vol. 58 (1997), p. 1103. On appeal, the Supreme Court of Ohio, although concluding that the program did not violate the Establishment Clause, held this particular statute, which was part of an omnibus appropriations bill, invalid under a state constitutional provision that no bill enacted by the legislature contain more than one subject. 88 Ohio St. 3d 1, 711 N.E.2d 203 (1999). For an additional recent decision rejecting federal constitutional challenges to other types of government assistance plans that include sectarian schools, see *Kotterman* v. *Killian*, 972 P.2d 606 (Az.) cert. denied, 1999 WL 278906 (1999) (tax credit).

48. *Rosenberger*, p. 863 (Souter, J., dissenting).

49. Choper, "Dangers to Religious Liberty," p. 725.

50. Jesse H. Choper, *Securing Religious Liberty* (University of Chicago Press, 1995), pp. 176–77.

51. *Church of Lukumi Babalu Aye, Inc.* v. *City of Hialeah*, 508 U.S. 520 (1993).

52. Ibid., p. 532.

53. See Bruce Cooper, "The Changing Universe of U.S. Private Schools," in Edward H. Haerbel, Thomas James, and Henry M. Levin, eds., *Comparing Public and Private Schools* (New York: Falmer, 1987).

54. See *Employment Div., Dept. of Human Resources of Ore.* v. *Smith*, 494 U.S. 872 (1990).

55. William H. Clune, "The Constitution and Vouchers for Religious Schools: The Demise of Separatism and the Rise of Nondiscrimination as Measures of State Neutrality" (University of California—Berkeley, Earl Warren Legal Institute, 1999), p. 10.

56. See Stephen Sugarman's chapter, this volume.

57. See Robert C. Post, "Subsidized Speech," *Yale Law Journal*, vol. 106 (1996), pp. 151, 166.

58. *Rust* v. *Sullivan*, 500 U.S. 173, 194 (1991).

59. *National Endowment for the Arts* v. *Finley*, 118 S.Ct. 2168, 2179 (1998), referring to *Regan v. Taxation with Representation of Washington*, 461 U.S. 540 (1983).

60. In *Finley*, the Court, after narrowly interpreting a congressional mandate—that in awarding grants the NEA take into consideration "general standards of decency and respect for the diverse beliefs and values of the American public" (p. 2171)—as being only "advisory" and a "vague exhortation" (pp. 2176, 2177), held that the law was not facially unconstitutional. In doing so, it emphasized that this provision "imposes no categorical requirement [that the NEA] deny funding on the basis of viewpoint discriminatory criteria" (p. 2176).

61. Post, "Subsidized Speech," p. 151; *Rosenberger*, p. 833, referring to *Rust* v. *Sullivan* (upholding denial of federal funds to family planning projects that counsel abortion).

62. *Rosenberger*, p. 834 (emphasis added). "Indiscriminately" was added by the Court to its description of *Rosenberger* in *National Endowment for the Arts* v. *Finley*.

63. For discussion of the difficulty in characterizing government subsidies under these circumstances, see Randall P. Bezanson, "The Government Speech Forum: *Forbes* and *Finley* and Government Speech Selection Judgments," *Iowa Law Review*, vol. 83 (1998), pp. 953, 962.

64. See the decisions forbidding government-sponsored prayers in public schools. *School*

District v. *Schempp*, 374 U.S. 203 (1963); *Engel* v. *Vitale*, 370 U.S. 421 (1962). See also *Flast* v. *Cohen*, 392 U.S. 83, 104–05 (1968) ("Our history vividly illustrates that one of the specific evils feared by those who drafted the Establishment Clause and fought for its adoption was that the taxing and spending power would be used to favor one religion over another or to support religion in general").

65. *McGowan* v. *Maryland*, 366 U.S. 420, 442 (1961) ("The 'Establishment' Clause does not ban federal or state regulation of conduct whose reason or effect merely happens to coincide or harmonize with the tenets of some or all religions").

66. See Choper, *Securing Religious Liberty*, pp. 106–12.

67. *Church of the Lukami Babalu Aye* v. *City of Hialeah*, p. 532.

68. *Witters* v. *Washington Department of Services for the Blind*, 474 U.S. 481 (1986); *Witters* v. *State of Washington Comm'n. for the Blind*, 112 Wash. 2d 363, 771 P.2d 1119 (1989); *Jackson* v. *Benson*, 570 N.W. 2d 507 (Wis. App. 1997) (holding school choice program permitting state payments to all private schools, including sectarian ones, violative of state constitution); *Chittenden School District* v. *Vermont Department of Education*, 1999 WL 388244 (Vt. June 11, 1999) (inclusion of religious schools in a private school tuition reimbursement program violates the state constitution's compelled purpose provision). See generally Frank R. Kemerer, "State Constitutions and School Vouchers," *West's Education Law Reporter*, October 2, 1997.

69. My colleague Robert Post has suggested that the Court might uphold the state constitutional provision by finding that the state's interest, in embodying in its constitution a higher wall between church and state than that erected by the Establishment Clause, is "compelling."

70. *Rosenberger*, p. 834.

71. Ibid., p. 833.

72. *Rust* v. *Sullivan*; for quotations that follow, see pp. 178, 179, 180, 193.

73. *Rosenberger*, p. 833.

74. See note 62 and accompanying text.

75. *Rust*, p. 210 (Blackmun, J., dissenting). "In addition to requiring referral for prenatal care and adoption services, the regulations permit general health services such as physical examinations, screening for breast cancer, treatment of gynecological problems, and treatment for sexually transmitted diseases."

76. For two recent rulings upholding Maine's exclusion of sectarian schools from its education tuition program, see *Strout* v. *Albanese*, 178 F.3d 57 (1st Cir. 1999); *Bagley* v. *Raymond School Dep't*, 728 A.2d 127 (Me. 1999). In October 1999, the U.S. Supreme Court declined to hear both cases.

77. The few decisions of the Supreme Court that have involved deliberate disfavoring of persons or groups because of their religious beliefs (or absence of such beliefs) have employed the test of strict scrutiny, either expressly or implicitly, to invalidate the regulations. See *Church of the Lukami Babalu Aye* v. *City of Hialeah*, 113 S.Ct. 2217 (1993) (holding that government may not forbid ritual animal sacrifice); *McDaniel* v. *Paty*, 435 U.S. 618 (1978) (holding that a state may not disqualify members of the clergy from being legislators); *Larson* v. *Valente*, 456 U.S. 228 (1982), reh'g denied, 457 U.S. 1111 (1982) (holding that a state may not impose registration and reporting requirements only upon religious organizations that solicit more than half their funds from nonmembers); *Torcaso* v. *Watkins*, 367 U.S. 488 (1961) (holding that a state may not require notaries public to take an oath of belief in God).

78. See chapter by Robert O'Neil, this volume.

79. *Rendell-Baker* v. *Kohn*, 457 U.S. 830 (1982); *Blum* v. *Yaretsky*, 457 U.S. 991 (1982).

80. *Rendell-Baker* v. *Kohn*; 42 U.S.C. § 1983.

81. *Rendell-Baker*, 457 U.S., p. 840.

82. Ibid., p. 841.

83. Ibid., p. 842, quoting *Jackson v. Metropolitan Edison Co.*, 419 U.S. 345, 353 (1974).

84. Ibid., pp. 842–43.

85. On the other hand, the world of elementary and secondary education that would exist under a system in which some (or all) "private" schools rely on vouchers (or other forms of public financial assistance) for their major (or exclusive) source of support would be radically different than the state of affairs at the time of *Rendell-Baker*. For example, it might be (at least in some school districts) that what used to be private schools, whether sectarian or secular, would all become charter schools, in that they would be fully funded by government with structures that place substantial authority over charter schools beyond the direct power of local school boards (see Robert O'Neil's chapter, this volume). As O'Neil suggests, existing state action precedent may not control under those circumstances.

86. *Norwood v. Harrison*, 413 U.S. 455 (1973). Quotations that follow are on pp. 467 (emphasis added), 466, 465, 468.

87. *Employment Division, Department of Human Resources of Oregon v. Smith*, pp. 872, 879.

88. Compare *NLRB v. Catholic Bishops*, 440 U.S. 490 (1979) (constitutional issue avoided by construing National Labor Relations Act's collective bargaining requirements not to cover lay teachers employed by parochial schools).

89. Of course, many regulatory laws will contain exemptions for religious organizations. For example, the federal antidiscrimination law, Title VII of the Civil Rights Act of 1964, exempts religious organizations from its general prohibition against discrimination in employment on the basis of religion. See *Corporation of the Presiding Bishop of the Church of Jesus Christ of Latter-Day Saints v. Amos*, 483 U.S. 327 (1987) (upholding Title VII exemption against Establishment Clause challenge).

90. *Employment Div., Dept. of Human Resources of Ore. v. Smith*, pp. 881–82 ("The only decisions in which we have held that the First Amendment bars application of a neutral, generally applicable law to religiously motivated action have involved not the Free Exercise Clause alone, but the Free Exercise Clause in conjunction with other constitutional protections").

91. *Pierce v. Society of Sisters*, 268 U.S. 510 (1925). The Court invalidated Oregon's statute compelling attendance in a public school from age eight to sixteen as unreasonably interfering with the parents' substantive due process right to direct the education of their children. See also *Wisconsin v. Yoder*, 406 U.S. 205 (1972); *Smith*, p. 881. Other cases identified as hybrids in *Smith* were *Cantwell v. Connecticut*, 310 U.S. 296 (1940) (free speech, free press, and free exercise), and *Murdock v. Pennsylvania*, 319 U.S. 105 (1943) (free speech and free exercise). The last quotation is from *Smith*, p. 881, n. 1 (quoting *Yoder*, p. 233).

92. *Pierce*, p. 534 (emphasis added).

93. Michael McConnell, "Free Exercise Revisionism and the Smith Decision," *University of Chicago Law Review*, vol. 57 (1990), pp. 1109, 1121 (referring to *Wisconsin v. Yoder*, pp. 215–16: "Thus, according to *Yoder* parents have no right independent of the Free Exercise Clause to withhold their children from school"). See generally Jesse H. Choper, "The Rise and Decline of the Constitutional Protection of Religious Liberty," *Nebraska Law Review*, vol. 70 (1991), pp. 651, 675–76.

94. *Pierce* involved a challenge by the Society of Sisters, "an Oregon corporation, organized in 1880, with power to care for orphans, educate and instruct the youth, establish and maintain academies or schools, and acquire necessary real and personal property" (pp. 531–32). See also *Michael H. v. Gerald D.*, 491 U.S. 110, 121 (1989) (Scalia, J., joined by Rehnquist, C.J., and O'Connor, J., and Kennedy, J., citing *Pierce* with approval).

95. See *Pierce*, p. 534 (listing many ways in which the state could reasonably and permissibly regulate nonpublic schools). See note 97 and accompanying text.

96. Maynard Bemis, "What Is Discrimination?" *Phi Delta Kappan*, vol. 42 (1961), p. 329.

97. *Pierce*, p. 510.

98. See generally Kathleen Sullivan, "Unconstitutional Conditions," *Harvard Law Review*, vol. 102 (1989), p. 1413.

99. *Pierce*, p. 534.

100. *Pierce, p. 535; Employment Div., Dept. of Human Resources of Ore. v. Smith*, p. 872; *Prince v. Massachusetts*, 321 U.S. 158, 168 (1944).

101. *School Dist. v. Schempp*, p. 242 (Brennan, J., concurring).

102. See Bezanson, "The Government Speech Forum," p. 976 ("government's expressive presence must not work to exclude competing views from the marketplace").

103. While a general regulation and the condition on funding in the hypothesized circumstances may be similarly coercive, they are not identical in operative effect. On the one hand, if a general regulation is disobeyed, the violating school may be found guilty of a crime. On the other hand, a criminal prosecution may not result in the school's closing, as would be true if funding that was necessary to the school's survival were cut off.

104. See note 59 and accompanying text.

105. *National Endowment for the Arts v. Finley*, p. 2179 (quoting *Simon and Schuster, Inc. v. Members of New York State Crime Victims Board*, 502 U.S. 105, 116 [1991]).

106. *Rust v. Sullivan*, p. 197.

107. Ibid., p. 196.

108. *F.C.C. v. League of Women Voters*, 468 U.S. 364 (1984). Also see *Rust*, p. 197.

109. *Rust* (quoting *League of Women Voters*, p. 400) (emphasis added). Although this was certainly part of the opinion in *League of Women Voters*, the Court's primary emphasis was the nature of the speech at issue, with the Court recognizing early and often that the condition was "directed at a form of speech—namely, the expression of editorial opinion—that lies at the heart of First Amendment protection" (p. 381). Chief Justice Rehnquist, the author of *Rust*, dissented in *League of Women Voters*.

110. *Maher v. Roe*, 432 U.S. 464 (1977); and pp. 474–75, n. 8.

111. *Harris v. McRae*, 448 U.S. 297 (1980); and p. 317, n. 19.

CHAPTER NINE

Race and School Choice

BETSY LEVIN

A politically and educationally diverse group of people, often for different and somewhat inconsistent reasons, is increasingly advocating school choice. As the school choice movement expands—and as a variety of alternatives to the assigned public school develops, whether magnet or other special emphasis alternative public schools, voucher programs, or charter schools—concern has been expressed about what impact this movement is likely to have on racial and ethnic minorities and the economically disadvantaged and on opportunities for enhancing racial justice.[1]

This chapter explores whether the objectives of racial and economic justice will be advanced or impeded by school choice, which kinds of choice are likely to be most advantageous, and which coalitions of interests are most likely to accomplish them. Among the issues examined are the politics of school choice, including the differences of views between national civil rights groups and their allies, on the one hand, and local community-based groups and parents, on the other. To what extent has the history of the use of choice in preserving segregation, and the context in which school choice has been promoted more recently (including its relationship to ideologies not always compatible with the interests of minorities and the poor), colored perceptions of whether these groups will benefit from the growing choice movement?

I wish to thank Jennifer Lynn Golub and Christopher M. McNally, students at the University of Baltimore School of Law, for their very able research assistance. I also wish to acknowledge Christopher Edley for the ideas and insights that formed the background for this chapter.

Among the issues raised are the extent to which choice is now exercised by racial and ethnic minorities and what conclusions, if any, can be drawn from that experience with regard to the impact of any substantial increase in school choice. What are the perceived advantages of choice to these communities? Will those advantages be retained as the movement expands? In answering these questions, concerned communities will have to address such issues as whether choice is likely to increase racial and economic isolation; whether admissions criteria or other factors will limit access for racial and ethnic minorities; whether the supply of choice opportunities will grow to meet the demands of racial and ethnic minorities at the same pace as for nonminorities; whether there are likely to be inequalities in the information available to racial minorities or the poor; whether educational opportunities are likely to be enhanced, including whether choice schools available for racial minorities will be staffed by teachers of appropriate quality and experience; and whether adequate resources will be available to allow equality of opportunity for choice for minority and poor parents.

A Historic Perspective on School Choice

For at least a decade and a half after the Supreme Court's decision in *Brown v. Board of Education* black students remained almost completely segregated in the South as school boards and state legislatures tried various measures to evade the command of *Brown*, such as minority to majority transfer arrangements and other pupil placement laws that perpetuated segregation within the public school system.[2] When those measures were struck down by the courts, states enacted laws providing for the closure of public schools while subsidizing private school attendance through tuition grants and by assisting private, segregated academies in school districts that were required to desegregate.[3]

The massive withdrawal of white students to these private academies was initially funded by state tuition grants.[4] After court decisions holding such funding unconstitutional, the schools relied on tuition fees, with the burden on parents being relieved by state and federal tax exemptions, free transportation, state-owned textbooks and supplies donated by various government entities (often transferred from the public school system), the use of public facilities, and so on.[5] The establishment of these segregated academies resulted not only in the withdrawal of white students from the public schools but also the withdrawal of substantial financial support from public schools, resulting in the public schools being stigmatized as inferior.[6] One case study of a county in Alabama found that segregated academies drew their enrollment disproportionately from whites at the higher socioeconomic levels, meaning that the public schools were not only increasingly racially isolated but economically isolated as well.[7] Many choice opponents today express the fear that school choice will similarly lead to the racial and economic isolation of students remaining in the traditional public schools.

Despite state undermining of desegregation and local support of the segregated academies, with the enforcement of Title VI of the Civil Rights Act and the unanimous Supreme Court decisions in *Green* v. *County School Board* and *Swann* v. *Charlotte-Mecklenburg Board of Education,* the South began to experience significant desegregation in a number of communities.[8] After the Supreme Court's decision in *Keyes* v. *School District No. 1, Denver,* some desegregation also began to occur in school districts in the North and West.[9]

This relatively brief period of progress began to be challenged by political forces, however. As part of Richard Nixon's "southern strategy," he criticized court-ordered busing and advocated "freedom-of-choice" plans.[10] Antibusing amendments proliferated in Congress, and finally, the Supreme Court itself put on the brakes. With the five-to-four decision in *Milliken* v. *Bradley,* which limited desegregation remedies to the predominantly minority school district of Detroit and barred (except in unusual circumstances) the use of interdistrict remedies that would include the predominantly white suburban districts, central city school districts became increasingly minority.[11] The exception was the South, where in many states school districts were countywide or metropolitan-area-wide.

The southern strategy appeared to be a feature of the 1980s as well. During the 1980 presidential campaign, Ronald Reagan opposed court-ordered busing and revived the idea of tuition vouchers and tuition tax credits.[12] Under both the Reagan and Bush administrations, the Department of Justice pursued a strategy of ending court-ordered desegregation. During the 1980s, when the Supreme Court moved to address issues of "unitary status," desegregation decrees began to be dismantled even in the South.[13] In the 1980s and 1990s, not only has racial and ethnic school segregation increased substantially, but central city school districts have also become increasingly economically segregated.[14] By 1986, only 3 percent of the nation's white school-aged children were enrolled in the twenty-five largest urban districts.[15] Even in the remaining integrated schools in the large urban districts, gifted and talented within-school programs that are predominantly white and middle class have proliferated.[16]

The Present Goals of Choice Proponents

One difficulty in talking about the politics of school choice is that different groups support school choice as a means of accomplishing very diverse goals. These very different types of choice—from unregulated vouchers to charter schools to controlled choice within a public school system to magnet schools—will not satisfy every goal. The various rationales underlying school choice do not always fall into separate and distinct categories, and some proponents may advocate choice for more than one reason. At the extremes, some of the goals appear inconsistent and conflicting. One commentator has developed four categories of school choice policies: education driven, economics driven, policy driven, and governance driven.[17] Education-driven choice is grounded in perceived differences in learning styles of children and in the amount of structure they need as well as opportunities for parental choice in accordance with family values and orientations. Economics-driven choice reflects the view that the problems of public schools are due to "their noncompetitive, monopolistic, and no-incentives status" and that the market approach, by requiring public schools to compete with private schools, will reform public education and force bad schools out of business. Some private school users and operators favor vouchers primarily as a way of obtaining public subsidies. In the last two decades, the Catholic Church has been an active proponent of choice.[18]

Policy-driven choice is directed toward equity-based initiatives. These can include vouchers based on a family's income and willingness to invest in education, or what are characterized as ways of equalizing opportunities for families to find a good school or to enable their children to escape a bad one.[19] Governance-driven choice is characterized as the "desire to remove education from the arena of collective decision and return its control to individuals," or the "libertarian case for choice." Some choice proponents in this category are said to be advocates of market control, rather than political control, while others advocate choice on the ground that shifting control from school officials to parents will enhance accountability. Obviously, with so many different goals, there is little agreement on what kinds of choice are desirable.[20]

Because of the diversity of goals and diversity of forms that school choice might take, it is difficult to read too much into the Gallup poll results, in which 72 percent of blacks said they favored the right to choose a private school at "government expense" (and 62 percent favored the government paying the tuition for any private or church-related school a parent chose),

especially since a much higher percentage of blacks—more than double that
of the public as a whole—would give grades of A or B to the nation's public schools.[21] Polling data may be distorted by the language used and by an
untutored sense of what the consequences of various policy options might
be. Nevertheless, it is clear that a large number of minority parents whose
children now attend schools with diminishing resources and a higher proportion of less credentialed and probationary teachers or teachers inexperienced in the fields they are assigned to teach see choice as a possible way
out of a deteriorating system and a way of improving educational opportunities for their children.[22] As a later section of this chapter notes, many
minority students already are enrolled either in private schools or in public schools of choice.

Robert Bulman and David Kirp, in their chapter in this volume, describe
how the notion of choice has been repackaged so that it appeals to a broader,
more ideologically diverse constituency and thus has acquired a new political legitimacy.[23] Clearly, hooking choice to equity considerations and moving away from an emphasis on unregulated tuition vouchers to a broader
range of more or less regulated types of choice (including various forms of
public school choice) has expanded its political base, including many minority parents, community activists, and local politicians of color. While minority communities and local politicians increasingly have supported voucher
programs, the leadership of some of the national civil rights groups has
either opposed such programs or been silent.[24] Major factors in the latter's
opposition to vouchers include the pernicious history of the use of vouchers to maintain segregation and the political ideology of many of the proponents of vouchers, which often includes opposition to other programs
endorsed by the civil rights movement. In North Carolina, members of the
state legislature's Black Caucus are aligned with the state teachers' union
in calling for the closing of those charter schools that are predominantly
African American, while minority parents whose children attend these
schools are aligned with various conservative organizations to maintain the
schools.[25]

As noted above, the first tuition voucher programs were proposed by
southern state legislatures to replace public schools with a private school
system in order to forestall court-ordered desegregation.[26] Freedom of
choice was a clear euphemism for a method of maintaining segregated
schools and for placing the burden of desegregation on minority parents
rather than on school officials; this method was later part of the southern
strategy.[27] Not surprisingly, then, advocates of voucher programs and other

forms of school choice, particularly unregulated forms, were viewed with suspicion by some civil rights leaders. Although choice within the public school system has greater acceptance, there is still concern that, unless there are certain safeguards, choice will result in increased racial and economic stratification.

When first revived in the 1980s by the Reagan administration, tuition vouchers and tax credits were coupled with an antigovernment, promarket, and antiunion ideology; calls for drastic cuts in or even the repeal of a whole array of social welfare programs; and an increasing gap between the highest and lowest income groups. In the area of education, arguments were increasingly being heard that suggested that equity and excellence were mutually inconsistent. By the early 1990s, civil rights leaders not only found little political support for the civil rights agenda they had long espoused but also saw large numbers of judges appointed by the Reagan-Bush administrations, who reflected much of that ideology, beginning to dismantle the school desegregation and affirmative action programs that the national civil rights groups had fought so hard to put in place. Considering who were its most avid proponents, it is not difficult to understand why many national civil rights groups and their allies did not trust school choice proposals. The question is whether decoupling school choice from its emphasis on unregulated tuition vouchers and its market-driven ideology, and moving to other varieties of school choice, such as charter schools, will garner more support from these groups.

On the other hand, it is also not difficult to understand why some minority community activists and parents, less interested in the abstract ideals of improved race relations and social cohesion than in improving education for their own children now, began to turn their backs on the national civil rights leadership and to support school choice. Sentiment for school choice on the part of some minority communities can be attributed in large part to the failure of *Brown* to desegregate the public schools after three or four decades, the failure to provide additional resources to those schools that had been separate and *un*equal, and the failure to improve student achievement. The growing economic, as well as racial, isolation of central cities meant that all of the social problems caused by concentrations of poverty were reflected in inner-city schools. Added to these concerns was the growth of black separatist views, or cultural nationalism, which considered that the curriculum of the public schools, perceived to be oriented toward white and middle-class students, impeded the learning of poor, minority children, especially when taught by an aging teaching population that was disproportionately white compared to the student population. These separatist views were sometimes manifested in the educational arena by movements to establish African American male academies or Afrocentric curricula.[28] Not surprisingly, these factors have led some to seek government support for abandoning the public schools in the inner cities. A recent example of the split between national civil rights (or even state civil rights) organizations and community-based leadership and minority parents is the controversy over the voucher program recently signed into law in Florida. That program would pay tuition for children at the lowest-rated public schools in the state to attend private schools, including those that are religiously affiliated. The Florida state NAACP, joining with the state teachers' unions, the ACLU, and other groups, filed a lawsuit challenging the law the day after it was signed, while the Urban League of Greater Miami (in opposition to its own national organization) has retained the Institute for Justice, a conservative legal foundation, to represent it in defending the law.[29]

Broadening school choice has clearly won more converts. Public school choice was seen as enhancing opportunities for students with specialized interests and, for some, as a way of attracting a more diverse student body, especially in cities with rigidly segregated residential areas. Thus equity considerations, coupled with opportunities for choosing schools or programs that might offer curricula related to the child's interest or learning style and some sense of control on the part of students and parents, have expanded the base of support for school choice programs. Charter schools, in particular, with their freedom from some of the budgetary and curricular restraints imposed by local and state regulations (not unlike the earlier school site management programs, or site-level governance), were seen as a way of energizing parents, students, and teachers.

Private school tuition voucher programs are still on the agenda, but broadening the types of choice (with charter schools being somewhere between vouchers and magnet schools) has helped reduce concerns about the conservative, market-driven ideology and the fear that some of its roots were in the desire either to escape desegregation or to provide subsidies for religiously affiliated schools (which were believed to be the principal factors motivating the earlier tuition voucher movement). However, the market-driven ideology with its emphasis on public support for competing private schools that would challenge, or eliminate, the public school system persists as an important component of the choice movement. Thus it is not clear whether the regulated plans specifically designed with minority and low-income children as the beneficiaries (in Milwaukee and Cleveland, for example) will continue to receive white and middle-class political and financial support unless opportunities for school choice include much more broadly based, and less regulated, choice programs. It should be noted that, at this point, school choice seems not to be as significant a factor in suburban or rural areas (magnet schools are clearly an urban phenomenon) or in the South or in the more rural states in the West.[30]

The differently motivated proponents of school choice may find that the compromises that have been necessary to achieve the limited opportunities for choice now available may no longer be acceptable. The real question is whether the divergent goals of school choice for racial and ethnic minorities and some of the other proponents eventually will split the movement for school choice into different and competing camps, severing the alliances that might have brought about more widespread choice opportunities. Some believe that the conservative, market-driven advocates of tuition vouchers may have joined forces with the advocates for vouchers for low-income minority children in inner-city school districts only as a way of getting a foot in the door for more widespread and unregulated voucher programs. While not an exact analogy, it is useful to recall that the community control movement in New York City in 1967–69 that eventually split that city apart had its roots in a joint effort by the teachers' union and the black community. The teachers' union initially had thought it could use the black community to help it in its fight to gain more power from the central administration, but when the black community activists and some of the parents evidenced different goals, the coalition split apart violently.[31] On the other hand, the burgeoning charter school movement may be perceived as more neutral territory around which both the market-driven and equity-driven proponents can coalesce, as Bulman and Kirp, in their chapter, suggest is happening.

Racial and Ethnic Minorities and School Choice

To what extent do minority communities pursue school choice options today, and what is the nature of those options? What conclusions, if any, can be drawn about the future of school choice for racial and ethnic minorities based on this information? As noted elsewhere, school choice plans may include a wide variety of programs: tuition vouchers that can be used in either private or public schools (Cleveland); charter school programs that permit private schools to convert to public school status (Arizona); charter schools limited to new or existing public schools (California); magnet schools within the public school system, either as separate schools or as schools within schools, generally in urban areas and often part of a court-ordered desegregation plan; interdistrict transfers (St. Louis and its suburbs); and controlled-choice districts (Cambridge, Mass.). By design, some of these may encourage a higher percentage of minorities than private schools generally (Cleveland). Jeffrey Henig and Stephen Sugarman, in their chapter in this volume, suggest that, even if families who choose schools through their choice of residence are excluded, nearly one-fourth of school-age children (or their families) choose their schools. Their data, however, do not indicate how many of those children are racial and ethnic minorities nor what types of school choice program they are most likely to choose.

While data are sketchy with regard to the number of minority students in private schools of choice, there are some indications from existing studies as to who takes advantage of what kinds of choice opportunities. Data show that 12 percent of the total number of children in school attend private schools (and another 1 to 2 percent of school-aged children are being home schooled).[32] Most students enrolled in private schools attend religiously affiliated schools.[33] Although in the 1960s the majority of these schools were Catholic, Catholic schools have experienced a substantial drop in students and in the number of schools since then, while the number of Christian evangelical schools has increased dramatically.[34] Although the percentage of blacks and Hispanics enrolling in private schools increased between 1972 and 1995, the percentage of racial and ethnic minorities relative to nonminorities is still much greater in public schools than in private schools.[35] In 1995 blacks and Hispanics comprised only 17.1 percent of students enrolled in private schools, compared to 31.1 percent of students enrolled in public schools. About 41.2 percent of private schools have a student enrollment of less than 5 percent minority students; 15.6 percent have a student enrollment of 50 percent or more minority.[36] (Almost no data exist regarding numbers of minority children being home schooled, although what little data do exist suggest that the numbers are very small.)[37] Blacks and Hispanics constitute 56.1 percent of those enrolled in public schools in central city school districts.[38] The high correlation between poverty and race in central cities means that the racial isolation of many central city schools is compounded by socioeconomic class isolation.

One study indicates that African Americans are more likely to take advantage of choice in the public sector, while whites and Asian Americans are more likely to take advantage of expanded opportunities for choice in the private sector.[39] However, even if a smaller percentage of minorities relative to the percentage of nonminorities is enrolled in private schools, this may say little about whether minorities will opt for private alternatives to their assigned public schools when given the opportunity. To what extent are racial and ethnic minorities electing choice plans today?

Some of the data analyzed by Frank Kemerer in this volume suggest that, in most cases, a higher proportion of racial and ethnic minorities attend charter schools than attend private schools: a study of charter schools in ten states shows that 14 percent of the students enrolled were African American and 25 percent were Hispanic. However, those data do not tell us the proportion of whites and nonwhites in individual alternative schools in those states. Perhaps a more important factor for predicting not only whether minorities will take advantage of an expanded choice movement but also whether choice is likely to increase or decrease racial and economic stratification is *why* parents choose a school other than the one assigned. Who chooses, and why they choose, is discussed later in the chapter.

Advantages

Most studies of minority parental and student satisfaction with school choice programs, particularly tuition voucher experiments and charter schools, cite as positive factors the small size of the school.[40] Size of classroom, sense of community, especially in the first year of a start-up school (and the sense of greater ownership that choosing a school gives to parents and students), more involved and caring teachers, the belief that the individual needs of the particular child are given greater attention, and the adaptation of the curriculum to ethnic and cultural considerations are also factors. In addition, many minority and low-income parents report that they sought alternative schools because they felt their child's previous school was unsafe.[41] Advocates of school choice also point to the increased parent involvement in their child's education, which is likely to occur in many school choice programs, and to the advantage to many working-class families of schools that operate well past the hours that public schools operate.[42] Some students and parents like the fact that choice schools often have a single, clear mission and hence a greater focus than do schools in the public school system. In general, parent and student satisfaction with choice schools appears to be substantial.

One of the major arguments for expanding school choice is that it will improve student achievement. However, as Jeffrey Henig points out in his chapter in this volume, it is difficult at this point to draw firm conclusions of improved academic achievement. Many programs have been in existence for only a short time, so that gains are not yet measurable. And since not all of the choice schools administer the same achievement tests given by the public schools in the district or state in which the choice school is located, it is not easy to make comparisons. There is such a diversity of choice schools, with diverse missions, and designed to appeal to students with different needs, that one cannot generalize as to the appropriate outcomes to measure. One advocate of charter schools is reported as saying, "We don't just have apples and oranges. We've got lots of apples, oranges, tangerines, and bananas."[43] As the author of that article notes, charters may be designed to serve only deaf students, home-schooled students, students in on-line computer schools, or juveniles who have been convicted of crimes. With such tremendous diversity, it is difficult to measure overall achievement gains of choice schools and compare them to traditional public schools. Better ways of assessing and comparing student achievement over time need to be developed before any conclusions can be drawn. However, several studies have found preliminary indications of achievement gains in students attending choice schools, and others show that at least attendance and retention have improved for disadvantaged children—certainly a necessary, if not sufficient, condition for improving academic achievement.[44]

Disadvantages

One of the major issues in the debate about school choice is whether certain school choice options will lead to increased racial and economic isolation. Although the statistics indicate increasing enrollment of minorities in private schools (the percentage increase, however, is less than that of non-minorities), as well as in public school choice plans (especially magnet school programs), that does not necessarily mean that the individual schools are less racially or economically stratified than the public schools these students previously attended. In one study, the researchers contend that their data show that more students of color and more low-income students are being served by charter schools than are white students. However, some of the comparisons are with the student population of public schools in the state as a whole, rather than with that of the central city school districts.[45] Often the data do not distinguish among the states, although charter schools in some states serve a much lower proportion of minority and low-income students, compared to the traditional public schools, than they do in other states.[46] Moreover, the data do not indicate whether the individual schools are more or less segregated than the public schools from which the students came. Some commentators point out that, inasmuch as the public schools are already heavily racially and economically segregated, segregated charter or tuition voucher schools would not change the picture substantially.[47]

One cannot draw any firm conclusions at this point, in the face of conflicting evidence (and of course it should be kept in mind that different types of choice plans may lead to either more or less segregation), with regard to whether school choice plans will lead to increased racial and ethnic stratification. An analysis of magnet school programs in Cincinnati, Nashville, and St. Louis finds that the percentage of black students enrolled in magnet schools is roughly the same as the percentage of black students in the school districts as a whole.[48] Another study, however, based on a 1990 resurvey of a subsample of the National Educational Longitudinal Study of 1988, found that either African Americans and Hispanics who attend magnet schools are likely to be more segregated from whites than in assigned public schools or that the level of segregation remains unchanged; in addition, the assigned public school has on average a somewhat higher proportion of whites than does the corresponding magnet school.[49] On the other hand, another study based on the National Educational Longitudinal Study of 1988 finds choice schools (which includes all schools of choice, not just magnet schools within the public school system) are more racially diverse than traditional public schools.[50] Finally, some studies of magnet school programs, particularly secondary school magnet programs that are schools within schools, conclude that they reinforce racial stratification.[51] Thus although some studies suggest that some school choice plans (particularly those that require some racial balance) may not necessarily increase racial stratification, the evidence is mixed. Moreover, it is important to note that many studies do not distinguish among the classroom, the school, and the school district with regard to racial and ethnic diversity.

The evidence of increased economic isolation resulting from school choice programs is more uniform, however. For example, the study of magnet school programs in Cincinnati, Nashville, and St. Louis finds that poor children remain more highly concentrated in nonmagnet than in magnet schools, even with special efforts to inform and attract students from poor families.[52] In the communities studied, researchers found that families of children in magnet schools have higher income and educational levels than those in the assigned public schools and that children in magnet schools are more likely to live in two-parent households with at least one parent employed. Even when the comparison is limited to minority parents, "positive correlations between magnet school attendance and higher socioeconomic status hold true." In other words, when minority parents are given a choice, those of higher socioeconomic status are more likely to choose magnets than those who are poorer and less educated. The study concludes that magnets, by and large, have contributed to a new phenomenon—schools that have achieved a measure of desegregation by race but that remain largely segregated on the basis of income.[53]

In a study of a program involving transfers from inner-city schools in St. Louis to suburban (predominantly white, middle-class) schools, the investigator found that students who remained at their assigned urban high school came from more disadvantaged backgrounds than those who participated in the choice program.[54] Transfer students were more likely to be from families with fewer children, and their parents were more likely to have graduated from high school and to have the highest-status jobs. Moreover, parents whose children remained in the assigned school not only had higher unemployment rates or jobs entailing more menial labor, they also were less likely to have had some experience in the world outside the city boundaries than parents of transfer children. The author of the study concludes that parents who elect to enroll their children in the school choice plan are more assertive and have a greater belief in the importance of education than do nonchoice parents, who are more likely to feel powerless or alienated and to lack a sense of control and an ability to act on their child's behalf.[55] The study also found that racial separatist attitudes influenced the decision of nonchoice parents not to send their children to white suburban schools.[56]

An evaluation of Milwaukee's voucher experiment, which was designed solely for low-income students, found that even among the poor, "parents seeking to get into the program are more educated, more involved, and have higher educational expectations than the average parent."[57] They also have smaller families than those who do not want to participate in the program. Choice parents were significantly more likely to have done volunteer work for the public school their child had previously attended than nonchoice parents, suggesting that, as in other studies, the parents are more likely to believe in the importance of education and to feel less alienated and powerless.[58] The result, of course, is that this cadre of public school volunteers is removed from the traditional public schools.

These and other studies suggest that, even when choice options are designed specifically for low-income students, those students who remain behind in their traditional public schools are more likely to be at the bottom economically, with significant numbers of them from the most alienated and powerless families. Several studies of choice in other countries reinforce this conclusion. A study in Scotland found that parents who participated in choice programs had significantly higher levels of education, more prestigious occupations, and smaller families than parents who did not participate in the program; the study concludes that "choice may have caused an increase in segregation along social class lines."[59]

In light of the conflicting evidence, before any projections are made about the extent to which an expanded choice movement may increase or decrease racial and economic stratification, both in the choice schools and the assigned public schools, the reasons parents now give for choosing schools as well as the adequacy of information available to different racial and socioeconomic groups should also be considered. These two interrelated issues are discussed below.

Much of the research is in agreement not only with regard to the difference in amount and quality of information available across socioeconomic groups but also with regard to the difference in sources and types of information used by parents of different socioeconomic groups. The authors of one article note that research shows that members of "dominant-status groups," defined as white and wealthy, "will have greater market resources, including time, money, information, educational backgrounds, political clout, and personal connections, and far fewer market constraints," which will give them an "advantage in the competition against members of subordinate status groups for seats in the most demanded schools."[60] Even among nonwhite and low-income parents, those with less disadvantaged backgrounds will have better sources of information. For example, the study of the transfer program in St. Louis reveals that students who stayed in their assigned urban high schools not only came from more disadvantaged backgrounds than those who participated in the transfer program but also that their families had less information on the school choice program than those who chose to transfer.[61]

One report on participation in magnet schools concludes that the lower participation rates of the poor in the three districts studied

is not a result of the failure of the school districts to provide information about magnet opportunities. The districts studied use many techniques of affirmative outreach (such as newsletters, brochures, advertising campaigns) in an effort to make parents and students aware of the program. However, the research showed that higher-income parents have available to them a wider variety of sources of information than low-income families. Access to people knowledgeable about schools either through their social networks or contacts at the work place often gives middle-class parents a basis for choice not available to those less well-off. Higher-income families who have cars and flexible working hours are better able than others to visit schools before making a choice.[62]

Some commentators note that, over time, poor parents may become as knowledgeable as higher-income parents, but they do not initially have the same level of information.[63] Thus it has been suggested that the use of a first-come, first-served selection criterion disadvantages those who do not have information early—usually those of lower socioeconomic status.[64]

Advocates of the market-driven approach to school choice programs, who believe that educational improvements will result through competitive market forces, and that bad schools will be driven out of business, assume that parents act rationally and choose schools based on "the quality of the academic program offered and the match between teaching styles and their child's individual needs."[65] Two researchers challenge the rational choice theory on the ground that it is distorted by racial and class bias. They review research showing that "race- and class-based views of image and status affect parents' perceptions of 'good' and 'bad' schools," noting that alienated parents with the least education are "inhibited from gathering information that would allow them to make decisions based on school-quality factors as opposed to school location and convenience." An upwardly mobile family, they argue, might rationally choose a school because of its social clout, while an isolated and alienated black family might equally rationally choose to remain in a predominantly black public school because of its familiarity and comfort level. It is unlikely, they suggest, that choices based on these nonacademic factors will lead to any significant educational improvement.

Other studies of the reasons for attending private schools also show that the perceptions of the academic quality of public schools have little or no apparent impact on private school enrollment but that race and class do affect choice. The percentage of minority students enrolled in the public schools has a significant effect on the decision of white parents to enroll their children in private schools.[66] Studies show that the percentage of minorities in choice schools similarly affects decisions, with white parents choosing schools with low percentages of minority students and minority parents seeking schools with high percentages of minority students.[67] Even those minority parents who choose schools where there are few children of their own race do so because of the perceived quality of predominantly white and middle-class schools. In the public school transfer program in St. Louis, transfer parents were found not to have any more factual information than nontransfer parents regarding the academic quality of the transfer school. Decisions were based on impressions, rather than objective information, with the decision to send a child to a suburban school apparently based on the assumption that a school in a wealthier, higher-status (white) neighborhood would be better and have more resources than the inner-city assigned school (whether this was actually true or not). Assessments of school quality appeared to be based primarily on the race of the students enrolled.[68]

Several studies in other countries support these observations. For example, a study of school choice in the Netherlands indicates that, regardless of class, parents are likely to consider that a school is of high quality because of the socioeconomic mix of students rather than the school's academic performance.[69] This study found that schools with high immigrant enrollments were experiencing white flight, noting that one public elementary school reached almost 100 percent non-Dutch enrollment soon after the non-Dutch enrollment had reached 50 percent. The author concludes that Dutch parents are using choice to abandon schools with substantial nonwhite immigrant enrollment. A study in Scotland found that parents selected schools that comprised a student body of a somewhat higher socioeconomic status than their own but that only marginally benefited their children in terms of academic attainment.[70]

Other factors affecting private school enrollment include religious preference, proximity to home or work, concern about sending a child to a school in an unfamiliar area, availability of transportation, or the parents' perception of their child's need for individual assistance. It has been noted that the decisionmaking process would probably be no different even if families had more factual information about choice options.[71]

Contrary to the results of many of these studies, the principal reasons given by parents for seeking to enroll their children in the Milwaukee voucher experiment are educational quality of the chosen school and greater discipline. Also important, however, are location of the choice school and frustration with public schools.[72] A report assessing charter schools nationally suggests that more than 50 percent of parents choose charter schools because of the small size of the school or the classes.[73] When the responses are broken down by racial and ethnic background, however, the range among minority parents who cite size of school or class as the reason for choosing charter schools is considerable, from 71.4 percent for Native American parents to 41.2 percent for Hispanic parents. A much smaller percentage of parents in this survey gave as other reasons the fact that the previous school was unsafe, that the child's special needs were not being met at the previous school, or that the child was not doing well in the previous school. Again, there were racial and ethnic differences in the responses: 14 to 18 percent of white, black, and Native American parents felt that their child's previous school was not safe, while more than 25 percent of Hispanic and Asian American parents gave safety as their reason. When responses are analyzed by income, 25 percent of low-income parents chose a charter school because they felt their child's previous school was unsafe, while only a little over 10 percent of upper-income parents sent their child to a charter school for this reason.

Apart from race or class concerns, which appear to be a major factor in choosing a school, with many parents equating the quality of the academic program with the composition of the student body, the studies suggest that parents probably look less to curricular or other educational innovations and academic quality of the educational program than they do to the size of the school and the classes and the fact that their child gets more individual attention from the teacher (which is in part related to size).

A number of commentators suggest that the use of a first-come, first-served selection criterion disadvantages those who do not obtain as much information as early as others—who are more likely to be those of higher socioeconomic status.[74] Many charter school laws provide that preference should be given to siblings of students currently enrolled in the school, potentially disadvantaging those parents who do not get as much information as early as others. The application process and forms themselves may deter economically disadvantaged families from applying.[75] Clearly, schools that use academic achievement test scores or other measures of academic achievement will disproportionately exclude minorities and low-income students.[76] Some choice school plans allow students to be excluded on the basis of their record of behavior at their prior school, which would limit choice at those schools to those who had been able to conform to the standards of the traditional public school to which they were assigned.[77] Behavior potentially could include the student's prior attendance record.

Some charter schools expect parents to contribute a certain number of hours of volunteer work on behalf of the school, sometimes known as sweat equity, both to increase the involvement of parents in the school their child attends and to provide in-kind support for the school.[78] If this is made a condition of admission, it may act as a substantial barrier for single-parent families or for those families in which both parents work in jobs that do not allow the flexibility that some professional positions might permit. The buy-out option offered by some schools whereby parents who do not have the time to volunteer either would pay others to do their share of volunteer work or contribute financial support directly to the school obviously would also not be a feasible option for low-income parents. An admissions criterion requiring parents to commit to volunteer time on behalf of the school thus may limit access for children from low-income, single-parent families.

With regard to tuition voucher programs, if the amount of the voucher does not cover the entire cost of tuition, it will be difficult for low-income students to take advantage of those programs unless schools were required to take a certain number of students without charging them the difference between the voucher and full tuition. Most private schools would be likely, at best, to accept only a limited number of such scholarship students. Larger families would be particularly disadvantaged in these circumstances. A number of studies of voucher experiments, even those designed solely for low-income students, found that parents seeking to participate had smaller families than those who did not, even without the barrier created by having to supplement the voucher.[79] Charter schools and choice within the public school system do not present the same problem as voucher programs, because they are not tuition dependent. In many cases, charter schools get the same amount per pupil as the districtwide average or statewide average per pupil expenditure and often are allowed to raise funds privately. As is apparent from the differences between middle-class and inner-city public schools in the financial and in-kind support they receive from their parent-teacher associations (PTAs), however, these differences in fund-raising ability among charter schools may persist and may even be exacerbated, since charter schools' fund-raising efforts go well beyond that of the traditional PTA.

Another important issue concerning the adequacy of resources is whether the state or school district will ensure transportation for all who want to choose schools, regardless of where they are located within the district or even within another district. The lack of transportation clearly will affect student and parent choice of schools.[80] Those families who can afford transportation or who have both the time and the means to provide their own transportation for their children will be favored. Since few programs involve complete subsidy of the transportation needs to maximize choice for low-income families, poor families and those isolated within the inner city may not have equal access to choice opportunities.

Some studies show that the lack of start-up money and the difficulty in obtaining funding for a building may also impact adversely on charter school organizers in states in which private entities are allowed to organize charter schools.[81] This lack of capital may affect low-income communities wanting to establish a charter school more than it will affect better-off communities.

School choice will have a substantial impact on the traditional public schools in central city districts by exacerbating the economic isolation and, in some circumstances, the racial isolation of those schools. Most studies show that many school choice programs leave the traditional public schools increasingly economically isolated. Even among students from low-income families, those who leave the assigned public school are more likely to come from two-parent families who are employed, better educated, more assertive, and have a greater belief in the importance of education and a sense of control than the families of students who remain behind. One commentator, analyzing New York City's magnet schools—even though choice is controlled and the schools are quite limited in opportunities for selectivity—found that the remaining schools became "pockets of concentrated disadvantage."[82] The impact on the education of children where race and poverty are concentrated is well documented.

A second, and related, concern is the impact of school choice on the improvement of education in the traditional public schools. Parents whose children remain in assigned schools have been shown to be alienated and to feel powerless. Since several studies have found that parents who participate in choice programs are likely to have been more involved in their children's education at their prior school, and are the more assertive parents who believe in the importance of education, the traditional schools lose not only those parents who have volunteered to work in the schools but also those parents most likely to press for reform.[83]

Another concern is the effect that school choice may have on the resources available to the traditional public schools. Certainly those who are suspicious of school choice (at least choice programs that include private schools) because of its history in the South, in which resources were drained from public schools to support private, segregated academies, and the continued underfunding of predominantly black public schools raise that concern. Studies even of choice within public school systems suggest that there is some adverse impact on resources available to the remaining public schools. Even within the limited public choice involved with magnet schools, researchers find that magnet schools have higher costs—including transportation, new equipment, teacher retraining, and smaller class size—than the traditional public schools.[84] Some argue that magnet school programs thus drain resources and also the best teachers from other schools.

A study of choice among rural school districts in Minnesota suggests some of the adverse financial implications for the public school system.[85] Districts that lost students as a result of the choice program lost funding, which meant either fewer resources for educating those students who remained or increased local taxes. An unexpected consequence of the competition that proponents of school choice tout as a way of reforming the public school system or getting rid of the failures is that some superintendents begin to allocate more of their budget to marketing and public relations, diverting resources from the academic program. The analyses of this study and of a study of charter schools in which some school districts also increased their marketing and public relations efforts in response to competition from charter schools raise concerns about the possible negative effects of competition arising from choice programs.

A concern that has been given somewhat less attention by those who are currently writing about school choice is the potential impact on teachers of color. One of the negative aspects of school desegregation in the South was the displacement of most black school administrators who had previously held positions in the dual system. When the dual system was disestablished, they lost their positions to white administrators. Many black teachers, who were deemed redundant after desegregation, also lost their positions. Today, African Americans constitute approximately 7.3 percent of teachers nationally; they are concentrated in the central city school districts, which is the highest-paid sector. In the private sector, black teachers constitute only 2.2 percent of the teaching force; not only is there a substantial salary differential between public and nonpublic schools, but benefits for private school teachers are also sharply limited.[86] To what extent would a substantial increase in nonpublic school choice opportunities affect this middle-class sector of the African American community? To what extent would there be more limited opportunities for black children to be exposed to teachers of their own race at some point during their schooling in nonpublic choice schools? The lack of benefits and the in-kind compensation offered by many private schools may attract fewer males and encourage greater feminization of the teaching force, in spite of the fact that one of the concerns of the black community is lack of male role models in the schools. This pattern may also affect those charter schools organized under state laws that permit charters to be granted to private entities or that permit charter schools to hire noncredentialed teachers.

Are teachers who bring energy and commitment to their jobs likely to remain in public schools with already limited resources, as more upwardly mobile, motivated, and active parents exit, leaving behind children impacted by poverty and the sense that education is less relevant to their lives? Central city school districts are already experiencing severe shortages of qualified teachers and teachers with experience in the fields they are assigned to teach. One potential effect of an expansion of the school choice movement may be to exacerbate the problem.

A Model School Choice Design

The expansion of the school choice movement poses several risks to equality of educational opportunity for racial and ethnic minorities and the poor. This section presents features that may minimize some of those risks. Of course, school choice includes such a diversity of goals, programs, organizational structures, and governance and financing mechanisms that it is impossible to generalize. Some choice programs clearly offer educational and other opportunities for minority children that they are not able to get in the traditional public schools to which they are assigned, at least as those schools are now organized and financed.[87] It is also clear, from the disadvantages outlined above, that school choice programs must include certain safeguards if minority and poor children are to have equal access to these opportunities. On the other hand, excessive regulation may frustrate the promise of school choice to improve education, so the safeguards should be no more than are necessary to ensure equality of access and opportunity.

Ensuring that Choice Does Not Increase Racial and Economic Stratification

Many school choice programs appear to increase racial and ethnic stratification, at least in certain circumstances, and are even more likely to increase economic segregation. Obviously, some choice schools will remain predominantly one race because of the mission of those schools and the type of curriculum (for example, a school that emphasizes an Afrocentric curriculum), as Frank Kemerer points out in his chapter in this volume. The effort should be to minimize factors that lessen diversity on bases other than choice grounded in personal preferences, values, interests, and perceived needs.

Several state charter school laws expressly prohibit discrimination on the basis of race or national origin (as well as other grounds) in the admission of students. Such provisions, alone, are not likely to have much effect on the diversity of the student body. Other states, in order to ensure that school choice does not lead to increased segregation, include racial balance provisions in legislation providing for school choice. Some statutes require that the charter school's racial and ethnic balance reflect that of the school district as a whole.[88] Others provide that the school's balance not deviate more than 10 percent from that of the district in which it is located.[89] Frank Kemerer notes some of the limitations to attaining diversity under these laws, such as the fact that the charter school might be located in a predominantly white suburban school district or a predominantly minority central city district. In addition to the fact that the requirement may be ineffective, there are substantial legal barriers to a school's selecting students to maintain a racially balanced student body.

There have been a number of challenges to the use of racial preferences in admissions to magnet schools or other specialized choice schools within the public school system. One recent case was brought by white parents who sued when their children were denied admission to a magnet school on the basis of their race. School officials, to ensure that the school's enrollment reflected the racial composition of the school district as a whole, had used a lottery system weighted by race to compensate for a disproportionately white applicant pool. The district court held that the school could not use race-conscious admissions policies, finding that under the strict scrutiny standard of review, the school system did not meet its burden of demonstrating that a compelling interest was served.[90] Other cases challenging the use of race-conscious admissions policies to ensure racial balance in alternative or choice schools reached similar results or were settled.[91] Nevertheless, an argument can be made that admissions programs that consider race as one factor among a number of criteria might survive constitutional scrutiny.[92] This area of the law is obviously very unsettled at this point.

Laws requiring that the racial and ethnic balance in choice schools reflect that of the school district as a whole also present problems for schools that may offer programs that appeal primarily to minority students and their families. For example, North Carolina's charter school law includes a requirement that the charter schools established under the act reasonably reflect the racial composition of the school district in which they are located. However, recent estimates are that twenty-two of the sixty charter schools in North Carolina may violate this requirement because they are more than 85 percent African American. This has led to an alliance between the state teachers' union and members of the state legislature's Black Caucus, who are calling for the law to be enforced or that the charter schools be closed, while in the other camp are minority parents whose children attend these charter schools, Republican members of the state legislature, and such conservative organizations as the North Carolina Foundation for Individual Rights (which has challenged affirmative action at the university level).[93] One school, which is now 99 percent black, originally had white parents sign up for the lottery as well, but they dropped out when they learned that the school was to be located in a black neighborhood.

If the means that states have used to ensure racial diversity in choice schools are constitutionally questionable, can measures to ensure diversity of socioeconomic background be taken? The Supreme Court has held that classifications based on wealth, unlike race, are not strictly scrutinized by the courts, so that such measures are much more likely to be found constitutional.[94] One suggestion is to require that the proportion of students eligible for the free or reduced-price lunch program reflect the proportion in the school district as a whole.[95] The Kansas charter school law has adopted this approach, requiring that a charter school be reasonably reflective of the socioeconomic composition of the school district in which it is located.[96] Frank Kemerer suggests another approach: a 20 percent set-aside for students whose families qualify for federally assisted school lunches as a condition of receiving public funds (whether as a charter school or through a tuition voucher program). The only decision to date that has questioned the use of socioeconomic preferences for admission is one in which the district court had previously struck down a lottery weighted by race and ethnicity in order to have a magnet school whose enrollment approximated that of the general school population. The judge found that changing the weighted lottery to use first-language and family income classifications was attempting to achieve the same end that had earlier been ruled unconstitutional. The judge viewed the first-language criterion as a proxy for a national origin classification and said that the family income classification, which he characterized as creating "a rigid dichotomy between students who qualify for free or reduced lunch and all other students," did not make the weighted system constitutional.[97]

Some state statutes have specified that a certain percentage of at-risk students must be served. The Colorado Charter School Act defines an at-risk student as a pupil who, because of physical, emotional, and socioeconomic or cultural factors, is less likely to succeed in a conventional educational environment. The law, however, mandates only that a percentage of the charter schools that are established under the act serve at-risk children, rather than requiring each choice school to take a certain percentage of at-risk children.[98]

To minimize the socioeconomic isolation of students in traditional, assigned schools, all parents in a broader choice program should be required to choose among available options, with admission to the school of one's choice to be made by lottery rather than simply assigning parents who do not choose to neighborhood schools. Requiring all families to make a choice at the same time (assuming that adequate information and some assistance with applications are provided) will reduce the extent to which those who receive information late will be kept out.

Adequate and Accessible Information

Because of the differences in amount, quality, sources, and types of information available to and used by parents of different socioeconomic levels, it is important to provide information tailored to the ways different groups gather and use information. States should promulgate standards for developing information and for its dissemination and should fund dissemination services. It has been suggested that recruitment and counseling centers be established that would not only disseminate information about choice options in the community but would also provide assistance with the actual applications.[99] Establishing these centers in places where parents live or do business and through media (grocery stores, gas stations, doctors' offices, public housing offices, newsletters, radio, including ethnic radio stations), and locating these centers near public transportation, having evening hours, and employing community residents would help to reach those at all socioeconomic levels.[100] To reach low-income and first-language-minority parents, in particular, intensive outreach efforts will be needed. It may be important to provide opportunities, including transportation, to enable parents to visit choice schools.[101] Finally, requiring choice schools to provide key information in an accessible and standardized format would enable parents to make comparisons among schools more easily, for example, mission, teaching philosophy, location and availability of transportation, when school was established, ages served, governance structure, size of school, average class size, student-teacher ratio, outcome measures, and retention rates for both students and teachers.

Selection Criteria

Some states' charter laws expressly prohibit schools from using academic ability as an admission criterion.[102] Rather than prohibiting choice schools from considering any measure of academic ability regardless of the emphasis of the school, the use of standardized test scores or other academic achievement measures should be permitted where appropriate to the nature of the program—for example, a high school that specializes in mathematics and science. However, these measures of academic achievement should be allowed only if used in combination with other criteria that might predict success in that program, so as to ensure opportunity for those who have the interest and the ability but whose prior educational experiences are inadequate.

To avoid penalizing those who obtain information late—most likely minority and low-income parents—a lottery system rather than a first-come, first-served admissions system should be employed. The federal Charter Schools Act minimizes the use of exclusionary admissions criteria by restricting funds to those schools that use a lottery system for admissions.[103] Similarly, efforts should be made to ensure that preferences for siblings of currently enrolled students do not disadvantage parents who acquire information late. Requiring all parents to make a choice at the same time will minimize the extent to which this will occur. Finally, admission of a student should not be conditioned on the ability of a parent to volunteer time, although parental involvement can and should be encouraged in various ways.

Equality of Resources

If the choice program is a tuition voucher program that includes private schools, participating schools should be required to admit a certain percentage of low-income students without requiring that the voucher be supplemented. Some voucher proposals specify that participating schools cannot charge anyone attending the school under the plan more than the amount of the voucher, but other voucher proposals do not limit the amount of tuition that a school may charge. Obviously, these latter proposals would sharply limit the participation of low-income and large families.

Transportation should be fully subsidized by the state in order to provide equality of access for low-income families to any choice school, including those outside the school district. Further, states should fund both recruitment and counseling centers that are easily accessible to minority and low-income communities and the dissemination of information about various programs, perhaps including transportation for parents to enable them to visit schools in which they are interested before making a choice.

Another important factor in ensuring that racial-ethnic minorities and the poor are not disadvantaged by expanding opportunities for diverse school choice programs will be performance accountability, which will necessitate the development and application of fair and meaningful outcome measures and regular evaluation of the schools and their programs.

Finally, states and school districts must ensure that the resources of those assigned public schools with large concentrations of low-income students are increased and directed toward overcoming the educational deficits exacerbated by concentrated poverty. States must ensure that students remaining in their assigned public schools do not have a disproportionate number of unqualified teachers.[104] They should also ensure that the already severe shortage in central city schools of qualified teachers and teachers trained in the fields they are assigned to teach is not heightened by an expanding school choice movement.

Conclusion

This chapter examines the potential impact of an expanded school choice movement on racial and ethnic minorities and the economically disadvantaged, including whether the current political coalitions are likely to advance or impede the objectives of racial and economic justice. Linking choice to equity considerations, and moving away from an emphasis on unregulated tuition vouchers to a broader range of more or less regulated types of choice, has expanded its political base to include many minority parents, community activists, and local politicians of color. On the other hand, the leadership of some of the national civil rights groups has either continued to oppose such programs or remained silent, largely attributable to the history of school choice and the political ideology of its proponents. Although broadening the types of choice may help to reduce the concerns of civil rights groups about the conservative, market-driven ideology that motivated the earlier tuition voucher movement, the question is whether school choice will continue to receive broad-based support. The widely divergent goals of school choice proponents eventually may sever the alliances that might have brought about increased opportunities for school choice. On the other hand, the rapidly emerging charter school movement may be perceived as neutral territory around which both the market-driven and equity-driven proponents can coalesce.

The chapter also explores both the advantages of school choice for racial-ethnic minorities and the economically disadvantaged and the potential disadvantages for these communities and ways in which some of those disadvantages might be minimized. Most surveys of minority parents and students involved in school choice programs find substantial satisfaction with their chosen schools. Among the positive factors cited are the small size of both the school and the classroom, a sense of community, involved and caring teachers, a safe school environment, attention to children's individual needs, and the adaptation of the curriculum to ethnic and cultural considerations. It is difficult at this point, however, to draw any firm conclusions about the role of school choice in improving academic achievement, although some studies find preliminary indications of achievement gains and others show that at least attendance and retention have improved.

One of the principal issues in the debate about school choice is whether it will lead to increased racial and economic isolation. With regard to increased racial stratification, the research yields mixed results, with some studies showing increased segregation. However, evidence of increased economic isolation resulting from school choice is substantial. In general, even among low-income and minority parents, those who opt out of the assigned public school have higher income and educational levels than those whose children remain behind. They are also more assertive and more likely to believe in the importance of education and to feel less alienated and powerless than nonchoosing parents.

The question of increased racial and economic stratification is related to the reasons parents give for selecting schools. The racial and socioeconomic composition of the student body has the greatest effect on school choice decisions, with white parents choosing schools with low percentages of minority students and minority parents often seeking schools with high percentages of minority students. Many parents appear to equate the quality of the academic program with the composition of the student body. Also related to the issue of racial and economic separation is the difference among socioeconomic groups in the amount and quality of information available to them about choice schools and in the sources and types of information they use.

This chapter recommends several ways of achieving greater racial and economic balance in choice schools as well as ways of addressing the disparities in information about them. Additional recommendations include regulating admissions criteria that would limit access of low-income and minority students and providing the resources necessary both to ensure equality of access to choice schools for these groups and to ensure that students who remain in assigned public schools are not disadvantaged.

In conclusion, although certain types of choice programs are likely to enhance educational and other opportunities for racial and ethnic minorities, the minimum safeguards recommended in this chapter are necessary to ensure equality of opportunity for all children, whether they and their parents avail themselves of expanded options for alternative schools or choose to remain with their assigned public schools.

Notes

1. The variety of alternative plans called school choice is described in detail in the chapter by Jeffrey Henig and Stephen Sugarman, this volume.

2. *Brown* v. *Board of Education*, 347 U.S. 483 (1954).

3. *Griffin* v. *County School Board*, 377 U.S. 218 (1964); *Hall* v. *St. Helena Parish School Board*, 197 F.Supp. 649 (E.D. La. 1961); aff'd mem., 368 U.S. 515 (1962); *Norwood* v. *Harrison*, 413 U.S. 455 (1973).

4. Seven southern states enacted tuition grant laws. See Helen Hershkoff and Adam S. Cohen, "School Choice and the Lessons of Choctaw County," *Yale Law and Policy Review*, vol. 10 (1992), pp. 1, 6.

5. Note, "Segregated Academies and State Action," *Yale Law Journal*, vol. 82 (1973), pp. 1436, 1446–47; Hershkoff and Cohen, "School Choice and the Lessons of Choctaw County," pp. 3, 8.

6. "Segregated Academies and State Action," pp. 1452–53; Hershkoff and Cohen, "School Choice and the Lessons of Choctaw County," pp. 8, 13.

7. Hershkoff and Cohen, "School Choice and the Lessons of Choctaw County," p. 13.

8. Civil Rights Act, 42 U.S.C.A., section 2000d and the following (West 1994). *Green* v. *County School Board*, 391 U.S. 430 (1968); *Swann* v. *Charlotte-Mecklenburg Board of Education*, 402 U.S. 1 (1971).

9. *Keyes* v. *School District No. 1, Denver*, 413 U.S. 189 (1973). During this period, public school choice (magnet schools) was sought as an alternative to mandatory pupil assignment in court-ordered desegregation remedies, urged by those who wanted to minimize the effects of desegregation decrees. Others advocated magnet schools as a way of attracting white parents back into public school systems following desegregation in the hope that it would promote integration.

10. Molly Townes O'Brien, "Private School Tuition Vouchers and the Realities of Racial Politics," *Tennessee Law Review*, vol. 64 (1997), pp. 359, 391.

11. *Milliken* v. *Bradley*, 418 U.S. 717 (1974).

12. O'Brien, "Private School Tuition Vouchers," p. 392.

13. *Board of Education of Oklahoma City Public Schools* v. *Dowell*, 498 U.S. 237 (1991); *Freeman* v. *Pitts*, 503 U.S. 467 (1992).

14. This has been well documented by Gary Orfield over the last decade. See generally Gary Orfield and Susan E. Eaton, *Dismantling Desegregation* (New Press, 1996), pp. 53–71. See also Gary Orfield, *The Growth of Segregation in American Schools* (Alexandria, Va.: National School Boards Association, 1993); Gary Orfield, Franklin Monfort, and Melissa Aaron, *Status of School Desegregation, 1968–1986* (Alexandria, Va.: National School Boards Association, Council of Urban Boards of Education, 1989); Gary Orfield, Franklin Monfort, and Rosemary George, "School Segregation in the 1980s," *IDRA Newsletter* (November 1987), pp. 3–5, 9.

15. Orfield and Eaton, *Dismantling Desegregation*, pp. 62–63.

16. Patrick Welsh, "Fast-Track Trap: How Ability Grouping Hurts Our Schools, Kids, and Families," *Washington Post*, September 16, 1990; Jeannie Oakes, *Keeping Track: How Schools Structure Inequality* (Yale University Press, 1985).

17. Mary Anne Raywid, "Choice Orientations, Discussions, and Prospects," in Peter W.

Cookson Jr., ed., *The Choice Controversy* (Newbury Park, Calif.: Corwin, 1992), pp. 5–7.

18. Kevin J. Dougherty and Lisabet Sostre, "Minerva and the Market: The Sources of the Movement for School Choice," in Cookson, *The Choice Controversy*, p. 33.

19. The following is based on Raywid, "Choice Orientations, Discussions, and Prospects," pp. 9–12.

20. See, for example, Kevin B. Smith and Kenneth J. Meier, *The Case against School Choice* (Armonk, N.Y.: M. E. Sharpe, 1995), pp. 1–13.

21. Lowell C. Rose and others, "The Twenty-Ninth Annual Phi Delta Kappa/Gallup Poll of the Public's Attitudes toward the Public Schools," *Phi Delta Kappan* (September 1997), p. 41. When the question was framed as to whether students and parents should be allowed to choose a private school to attend at public expense rather than government expense, 51 percent of nonwhites were in favor (compared to 44 percent of the public as a whole). Inexplicably, when the *public expense* version of the question was posed, eighteen to twenty-nine year olds were most likely to oppose this form of choice (62 percent), but when the term *government expense* was used, this demographic group was most likely to favor choice (70 percent). And when a question most directly associated with vouchers was asked (whether the government should pay all or part of the tuition for any private or church-related school), although the general public was evenly divided (49 percent in favor and 48 percent opposed), among the groups favoring vouchers were women, nonwhites (61 percent), lower-income groups, younger people, and those who live in the South; those opposed included men, those living in the West, and suburban residents.

A 1998 survey by the Joint Center for Political and Economic Studies found that 48 percent of African Americans favored the use of state funds for private school tuition, with 40 percent opposed. By contrast, whites opposed the use of such funds for vouchers for private schools by a margin of 50 percent to 41 percent. Steven A. Holmes, "Black Groups in Florida Split over School Voucher Plan," *New York Times,* May 30, 1999.

22. Lori Olszewski, "Help Wanted at Schools: Severe Shortage of Trained Math and Science Teachers Strains State Educational Resources," *San Francisco Chronicle*, October 6, 1998; DeNeen L. Brown, "Third Graders Mark Time during Parade of Teachers," *Washington Post*, December 9, 1995. See also Orfield and Eaton, *Dismantling Segregation*, pp. 68–69. In general, polls show that low-income African Americans are more likely to support the concept of publicly funded choice than middle- and higher-income, college-educated African Americans. Holmes, "Black Groups in Florida Split over School Voucher Plan." See also Clarence Page, "The Voucher Question in Florida Voucher Plan Splits Black Groups," *Tulsa World*, June 13, 1999.

23. See also Dougherty and Sostre, "Minerva and the Market," p. 28.

24. Ibid., p. 32.

25. David Dent, "Diversity Rules Threaten North Carolina Schools That Aid Blacks," *New York Times*, December 23, 1998.

26. Milton Friedman introduced his proposal to privatize education through a system of tuition vouchers only a year after *Brown* v. *Board of Education*. See O'Brien, "Private School Tuition Vouchers," pp. 359, 385. O'Brien notes (pp. 384–85) that even before *Brown* a number of southern states considered legislation to provide grants to individuals to use at private schools and to cut off funds to public schools if a black student were admitted to a white school.

27. See *Green* v. *County School Board*, 391 U.S. 430 (1968).

28. *Garrett* v. *Board of Education*, 775 F.Supp. 1004 (E.D. Mich. 1991); Donald O. Leake and Brenda L. Leake, "African American Immersion Schools in Milwaukee: A View from the Inside," *Phi Delta Kappan* (1992), p. 783; Donald O. Leake and Brenda L. Leake, "Islands of Hope: Milwaukee's African American Immersion Schools," *Journal of Negro Education,*

vol. 61 (1992), p. 24; Kenneth W. Brown, "The Educational Crisis of African American Males," *Journal of Law and Education*, vol. 25 (1995), p. 517; Charles Vergon, "Male Academies for At-Risk Urban Youth: Legal and Policy Lessons from the Detroit Experience," *West's Education Law Reporter*, vol. 79 (1993), p. 351; Robert L. Steele, "All Things Not Being Equal: The Case for Race Separate Schools," *Case Western Reserve Law Review*, vol. 43 (1993), p. 591; Note, "Creating Space for Racial Difference: The Case for African-American Schools," *Harvard Civil Rights–Civil Liberties Law Review*, vol. 27 (1992), p. 187; Walter Gill, "Jewish Day Schools and Afrocentric Programs as Models for Educating African American Youth," *Journal of Negro Education*, vol. 60 (1991), pp. 566, 571; Steven Siegel, "Ethnocentric Public School Curriculum in a Multicultural Nation: Proposed Standards for Judicial Review," *New York Law School Law Review*, vol. 40 (1996), p. 311; Sonia R. Jarvis, "*Brown* and the Afrocentric Curriculum," *Yale Law Journal*, vol. 101 (1992), p. 1285; Molefi K. Asante, "The Afrocentric Idea in Education," *Journal of Negro Education*, vol. 60 (1991), p. 170.

29. Holmes, "Black Groups in Florida Split over School Voucher Plan"; Linda Kleindienst, "Foes Sue to Prevent Vouchers," *Orlando Sentinel*, June 23, 1999.

30. Valerie E. Lee, Robert G. Croninger, and Julia B. Smith, "Equity and Choice in Detroit," in Bruce Fuller and Richard F. Elmore, eds., *Who Chooses? Who Loses? Culture, Institutions, and the Unequal Effects of School Choice* (Teachers College Press, 1996); Rolf K. Blank and others, "After Fifteen Years: Magnet Schools in Urban Education," in Fuller and Elmore, *Who Chooses? Who Loses?*

31. See Betsy Levin, *And Then There Were the Children: An Assessment of Efforts to Test Decentralization in New York City's Public School System* (Ford Foundation, 1969).

32. Derived from data projected for 1998; National Center for Education Statistics, *The Condition of Education, 1998* (U.S. Department of Education, 1998), p. 132. The number of children being home schooled was projected to be 1 million for the 1997–98 school year; Patricia M. Lines, "Home Schoolers: Estimated Numbers and Growth," in National Center for Education Statistics, *The Condition of Education, 1998*. Home-schooling statistics from the Home School Legal Defense Association show a somewhat higher number (1.23 million); Brian Ray, "Home Education across the United States" (http://www.hslda.org/nationalcenter/statsandreports/index.stm), 1997.

33. Only about 15 percent of those who attend private schools attend secular schools; National Center for Education Statistics, *Digest of Education Statistics, 1997* (U.S. Department of Education, 1997), table 61, 1993–94 school year.

34. Students attending Catholic schools still comprise 60 percent of those attending religiously affiliated schools, but only 41 percent of the religiously affiliated schools are Catholic; National Center for Education Statistics, *Digest of Education Statistics, 1997*, tables 61 and 59.

35. National Center for Education Statistics, *The Condition of Education, 1998*, p. 134.

36. National Center for Education Statistics, *Digest of Education Statistics, 1997*, table 59.

37. In one study based on a survey of home schoolers that included 1,657 families drawn from all fifty states, the District of Columbia, and three U.S. territories, with between 3 percent and 6.5 percent of the sample drawn from each of seven states (including Texas, California, New York, and Ohio, with fairly large populations of minority school-aged children), 96 percent of the surveyed parents were white, 1.5 percent were Hispanic, 1 percent were Asian American, and the percentage of African Americans was substantially less than 1 percent. Brian D. Ray, *Strengths of Their Own: Home Schoolers across America* (Salem, Ore.: National Home Education Research Institute, 1997). Clearly, more data on which types of students select which types of schools, where, and why, need to be collected and analyzed. This area needs much more research before appropriate policies can be made.

38. The data are for 1995; National Center for Education Statistics, *The Condition of Education, 1998.*

39. Stephen Plank and others, "Effects of Choice in Education," in Edith Rasell and Richard Rothstein, eds., *School Choice: Examining the Evidence* (Washington, D.C.: Economic Policy Institute, 1993). Their study was based on a 1990 resurvey of a subsample of those surveyed for the 1988 National Educational Longitudinal Study.

40. In 1995, the average enrollment in charter schools was 287 students, and most of them were elementary schools; Linda Jacobson, "Under the Microscope: As Charter Schools Flourish, the Big Question for Researchers Is, Do They Work?" *Education Week,* November 6, 1996. The U.S. Department of Education's report on charter schools in ten states notes that 62 percent of the charter schools enroll fewer than 200 students. *A Study of Charter Schools: First-Year Report* (U.S. Department of Education, 1997).

41. Gregg Vanourek and others, *Charter Schools in Action Project: Final Report,* pt. 5 (New York: Hudson Institute, 1997).

42. Bruno V. Manno and others, "How Charter Schools Are Different: Lessons and Implications from a National Study," *Phi Delta Kappan* (1998), p. 488.

43. Jacobson, "Under the Microscope."

44. Vanourek and others, *Charter Schools in Action*; Peter W. Cookson Jr. and Sonali M. Shroff, *Recent Experience with Urban School Choice Plans,* Digest 127 (ERIC/Clearinghouse on Urban Education, 1997). See also Jeffrey Henig's discussion, this volume, regarding conflicting findings on student achievement in the Milwaukee and Cleveland voucher programs.

45. Both a Hudson Institute study (Vanourek and others, *Charter Schools in Action)* and a U.S. Department of Education study *(A Study of Charter Schools: First-Year Report)* compare the racial and ethnic background of students in charter schools with that of all public school students in the country and find that, although the percentage of minority students in all public schools is 34.0 percent, minorities comprise 49.6 percent (Hudson) or 48.4 percent (U.S. Department of Education) of charter school students. Since most of the charter schools are located in central city districts, and many are designed for minority students, these comparisons do not tell us much. They certainly do not tell us, contrary to what the authors of the Hudson Institute report contend, that these data show that charter schools are not creaming the best students from the public schools. Other studies compare the percentage of minorities served by choice programs with the percentage of minorities attending public schools in the central city school district in which the choice programs are located. Paul E. Peterson, "School Choice: A Report Card," in Paul E. Peterson and Bryan Hassel, eds., *Learning from School Choice* (Brookings, 1998). Peterson notes that most choice programs in central city districts are specifically designed to serve low-income students and that their predominantly minority background reflects that of the school district in which the choice programs are located. Following are some of his data on central city choice programs, with the minority population of that city's public schools in parentheses (ibid., tables 1-1, 1-3): Milwaukee has 73 percent African American and 21 percent Latino (73 percent), Cleveland has 65 percent African American and 5 percent Latino (78 percent), New York City has 48 percent African American and 45 percent Latino (82 percent), San Antonio has 4 percent African American and 82 percent Latino (public school percentage not given); only Indianapolis has less than 50 percent, with 41 percent African American and 4 percent Latino (56 percent).

46. In Georgia and Colorado, the proportion of minority and low-income students in charter schools is substantially lower than the proportion in traditional public schools; in Arizona, the proportion is higher. Note, "Charter Schools, Equal Protection Litigation, and the New School Reform Movement," *New York University Law Review,* vol. 73 (1998), p. 1290.

47. Caroline M. Hoxby, "Analyzing School Choice Reforms That Use America's Traditional Forms of Parental Choice," in Peterson and Hassel, *Learning from School Choice,* p.

151. See also Dennis Epple, "Stratification by Income, Race, and Outcomes in Chicago Public Schools" (Washington, D.C.: National Academy of Sciences, 1998).

48. Corrine M. Yu and William L. Taylor, eds., *Difficult Choices: Do Magnet Schools Serve Children in Need?* (Washington, D.C.: Citizens Commission on Civil Rights, 1997).

49. Plank and others, "Effects of Choice in Education," p. 129.

50. Mary Erina Driscoll, "Choice Achievement and School Community," in Rasell and Rothstein, *School Choice*, pp. 154–55.

51. Susan E. Eaton, "Slipping toward Segregation," in Orfield and Eaton, *Dismantling Desegregation*, p. 219. A study of these programs in Montgomery County, Maryland, found that the magnet schools were predominantly white and Asian, while the larger schools in which the magnets were located were predominantly African American and Latino (ibid., p. 207). This was attributed in part to the failure to provide all parents with equal information. Latino parents were found to be the least well informed and white parents the most (p. 224).

52. Yu and Taylor, *Difficult Choices*, p. 2.

53. Ibid, p. 27. See also R. Kenneth Godwin, Frank R. Kemerer, and Valerie J. Martinez, "Comparing Public Choice and Private Voucher Programs in San Antonio," in Peterson and Hassel, *Learning from School Choice*, pp. 296–97, which notes a similar sorting by race and socioeconomic status in a districtwide thematic choice program operated by the San Antonio public school district.

54. Amy Stuart Wells, "The Sociology of School Choice," in Rasell and Rothstein, *School Choice*.

55. Ibid., p. 36. Amy Stuart Wells and Robert L. Crain, "Do Parents Choose School Quality or School Status? A Sociological Theory of Free Market Education," in Cookson, *The Choice Controversy*, p. 78, note that powerlessness and alienation are key factors in decisions of those minority or poor parents who remain in their assigned neighborhood school even though a choice of a better school is available.

56. Wells, "The Sociology of School Choice," p. 39.

57. John Witte, "The Milwaukee Parental Choice Program," in Rasell and Rothstein, *School Choice*.

58. Ibid., pp. 83–84.

59. J. Douglas Willms and Frank H. Echols, "The Scottish Experience of Parental School Choice," in Rasell and Rothstein, *School Choice*, pp. 49, 50, 61.

60. Wells and Crain, "Do Parents Choose School Quality or School Status?" p. 76.

61. See Wells, "The Sociology of School Choice."

62. Yu and Taylor, *Difficult Choices*, p. 2. Peter W. Cookson, *School Choice: The Struggle for the Soul of American Education* (Yale University Press, 1994), pp. 91–92, agrees that there is a gap between the poor and the nonpoor in acquiring information and that the two groups of parents rely on different sources of information.

63. See, for example, Cookson, *School Choice*, pp. 91–92.

64. Peterson, "School Choice," p. 17.

65. Wells and Crain, "Do Parents Choose School Quality or School Status?" pp. 65, 66, 69, 70.

66. Kevin B. Smith and Kenneth J. Meier, "School Choice: Panacea or Pandora's Box?" *Phi Delta Kappan* (1995), p. 312.

67. Jeffrey R. Henig, "The Local Dynamics of Choice: Ethnic Preferences and Institutional Responses," in Fuller and Elmore, *Who Chooses? Who Loses?* p. 105. See also Wells, "The Sociology of Choice," p. 35.

68. Wells, "The Sociology of Choice," pp. 40–43.

69. Frank Brown, "The Dutch Experience with School Choice: Implications for American Education," in Cookson, *The Choice Controversy*, pp. 178–79.

70. Willms and Echols, "The Scottish Experience of Parental School Choice," p. 49.

71. Wells, "The Sociology of School Choice," p. 35.

72. Witte, "The Milwaukee Parental Choice Program," p. 79.

73. Vanourek and others, *Charter Schools in Action Project*, tables 4 and 5.

74. Peterson, "School Choice," p. 17. See also *Villanueva v. Carere*, 85 F.3d 481, 488 n.3 (10th Cir. 1996).

75. *Villanueva v. Carere*, 873 F. Supp. 434, 449 (D. Colo. 1994); aff'd, 85 F.3d 481 (10th Cir. 1996).

76. Some charter school laws, but not all, prohibit charter schools from discriminating on the basis of academic achievement. See Mass. Gen. Laws, chap. 71, section 89(I) (1997). However, the Massachusetts law also includes a provision that a charter school may establish reasonable academic standards as a condition for eligibility for applicants.

77. The Texas open-enrollment charter school law allows charter schools to exclude students who have a documented history of discipline problems. Texas Education Code Ann., section 12.111 (6) (West 1998).

78. Manno and others, "How Charter Schools Are Different," p. 488. See also *Villanueva v. Carere*, 85 F.3d 481, 484 (10th Cir. 1996).

79. See the analysis of the Milwaukee voucher experiment, Witte, "The Milwaukee Parental Choice Program," p. 70.

80. Stuart Biegel, "School Choice Policy and Title VI: Maximizing Equal Access for K–12 Students in a Substantially Deregulated Educational Environment," *Hastings Law Journal*, vol. 46 (1995), p. 1533.

81. Jacobson, "Under the Microscope," p. 21.

82. Robert L. Crain, "New York City's Career Magnet High Schools," in Rasell and Rothstein, *School Choice*, p. 265.

83. Jeanne M. Powers and Peter W. Cookson Jr., "The Politics of School Choice Research: Fact, Fiction, and Statistics," *Educational Policy*, vol. 13 (1999), pp. 104, 115.

84. Yu and Taylor, *Difficult Choices*, p. 9, note that Houston spends $400 to $1,300 more per student on its magnet school program. See also Orfield and Eaton, *Dismantling Desegregation*, p. 103; Blank and others, "After Fifteen Years," pp. 164–65.

85. Powers and Cookson, "The Politics of School Choice Research," pp. 115–16.

86. Discussion in this paragraph is from Sharon Keller, "Something to Lose: The Black Community's Hard Choices about Educational Choice," *Journal of Legislation*, vol. 24 (1998), pp. 67, 96–97.

87. See Yu and Taylor, *Difficult Choices*, p. 1; Vanourek and others, *Charter Schools in Action Project*.

88. California Education Code, section 47.605 (b)(G) (West 1999); North Carolina General Statutes, section 115C-238.29F (g)(5) (1997). Both these laws specify racial and ethnic composition of the general population in the school district, rather than the student population. Kansas law requires the charter school to be reasonably reflective of the socioeconomic composition of the school district as well as its racial composition. Kansas Statutes Ann., 72-1906(d)(2) (1997).

89. South Carolina Code Ann., section 59-40-50 (B)(6) (Law Co-Op 1998); Nevada Revised Statutes, 386.580(2) (1997).

90. *Tito v. Arlington County School Board*, 1997 U.S. Dist. LEXIS 7932 (E.D. Va.). The Supreme Court has held that all racial classifications are subject to strict scrutiny by the courts, requiring the government to demonstrate that the classification serves a compelling state interest and that the use of the classification is narrowly tailored to achieve that goal for it to be found constitutional. *Adarand Constructors, Inc. v. Peña*, 515 U.S. 200 (1995).

91. *Wessman v. Gittens*, 160 F. 3d 790 (1st Cir. 1998) (admission to academically elite

school based on standardized test scores plus racial-ethnic guidelines held unconstitutional); *Ho v. San Francisco Unified School District*, 965 F.Supp. 1316 (N.D. Cal. 1997) (court denied motion for summary judgment in case brought by Chinese Americans challenging racial-ethnic guidelines for admission to academically elite school; case settled with school officials being directed to develop new assignment plan in which no student could be assigned to a particular school on the basis of race or ethnicity, ending priority given to African American and Latino students in school assignments); *Equal Open Enrollment Ass'n v. Akron City School District*, 937 F.Supp. 700 (N.D. Ohio 1996) (court enjoined school district's policy of barring white students from transferring to nearby suburban districts while allowing black students to do so in order to prevent white flight). But see *Eisenberg v. Montgomery County Public Schools*, 19 F.Supp. 2d 449 (D. Md. 1998) (court denied preliminary injunction in challenge to district policy denying transfer from assigned school to magnet school on grounds of racial balance).

92. Note, "The Constitutionality of Race-Conscious Admissions Programs in Public Elementary and Secondary Schools," *Harvard Law Review*, vol. 112 (1999), p. 940. But see *Hopwood v. Texas*, 78 F.3d 932 (5th Cir. 1996).

93. Dent, "Diversity Rules Threaten North Carolina Charter Schools."

94. But see *Tuttle v. Arlington County School Board*, 1998 U.S. Dist. LEXIS 19788 (E.D. Va.), in which the court held that a magnet school's use of a lottery weighted by family income, together with using first language, violated both the Due Process and Equal Protection Clauses.

95. Yu and Taylor, *Difficult Choices*.

96. Kansas Statutes Ann., section 72-1906 (d)(2) (1997).

97. *Tuttle v. Arlington County School Board*.

98. Colorado Revised Statutes, sections 22-30.5-109 (2)(a) (1999); 22-30.5-103 (1999).

99. The Cambridge, Massachusetts, regulated-choice program has established information centers to assist families. The White Plains, New York, school district also has an information center for parents and an aggressive outreach program. Raquel Aldana, "When the Free-Market Visits Public Schools: Answering the Roll Call for Disadvantaged Students," *National Black Law Journal*, vol. 15 (1997–98), pp. 26, 44.

100. Yu and Taylor, *Difficult Choices*, pp. 28–29.

101. Ibid., p. 22.

102. For example, Minnesota Statutes Ann., section 120.064 (1998).

103. 20 U.S.C., section 8066(1)(H).

104. Yu and Taylor, *Difficult Choices*, p. 29.

CHAPTER TEN

Teachers, Teachers' Unions, and School Choice

WILLIAM G. BUSS

Teachers engage in collective bargaining through union organizations, which are a significant political force in education at all levels of the government in the United States. Teachers' unions are naturally suspicious about educational reform because of its threat to their influence. At the same time, teachers' unions are outspoken about the problems confronting American public schools and, in various ways, cautiously support change. School choice could both influence and be influenced by the development of new forms of unionism that are being advocated and, in a limited number of places, being tried. A critical variable will be the individual choices of countless numbers of teachers who must decide whether their professional satisfaction and job security will be furthered best by greater individual autonomy or by traditional union representation.

A union's traditional role as the collective bargaining agent could be dramatically impacted by school choice, but the actual impact will depend on the nature and scope of choice that is actually implemented. To the extent that school choice in the United States involves a substantial amount of privatization and decentralization, the impact could be profound. Such a shift in the way education is delivered on a significant scale could entail forcing teachers' unions into the domain of private labor law, where they have had little influence in the past; and it could bring about significant changes resulting from a restructuring of the appropriate unit of bargaining, the scope of bargaining, and the security arrangements under which teachers' unions have been assured that a high proportion of teachers would become union members and pay union dues.

The Problem of School Choice for Teachers' Unions

Labor unions gain their strength as well as their identity by subordinating individual differences to group ends. Unions protect individual workers by including all individuals in the group and eliminating outside rivals for workers' jobs. Unions reduce the incentive for competition among workers by imposing uniform terms and conditions of employment on all workers doing the same tasks. To achieve such uniformity, unions attempt to reach agreements with employers that standardize work and the rewards for work. The willingness of workers to accommodate themselves to established standards depends on the attractiveness of those standards in terms of compensation and working conditions, and it may also depend on workers' sense of being a part of the union and of participating in the formulation of the governing standards.

The two major teachers' unions in the United States, the National Education Association (NEA) and the American Federation of Teachers (AFT), are organized at the national level, with state and local affiliates.[1] At the present time, the NEA and the AFT are separate organizations. Despite a significant negative vote at the 1998 NEA convention, the NEA and AFT continue to work on an elaborate merger process and may eventually become a single national organization.[2] Like other unions, these organizations are active participants in the political process at all levels, and because of their numbers, their political influence is often significant.[3] State and local affiliates obtain support from the national union but also have some independence from national positions.[4] Union political power at the local level has a unique compounding effect in that teachers' unions are active and influential participants in electing the school board members who sit across the bargaining table from them.[5]

Teachers' Unions in Opposition to School Choice

To the question, Are teachers' unions in favor of school choice? the simple answer is no. Reports about school choice aimed at a popular audience nearly always include an offhand comment indicating that it is common knowledge that teachers' unions are opposed to this or that educational reform measure.[6]

The opposition of teachers' unions to many educational reforms currently being advocated and tried may seem obvious and inevitable. Since teachers' unions at the present time occupy a powerful position in public education, they are not likely to want changes that would weaken or destroy that power. Moreover, it is an important purpose of unions to increase teachers' pay and benefits and to reduce workload. Educational reforms often push in the opposite direction. Innovations cost more (reducing the available educational resources from which teacher pay and benefits must come) or want teachers to work harder (more one-to-one teaching, more feedback on written student work, and so on) for less money.[7] Teachers' unions are faulted for being part of the unwieldy educational bureaucracy—rule bound, formalistic, hierarchical, stifling of flexible managerial direction and individual teacher initiative. Unions oppose broad discretion for principals to hire, fire, assign, and control; and they resist merit pay or other salary differentials that would reflect real differences in educational value based on the scarcity of teachers of particular subjects or on the difficulty of some fields of knowledge.[8]

These objections to the effect of unionization on the efficiency of an enterprise are not unique to education or even to public employment.[9] Nevertheless, teachers' unions are singled out because of the importance of education, its perceived failures and the resulting attention to educational reform, and the fact that all children are compelled to attend school and, practically speaking, most children are forced to attend public schools. Furthermore, in one respect the impact of teachers' unions on education is unique. A union's substantial influence on school board elections means that it is in an especially strong position to protect its own interests directly by presenting its position at the bargaining table and in the political arena and indirectly by controlling or at least modulating opposition to its positions by the employer–school board representatives at the bargaining table. Unlike its private sector counterparts (absent expanded school choice), union demands at the bargaining table are not constrained by the competition of the marketplace. The school board *employer* is constrained in resisting union demands because school board members may have to face the union's political power in the next election.[10]

Union resistance to school choice is also much in evidence in the opposition of teachers' unions, through litigation or otherwise, to particular choices; in their attempt to prevent the enactment of charter laws or, failing that, to weaken the law enacted; in their attempt to prevent voucher programs, particularly those that include religious schools; and in their strong resistance to contracting out to private entities (whether or not based on a charter statute).[11]

Teachers' Unions in Support of School Choice

Teachers' unions say they are for educational quality, and they readily concede the need for change.[12] They do not concede that a union's role as an advocate of teacher collective bargaining rights is inconsistent with educational reform. Their arguments against certain school choices are not inherently implausible: they have frequently argued that school choice will further weaken public schools, leaving them as schools of last resort for the most needy students—the poor, racial minorities, students with disabilities, those least politically able to defend their own interests. Union opposition to particular school choices can be defended by nonfrivolous arguments based on principle, such as violation of the separation of church and state or the undermining of racial integration. The union position has typically found respectable allies, such as the American Civil Liberties Union, the National Association for the Advancement of Colored People, disability rights advocates, and defenders of democratic education.[13]

Both the NEA and the AFT have sponsored or participated in charter schools.[14] The AFT has been willing to grant exceptions from some provisions of the collective bargaining agreement in the interest of educational experimentation.[15] Both the AFT and the NEA have cautiously and qualifiedly endorsed charter school legislation when, not surprisingly, the particular charter provisions are consistent with what the union finds compatible with its interests.

The Rhode Island charter statute has been cited by the AFT as a "good" charter law.[16] It permits charters to be granted only to public schools, requires charter schools to be within the collective bargaining unit, gives primary responsibility for granting a charter to the local school board, and requires that the collective bargaining agent's objections to a charter proposal be considered and answered by the deciding government bodies.[17] A charter may be granted to an existing school under the Rhode Island statute only if the affirmative vote of two-thirds of the certified teachers assigned to the prospective charter school (not two-thirds of the voters) approve; only if that same absolute two-thirds approve any departure from existing statutes, regulations, or the collective bargaining agreement; and only if the proposal receives the affirmative support from "a number of certified teachers employed within the school district at least equal to two-thirds (2/3) of the numbers of teachers that will be required to staff" a proposed school.[18]

Teachers' Unions in Tension with School Choice

In their strong case against union obstruction of educational reform, John Chubb and Terry Moe say,

> teachers are said to be protected from arbitrary evaluations by incompetent or biased administrators and politicians. Yet whatever the merits of these arguments, it must also be said that strict seniority systems can protect mediocrity among teachers and prevent principals from organizing schools according to their best professional judgment.[19]

This nexus between teachers' interests and educational reform runs in both directions, and the legitimate concern of teachers is evident when the words of Chubb and Moe are turned around:

> Administrators are said to be prevented from eliminating mediocrity and organizing schools according to their best professional judgment by the union-imposed system of strict seniority. Yet whatever the merits of these arguments, it must also be said that seniority protects teachers from arbitrary evaluations by incompetent or biased administrators and politicians.

The value of breaking the stranglehold of top-down bureaucracy is easy to recognize. Rewarding superior and imaginative teachers over those who are incompetent, indolent, or just burned out is very appealing. But managerial flexibility will not inevitably be used wisely or even fairly. Wide discretion to treat individual employees differently is not a sufficient condition for bringing about employer abuse, but it is almost always a necessary condition. For these purposes, what Paul Weiler has said about private sector collective bargaining is likely to apply to teacher–school board collective bargaining as well: "A more egalitarian distribution of wages, rewards for long service in the design of fringe benefits and the allocation of desirable jobs, protection against unfair treatment and dismissal. . . are emphasized much more in union than in comparable nonunion firms." Because of the threat of collective action through unionization, according to Weiler, long-service employees are protected from a significant fact of life about most employer-employee relationships: "The firm"—and also the school board— "can lose and replace any one employee much more easily than the employee can lose and replace his job with the firm."[20]

These observations do not demonstrate that school choice is a bad thing, nor that teachers' unions always oppose school choice or are always right when they do so. For the private sector, Weiler concedes that the effect of unionization on productivity and efficiency is controversial; the effect of teachers' unions on educational outcomes is similarly inconclusive.[21] The critical point is that unions, which partly define themselves as representatives of teachers in classic industrial collective bargaining terms, will be deeply suspicious of a movement whose strongest arguments sound in the competition between school employers and in the value of managerial discretion to hire, fire, and direct the work force.

Teachers and Teachers' Unions

The strength of union solidarity faces out toward school boards at the bargaining table and toward decisionmakers in the political arena; and it faces inward to individual teachers. Teachers as a group are advantaged by group solidarity, but group solidarity is a blunt strategy, which does not always leave room for individual differentiation. Whether the interests of teachers and unions diverge or converge (and to what degree) depends on which teacher, on which issue, and with which solution. Teachers' unions may help individual teachers to have greater freedom, autonomy, and dignity; and they may do just the opposite. To the extent that teachers see the union as the source of higher salaries and benefits and better working conditions, they will tend to see their interests as the union's interests, and vice versa; to the extent that teachers see the union as a source of bureaucratic top-down uniformity, they may see their interests as diverging from the union's.

Any generalization is going to be an overgeneralization: however true this or that conclusion may be for most teachers most of the time, it will not be true of all. Indeed, for many individual teachers, the identity with or alienation from union interests will be partial and mixed. As a group, teachers cannot be assumed to be eager to abandon the status quo or to be held back from innovation by their union. Paul Hill and Dean Millot, referring to an analysis of the implementation of principles advocated by Ted Sizer in the Coalition of Essential Schools, describe the responses of teachers who had worked with the coalition for three years: one-third enthusiastic, one-third indifferent, one-third hostile.[22] Under the progressive leadership of Adam Urbanski, president of the Rochester Teachers' Union (RTU) and vice president of the AFT, the RTU and the Rochester School District negotiated a collective bargaining agreement that included elaborate provisions for teacher evaluations, significantly involving peer review.[23] Chilled by the threat of negative reviews, the teachers refused to ratify the agreement by a vote of 849 against, 774 for (with nearly 1,000 teachers not voting).[24]

A New Breed of Teachers' Union?

Paralleling the commentary on private sector collective bargaining, a number of scholars of teacher–school board collective bargaining advocate a more cooperative and less adversarial approach, which places much more emphasis on teachers' responsibility for the quality of education; and there has been some movement toward cooperative, or collaborative, collective bargaining by teachers' unions.[25] A fundamental modification of union–school board collective bargaining relationships is treated as a part of some proposals for school choice.[26] Charles Kerchner argues that teacher–school board collective bargaining has gone through two stages (meet and confer, and adversarial collective bargaining) and now is moving into the third stage, which involves a cooperative relationship between teachers as professionals and school boards. Together, as guardians of the public interest, these two actors must jointly pursue what is good for the education of children.[27] Kerchner and colleagues explain this recommendation in terms of the change that has already taken place between the industrial society and the "knowledge" society.[28]

In *The United Mind Workers*, Kerchner and his colleagues propose a significant change in the way the teachers' union would represent teachers: the union would represent the same group of teachers as before, but in place of the one collective bargaining agreement covering all of the teachers in the district, there would be one umbrella contract and a series of satellite contracts. A "thin" districtwide contract would recognize the union as the exclusive bargaining representative and would set basic salary levels; separate compacts at the school level would spell out the details of the educational plan for that school through a process of negotiation that would place all matters of educational concern on the bargaining table.[29] Teachers would be hired at the school level through a union hiring hall, such as those in the construction and maritime industries; and the proposal would give the union a monopoly in supplying teachers. All teachers would have to be members of the union or pay a fee in lieu of the membership fee.[30]

Under the Kerchner proposal, each school would be a public school operated by a vaguely described community of interested parents, citizens, teachers, administrators, and union representatives. Paul T. Hill and his colleagues, in *Reinventing Public Education*, propose an educational model that moves decisionmaking to the school level in a somewhat different fashion. The Hill proposal stresses a contract arrangement under which a contractor, public or private, would be engaged to operate each school.[31] Public schools could contract out the management and supply of teaching services, just as they can contract out the delivery of transportation services or food in the cafeteria. Under the Kerchner proposal, the union might perform various services as the operator of a hiring hall to ensure the quality of the teachers supplied, but it would have no role in the ongoing supervision of the teaching services once teachers were selected and assigned to a school. Under the Hill proposal, however, the union's role would be potentially much more radically altered: the union might simply operate a hiring hall to supply teachers (as in the Kerchner proposal), but it might also be one of the possible contractors that would assume direct responsibility for the operation of the teaching work force.[32] Under this conception, the union would operate in competition with "other employers" and suppliers of teachers to operate a public school. Under the Hill model, in setting the terms of the school-level contract, the union *as an independent contractor* would sit across the table from the representatives of the school district; but then, when deciding how to allocate the contract price among teacher salaries and all other educational expenses, the union *as an employer* would be sitting across the table from the teachers.[33]

These proposals contemplate significant changes in the law. The Hill proposal acknowledges that the current law may have to be changed, at least in some states, to enable school boards to contract out teaching services.[34] In an unusual case in Wilkinsburg, Pennsylvania, a school district hired a for-profit contractor to supply teaching services for a school with extraordinarily poor student performance. All of the regular teachers were discharged; only a few of them were rehired by the private contractor. The NEA and its state and local affiliates initiated legal actions alleging that the school district had exceeded its statutory authority. The Pennsylvania Supreme Court remanded the case because the lower court had granted a temporary restraining order against the school district without providing an adequate hearing.[35] On the remand, and after the Wilkinsburg schools had been operated by the private contractor for three years, the union succeeded in convincing the trial court that the subcontracting had exceeded the school district's authority. That court was influenced by the fact that, during the litigation, Pennsylvania had adopted a charter act that prohibited for-profit schools from obtaining a charter.[36]

The case appears to have ended without fully resolving an important constitutional issue. The district argued that it had the statutory authority to subcontract but that, if it lacked such authority, the statute was uncon-stitutional, as applied, on the ground that it would prevent the district from meeting its state constitutional obligation to provide a "thorough and effi-cient" education for its children.[37] The Pennsylvania Supreme Court never had to decide whether the school district had this statutory authority. In explaining its decision to remand the case, the court said that the ultimate test of legality was the best interest of the child.[38] The court's opinion appeared to concede the possible validity of the district's argument based on the state constitution.[39] This is a conclusion with potentially far-reaching consequences for educational reform and teachers' unions. A parallel con-clusion could be reached under other state constitutions, a conclusion that would free school districts to privatize teaching services for poorly per-forming school districts without regard to statutory limitations.

The Kerchner proposal acknowledges that the replacement of the gener-ally prevailing industrial-style collective bargaining in school board–teachers' union relationships could not be accomplished easily and perhaps not at all without substantial revision of existing law.[40] *The United Mind Work-ers* recommends seven distinct changes in current labor law, concerning such things as the appropriate unit for collective bargaining, the treatment of company-assisted unions, the regulation of union hiring halls, and the scope of collective bargaining.[41] Changes as radical as those proposed by the Hill and Kerchner groups depend not only on revisions of existing law—over possible significant union resistance—but also on the union's drastically modifying its mode of operation and, even more, its conception of itself. They contemplate a very different sort of union than the one that now rep-resents teachers at the bargaining table with school boards. Just as the union impedes school choice, school choice may drastically impact on teachers' unions. The world changes, and a very different teachers' union is imagin-able, but possible change is not to be confused with existing reality.

The preface of *The United Mind Workers* states, "This is a book about teachers' unions, not as they are, but as they might be."[42] Reporting on sev-eral case studies in an earlier work, Kerchner and his co-author wrote, "The story we tell is unfinished. The changes in labor-management relationships we describe exist in no more than a few hundred of the nation's 16,000 school districts."[43] Robert Chanin, general counsel of the NEA, responded to Kerchner's vision of the future of teachers' unions with respectful skep-ticism. According to Chanin, there will be a continuing need for good old hard-headed, adversarial, collective bargaining. Chanin forthrightly con-cedes that there will be times when educational reform and collective bargaining are on a collision course and that the NEA may have to opt for collective bargaining when that happens.[44]

Teachers' unions, like other organizations and interests, will influence the choices that become available through litigation and lobbying. Through propaganda and promotion, teachers' unions (and others) will also influence the choices, as preferences, that consumers of education come to have; and they will even influence consumers' expectations and the perception of educational success.

Teachers' Unions' Response to School Choice

The precise response of teachers' unions to specific school choice proposals will depend on a number of variables other than the union's abstract position on school choice. Five such variables are briefly considered here.[45] First, the strength of the movement for school choice, in general or for some particular approach, will significantly shape the union response. The greater the strength of the movement, the more careful the union will have to be in advancing its opposition and the more likely the union will be to make strategic compromises rather than to present confrontational opposition. This variable will certainly influence the union's rhetoric, and it is likely to influence the union's strategy as well.

Second, the other side of the same coin is the union's own strength under the circumstances, and that especially means the solidarity of the union's position among its members. The greater the solidarity in relation to any particular proposal for change, the more likely it will be to take an unqualified stance. In this respect, the union's strength might vary from one affiliate to another, and that might determine whether a response to a particular school choice proposal is taken nationally or is varied from place to place.

Third, the particular proposal (or the particular dimension of the proposal being considered) will be an important variable. To take a very broad example, both of the national teachers' unions have opposed educational vouchers absolutely, but they have opposed only certain provisions in laws authorizing charter schools. A narrower example is illustrated by the unions' opposition to the contracting out of teaching services. The unions would be less resistant to a law providing such contracting if only nonprofit entities were permitted to make such contracts, but they will resist more strenuously if such contracts are open to for-profit entities, which are likely to be seen as a greater competitive threat to teaching jobs. Issue by issue, differences are particularly likely to occur from one affiliate to another. If the union leadership in a particular affiliate has decided that a particular form of change is desirable for the union, or at least not harmful, that choice might not be opposed at a state or local level even though it is out of harmony with the national union's position.[46]

Fourth, the local union's position may be influenced by the intense preferences of a substantial number of teachers in a particular school district or school. In this situation, the union might not itself be inclined to adopt a particular change, but it might be willing to facilitate the change for a group of teachers in one school or a small number of schools. This might result from a straightforward inclination to support teachers in their professional endeavors, recognizing the value to them of experimentation and independent action. Or it might simply be a tactical judgment that a divergent group should be accommodated to avoid divisiveness, without a major risk that this would be the first step down the wrong path, especially as long as the prevailing pattern of charter laws is to limit the total number of charter schools. Union acquiescence in charter law experimentation, including the granting of waivers from the union contract to charter schools, may illustrate this variable in action.

Fifth, the stage of the union's involvement with a particular issue will often influence its conduct. If a school choice to which the union objects requires legal authorization through statutory change, the union will oppose the change through lobbying or will support a change only in the weakest or least objectionable form.[47] Somewhat similarly, if a school choice to which the union objects is not within the scope of bargaining, the union may exert political pressure to bring it within the framework of collective bargaining to prevent the employer from making that change unilaterally. On the other hand, if an objectionable school choice is proposed by the school board at the bargaining table, or if the union can find a way to oppose it within the bargaining process, then union opposition will be manifested in bargaining strategy—by opposing any agreement on that item or, as a fallback, by supporting an agreement that weakens the proposed change or that exacts a substantial concession for agreement.

School Choice and Collective Bargaining

In its traditional role as collective bargaining representative, the teachers' union is threatened by any school choice that tends to erode its membership, its financial support, or its political leverage. If students are offered a choice of school A over school B and they vote with their feet by choosing school A, that will eventually mean that teachers will be in school A and not school B—or at least relatively speaking, more teachers will be teaching in school A and fewer in school B. That might mean that the very same teachers, literally, will move from school B to school A; or it might mean that teachers at school B will be out of jobs and different teachers will be hired at school A. Or more realistically, it will mean varying combinations of these shifting arrangements.

Although the schooling alternatives that become available to students and their parents will depend heavily on teacher preferences, in the remainder of this chapter I talk about all of these arrangements in terms of the teachers at school B following the students to school A. The union, in turn, will attempt to follow the teachers in order to continue to represent them or the teachers who have taken their place. I examine five dimensions of teacher–school board collective bargaining that tend to bring about a B-to-A following phenomenon and thereby threaten to weaken the union's strength: (1) the public employer, private employer distinction, (2) the appropriate unit of collective bargaining, (3) exclusive representation, (4) the scope of bargaining, and (5) union security arrangements.

Public and Private Employers

The great landmark change in labor relations law in the United States came in 1935 with the enactment of the National Labor Relations Act (NLRA), known as the Wagner Act.[48] Under that statute, employees were given the right to self-organization, to participate in collective bargaining, and to be protected from employer discrimination against employees who exercised their organizational and bargaining rights.[49] But this statute does not apply to an employee of a person not defined as an "employer" in the act, and this definition expressly excludes federal, state, and local government bodies.[50] Much later, beginning in the late 1960s, states began enacting statutes dealing with collective bargaining by public employees.[51] Thirty-four states have bargaining laws; seven states do not, but permit bargaining; and nine states prohibit teacher–school board collective bargaining entirely.[52] Of those states with authorizing laws, some enacted separate laws covering only teachers and others enacted laws governing public employees generally (including public school teachers). Despite many state-to-state differences, these public employee collective bargaining statutes were modeled on the NLRA, except that public employees were generally denied the right to strike and, instead, were given some form of impasse procedures (mediation, fact finding, arbitration).[53]

How would this legal framework be affected by the availability of school vouchers or charter schools? If a sufficient number of students exchange their school vouchers for a private education, the need for public school teachers will be reduced and the need for private school teachers will be increased. An exodus of teachers from public schools would also mean their exodus from the jurisdiction of public employment bargaining laws. The union could not simply continue to represent the private school teachers even if those teachers all came directly from a school in which they were previously represented by the union. The union's right to represent any group of teacher-employees is employer specific, and any existing collective bargaining agreement would cover employees in relationship to a particular employer, so the teacher-employees of the new employer would have to be "organized" into the union anew. A new organizational effort would mean costs in time and money for the union and, in many cases, the need to convince the teachers again that it is in their interest to have collective bargaining and to have the union (or a particular union, if there is any rival on the scene) represent them. Even without a rival union, the unique power and advantages of the teachers' union in public education would not necessarily apply in the private setting, and the teachers most likely to follow the students into private schools are not likely to have union sympathies. Thus the advantages of unionization might be hard to sell.

Even if the union were to end up representing the same number of teachers, it would be a less desirable situation for the union in at least three respects. First, it would lose the bargaining leverage that goes with political power over school board members since, for private schools, it would not be able to participate in the election of the school managers. Second, coverage by national labor law would involve not only the NLRA but also the Landrum-Griffin Act, which requires accounting for union finances, for which there is no equivalent at all in state laws regulating public employment bargaining.[54]

Third, the teachers who have moved to a private school will have moved from one labor law regime to another. Given the fact that the state statutes authorizing public employment collective bargaining are generally modeled after the private sector NLRA, there will be much commonality between the two regimes. But just as there are sometimes significant differences from one state public employment law to another, so inevitably will there be differences between the existing state law that covers teachers in public education and the national labor law that covers private employees. One important difference is likely to be in the administration of the two laws, the difference between a state public employment relations board and the complex regionally administered National Labor Relations Board (NLRB).[55] Under the best of circumstances, where there is both a public and a private labor law in effect, the union would be required, permanently, to deal with two administrative structures and two administrative agencies in every state. In states that have no public employment collective bargaining law, there might be some advantage to the union when employees move into private schools subject to the NLRB's jurisdiction. It is also possible, however, that the private school in which the voucher is used will be too small to come within the NLRB jurisdiction, either because of the NLRB's own administration or because the labor relations involved do not have a substantial effect on interstate commerce.[56]

A still different, and potentially greater, problem for the union would be presented by the inclusion of religious schools in the voucher scheme.[57] As these schools now account for a great disproportion of private schools (roughly 85 percent), their inclusion would greatly increase the number of nonpublic school options and, thus, the potential for a more substantial reduction in the number of teachers represented by the union in public schools.[58] Furthermore, were the union to try to follow these teachers who move from the public school for which the union is the bargaining representative to the new religious school, it would be faced with an impediment to using the machinery of the NLRA. In *NLRB v. Catholic Bishops of Chicago,* the Supreme Court held that the NLRA did not cover religious schools.[59] The Court construed the statute so as to avoid a violation of the Establishment Clause that might result if religious schools were treated as private employers under the NLRA. The *Catholic Bishops* case does not prohibit a union from representing lay teachers in a religious school, and several recent cases in other courts have held that there is no constitutional barrier to such representation.[60] But as long as the *Catholic Bishops* case is not changed by a judicial reinterpretation or statutory amendment, the union could not invoke the legal provisions of the NLRA to aid its attempt to organize and represent the religious school teachers. Neither a statutory amendment nor a judicial revision of *Catholic Bishops* seems at all likely.

At first blush, it appears that none of these effects would result from the implementation of a school charter plan. Charter schools are simply public schools operated under a different public governing structure, and therefore it would appear that the teachers would still be public employees and that the union could continue to represent them under public employment bargaining laws. But appearances may be deceiving, and a much more complex question would be presented if a charter is granted to a private entity (or even in the absence of a charter statute, if the school district enters into a contract with a private entity to operate one or more schools).[61] The terms of the charter (or contract) may provide that the private contracting party is engaged to manage the schools and to determine which teachers will be hired to teach in the schools. Under such an arrangement, the teachers may be hired by the school district and continue to be public employees of the school district, in which case the state's public employment bargaining statute, if any, would govern the labor relations of the teachers.

If, however, the teachers are hired by the private charterer or contractor and supplied to the school, the teachers would be employees of a private employer. Indeed, even if the teachers are professional independent contractors performing services for a school, they might be regarded as employees of a private manager who exercises extensive control over the teachers in securing their teaching contracts and in determining the terms of their teaching activity.[62] Under either of these assumptions, the teachers would be the employees of a private employer in much the same fashion as are employees of a contractor hired by the school system to make repairs on a school building or to provide food services in the cafeteria. If that is so, then the employees' organizational and collecting bargaining rights (if any) would arise under the NLRA, and if the teachers' union represented them for purposes of collective bargaining, it would have to do so through the private contractor employed under the legal regime governed by the NLRA. Under this view of the educational structure, the labor relations of the teachers would be subject to regulation like any other private employment relationship even though the schools would be public schools and subject to regulation as agencies of the state. (As "state actors," these public schools also would be subject to constitutional limitations, for an extended discussion of which, see Robert O'Neil's chapter in this book.)

The Appropriate Bargaining Unit

The determination of the appropriate unit for collective bargaining is a critical decision in the establishment and administration of a union-employer collective bargaining relationship under public employer bargaining statutes, as well as under the NLRA.[63] The "appropriate unit" is both a voting and a governing unit of employees. A union becomes the representative of a group of employees for purposes of collective bargaining when a majority of the employees who participate in the election (held under the auspices of the government agency responsible for administering labor relations) votes for the union. A critical question is, Which employees are eligible to vote? The answer is that all employees in the appropriate unit may vote. The appropriate unit is usually based on a variety of factors, including what the union requests and has organized, the efficiency of the employer or governing unit, employee preferences, and the community of interests among employees.

In collective bargaining by public school teachers, the unit is almost always all of the teachers in a school district.[64] In principle, there could be a multiple-employer collective bargaining unit cutting across school districts (though that would raise questions about the legal power of a school board to agree to share power to make public policy for the district with an "outside" entity not elected by the voters of the district).[65] On the other hand, there could be a bargaining unit consisting of one or more—but less than all—of the schools in the district. Whether part-time teachers, teaching assistants, or other professional school employees (such as psychologists and nurses) should be included in the same unit as teachers may also be a unit determination question. Of course, every change in the unit is a change in who is eligible to vote and, potentially, a change in the union's strength and in the interests that an elected union must represent. Furthermore, except when the union happens to have support in one or more schools but not in others, there is an advantage in larger units as a result of efficiencies of scale.

After the appropriate unit is determined, a vote within that unit is taken, and if a majority of voting teachers select a union to represent them, the unit becomes a governing unit. That is, after the vote, the appropriate unit now describes the group of teachers who are represented by the union in bargaining, and it describes the group of teachers who are covered by the collective bargaining agreement, if and when an agreement is reached. For both purposes—bargaining and contract administration—a teacher who is in the appropriate unit is represented by the union whether or not that teacher is a member of the union.

In terms of the appropriate bargaining unit dimension, the impact of school choice on the teachers' union as the collective bargaining agent is straightforward. If teachers follow student voucher bearers to a new school or if teachers follow students transferring to a charter school, the union will feel no direct impact as long as the transferee school is part of the previously existing bargaining unit. This might be true of an existing school already in the bargaining unit or of a new school that is determined to be an accretion to the existing unit. If, on the other hand, teachers follow students out of the bargaining unit, the union immediately ceases to be the representative of those teachers. This could occur when vouchers are exchanged for education at a private school or at a public school that is not in the existing bargaining unit (and that could be part of another established bargaining unit, in which teachers are represented by the same union or by a different union or by no union). A private school receiving vouchers might be too small to come within the protection of the NLRB jurisdiction, but several voucher private schools in one area might be treated by the NLRB as a multiemployer unit.[66]

A direct adverse effect on the union would also be felt under a charter plan if the students, followed by their teachers, transfer to a school outside the existing unit or that is determined to be outside the existing unit as part of the terms of the charter or governing law. It would also be possible for the law that authorizes charter schools (or schools by contract) to permit the teachers in the charter or contract school to determine or influence whether that school would be part of the existing bargaining unit. For example, under the Minnesota charter statute, the appropriate unit would be either the charter school itself or the school district, depending on the agreement among teachers, school directors, the bargaining agent, and the sponsoring district board.[67]

Because teachers who opt to teach in charter schools are likely to be in the subset of teachers who are pursuing innovation and autonomy and, accordingly, likely to be teachers who feel little need for union protection or desire for union involvement, they would be unlikely to choose a bargaining unit that favored union representation. But a charter law that requires charter school teachers to be certified or requires a charter to be approved by a substantial percentage of teachers in the school district will dilute the preferences of those teachers seeking reform and will make inclusion of the charter school in an already unionized bargaining unit more likely.[68]

The appropriate unit dimension might also come into play in connection with teacher involvement in innovative managerial arrangements in a charter school. Although a charter law such as New Hampshire's might restrict teachers who serve on the governing board from participating in various matters, most charter statutes would permit teachers to perform managerial functions.[69] School principals are ordinarily regarded as supervisors and, as such, excluded from a bargaining unit of teachers.[70] If a charter school had a "head teacher" instead of a principal, the union might not want such a principal substitute to be a part of the bargaining unit. On the other hand, if a *group* of teachers were managing a charter school in a cooperative, nonhierarchical arrangement, the union might be precluded from representing these teachers because of the Supreme Court's decision in *NLRB* v. *Yeshiva University*. The *Yeshiva* case held that university-level teachers were not employees under the NLRA because, through the Yeshiva University's governing structure, they participated in management decisions and were thus managerial employees.[71] If the theory of the *Yeshiva* case is deemed to apply to such a charter school arrangement, the teacher-managers would be treated as nonemployees and thus would not be eligible to be in a bargaining unit represented by a union.

Exclusive Representation

The pervasive view in American labor law is that, once selected, the union is the exclusive representative of all of the employees in the appropriate unit.[72] That does not mean that the employees must join the union nor even that they cannot belong to some other union. It means that for all matters that are subject to bargaining and for the implementation of any bargain struck, the exclusive representative alone is entitled to deal with the employer. For every teacher represented by a teachers' union, it means that the teacher, acting alone or through any other organization, may not strike a separate deal. Without the union's authorization to the contrary, the collective agreement represents the maximum benefit for all teachers as well as the minimum that all may claim. As the Supreme Court said long ago,

> The practice and philosophy of collective bargaining looks with suspicion on such individual advantages. . . . Increased compensation, if individually deserved, is often earned at the cost of breaking down some other standard thought to be for the welfare of the group, and always creates the suspicion of being paid at the long-range expense of the group as a whole.[73]

Patently, this philosophy will not look kindly on merit pay any more than it will look kindly on teachers who are willing to receive less pay for more freedom. It is important to recognize that educational reforms push in both directions. For many reformers, including many teachers, school choice means recognizing differences among teachers such that some teachers should be paid more because they are more meritorious or because they have more valuable knowledge or simply because they happen to teach in an area for which teachers are scarce. At the other extreme, school choice often means giving teachers greater autonomy but paying them less simply because the schools that are willing to try something different often operate on more limited budgets.[74] Teachers in such schools may be willing to give up higher pay for greater autonomy. The schools created to provide greater school choice often pursue policies in which top-down control is loosened and teachers are given much greater flexibility and discretion. Escaping the restrictions of the master labor-management contract may be an important motivation for creating or joining an independent school through a charter provision or otherwise.

As a general proposition, all of these tendencies will be discomforting to teachers' unions. When some teachers are willing to teach for less, and perhaps to put in longer hours as well, that undermines the union's attempt to demand more for all. But if some teachers are permitted to demand and receive more than the group, that too leaves less for the whole and sets a precedent of playing one group against another. Any general move for greater flexibility complicates the union's attempt to set higher standards for all.

It does not quite follow that the teachers' union will adamantly resist all such efforts to pay more to some teachers than to others; much less does it follow that the teachers' union will abstractly oppose any form of rewarding meritorious teaching or achieving greater flexibility. The union does not want to be seen as a force in opposition to teachers' flexibility and autonomy. Indeed, unions have waived compliance for some contract provisions for some charter schools. What does follow is that the union will resist the multiplication of distinctions among teachers and the recognition of any distinctions except when the case for doing so is very strong. Even more, the union will want to control the making of distinctions. It will want to do that by bargaining about the criteria and the process for making distinctions, and it will want to be involved in the administration of any machinery set up for making them. It may well be that the mixed reception of peer review within the union results from the fact that it involves both the negative dimension of making distinctions between teachers and the positive dimension of making distinctions through union-controlled methods.[75]

The union's power of exclusive representation affects the enforcment of collective bargaining agreements as well as the substance of the agreements. It does so by preventing teachers from dealing individually with the employer in a way that circumvents and subverts the union's representative status. When the subject of discussion touches upon matters covered by the collective agreement, such as grievances about working conditions, individual teachers must deal with the employer through the union or in a manner specified in the collective agreement. The control of employee grievances is central to the function of the exclusive union representative. Once again, how the grievance process is arranged and managed is a matter of negotiation. The employer generally, and advocates of school choice in particular, may want managerial employees to have great flexibility in handling grievances, and they may bargain for such flexibility and control. But the union is not likely to yield to such desires and (if it has the bargaining leverage) almost surely will not yield without exacting a substantial price in return. All of which is to repeat the refrain that a teachers' union in a strong position will often have good reasons to impede the road to school choice.

One might wonder whether this feature of exclusive representation is qualified for collective bargaining in education because of the applicability of the First Amendment to the relationship between public school teachers and their school boards, which are state entities.[76] It might seem that the state's action, through statute and collective agreements, of granting teachers' unions the exclusive right to speak for teachers in dealing with school boards concerning teachers' conditions of employment would be a violation of teachers' freedom of speech. But constitutional rights are never absolute, and public school teachers' free speech rights have been found to qualify the general principles of exclusive representation very little. The principle of exclusive representation cannot be used as a justification for denying speech opportunities to teachers that are available to members of the public generally.[77] The opportunity to communicate with the school board concerning collective bargaining matters or to use school facilities to communicate with teachers, however, may be reserved for the exclusive bargaining representative and denied to individual teachers desiring to speak for themselves or for other teachers.[78]

Furthermore, meager as these First Amendment limitations on exclusive representation in the public sector are, they will sometimes apply to private, as well as public, sector collective bargaining. These limitations would apply directly to the private sector if, under the totality of the applicable regulatory scheme, the receipt of state funds in exchange for educational vouchers or the receipt of a school charter provides a sufficient basis for treating private schools as state actors.[79] Comparable limitations might also apply to private schools that were covered by the NLRA, as a matter of statutory interpretation adopted to avoid a First Amendment issue, on the theory that the union's exclusive representation power was created by state action in the form of federal legislation and thus the state would have caused any First Amendment abridgement of employee speech.[80]

The Scope of Bargaining

Once a union has been selected as a bargaining representative, the union and the employer have a mutual duty to bargain in good faith. But bargain about what? Well, whatever the statute says they must bargain about. That is the scope of bargaining; or at least that is the starting point in understanding the scope of bargaining.

The conventional wisdom in labor law is that every subject about which one or both of the bargaining partners might want to bargain can be categorized as a mandatory, a permissive, or a prohibited subject.[81] The parties *must* bargain about mandatory subjects. The NLRA defines these as "wages, hours, and other terms and conditions of employment."[82] Public bargaining statutes may define mandatory subjects in this way, or the wording may be a little different, or the public bargaining statute might consist of a laundry list of mandatory subjects, or the statute might combine openended language like that in the NLRA with a laundry list.[83] To say that the parties must bargain in good faith about whatever comes within this mandatory category means, first of all, that the parties must make a bona fide effort to reach agreement about these subjects. In addition, this duty takes away the freedom that the employer would otherwise have to set the terms and conditions of employment in the manner that the employer believes would be best for the good of the enterprise, whatever it is. In the union–school board context, the school board must bargain in good faith about these mandatory subjects and refrain from making unilateral changes in them (until the parties have bargained to impasse).

The school board may unilaterally decide about most nonmandatory subjects, however. The line separating mandatory and nonmandatory subjects in teacher–school board collective bargaining is also the line between conditions of employment and educational policy. The line is a blurry one because of the substantial overlap between these two big categories. Many nonmandatory subjects are called permissive because the parties are free to bargain about those things if they choose to. Neither party may condition its bargaining about any mandatory subject on the other party's concession to bargain about any permissive subject.[84] The dynamics of the bargaining process, however, undercuts the ability to make a sharp distinction between a voluntary agreement and a coerced agreement to bargain about a permissive subject. Suppose that selection of textbooks is a permissive subject and that the teachers have a strong desire to influence the selection process. The teachers' union representative might say to the school board, "Well, you know how important textbook selection is to the teachers. We know that it is a permissive subject, and of course we would not attempt to put pressure on you to bargain about the selection process. Nevertheless, it is obvious that continued use of the current books puts all sorts of extra burdens on the teaching staff that entails an inefficient use of their time. So naturally if we assume that the old books are going to be used, more preparation time will have to be built into the schedule (and I believe we all agree that preparation time is a mandatory subject)." No doubt an argument could be made that the union, in this imaginary illustration, is conditioning its mandatory subject bargaining and thus is bargaining in bad faith. Yet the argument is far from a sure winner, and making the argument through a potentially prolonged litigation process would rarely be in the school board's interest.

There is another dimension to permissive bargaining that gives the union even more leverage in forcing permissive subjects about which the union wants to bargain onto the bargaining table. Although the employer is not obligated to bargain about permissive subjects, it will ordinarily be obligated to bargain about the *effect* of decisions concerning permissive subjects on the terms and conditions of employment.[85] Thus in the textbook selection example, once the school board unilaterally makes a decision about textbooks, the union has a right to bargain about the effect of that decision on teacher preparation time. Indeed, the Supreme Court has stated that the duty to bargain about effects must be performed "in a meaningful manner and at a meaningful time."[86] That often means, or could be plausibly claimed to mean, that bargaining about effects must occur before the decision is implemented; and that is only a short step from saying that it must be bargained about before the decision is finalized (before the decision is made). Given the union's ample capacity to reach by indirection what it cannot reach directly, the actual scope of bargaining may be considerably enlarged. It is only necessary to add the complicating twist that the union's interest in expanding the actual bargaining to reach permissive subjects does not depend on its passionate desire (or that of the teachers represented) concerning any particular permissive subject. On the contrary, it is in the union's interest to have many subjects on the table so that it has many subjects for which it can make concessions in order to get those things that it most wants.

Prohibited subjects, the third part of the tripartite division of potential subjects of bargaining, are those subjects about which the parties may not bargain even if they want to. This third category is relatively small; it is dependent upon the interpretation of statutory language; and in the context of collective bargaining by teachers' unions, it is significantly influenced by judgments about which items of education policy involve public interests that cannot be traded away by the board of education.

The scope-of-bargaining dimension may affect school choice issues in two ways. First, when choice brings about a restructuring of the educational enterprise, the scope of bargaining may also change. If, for example, the union ends up bargaining with a private employer, the subjects about which the parties must bargain will be defined by a different statute—the NLRA instead of a particular state public bargaining statute—and possibly contain different language. The difference might be great or small; it might favor or disfavor the union. But all other things being equal, it would produce a change and in that sense a disruption of the status quo. If the structural change simply involves the removal of one or more schools from the preexisting bargaining unit, the definition of the mandatory subjects would not change, but the process of bargaining might change what is available to be traded at the bargaining table.

A second kind of interplay between school choice issues and the scope-of-bargaining dimension concerns the *creation* of choice rather than the *effect* of it. One illustration of this interrelationship could occur under charter statutes that condition the granting of a charter on the approval of a vote by teachers. A contract proposal from the school board concerning the procedure for taking such a vote (or for the union's endorsement of a positive vote) might well be a permissive subject of bargaining about which the union could refuse to bargain (or agree to bargain only in exchange for some concession).[87]

A more fundamental example of the way the scope of bargaining might determine the creation of school choice is provided by the various proposals for operating schools through subcontracting.[88] If the school board is not permitted to contract out the management or the supply of teaching services to a private entity, the union will lobby hard against the creation of such authority.[89] If such subcontracting is permitted (now or in the future), there would be a distinct question whether the school board may or must bargain about its decision to do so. Even if the decision to subcontract is regarded as a permissive (or even prohibited) subject of bargaining, the effect of that decision would be a mandatory subject of bargaining.[90] One way or the other, the union is likely to bargain hard against such an innovation. As discussed earlier, bargaining about effects gives the union considerable latitude in bringing a nonmandatory subject into the bargaining process; that latitude will be fully used. In labor relations generally, the contracting out of bargaining unit work is everywhere and always regarded as a fundamental threat to the union.

Union Security Arrangements

The problem of the free rider arises in all American labor law contexts because of the pervasive adoption of the principle of fair representation. As we have seen, a union is the exclusive bargaining representative for all of the employees in the appropriate bargaining unit, whether or not they are union members. All employees are precluded from representing themselves or being represented by a rival union in connection with their terms and conditions of employment. To protect the interests of all bargaining unit employees in view of this disability, the bargaining representative has a "duty of fair representation" to represent all employees fairly, without regard to their union status.[91] If that were the end of the story, it would mean that union members who pay union dues would be subsidizing the benefits of collective bargaining for nonmembers, who do not pay union dues. That would make the nonmembers free riders, a result that would not only seem unfair but that would create a substantial incentive not to be a union member and consequently would tend to undermine the stability of the collective relationship.[92]

Under American labor law, the closed shop, under which only union members are eligible to be hired by certain employers, is generally prohibited.[93] The NLRA formally permits a union shop, under which an employee must become a union member after being hired by the employer and if required by the collective bargaining agreement.[94] Yet in practice the operation of a legal union shop is so restricted that what can be enforced amounts only to an agency shop, an arrangement that requires nonmembers, as a condition of employment, to pay the equivalent of union dues. As the Supreme Court explained it, in the statutory authorization to condition employment on union membership, "membership" has been "whittled down to its financial core."[95] In the public sector, the agency shop (where it is permitted by state law) is constitutionally qualified in order to protect an employee's right of freedom of speech and association, which includes a freedom not to speak or associate.[96] The Court has reasoned that requiring a public employee to pay the equivalent of the entire full union dues would coerce an employee to support political views that the employee does not hold and thus would violate the employee's First Amendment rights. The Court concluded, nevertheless, that it is permissible to require employees to pay for the representational services that the union provides for all members of the bargaining unit under its duty of fair representation.

The Court's conclusion, in short, requires that a distinction be made between the cost of union activity that goes into negotiating the collective bargaining agreement and administering grievances, on the one hand, and union activity that involves lobbying and participation in the political process, on the other. This distinction has been criticized as wrong in principle and unworkable in practice—and indeed as productive of the union's manipulation of its accounts.[97] But the Court has stuck to the distinction and has attempted to clarify and elaborate it in subsequent cases.[98]

Given this division between expenditure of union funds on collective bargaining work (the bargaining process and contract administration, including the processing of employee grievances) and expenditure of union funds on political action (legislative lobbying and participation in political campaigns), the union collects higher agency fees to the extent it is able to treat the collective bargaining and grievance administration activity as a relatively larger proportion of its work. Moreover, the smaller the difference between the part of the union's activity for which an agency fee can be charged and the remainder of the union's activity that must be paid out of union dues not chargable to nonmembers, the greater the incentive to teachers to become members. Some benefits are available to members alone. For example, participation in union affairs in setting the union agenda is available only to members. Even assuming that the union scrupulously avoids any discrimination against nonmembers, there may be choices at the bargaining table or in grievance administration that will tend to favor one group of employees over another. And no doubt some teachers will wonder whether the union always follows a policy of nondiscrimination between union members and teachers who are not in the union. These considerations will tend to draw more teachers into full union membership. When that happens, the union not only receives the additional revenues amounting to the difference between the agency fee and full union dues but also strengthens its position at the bargaining table and in the political arena.

When the union–school board collective agreement includes a checkoff provision, membership dues or agency shop fees are deducted from a teacher's paycheck and paid directly to the union.[99] Under a checkoff provision, the employer, in effect, does the bookkeeping, banking, and collecting for the union. Plainly, such an arrangement is extremely valuable to the union. It ensures a regular flow of the fees that support the union's operation, and it saves the union the time-consuming and expensive task of collecting these revenues. Furthermore, it saves the union the cost of being the unwelcome collection agency and avoids calling to the attention of employees the cost of being a union member or of paying for its representation.[100]

The impact of school choice on these vital sources of union economic strength is obvious and straightforward. Any substantial break in the status quo may erode the arrangement under which the fees automatically flow from teachers to union. This might happen to some extent merely as a result of the fact that choice is in the air. When routines are broken in one way, that can become a motivator for breaking them in other ways. More concretely, the automatic flow of union dues and agency fees into the union's budget would be directly disrupted to the extent that teachers, following vouchers or moving to charter schools (or separate contract schools), move out from under the existing (and to some extent habitually renewed) collective bargaining agreements. This direct effect on union revenues will be great or small depending upon the nature and extent of the school choice that is created and implemented. In some situations, it will be possible for the union to follow teachers to the choice schools, to obtain their votes in a new union representation election, and to obtain their membership fees and related agency fees and the approval of a dues checkoff arrangement with the new public or private employer. But that prospect will be very uncertain and very unappealing to the union and an unattractive alternative working against the school choices that would produce those unwanted effects.

Conclusion

School choice programs that are on the drawing boards and that are working their way into practice could profoundly threaten the collective bargaining role of the traditional teachers' union in terms of membership, wealth, and power. It is much too early to know whether charter schools will be just another passing fad in education, whether the Milwaukee case approving the use of vouchers in religious schools will signal a new life for school vouchers, or whether any combination of the far-reaching reinventions of public education will become the core of a new "one best system." It is clear, however, that school choices are conceptually multiplying while the overwhelming number of children continue to go to the same old schools. It is highly unlikely that teachers' unions will reinvent themselves in any fundamental way unless innovative ideas truly become a mass movement. Teachers are an important part of the choice movement. Whether school choices have a deep attraction to teachers will influence both the magnitude of the movement and the union's response.

Notes

1. Myron Lieberman, *The Teacher Unions* (Chicago: Free Press, 1997), pp. 1–2, 10–16.

2. The two unions, after years of jurisdictional disputes and raiding attempts, have been trying to merge. Steven Greenhouse, "Teachers' Groups Plan to Merge, Creating Nation's Largest Union," *New York Times*, January 27, 1998. The merger effort suffered a setback when a merger proposal received only 42 percent of the votes of the delegates to the NEA national convention. Steven Greenhouse, "Teachers Reject Merger of Unions by Large Margin," *New York Times*, July 6, 1998. Insufficient organizational democracy and affiliation with the AFL-CIO were the reasons cited for disapproval. The NEA delegates have instructed their leaders to continue to work for a merger on different terms. Steven Greenhouse, "Teachers Urge Union Leadership to Try Again on Merger Plan," *New York Times*, July 7, 1998.

3. The merged union would have more than 3 million members—approximately 2.3 million from the NEA and 950,000 from the AFT—making it the largest union in the United States. Both the NEA and the AFT endorsed President Clinton when he ran for reelection in 1996. See Jacob Weisberg, "Where's the Party?" *New York*, September 9, 1996, p. 40 (characterizing the AFT and the NEA as "the party's single most powerful interest group"); editorial, *America*, September 21, 1996, p. 3; David Gergen, "Before Crusaders Charge Off," *U.S. News & World Report*, February 17, 1997, p. 6.

4. See Lieberman, *The Teacher Unions*, pp. 51–65. In connection with the now defunct AFT-NEA principles of unity for the merger, state and local affiliates were permitted to decide whether to establish an affiliation with the AFL-CIO federation of labor unions. See Principles of Unity for a United Organization (www.aft.org), April 29, 1998.

5. John E. Chubb and Terry M. Moe, *Politics, Markets, and America's Schools* (Brookings, 1990), p. 48; Lieberman, *The Teacher Unions*, pp. 76, 228–29.

6. Adam Cohen, "Victory for Vouchers," *Time*, June 22, 1998, p. 38; Michael Winerip, "Schools for Sale," *New York Times Magazine*, June 14, 1998; Thomas Toch, "The New Education Bazaar," *U.S. News & World Report*, April 27, 1998, p. 34. The AFT has tended to project a greater receptivity to reform; see for example Thomas Toch, *In the Name of Excellence* (Oxford University Press, 1991), pp. 134–204. It is doubtful, however, if there are significant differences in the position of the two unions on most school choice issues; see Lieberman, *The Teacher Unions*, pp. 27–28, 191–206.

7. Education Commission of the States, *Charter Schools: Initial Findings* (Denver: March 1996).

8. Chubb and Moe, *Politics, Markets, and America's Schools*, pp. 25–26, 48–51; Lieberman, *The Teacher Unions*, p. 186; Paul T. Hill and Marc Dean Millot, *Potential Sources of Union Opposition to NASDC Design* (Arlington, Va.: New American Schools Development Corporation, 1993), p. 15.

9. See Paul C. Weiler, *Governing the Workplace: The Future of Labor and Employment Law* (Harvard University Press, 1990), pp. 11–12, 187–88, 221.

10. See Chubb and Moe, *Politics, Markets, and America's Schools*; Lieberman, *The Teacher Unions*. In Duluth, Minnesota, as part of a dispute involving the exclusion from the union bargaining unit of a charter school operated by the Edison Project (a private, for-profit company), the local AFT affiliate was unsuccessful in two litigation challenges but succeeded in electing four union-supported candidates to the school board. *Duluth News-Tribune*, December 30, 1997 (www.duluthnews.com/dnt/news/edi 1230.htm), June 11, 1998. In Wilkinsburg,

Pennsylvania, an attempt to privatize the provision of teaching services was defeated in court and ultimately resulted in the election of an antisubcontracting school board majority (Ronald N. Watzman, legal representative of Wilkinsburg and Pennsylvania Education Associations, telephone interview with author, July 16, 1998).

11. *Council of Organizations and Others for Education about Parochiaid, Inc.* v. *Engler*, 455 Mich. 557, 566 N.W.2d 208 (1997) (union challenge to validity of charter law); *School District of Wilkinsburg, Pennsylvania* v. *Wilkinsburg Education Association*, 542 Pa. 335, 667 A.2d 5 (1995)(union challenge to validity of subcontracting); *Jackson* v. *Benson*, 578 N.W.2d 602 (1998)(union challenge to vouchers for religious schools in Milwaukee); *Simmons-Harris* v. *Goff*, 86 Ohio St. 3d 1, 711 N.E.2d 203 (1999)(same, in Cleveland); Gary K. Hart and Sue Burr, "The Story of California's Charter School Legislation," *Phi Delta Kappan* (September 1996), pp. 37–39 (describing union efforts to weaken charter legislation); Lieberman, *The Teacher Unions*, pp. 117–18 (describing union opposition to subcontracting in Baltimore and Hartford); Hill and Millot, *Potential Sources of Union Opposition*, pp. 8–9 (same). See also David Kirp and Robert Bulman's chapter in this book (describing union opposition to OEO's experimental voucher plan).

12. Albert Shanker, president, AFT, "State of the [AFT] Union Address," August 2, 1996, Cincinnati, Ohio (www.aft.org), June 17, 1998; Steven Greenhouse, "Teachers' Leader Seeks New Path," *New York Times*, July 4, 1998 (referring to NEA president Bob Chase).

13. *Jackson* v. *Benson*, 578 N.W.2d 602 (1998) (ACLU and NAACP among coplaintiffs with the Milwaukee Teachers' Education Association); Jay P. Heubert, "Schools without Rules? Charter Schools, Federal Disability Law, and the Paradoxes of Deregulation," *Harvard Civil Liberties–Civil Rights Law Review*, vol. 32 (1997), pp. 301, 308–10. Laura Rothstein's chapter in this book contains a fuller discussion of the disability issue. See also Amy Gutmann, *Democratic Education* (Princeton University Press, 1987), pp. 65–70, 79–84.

14. Shanker, "State of the Union Address"; NEA Center for the Advancement of Public Education, *The NEA Charter School Initiative* (Washington, D.C.: 1996), and (www.nea.org), June 1, 1998.

15. AFT resolution on charter schools adopted at AFT convention, July 1994.

16. AFT press release, "Charter School Laws: Do They Measure Up?" (www.aft.org), June 1, 1998.

17. Rhode Island Statutes, sections 16-77-3(a)(b)(e), 16-77-4 (b)(12), 16-77-5(c).

18. Ibid., sections 16-77-3(c), 16-77-4.1, 16-77-4.2 ("teachers must state their desire to transfer to the charter public school . . . and to teach under the terms of the charter").

19. Chubb and Moe, *Politics, Markets, and America's Schools*, pp. 154–55.

20. Weiler, *Governing the Workplace*, pp. 181, 183.

21. Compare Chubb and Moe, *Politics, Markets, and America's Schools*, pp. 150–55, with F. Howard Nelson, Michael Rosen, Brian Powell, *Are Teachers' Unions Hurting American Education?* (Milwaukee: Institute for Wisconsin's Future, 1996).

22. Hill and Millot, *Potential Sources of Union Opposition*, p. 9.

23. Adam Urbanski, "Real Change Is Real Hard: Lessons Learned in Rochester," *Stanford Law and Policy Review*, vol. 4 (1993), p. 123. See also Julia E. Koppich, "Rochester: The Rocky Road to Reform," in Charles T. Kerchner and Julia E. Koppich, eds., *A Union of Professionals: Labor Relations and Educational Reform* (Teachers College Press, 1993).

24. Urbanski, "Real Change Is Real Hard," p. 130.

25. A recurrent focus of attention has been the importance of softening the barrier stemming from the National Labor Relations Act's prohibition of company-dominated and, particularly, company-assisted unions. The ideal of the Tennessee Saturn plant is frequently invoked. See Weiler, *Governing the Workplace*, pp. 29–37, 203–24; Charles Kerchner, Julia Koppich, and Joseph Weeres, *United Mind Workers: Unions and Teaching in the Knowledge*

Society (San Francisco: Jossey-Bass, 1997), pp. 39, 184–85; Hill and Millot, *Potential Sources of Union Opposition;* Lieberman, *The Teacher Unions,* p. 247; Kerchner and Koppich, *Union of Professionals;* NEA, *Negotiating Change: Education Reform and Collective Bargaining,* Studies in Collective Bargaining (Washington, D.C.: 1992); NEA, *Collaborative Bargaining: A Critical Appraisal,* Studies in Collective Bargaining (Washington, D.C.: 1991).

26. Paul Hill, Lawrence C. Pierce, and James W. Guthrie, *Reinventing Public Education: How Contracting Can Transform America's Schools* (University of Chicago Press, 1997); Kerchner, Koppich, and Weeres, *United Mind Workers;* David S. Doty, "Forging New Partnerships: Teacher Unions and Educational Reform in the '90's," *B.Y.U. Education and Law Journal,* vol. 1994 (1994), p. 117.

27. Charles Taylor Kerchner, "Inventing Professional Unionism," in NEA, *Advancing the National Education Goals: The Role of Collective Bargaining,* Studies in Collective Bargaining (1993). The Kerchner analysis, like Weiler's for the private sector, is partly based on the suggestion that this third stage must be seen in the light of the professionalism of the first, or craft, stage, in contrast to the second, or industrial, stage. See Kerchner, Koppich, and Weeres, *United Mind Workers,* pp. 41–42; Weiler, *Governing the Workplace,* pp. 194–96.

28. Kerchner, Koppich, and Weeres, *United Mind Workers,* pp. 18–23, 33–35.

29. Ibid., pp. 128–37, 186–87.

30. The proposal does not indicate whether the fee payment would be required to comply with the existing constitutional law limiting the agency fee that could be charged. See text accompanying notes 95–98.

31. Hill, Pierce, and Guthrie, *Reinventing Public Education.*

32. Ibid., pp. 135, 158, 242.

33. Ibid., p. 158.

34. Ibid., p. 186. See also Hill and Millot, *Potential Sources of Union Opposition,* p. 20. Some charter laws appear to permit teachers' unions to obtain charters. See, for example, Illinois Statutes, chapter 105, section 5/27A-7(b) ("organization"); Kansas Statutes, section 72-1906(b)("entity"); New Jersey Statutes, section 18A:36A-4(a)("private entity").

35. *School District of Wilkensburg, Pennsylvania* v. *Wilkinsburg Education Association,* 542 Pa. 335, 340–41, 667 A.2d 5, 7–8 (1995). See also Kimberly Colonna, "The Privatization of Public Schools: A Statutory and Constitutional Analysis," *Dickinson Law Review,* vol. 100 (1996), p. 1027.

36. *Wilkinsburg Education Association* v. *School District,* GD95-05174 (Common Pleas, Allegheny County, August 6, 1997). In a separate action, the school district was found to have violated the collective bargaining agreement. See Watzman interview, note 10.

37. 542 Pa., p. 342; 667 A.2d, p. 8.

38. 542 Pa., p. 343; 667 A.2d, p. 9.

39. The two-justice dissenting opinion assumed that the majority had held that denial of school district power to subcontract teaching services would be unconstitutional under some facts. 542 Pa. p. 347; 667 A.2d, p. 11.

40. Kerchner, Koppich, and Weeres, *United Mind Workers,* pp. 178–92.

41. Ibid., p. 182.

42. Ibid., p. xi.

43. Kerchner and Koppich, *Union of Professionals,* p. 1.

44. Robert Chanin, "The Relationship between Collective Bargaining and Education Reform," in NEA, *Advancing the National Education,* pp. 14, 18.

45. No doubt other variables could be added—for example, whether the state law authorizes or permits collective bargaining. See Hill and Millot, *Potential Sources of Union Opposition,* p. 17.

46. In Kerchner and Koppich, *Union of Professionals,* the authors report various innov-

ative actions supported by local teachers' unions in particular school districts. Paul T. Hill, *How to Create Incentives for Design-Based Schools*, vol. 6 of *Getting Better by Design* (Arlington, Va.: New American Schools, 1994), pp. 6, 11, shows why union leaders at different levels might be affected differently by particular school choices.

47. Hart and Burr, "The Story of California's Charter School Legislation," pp. 37–39.

48. 49 Stat. 449 (1935), as amended; 29 U.S.C., sections 151–69 (1988).

49. Section 7; 29 U.S.C., section 157.

50. Section 2(2) and (3); 29 U.S.C., section 152(2) and (3).

51. Robert E. Doherty and Walter E. Oberer, *Teachers, School Boards, and Collective Bargaining: A Changing of the Guard* (Cornell University Press, 1967), p. vii; Robert C. O'Reilly, *Understanding Collective Bargaining in Education* (Metuchen, N.J.: Scarecrow Press, 1978); Morris A. Horowitz, *Collective Bargaining in the Public Sector* (New York: Lexington, 1994), p. 26.

52. See Lieberman, *The Teacher Unions*, p. 48, table 4-1.

53. Ibid., p. 47; Donald H. Wollett, Joseph R. Grodin, and June M. Weisberger, *Collective Bargaining in Public Employment*, 4th ed. (St. Paul: West, 1993), pp. 9–10; Anthony M. Cresswell, Michael J. Murphy, and Charles T. Kerchner, *Teachers, Unions, and Collective Bargaining in Public Education* (Berkeley, Calif.: McCutchan), 1980, pp. 151–83.

54. Lieberman, *The Teacher Unions*, p. 145; the Landrum-Griffin Act is the Labor-Management Reporting and Disclosure Act of 1959 (LMRDA), 29 U.S.C., sections 401–531 (1988).

55. Robert A. Gorman, *Labor Law, Unionization, and Collective Bargaining* (St. Paul: West, 1976), pp. 7–10.

56. Ibid., pp. 22–26 (NLRB will not take cases having only a minimal impact on commerce). The NLRA's applicability requires a finding of a question of representation or an unfair labor practice "affecting commerce," sections 9(c)(1), 10(a). Until quite recently, it would have been unthinkable that the scope of this language was subject to any constitutional limit on Congress's power to legislate in the labor relations area. See *NLRB* v. *Jones and Laughlin Steel Corp.*, 301 U.S. 1 (1937); *NLRB* v. *Friedman-Harry Marks Clothing Co.*, 301 U.S. 58 (1937). But the Supreme Court's decision in *United States* v. *Lopez*, 514 U.S. 549 (1995), opens up the possibility that the Court might find such a limit or at least read the statute to avoid the constitutional question. See *United States* v. *Five Gambling Devices*, 346 U.S. 441 (1953).

57. See Jesse Choper's chapter in this book for a discussion of the relevant legal issues.

58. Further discussion of the numbers may be found in Jeffrey Henig and Stephen Sugarman's chapter in this book.

59. *NLRB* v. *Catholic Bishops of Chicago*, 440 U.S. 490 (1979).

60. *South Jersey Catholic School Teachers Organization* v. *St. Teresa of the Infant Jesus Church Elementary School*, 150 N.J. 575, 696 A.2d 709 (1997); *New York State Employment Relations Board* v. *Christ the King Regional High School*, 90 N.Y. 2d 244, 682 N.E.2d 960 (1997); *Catholic High School Ass'n* v. *Culvert*, 753 F.2d 1161 (2d Cir. 1985). See also Douglas Laycock, "Toward a General Theory of the Religion Clauses: The Case of Church Labor Relations and the Right to Church Autonomy," *Columbia Law Review*, vol. 81 (1981), pp. 1373, 1388–1402 (arguing that religious freedom includes a principle of church autonomy to control its own operations).

61. See text accompanying notes 31–39.

62. Concerning the line between employees and independent contractors, see Gorman, *Labor Law, Unionization, and Collective Bargaining*, pp. 28–31; Marc Linder, *Farewell to the Self-Employed: Deconstructing a Socioeconomic and Legal Solipsism* (Greenwood, 1992), chap. 4; Marc Linder, "Toward Universal Worker Coverage under the National Labor Relations Act: Making Room for Uncontrolled Employees, Dependent Contractors, and Employee-

like Persons," *University of Detroit Law Review*, vol. 66 (1989), p. 555. Generally, national labor policy preempts any inconsistent state labor law (Gorman, *Labor Law, Unionization, and Collective Bargaining*, chap. 32), but it is possible that the courts would interpret the NLRA's express exclusion of government employees as revealing a congressional intent to honor a state charter law provision that purports to make charter school teachers public school teachers. See also Wollett, Grodin, and Weisberger, *Collective Bargaining in Public Employment*, p. 70.

63. Cresswell, Murphy, and Kerchner, *Teachers, Unions, and Collective Bargaining*, pp. 161–65, 296–301; Wollett, Grodin, and Weisberger, *Collective Bargaining in Public Employment*, pp. 30–38; Kerchner, Koppich, and Weeres, *United Mind Workers*, p. 184; Gorman, *Labor Law, Unionization, and Collective Bargaining*, chap. 5.

64. Cresswell, Murphy, and Kerchner, *Teachers, Unions, and Collective Bargaining*, p. 163; Lieberman, *The Teacher Unions*, pp. 13–14.

65. Lieberman, *The Teacher Unions*, p. 250.

66. See note 65 and accompanying text.

67. Minnesota Statutes, section 120.064, subdivision 20. See also Florida charter law, section 228.056(12) (employees in unit determined by "structure of the charter school"). Compare Globe Machinery and Stamping Co., 3 N.L.R.B. 294 (1937) ("Globe" elections held under the NLRA permit craft union employees to vote, in the same election, to determine whether they want to be represented at all and also whether they want to be elected in a craft or an industrial unit).

68. See text accompanying notes 16–18.

69. See New Hampshire Statutes, section 194-B.14 (teacher trustee may not participate in collective bargaining matters).

70. Cresswell, Murphy, and Kerchner, *Teachers, Unions, and Collective Bargaining*, pp. 162–63; Wollett, Grodin, and Weisberger, *Collective Bargaining in Public Employment*, pp. 44–58.

71. *NLRB v. Yeshiva University*, 444 U.S. 672 (1980).

72. Lieberman, *The Teacher Unions*, p. 20; Gorman, *Labor Law, Unionization, and Collective Bargaining*, chap. 19.

73. *J. I. Case Co. v. NLRB*, 321 U.S. 332 (1944).

74. For more on these points, see notes 7 and 8 and accompanying text.

75. Greenhouse, "Teachers' Leader Seeks New Path," p. A7; Kerchner, Koppich, and Weeres, *United Mind Workers*, pp. 87–99, 121–22; Shanker, "State of the Union Address"; text accompanying notes 23 and 24.

76. *Pickering v. Board of Education*, 391 U.S. 563 (1968).

77. *City of Madison, Joint School District No. 8 v. WERC*, 429 U.S. 167 (1976).

78. *Minnesota State Board v. Knight*, 465 U.S. 271 (1984); *Perry Education Association v. Perry Local Educators' Association*, 460 U.S. 37 (1983).

79. For a further discussion of this issue, see Robert O'Neil's chapter in this book.

80. *Air Line Pilots Association. v. Miller*, U.S., 118 S.Ct. 1761 (1998) (holding that federal labor legislation must be interpreted in pari materia with First Amendment principles applicable to public employment agency shop limitations in order to preclude that legislation from violating the First Amendment). See also text accompanying notes 96–98.

81. Cresswell, Murphy, and Kerchner, *Teachers, Unions, and Collective Bargaining*, pp. 166–67; Gorman, *Labor Law, Unionization, and Collective Bargaining*, chap. 21.

82. Section 8(d); 29 U.S.C., section 158(d).

83. Wollett, Grodin, and Weisberger, *Collective Bargaining in Public Employment*, pp. 148–53.

84. *NLRB v. Wooster Division of Borg-Warner Corp.*, 356 U.S. 342 (1958).

85. June Weisberger, "The Appropriate Scope of Bargaining in the Public Sector: The Con-

tinuing Controversy and the Wisconsin Experience," *Wisconsin Law Review*, vol. 1977 (1977), p. 685.

86. *NLRB* v. *First National Maintenance Corp.*, 452 U.S. 666, 682 (1981).

87. *NLRB* v. *Wooster Division of Borg-Warner Corp.* (holding that a private employer's proposal concerning conditions under which a union would be allowed to strike was only a permissive subject over which the employer had no right to bargain because it affected the relationship between the union and the employees that the union represented).

88. See text accompanying notes 31–33.

89. See text accompanying notes 34–39.

90. See text accompanying notes 85 and 86. Believing that it is essential that a school board be able to subcontract the operation of schools free of any union resistance, Myron Lieberman, *Public Education: An Autopsy* (Harvard University Press, 1993), p. 276, argues that such contracting out should be a prohibited subject of bargaining.

91. Gorman, *Labor Law, Unionization, and Collective Bargaining*, chap. 30; Wollett, Grodin, and Weisberger, *Collective Bargaining in Public Employment*, p. 381.

92. Lieberman, *The Teacher Unions*, pp. 185–87, challenges the claim of unfairness.

93. Gorman, *Labor Law, Unionization, and Collective Bargaining*, chap. 28.

94. NLRA, section 8(a)(3); 29 U.S.C., section 158(a)(3).

95. *NLRB* v. *General Motors Corp.*, 373 U.S. 734, 742 (1963).

96. *Abood* v. *Detroit Board of Education*, 431 U.S. 209 (1977).

97. Steven Shiffrin, "Government Speech," *U.C.L.A. Law Review*, vol. 27 (1980), pp. 88–95; Lieberman, *The Teacher Unions*, pp. 5, 180–85.

98. *Air Line Pilots Assn.* v. *Miller*; *Lehnert* v. *Ferris Faculty Association*, 500 U.S. 507 (1991); *Chicago Teachers Union Local No. 1, AFT, AFL-CIO* v. *Hudson*, 475 U.S. 292 (1986).

99. Cresswell, Murphy, and Kerchner, *Teachers, Unions, and Collective Bargaining*, p. 173; Gorman, *Labor Law, Unionization, and Collective Bargaining*, pp. 670–73.

100. Lieberman, *The Teacher Unions*, pp. 162–64, describes this as the most valuable of several government subsidies of the union.

CHAPTER ELEVEN

School Choice and Students with Disabilities

LAURA F. ROTHSTEIN

For the five and a half million children with disabilities in special education and the children with disabilities not requiring special education but requiring reasonable accommodations, public education is not perfect, but it is substantially better than it was before 1975, when Congress enacted the Education for All Handicapped Children Act (EAHCA).[1] The EAHCA—since 1991 the Individuals with Disabilities Education Act (IDEA)—along with the nondiscrimination requirements of section 504 of the Rehabilitation Act and Titles II and III of the Americans with Disabilities Act (ADA) ensure that all students with disabilities are provided equal access to education.[2] Even with this comprehensive protection and substantial improvement in educational opportunities, problems still exist for students with disabilities.

Advocates for students with disabilities have become well organized and are a strong political force in pressing to resolve the problems that remain in ensuring equal and appropriate treatment of students with disabilities as well as in complying with special education mandates. These advocates, in addition to lobbying for additional appropriations for special education and against proposals by various parties to amend the laws to decrease the

Appreciation is expressed to Sterling Elza, Gus Pick, Joseph Acosta, and Jeremy Stone, all students at the University of Houston Law Center, and to Harriet Richman, faculty services librarian, for their research assistance.

protections available to students with disabilities, now face a new challenge. This new concern is the impact of school choice programs on students with disabilities.

Although school choice in the public sector has existed for some time, new types of choice program are being developed, and proponents are pressing for an increase in school choice opportunities. State and local educational agencies are responding by approving an increasing array of publicly funded school choices. The school choice trend raises substantial concern among advocates for students with disabilities. The concerns are twofold. First, will students with disabilities have the same access to school choice programs as students without disabilities? Second, if students with disabilities are not proportionately represented in school choice programs, and are thus disproportionately left behind in regular public schools, will this impermissibly violate the mandate for mainstreaming special education students?

The school choice trend also raises questions about whether the goals of school choice programs are irreconcilable with the goals of special education and equal access. It may be that certain school choice programs would violate the legal mandates of the IDEA, section 504, and the ADA. If that is the case, these laws may be a substantial barrier to the implementation of at least some school choice options. School choice, however, may offer an opportunity for choice advocates and advocates for students with disabilities to collaborate in pointing out insufficiencies in public school programs and in working together to find solutions.

Parents of students with disabilities often have the same motivations as other parents who might want their children to attend a school other than the neighborhood public school. First, like other parents they may simply have a preference unrelated to the student's disability. Second, they may seek an alternative because of the student's disability. If the child's disability requires special education or related services, and if the neighborhood school does not provide these services, parents may seek an alternative, most often in a private placement. Third, the parent of a student who is receiving special education and related services at a school other than the neighborhood school, but provided by the public agency, may want the program to be provided in the neighborhood school. The local educational agency, because of economies of scale, may find it administratively and financially preferable to provide that program at another site. At present, the courts seem to allow such clustering of students with disabilities for the sake of efficiency.[3]

The implications of school choice programs for students with disabilities depend to a large extent on the type and severity of the disability involved. Different disabilities require different levels of resources, knowledge, expertise, and awareness. Parents' decisions to seek choice will be affected by these factors. Similarly, the school's willingness or receptivity to permitting the choice may also depend on the type and severity of the disability, because educational programs for children with disabilities requires highly specialized training and perhaps expensive supportive personnel or equipment.[4] Their needs may also affect transportation costs.

School Choice and Legal Requirements for Children with Disabilities

It is too early to assess comprehensively the impact of school choice on students with disabilities: the legal requirements are too new, the number of charter and voucher schools are too few, and the length of time that such schools have existed is too short. There are, nonetheless, some indications of what is currently occurring and what is likely to occur in the future unless there are additional policy changes.

The Individuals with Disabilities Education Act

Before the early 1970s, the right to education for students with substantial disabilities had not been demanded on a large scale. The general practice was separation, either by denying education entirely or by placing children in special schools or separate special classes within regular schools.[5] As a result of litigation in the 1970s challenging such discrimination, the Individuals with Disabilities Education Act was enacted.[6] While it has been amended several times, most recently in 1997, the basic principles of the IDEA have not changed since its 1975 enactment (under its original title, the Education for All Handicapped Children Act.)[7] At the time of enactment, it was estimated that of the eight million children with "handicaps," approximately three million were being inappropriately educated and one million were entirely excluded from education. Those who were not separated or excluded were generally students with less substantial impairments, such as a those who needed speech therapy or those with mobility impairments not affecting learning ability.

The IDEA is a funding statute by which states are eligible for federal grants from the U.S. Department of Education if they submit a program plan containing a number of essential elements. Although every state has elected to apply for funding under IDEA, it is important to recognize that federal support does not compensate state and local educational agencies for the full costs of educating these students. State and local budgets must compensate for the difference. Funding is based on an average per pupil expenditure for all identified students.[8] The essential elements of IDEA are that the state must provide a *free, appropriate public education* (sometimes referred to as FAPE) to all age-eligible (referred to as the zero-reject principle) students in the least restrictive appropriate placement (sometimes referred to as mainstreaming) and that the education must be individualized to the child's needs.[9] Mainstreaming, or being educated with students without disabilities, is one of the primary principles of the IDEA. It was recognized in the IDEA that, to the maximum extent appropriate, children with disabilities are to be educated with children who are not disabled.[10] The value of peer interaction in developing social skills as well as academic skills is recognized by virtually all educators. The state plan must identify, locate, and evaluate all eligible children and have a system of personnel development.[11]

One of the most important elements of the state's plan, which must be submitted to receive federal funding under the IDEA, is procedural safeguards at the identification, evaluation, and placement stages.[12] These procedural safeguards include access to student records; notice and an opportunity for a hearing about identification, evaluation, and placement; and a right of review to a state administrative agency.[13]

> Children with disabilities protected under the IDEA are those with mental retardation, hearing impairments (including deafness), speech or language impairments, visual impairments (including blindness), serious emotional disturbance . . . orthopedic impairments, autism, traumatic brain injury, other health impairments, or specific learning disabilities . . . who by reason thereof, need special education and related services.[14]

The 1997 amendments add that children three through nine years of age may, at the state or local agency's discretion, include children experiencing certain developmental delays who require special education as a result of those delays.[15] It is estimated that approximately 5.5 million students meet this definition. Within that group, the numbers break out by disability group as follows:[16]

—Learning disability: 2,579,000
—Speech and language impairments: 1,022,000
—Mental retardation: 570,000
—Serious emotional disturbance: 438,000
—Multiple disabilities: 93,000

—Hearing impairments: 68,000
—Orthopedic impairments: 63,000
—Other health impairments: 133,000
—Visual impairments: 25,000
—Deafness and blindness: 1,000

Since 1975 an enormous body of judicial interpretation of these requirements has grown, including several Supreme Court decisions and a hand-
ful of amendments to the statute.[17] The 1997 amendments to the IDEA are
important because they include references to school choice issues.[18] When
parents place their child in a school chartered by the state or local educational agency, the public agency remains obligated to provide special education services and funding to students with disabilities in the same manner
that the local agency provides support to its other public school programs.[19]
Before the 1997 amendments, it was unclear what obligation the local educational agency had to children in charter schools. The obligation of the
public educational agency to fund all or part of the educational costs of a
student in a private placement, such as in a voucher system, depends on
whether the placement is made for reasons unrelated to the disability or to
ensure appropriate special education programs. The amendments limit the
obligation of the public agency to reimburse private school expenditures
when the placement is unilateral and based on personal preference rather
than on denial of appropriate special education.[20]

Because of financial considerations, public educational agencies will generally try to serve students with disabilities in their own public school programs. For students with certain special education needs, the public
educational agency may find that only placement in a private school is appropriate. This may be because the needs of the child are such that a program
is not available within the school system and the cost of developing a new
program is too high when compared to contracting to place a child in an
existing private setting. Such placements are probably most likely to occur
with students with severe psychological problems, drug or alcohol problems, autism, or sensory impairments (visual and hearing). When the placement is essential to meet special education needs, the public agency is
responsible for the cost.

Placements for students with special education needs are generally made
by contracting with the private school, rather than through voucher programs. In making such a placement, the public educational agency must
ensure that the educational program is provided at no cost to the parents.[21]
The placement must meet the least restrictive appropriate placement require-

ment of the IDEA and must be in a school that is either approved by the state educational agency or found to be appropriate within the educational guidelines of the state.[22] The private school with which the public school contracts for services must ensure that the standards of the IDEA are met. Parents generally do not oppose private school placements made by the public agency because these programs will generally be highly specialized. Occasionally, however, parents will seek to have students with highly specialized needs mainstreamed.[23]

Parents of students with disabilities may choose to place their children in private schools for reasons other than special education. They may think that the school offers better college preparation or that it is safer, or the school may offer religious training as part of the educational process. Placement in private schools may also happen because parents believe that the private program will provide appropriate special education without requiring that the child be given a stigmatizing label. The reason for the placement may affect the public educational agency's obligation to provide special educational services. When the public agency program offered is appropriate but parents enroll their children in private schools for reasons of personal preference, the parents are still entitled to some public special educational services. The 1997 IDEA amendments, however, limit this funding to the amount that is "equal to a proportionate amount of Federal funds made available" through the IDEA.[24] Although services provided to private schools are to be comparable in terms of quality of personnel, public agencies are not required to provide the same amount of service as they would for the student in a public setting.[25] The 1997 amendments also clarify that public services and funding can be provided at the private school, even if it is a parochial school.

The way these requirements work can be illustrated by considering a child placed by parents in a private college preparatory high school. The child may have a learning disability and need some intensive programing related to reading. If the public high school has an appropriate program available to the student, it will still have to provide this special education and related service to the student enrolled at the private high school, but the amount it must expend for this program will be limited to a proportionate amount that it would have spent had the student been educated at the public school. The problem with this formula is that the funding may be inadequate to cover the costs of a special education student in the private school with low numbers of students with this disability, due to the cost efficiencies of the public school. The private school may seek reimbursement from the parents for these additional costs. Under current legal requirements, the private school may be entitled to compensation from the parents, and the public agency would not be obligated for the additional expenses.

An alternative to the public agency providing or paying for a program at the private school is to provide certain programs at the public school and to have the student travel to the public school.[26] These various alternatives can present logistical and financial problems. If the program is provided at the private school, the public agency might either reimburse the private school for staffing costs or, if the numbers of students at the private school merit it, directly employ a staff member at the private school, the employee being appointed by the public agency. If the student is to travel from the private school to the public school, the obligation to provide transportation can become an issue. The 1997 IDEA amendments contemplate the public agency being responsible for costs, although costs can be included in determining whether the financial obligation to the private program has been met.[27] For example, if the proportionate federal IDEA expenditure is $3,000 for each special education child, and the child's special education needs at the private school are $2,500, the public agency would be required to spend up to $500 more to fund transportation of the child between private and public schools. The public agency would not be required to pay for the cost of transporting the private student to and from the student's home when the parents have chosen to place the student in a private school and when the public agency has made an appropriate public school program available. Because of the logistical, financial, and practical problems of transportation, it is more likely in most cases that the services will be provided on site whenever possible. When that is the case, private school personnel may be paid by the public agency, or the public agency may use its own personnel.[28] However, there is no requirement that the private school provide IDEA services. In this case, the parent has no alternative but to seek them from the public school.

When a publicly employed staff member is involved, it may well be an itinerant teacher who serves more than one school. The disadvantage of an itinerant teacher is the same as that of itinerant teachers for any purpose (such as music or art): weather problems and other logistical problems may interfere with attendance. This, of course, is a problem for all schools, both public and private, when there are only a few students at each school, making an itinerant teacher the only feasible alternative. It may be exacerbated, however, in the case of private school placements of special education students, when there may be enough students with a particular need at the public school to merit a full-time teacher but not at the private school.

Having the student travel from the private school to the public school or to some neutral site presents different problems. The obvious one is the time taken from educational programs to spend in transit. In addition, the bus ride can be exhausting and can affect the student even after the bus ride is over. For students who already spend time on the bus just getting to and from school at the beginning and end of the day, additional travel time has the potential of interfering with academic performance. This can be particularly problematic if the child has physical impairments that make travel difficult. The child with emotional difficulties affecting the ability to sit still for long periods of time or other behaviors that could be affected by bus rides will also be adversely affected by such an arrangement. With the recent judicial and statutory changes allowing publicly provided education to be given at a parochial school, it is probable that there will be a decrease in the number of private school students being transported to public schools. The fact that the public school apparently may now provide a program at a parochial school, however, does not mean that it must do so, if an appropriate program can be provided by bringing the student to the public school.

In addition to the obligations related to providing educational programs, the public agency remains responsible for what is referred to as the child-find requirement. Public educational agencies receiving federal financial assistance are required to have in place, and to implement in fact, programs to identify, locate, and evaluate all children with disabilities who reside in the state. This obligation includes those in private schools.[29]

Section 504 and the Americans with Disabilities Act

In addition to the requirements to serve students with disabilities under the IDEA, two nondiscrimination statutes have obligations for both public and private schools. Section 504 of the Rehabilitation Act of 1973 provides that recipients of federal financial assistance may not discriminate on the basis of disability.[30] All state educational agencies receive such assistance, as do many local school agencies. Such assistance is available to both public and private schools, and even some parochial schools (not receiving IDEA funds) receive federal financial assistance through school lunch programs.

Individuals protected under section 504 are those who have impairments that substantially limit one or more major life activities, have a record of such an impairment, or are regarded as being substantially limited.[31] Students must also be otherwise qualified, which would mean that they are age eligible and also that they do not pose a direct threat to the health or safety of others because of an infectious disease.[32] Section 504, unlike the IDEA, is a nondiscrimination statute and does not provide for the same level of educational benefits intended under IDEA, although some substantive and procedural safeguards similar to IDEA are envisioned in the section 504 model regulations applying to preschool, elementary, and secondary education.[33] Nonetheless, section 504 mandates that reasonable accommodations be provided. This does not require the lowering of educational standards or the fundamental alteration of school programs. For example, section 504 might not require that a child be given intensive speech therapy, while the IDEA would. Section 504 might require that attendance policies be waived for students with chronic health problems relating to a disability. Examples would include a child with asthma who might require an accommodation to the school's policy prohibiting self-medication or allowing a student using a wheelchair or one with severe arthritis who does not require special education to have an elevator key.

The Americans with Disabilities Act of 1990 (ADA) operates similarly to section 504 of the Rehabilitation Act.[34] The definition of who is covered is virtually identical, and requirements regarding other qualifications and reasonable accommodation are intended to be interpreted similarly to section 504.[35] The primary distinction between the ADA and the Rehabilitation Act for purposes of students with disabilities in schools is the application of the different titles to different types of school.

Title II of the ADA applies to state and local governmental agencies.[36] Virtually all public school programs (including charter schools funded by the state or local agencies) are subject to Title II of the ADA. Title III of the ADA applies to private schools whether they receive federal financial assistance or not.[37] Private schools operated by religious institutions are subject to different requirements. Title III includes what is known as the religious organization exemption, which provides that the Title III requirements do not extend to religious organizations or entities controlled by religious organizations.[38] The key issue for resolution becomes whether the religious organization controls the activities of the school. A parochial school that is found to be sufficiently controlled by the religious organization so as to be exempt from Title III of the ADA is still covered by section 504 if it receives federal financial assistance. Many parochial schools receive federally subsidized school lunches, and they would be covered by section 504 as a result.[39] Private schools not affected by the religious exemption, such as Montessori schools and private college preparatory schools, would be subject to Title III.

Private schools subject to Title III are also required to meet certain architectural access requirements. For facilities existing before the effective date, structural barriers (including architectural and communications barriers) must be removed to the extent that it is *readily achievable* to do so, a term meaning "easily accomplishable without much difficulty or expense."[40] If removing barriers is not readily achievable, the program must provide alternative methods of providing the service to the public.

Students with Disabilities in Schools of Choice

The consequences for students of legal mandates regarding students with disabilities, the impact of these legal mandates on school choice programs, and the realities of how these mandates are likely to work can be demonstrated by considering the various disabilities, the probable parental desire for choice, and the probable response by the school of choice for these various disabilities.[41]

Sensory Impairments

Students with significant sensory impairments, such as hearing or visual loss, may require expensive special education or related services.[42] For some, the program they need may be speech therapy or an interpreter. Others may need specialized teaching methods, depending on the severity of the impairment, the age of the student, and previous education. The child with a mild sensory impairment requiring speech therapy might be placed in a school other than the neighborhood school because the clustering of several students with these needs in one school permits the hiring of a single teacher. The parents of this child might want to have the option of having the child attend the neighborhood public school and thus would seek a transfer or open-enrollment option if such a program were available.

Parents of a child with significant sensory impairments might seek a different experience for their child. These parents may be dissatisfied with the educational programs offered by the public school, regardless of the location, and may want to place their child in a private school that provides what the parents believe to be better programs. For students in this group, the concern from the public school's perspective is cost. The charter school or the private voucher school may also lack the expertise or experience to deal with such special education students. These are the concerns for most of the disabled requiring special education.

Learning Disabilities, Related Impairments, and Mental Retardation

Some schools, both public and private, do an excellent job of providing appropriate programs for students with learning disabilities and other impairments affecting learning, such as attention deficit disorder (ADD), attention deficit hyperactivity disorder (ADHD), and mental retardation. Appropriate programming requires specific training and expertise. Some private schools specialize in programs for students with these disabilities. Some charter schools even may target this population, although there are questions about whether such targeting is permissible under special education mainstreaming principles. Many schools, however, lack either the expertise or the financial resources to provide appropriate programs for students in this population. Parents of these students who have found programs suited to their needs are unlikely to choose to apply to another program. Those who do want to choose, however, may face resistance from the school of choice. This resistance may be because of financial limitations or lack of expertise.[43]

Schools in a choice system that have academic requirements for admission are also less likely to admit many students with learning disabilities, even though inflexible entrance standards based substantially on standardized test scores may be challenged on the basis of disparate impact on students with learning disabilities.[44] Similarly, students with mental retardation are unlikely to meet academic eligibility standards.

Psychological and Behavior Problems

Parents of children with behavior problems, regardless of the cause, are usually looking for school personnel who understand these problems and are able to provide appropriate programs. Parents are unlikely to want to seek alternatives if they have already found appropriate programs.

On the other hand, those parents who do want to take advantage of school choice options available to students in general may find resistance from the transferee school. Some school choice programs may have admissions criteria that screen out students with behavior problems. Such screening out might be impermissible discrimination in some cases, although this issue has not been addressed yet by the courts.

Mobility Impairments

The student with a mobility impairment, such as a wheelchair user or one with severe arthritis or lupus, is most likely to be concerned about physical barriers and possibly accommodations relating to limited mobility. The student may need ramps and modified desks and accessible restrooms, elevators, classrooms, and lockers. The student may need an amanuensis to provide assistance in writing or perhaps computer technology. There may be a need to make exceptions to tardiness policies (when the student must change classrooms, as is often the case in middle and high school) and perhaps even attendance (when chronic health problems are related to the mobility impairment). It may also be necessary to modify physical education or even to waive it.

Many of these requirements would not be viewed as special education or even related services. Therefore, the student would not be covered under special education mandates. Students with only mobility impairments, and no special education needs, still would require the protection of the nondiscrimination and reasonable accommodation requirements in section 504 and the ADA.

The school program's response to including students in this population will probably vary. When the needs are primarily architectural access, the school's attitude toward accepting the student may depend on whether the building is currently accessible. Although legal mandates require most schools, both public and private, to ensure some degree of physical access, that does not mean that the school that may need to spend money on removing barriers will be enthusiastic about doing so.[45] Parochial schools not receiving federal financial assistance and falling within the religious organizations exemption of Title III of the ADA are not required to remove barriers under any federal law.

While the IDEA does not seem to require the school to provide educational programming in the neighborhood school to meet the least restrictive environment mandates, a choice program within a school system will probably be required to do so. If students with disabilities do not have the same options as their nondisabled peers, they do not have the same range of choice. This disparate treatment could violate both section 504 and the ADA.[46] The obstacles to school choice in these situations are thus different from those in which special education is involved. The parents may wish to have the choice of having their child attend a school in the neighborhood. Or they may wish to place the child in a public school facility not in the neighborhood because it is accessible.

Inaccessible school facilities within a choice system can present problems. Although the school may resist the placement of the student requiring barrier removal because of the cost, in most cases the necessary barrier removal or other accommodations (such as relocating classes) will have to be made. Otherwise, the choice program impermissibly discriminates against the student with a disability. The issue is more likely to be practical than legal, the question being whether the parents want to press for their legal rights or simply accept a placement at the accessible school, even if they would prefer another placement that better meets their needs and to which they are entitled. Although parents may legally be in a position to press for the inaccessible school to remove architectural barriers as required under section 504 or the ADA, undertaking litigation to achieve this goal can be formidable. Many parents may not know they have these rights. Finding and paying for an attorney to represent the student may be problematic.[47]

Health Impairments

Health impairments range from conditions that may not interfere on a daily basis with education to those that are more chronic in nature and that require modifications in attendance policies or auxiliary services, such as catheterization, suctioning, or therapy to loosen fluids in the lungs. These conditions include HIV, asthma, cancer, cystic fibrosis, diabetes, spina bifida, severe allergies, tuberculosis, hepatitis, and epilepsy. Like students with mobility impairments, not all students with health impairments require special education or related services (and are not covered by IDEA), but they do require reasonable accommodations (and would potentially be covered by section 504 or the ADA).

Access to school choice for children in this category may depend on a number of factors. While all of them are probably legally entitled to protection against nondiscrimination, the requirements to provide accommodations are much lower in terms of what would be expected of a school than if the child is identified as entitled to related services under the IDEA. For that reason, it can become important to determine whether the student is covered under the IDEA or only section 504 or the ADA. Attitudes are one factor affecting choice for this population. In the early 1980s the initial reaction to having a child with HIV in a school was fear. Although this attitude has changed, there is still a stigma attached to HIV and similar conditions. Schools, particularly preschools, may be reluctant to enroll students with these conditions because of concerns about danger to the health of others. It requires awareness and understanding on the part of school personnel to respond appropriately to legitimate concerns about transmission of communicable diseases and not to react to unfounded myths, fears, and stereotypes.

Students with conditions such as asthma or diabetes require accommodations to school policies relating to self-medication. Some require the school nurse to administer medication. For those whose needs are not substantial, there may be little problem with school choice options; but for those requiring more in terms of service or understanding, the parents may elect to stay with a program in which the needs are already being met, rather than face resistance from a private school or an unknown school, where the attitudes and willingness to accommodate may be less favorable. For students requiring expensive services, such as low-ratio attendant care to monitor suctioning needs for a student with cystic fibrosis, the school's concern will be cost. Not only do many public charter and private schools have budgetary limitations, but also their administrators and teachers may not be aware of the availability of appropriate services for students with these needs from outside sources, including from public schools.

A substantial body of case law addresses the public school's obligation to pay for related service and reasonable accommodations. A 1999 Supreme Court decision established that the school is obligated for these services even when they require specially trained personnel.[48] If public schools are not required to provide such services, it is unlikely that private schools will be required to provide them. In these cases the parents' insurance or some social service provider pays. Even when cost is not an issue, however, private schools may still be reluctant to have children with life-threatening conditions in the classroom because of concerns about liability.

Substance Abuse Impairments

Students with substance abuse impairments, such as alcoholism and drug addiction, present special considerations.[49] Although these students may need and benefit from special programs, like counseling, they may not be eligible for IDEA services. They may not even be entitled to accommodations such as waiver of attendance policies to receive counseling or rehabilitation under section 504 or the ADA. Even though these students may be considered to be disabled within nondiscrimination statutes, schools will not usually be required to excuse them from most behavior and conduct requirements. Violence and other unacceptable behavior, such as substance use at the school or within drug-free zones surrounding the school, need not be tolerated.[50]

Students already identified as eligible for special education or those identified as potentially eligible may not be subjected to disciplinary removal
without compliance with the IDEA protections.[51] Public schools (such as
magnet schools, charter schools, and open-enrollment schools) are clearly
subject to IDEA mandates; private schools are not. It could be argued, however, that private schools participating in voucher programs should be
required to comply with IDEA mandates because they receive at least some
public funding. This concept has not been tested in the courts. Disciplinary
procedural safeguards can present problems in a school of choice in which
the school is not familiar with what might make a child subject to these
protections.

Federal Disability Law and School Choice Programs

Although the legal protections appear to be in place to ensure that students
with disabilities have equal access to school choice programs within public education, the reality of implementing these legal mandates is problematic. It is not even entirely clear that the legal mandates fully provide
protection. If school choice programs do not provide equivalent access for
students with disabilities, these students will be disparately left behind.[52]
The result will be that the goal of mainstreaming will not be accomplished.
There will also be effects on budgeting, staffing, and physical facilities.

Challenges to Mainstreaming

With respect to eligibility for admission to school choice programs, it
would appear that any public school program (charter, magnet, open-
enrollment transfer) that categorically excludes students with disabilities or
even a certain type of disability violates the nondiscrimination provisions
of section 504 and the ADA.[53] The same would be true for a private school
subject to section 504 or to Title III of the ADA. It seems questionable
whether it is appropriate or legal for a public school system to participate
through vouchers with any private parochial school that discriminates on
the basis of disability, although this issue is not clearly resolved.

School choice programs with selective admissions criteria present another
problem. Having selective programs appears to be permissible, but criteria
that disparately screen out students with disabilities may be disallowed under
section 504 or the ADA.[54] Questions could also be raised if too many of
the specialized programs have a disparate impact on students with disabil-

ities, so that a disproportionate number of students in this population are ineligibile.

For students who need special education, the 1997 IDEA amendments theoretically ensure that the public agency provide special education in charter schools, although in practice this promise has not always been carried out.[55] There is less clarity about the guarantee of special education for students who wish to exercise open-enrollment transfers or magnet school options. Arguably, the 1997 amendments regarding the obligation with respect to charter schools would seem to indicate a policy of requiring the public agency to ensure that special education is available for any public school option, although that is not explicit in the statute. Students needing physical barrier removal or reasonable accommodations are substantially protected by the legal mandates under section 504 or the ADA.

If the legal protections are in place, then the question is, Why is there no assurance of equal access? The answer lies in the realities and practicalities of implementing legal requirements. For instance, charter school personnel are less likely than their public school counterparts to be aware of the special education and nondiscrimination mandates of federal law and to understand how these mandates apply to their programs. They may not even realize that these mandates apply at all. In addition, public schools already face a serious inadequacy in the number of available qualified special education teachers. If even more are needed to teach in choice schools, it seems legitimate to question whether special education is likely to be available to students requesting it in these settings.

Parents often face an uphill battle gaining entitlements for their children at their local public school, where the mandates are more clearly understood. They may be more than a little hesitant, as a result, to take on these battles in combination with school choice selection. Even parents who are willing to take on a legal fight must find an attorney willing to represent them. They must also have the financial resources to pay for such representation.[56] Parents are also often realistic about the emotional costs to themselves and their children in taking legal action as well as the potential residual bad feelings of the educational agency resulting from legal challenges. Although it may be too early to evaluate the actual effect on the behavior of parents of students with disabilities under the 1997 amendments, an initial U.S. Department of Education evaluation indicates that in general charter schools appear to serve a slightly lower proportion of students with disabilities, except in Minnesota and Wisconsin.[57] While this study was made before a number of states began chartering schools, the initial research should raise concerns.

Private school voucher programs are even more problematic because it is far from clear how education for students with disabilities will be provided in such arrangements. Categorical exclusion, the refusal to remove barriers to the extent required by section 504 or the ADA, and the denial of reasonable accommodations would seem to be challengable as violating nondiscrimination mandates; the obligation to ensure that special education is available is much less clear. To the extent that these private schools do not receive federal financial assistance and are exempt under the religious organization exemption, they will not be subject to the requirements of Title III or section 504. The public educational agency is obligated to provide some funding to support special education in the private school, but there are significant limitations. Arguably, any voucher system funded by a public agency should be required to ensure that additional funding for students with special education needs be provided along with the voucher. Without such supplementary funding, it is certainly questionable whether the program as a whole ensures that students with disabilities are not disparately adversely affected, in violation of nondiscrimination mandates. Such a theory has not yet been applied by a court to clarify whether a disparate impact test would invalidate voucher programs that do not ensure equivalent treatment of students with special needs.

Even assuming that the legal protections exist to ensure that students with disabilities have equal access to school choice programs, the reluctance of parents to assert their rights will result in students with disabilities being disparately left behind in the nonchoice school. The result may well be that the neighborhood school will be filled with the average and below-average student or at least those who are not identified as being gifted or high achieving. The result will be that one of the primary goals of special education, mainstreaming, will not be met.

Charter schools with specialized programs for students with disabilities have also been advocated. The problem with a charter school or any public school choice option geared primarily to students with a specific type of disability is that this undermines the mandate to mainstream students with disabilities. The values underlying mainstreaming include preventing stigma and providing socialization through peer modeling.[58] From a financial perspective, it may be more efficient to cluster students with certain disabilities, but such a plan can isolate students with disabilities in ways deemed unacceptable under the IDEA.

Challenges to School Choice Programs

Choice programs that must provide education to students with disabilities will be affected financially. Magnet schools and open-enrollment transfer programs may not be affected in the same way as individual schools, because the entire local or state educational agency budget will be available to subsidize certain costs, but charter schools and private schools funded through voucher programs will be affected.

With respect to the costs of providing special education and related services, the charter school will be entitled under the 1997 IDEA amendments to have the chartering entity provide that programming or pay for the costs of the programming. Depending on the chartering and other funding mechanism, however, certain facilities' costs will not be funded by the public agency. Thus a charter school in an inaccessible building may face the cost of removing architectural barriers, not a cost that would be contemplated under the IDEA and thus not the responsibility of the local or state educational agency. Similarly, the student who is disabled but not receiving special education would be entitled to reasonable accommodation without the public agency bearing financial responsibility for it. An example would be a student who is not entitled to service under the IDEA but who needs catheterization during the school day. The charter school would have this responsibility, unless it could demonstrate that it is unduly burdensome to provide the accommodation.

The result is that charter schools subject to transfer or open-enrollment requirements by state or local mandate may not exclude a child with expensive special needs simply because of the potential cost. Although the 1997 amendments to the IDEA clarify that the local educational agency must provide special education services and funding, these amendments do not address architectural barrier removal or reasonable accommodation issues under section 504 or the ADA for a student not entitled to services under the IDEA. A child with an orthopedic impairment requiring accessible physical facilities cannot be excluded simply because barriers might have to be removed. This can create a significant problem for the charter school because of the much smaller budgets that these schools have compared with large school districts.[59]

The financial burden on the private voucher school is somewhat different. Although the IDEA amendments require the public agency to provide "proportionate" funding for special education students whose parents choose a private school, such funding will not necessarily cover the total costs of special education. Thus the financial responsibility for the difference must be determined. Such costs are probably not legally the obligation of the private school, unless they are considered to be reasonable accommodations under the ADA. In that case, the private school would have to agree to absorb the costs or else demonstrate that it would be unduly burdensome to do so. In that event, the parents (or possibly insurance or other benefits programs) would pay. Like the charter school, private schools (except for those subject to the religious organization exemption and not receiving federal financial assistance) would be required to ensure architectural access for the student with a disability who is not in need of special education but who needs barrier removal.[60]

Providing education for students with disabilities also has personnel and administrative costs. Even if the public agency is required to provide or fund special education at either a charter school or a voucher private school, it may be problematic to find qualified personnel to do so. Programming for children with certain disabilities may require teachers with very specialized training. There may not be enough teachers with the required credentials or training to serve more than one school in a particular school district, thus requiring transportation to the school where the educational program is available. When this is the case, the student does not really have the same transfer choice as students without special education needs because the student would not be able to receive appropriate special education in the desired school. The burden will be on the school to demonstrate that it could not provide the appropriate program at the transferee school. If that burden is met, the student's choice is limited.

Challenges to Public Education Funding

Although many parents may not choose to exercise options because of the practical reasons set out previously, at least some will. The public budget will be affected because of basic efficiencies. In an educational program in which a public school system is allowed to cluster students with certain disabilities at one school, rather than providing special education or related services at several public schools (including magnet schools, open-enrollment transfer schools, and charter schools), there are obvious efficiencies. There will be less physical classroom space required, and a full-time teacher at one school for ten students is more efficient than three full-time teachers at three schools with only a few students at each site. Even if a student with a particular need does not require a full-time teacher to meet the needs all day, every day, it is clearly more efficient for that one teacher to be available at one site for all of the students who receive special education throughout the day.

The obligation to provide educational programming or funding to private schools is limited to a proportionate amount, so theoretically this should not affect the special education budget. In reality, however, because of efficiencies in staffing, there will be an impact. If a local school district has $300,000 in federal IDEA funds to spend, based on an average $3,000 per special education pupil expenditure and 100 students with disabilities, the cost of educating the student with expensive needs (the $50,000 residential placement student) can be offset by the lower-than-$3,000 cost of many of the remaining students, who, for example, may need only occasional speech therapy (at roughly $2,000 per student). When one of those "inexpensive" special education students goes to a private school, the public agency must provide programming to that school in at least a proportionate amount. The $2,000 cost per student for speech therapy at the public school is possible because of staffing efficiencies. If that student is now the only student needing speech therapy at the private school, the cost is likely to be higher than $2,000 (say $3,500). The public agency is not required to provide $3,000 to the private school for that student, but under the 1997 amendments it is apparently required to provide the actual cost (which may exceed what the actual cost would have been in the public school), at least up to the $3,000, if the cost of educating the student in that setting requires that amount. It is obvious that the $300,000 that may have been adequate to cover the special education costs of the 100 students if they all remained in the public school system will no longer be adequate if the less expensive students choose private placements.

The private student who is costly to educate (say a student whose educational costs are $15,000) will not be desirable to the private school program, because the maximum the public school would be obligated for is $3,000. If such a private school is part of a voucher program, a question is raised whether the parents of that student really have the same school choice opportunity if they are either denied enrollment (because the private school claims undue burden) or required to pay the difference themselves. One solution might be that, if the public agency approves a voucher program, it must agree to provide the additional funding costs to the private school receiving the voucher. The additional potential costs to the public school budget are obvious.

In addition to direct education costs, there are other potential budgetary implications for both public and private school choice programs if they must be open to students with disabilities pursuant to IDEA, section 504, and the ADA. For example, to the extent that schools provide transportation as part of a school choice program for students without disabilities, it would certainly be required to provide transportation to students with disabilities. While many students, such as those with learning disabilities, do not have specialized transportation requirements, those with mobility and some health impairments do. Transportation for students with these disabilities can be quite expensive. Again, some of the efficiencies of special transportation to a limited number of sites will be lost when when travel to more locations is required.

Other Issues

One of the possible benefits of implementing school choice and policy mandates for students with disabilities will be that private schools will remove architectural barriers. Existing disability policy arguably requires at least some barrier removal, even without school choice options, but the implementation of school choice options might increase the number of schools carrying out barrier removal plans. Under the ADA requirements for barrier-free design, public educational programs were required to remove barriers only to the extent necessary to make the program accessible when viewed in its entirety.[61] That could be interpreted to mean that as long as there is an accessible public grade school available in reasonably close proximity to a child with a mobility impairment, the student is not entitled to go to a neighborhood school that is not now accessible. Private schools are required to remove barriers to the extent it is readily achievable to do so, meaning without much difficulty or expense.

The implementation of a publicly funded school choice program, however, would seem to add new mandates to the barrier removal requirements. If any type of choice is available to regular students but not available to students with disabilities that require physical access or barrier-free design, nondiscrimination mandates would appear to be violated. For example, the student using a wheelchair who wants to apply to the magnet school program in math, a program available only in an inaccessible school facility, could not be turned away because the student could get a regular education at another site. Once the public agency offers something special or unique (even if it is just an open-enrollment transfer system), that program must be nondiscriminatory. With respect to private schools, it could be argued that public agencies should not be permitted to provide vouchers to private schools that are not accessible or that are not willing to remove barriers if a student with a mobility impairment chooses to enroll. This, added to the requirement that many private schools are subject to an ADA Title III mandate to remove barriers to some extent anyway, may pressure more private schools to make their educational facilities accessible.

Another area of concern is personnel training. There is already a significant need for more qualified special education teachers.[62] Implementation of school choice programs to ensure that students with disabilities have equal access to these programs will increase the demand for these teachers. If the political pressure for school choice is strong enough, and if school choice programs are not allowed to go forward without implementation of special education programming, perhaps advocates for school choice will join with advocates for students with disabilities in pressing for greater availability of special education professionals. Although the 1997 amendments to the IDEA provide for a number of incentives, such as scholarships, to increase the training and preparation of personnel, such efforts are not enough.[63] Studies indicate a much higher burnout rate for special education teachers than for regular classroom teachers.[64] Without an increase in number of trained professionals and without salary incentives, public schools will continue to find it difficult to attract and retain qualified special education teachers.

In addition, there is a continuing problem with adequate preparation for regular classroom teachers, administrators, and support personnel to teach students with disabilities. The goal of mainstreaming students with disabilities requires that regular classroom teachers have adequate training in behavior management; identification of disabilities for purposes of referral for testing; the legal requirements of the IDEA, section 504; and the ADA. School administrators must also understand and know how to implement these legal requirements. Support personnel, such as bus drivers, must also have some training. Unfortunately, there are few mandates to ensure such preparation. As a result, many regular educators are resistant to having students with disabilities in their classrooms, and many administrators do not implement legal mandates appropriately. If personnel preparation is inadequate in the regular school system almost twenty-five years after the passage of special education mandates, one might question whether school choice programs (such as charter schools and magnet schools) are prepared to meet the challenge.

In a number of cases the courts have addressed the right of a special education student to receive education in the neighborhood school.[65] These cases arise when the school district clusters several students with similar disabilities and needs at one regular school, which will not be the neighborhood school for some students. The claimants in these cases generally argue that being educated in the least restrictive environment—that is, mainstreaming—means being educated in their neighborhood school. Virtually all of the courts addressing this issue, however, have held that the least restrictive environment aspect of special education law does not mandate that the local school be the place for providing the education. The courts have determined that the mainstreaming mandate is met as long as students with disabilities are educated with students who are not disabled. Clustering is an efficient system of delivering special education, particularly in light of the scarcity of qualified personnel.

When school choice is part of the educational programming available to students in a school district or state, the theory for challenging the denial of being educated at a particular school changes. For example, if a school district has an open-enrollment transfer program allowing any student to elect to attend any school as long as space is available, the denial of participation in this program for special education students could be challenged as discriminatory under section 504 or the ADA. No longer is the theory solely a mainstreaming argument. There has been little, if any, litigation to date applying that theory in such cases.[66]

If the nondiscrimination theory is accepted as the basis for requiring schooling at specific schools (at least when school choice options are involved), more neighborhood schools may provide a fuller array of special education services. Again, choice advocates and special education advocates could join in pressing for this to occur. The realities of scarce numbers of qualified personnel and fiscal constraints, however, may make this difficult to achieve.

Policy Options and Political Realities

Given the challenges in implementing the goals of school choice and at the same time carrying out the legal mandates for educating students with disabilities, it is important to consider what policy changes might be necessary to meet both goals. In considering these policy options, however, it is essential to consider the political reality that such policy options would be approved.

Funding for Special Education

If students with special education needs or those with disabilities requiring physical barrier removal or costly reasonable accommodations are to be provided these services in choice programs, there will be a need for increased funding. There will also be a need for a change in the formula for funding these programs, at least in some cases. There is certainly a need to increase the salaries and support for special educators generally, as an incentive to increase the number of special educators in the system as a whole. Without such an increase, there are simply not enough people to provide the mandated level of services at both regular schools and choice schools. Because school choice is primarily a state or local option, such additional funding will probably have to come from the state or local educational agency implementing the choice program.

A change in formula funding may be necessary to carry out some choice options. This is primarily true for voucher programs. IDEA requires only that a proportionate level of funding be made available to a private school for a student with a disability; in some cases, such public funding to the private school will be inadequate to cover the actual costs. When this is the case, the private school might elect not to accept the student, or the parents might be faced with absorbing the additional costs themselves.

The IDEA provisions, however, do not address what happens in the case of a voucher program. A policy change mandating that the special education agency provide the actual cost of the education at the voucher school instead of only a proportionate amount would theoretically resolve that problem. Such a policy change would clearly result in a higher overall cost to the education budget. Policymakers would have to determine whether this funding would be from federal, state, or local sources and whether it would come from the regular or special education budget. It would seem that because voucher programs are a local option program, the local educational agency would be the entity required to absorb the difference out of its own budget (and that IDEA funding would not be available for this). A clarification in the IDEA statute might resolve this uncertainty.

Proportionate funding raises a long-standing problem with IDEA funding. The funding that is provided to the states is based on a pupil count multiplied by a dollar amount that represents an average cost. The per pupil average is the same regardless of the type of disability within each state. For example, a state with 100,000 eligible special education students might receive $3,000 per pupil from the U.S. Department of Education under IDEA, or a total of $30 million. A state with 10,000 eligible students would also receive $3,000 per pupil, or a total of $3 million. Most states pass these funds on to the school districts, using the same proportionate funding formula. The reason for formula funding is that the average per pupil cost is a reasonably efficient way to fund special education. The problem arises when a state or a local school district has a large number of students with disabilities requiring services that cost more than the average. This is particularly a problem for a small state or a small school district, with less opportunity to cross-subsidize such expenses.[67] One or two residential placements or students with expensive needs can break a school's budget.[68] This same funding formula does not work well in choice schools either.[69]

The examination of the funding mechanism within school choice options may thus result in a much needed reexamination of the formula funding for special education generally, a policy assessment that many believe is long overdue.

Eligibility Requirements

Although there has been little if any litigation challenging academic or other eligibility requirements in school choice programs, the trend toward increasing the number and type of school choice options will inevitably lead to such litigation. Challenges are likely to come from both students with learning disabilities and those with behavior problems. For example, a program (whether it is a magnet program, a charter school, or a voucher program) that has as an eligibility requirement the achievement of a particular score or grade point average could be challenged if it has a disparate impact on students with learning disabilities. Such challenges have occurred regarding eligibility requirements for National Collegiate Athletic Association scholarships. The result has been an agreement to make individualized assessments of these students to determine whether other factors indicate that the student meets the necessary academic achievement level.[70]

Schools with eligibility requirements related to behavior face different issues. For example, it is not unlikely that a voucher school or a charter school might accept all applicants but require that they must not have disciplinary problems. Such a restriction would have a disparate impact on students with an emotional disturbance or autism.

Policymakers will have to evaluate whether some adjustment in these restrictions should be allowed for special education students. Without consideration of the impact of certain eligibility requirements on students with disabilities, policymakers run the risk that such programs will result in a disparately high number of special education students being left out of choice programs and being overrepresented in nonchoice schools, thus violating mainstreaming goals.

One way to allow school choice programs to go forward without the fiscal and administrative burdens of educating students with disabilities would be to exempt them from such requirements. Such an exemption would surely have to occur at the federal level. While Congress could theoretically do so, politically it is extremely unlikely that such a measure could be approved. Special education and disability advocacy groups are well organized and very strong. Discriminating against children with disabilities does not generate good publicity. Even if Congress amended IDEA, section 504, and the ADA to allow such exemptions, it is questionable whether the Constitution would permit doing so.[71]

Conclusion

School choice options provide an interesting opportunity to experiment with alternative educational programs. This is particularly true for options like charter schools that allow for substantial changes in teaching methodology, teaching materials, and curriculum. Such experiments might well benefit students with disabilities. At the same time, there are significant tensions between school choice programming as it is evolving and mandates regarding educating students with disabilities. Current choice programs often operate in a way that is either directly or indirectly exclusionary. Such programs are directly exclusionary because of eligibility requirements or because they do not enable a student with a disability to receive an education within that choice option. When such exclusion is in violation of federal mandates, the programs are indirectly exclusionary because parents face formidable obstacles in using the legal system to ensure their rights of access. To the extent that choice programs result in disparately low participation by students with disabilities, these students will be disparately left behind in the regular school, thus violating the mainstreaming goal of special education.

Some of these tensions appear irreconcilable and will almost certainly result in litigation at some point unless these problems are resolved by policymakers. Public policy support for educating students with disabilities is strong and long-standing and thus is likely to trump school choice programs that run afoul of special education mandates. For that reason, policymakers who support school choice must carefully consider realistic policy options to anticipate inevitable challenges. One of the clearest ways to resolve these tensions is substantially increased funding. If policymakers are able to convince the public to provide the funding necessary for school choice programs to meet their obligations to students with disabilities, one wonders why this effort could not also result in additional funding for public schools generally.

There is disagreement about the reasons for the failure of public schools. An underlying philosophy of many school choice advocates is that competition will improve regular public schools. This expectation, however, overlooks the fact that regular public schools may be inadequate because they are underfunded. Even in the 1960s, before policymakers at various levels began mandating that schools provide special education, bilingual education, drug education, after-school care, child care for teenage mothers, school lunches, early childhood programs, and improved physical education, public education was not adequately funded in every school district.[72] The real competition problem is for qualified educators. Without adequate funding to attract the best and the brightest to be educators for students of all abilities, public education will continue to fail.

One of the driving forces behind school choice options is dissatisfaction with the current public education system. By allowing those students who are the easiest and least expensive to educate to leave the neighborhood public school and to use public dollars as vouchers or to fund magnet schools for these students, the most challenging and most expensive students will be left behind. There will be an even greater need for public dollars to appropriately educate them. We will only have delayed the necessity to adequately fund public schools. The public demand to fund each and every school appropriately is less likely to occur if those who are most able to understand how to take advantage of school choice options are no longer there.

The need for additional funding becomes obvious if students with disabilities are to be assured of their full legal rights within school choice options. This additional funding will have to come from somewhere. Policymakers will need to consider whether the effort to find additional public funding is best directed toward funding public education generally, thus eliminating many of the reasons that school choice has become desirable in the first place.

Notes

1. See Office of Special Education and Rehabilitative Services, *Annual Report to Congress on the Implementation of the Individuals with Disabilities Education Act* (U.S. Department of Education, May 1997); 20 U.S.C., sections 1400 and the following (1997); Public Law 102-119, 105 Stat. 587 (1991) (codifying the 1991 amendments).

2. See 29 U.S.C., section 794 (1997); 42 U.S.C., sections 12131 and the following, sections 12181 and the following (1997).

3. The courts have uniformly held that the IDEA does not mandate a right to have appropriate special education provided in the neighborhood school. *Flour Bluff Independent School District* v. *Katherine M.*, 91 F.3d 689 (5th Cir. 1996); *Murray* v. *Montrose County School District*, 51 F.3d 921 (10th Cir. 1995), cert. denied, 116 S.Ct. 278 (1995); *Schuldt* v. *Mankato Independent School District No. 77*, 937 F.2d 1357 (8th Cir. 1991); *Barnett* v. *Fairfax County School Board*, 927 F.2d 146 (4th Cir. 1991); *DeVries* v. *Fairfax County School Board*, 882 F.2d 876 (4th Cir. 1989).

4. Children needing speech therapy are generally the least expensive to educate among students eligible for special education; those with emotional disturbance are the most expensive. See Mei-lan E. Wong, "The Implications of School Choice for Children with Disabilities," *Yale Law Journal*, vol. 103 (1993), pp. 827, 832.

5. For a history of special education law, see Laura F. Rothstein, *Disabilities and the Law* (St. Paul, Minn.: West, 1997), sections 2.02–2.06; Laura F. Rothstein, *Special Education Law*, 3d ed. (Longman, 1999), chap. 2.

6. Public Law 105-17 (June 4, 1997).

7. Public Law 94-142 (1975); 20 U.S.C., sections 1491–97.

8. 20 U.S.C., section 1411(a)(2) (1997). The funding provided is 40 percent of the average cost of educating a regular education student.

9. 20 U.S.C., sections 1401(8) (1997), 1412(a) (1997), 1412(a)(5)(A) (1997), 1412(a)(4) (1997), 1412(a)(5)(A) (1997). For a review of the research supporting the value of mainstreaming for children with disabilities and those who are not disabled, see Wong, "The Implications of School Choice," pp. 841–42. Wong provides the following data on the relative costs of educating students with disabilities for the 1982–83 school year. The mean cost of providing a regular education to a regular education student was approximately $3,800 to $4,180. Speech-impaired children required $5,414; children with learning disabilities, $7,172; children with mental retardation, $7,853; children with emotional disturbances, $8,204; students with physical, hearing, visual, or health impairments, $10,791. Wong (p. 847) refers to Ellen S. Raphael and others, "Per Pupil Expenditures on Special Education in Three Metropolitan School Districts," *Journal of Education Finance*, vol. 11 (1985), pp. 69, 80.

10. 42 U.S.C., section 1412(a)(5) (1997).

11. 20 U.S.C., section 1412(a)(3) (1997).

12. 20 U.S.C., section 1412 (1997).

13. Important procedural and substantive protections also relate to the confidentiality of student records and information. This can be particularly important for students with stigmatizing conditions, such as HIV, drug or alcohol problems, and mental illness.

14. 20 U.S.C., section 1401(3) (1997).

15. 20 U.S.C., section 1401(3)(B) (1997).

16. Office of Special Education and Rehabilitative Services, *Annual Report to Congress*, table 52.

17. For a comprehensive discussion of the statutory provisions, the regulations, and the major cases involved in these developments, see Rothstein, *Disabilities and the Law*, chap. 2.

18. The most sweeping change involves discipline. Although students may not be completely removed from educational programs, new guidelines give schools more latitude in cases involving behavior problems; 20 U.S.C., section 1415(k) (1997). Other significant changes in the 1997 reauthorization include changes in what must be provided for transitional programs and the inclusion of extracurricular activities in the development of the individualized educational program; 20 U.S.C., section 1414(d)(1)(A)(vii)–(viii) (1997); and mediation as an additional tool for resolving disputes; 20 U.S.C., section 1415(e) (1997). The 1997 amendments also changed the mechanism for federal formula funding. The original statute provided for payment of an average per pupil amount to states presenting annual program plans satisfying the requirements. The new system provided for grants to be based on the most recent

population data, the effective date for the new system being primarily in July 1998; 20 U.S.C., section 1411 (1997). The most significant amendments for purposes of school choice occurred in 1997. The 1997 amendments, while not substantially changing the principles of the original 1975 statute, did respond to some concerns of educational agencies.

19. 20 U.S.C., section 1413(a)(5) (1997). For a careful analysis of the significant adverse impact on charter schools if the 1997 IDEA amendments had not been enacted, see Jay Heubert, "Schools without Rules? Charter Schools, Federal Disability Law, and the Paradoxes of Deregulation," *Harvard Civil Rights–Civil Liberties Law Review*, vol. 32 (1997), p. 301. Without the local agency's obligation to provide special education services and funding to the charter school, the charter school itself would have had this responsibility, one that financially would have been the death knell for many of these schools. See also Joseph R. McKinney, "Charter Schools' Legal Responsibilities toward Children with Disabilities," *West's Education Law Reporter*, vol. 126 (August 20, 1998), p. 565.

20. 20 U.S.C., section 1412(a)(10)(A) (1997).

21. 20 U.S.C., section 1412(a)(10)(B)(i) (1997). Parents sometimes dispute whether the school is providing an appropriate program and make unilateral placements in private schools, seeking reimbursement from the school for the costs incurred. These placements most often occur in cases involving learning disabilities, attention deficit disorder, attention hyperactivity disorder, and severe psychological problems, such as autism.

In an early Supreme Court case, *Burlington School Committee* v. *Department of Education*, 471 U.S. 359 (1985), it was established that the public agency must reimburse the parents for a unilateral private school placement in limited circumstances. Reimbursement is required if the private school offers an appropriate public education and the public school does not. The Court recognized that, as a policy, it is unreasonable to expect parents to wait—after what can be years of litigation—for a decision allowing the private school placement. Parents take some risk, however, because if it is shown that the school's offered placement was appropriate, the parent will have to pay for the private school expenses incurred during the dispute. 20 U.S.C., section 1412(a)(10)(C)(i) (1997).

The 1997 amendments to the IDEA place some limitations on the amount of reimbursement required even when the public agency does not provide appropriate education in a timely manner. The limitation reduces the payment when the parents do not reasonably give the public educational agency, acting in good faith, the opportunity to comply. 20 U.S.C., section 1412(a)(10)(C)(iii) (1997). The limitation or denial of payment is at the discretion of the hearing officer or the court.

22. 20 U.S.C., section 1412(a)(10)(B)(ii) (1997).

23. *Board of Education* v. *West Virginia Human Rights Comm'n*, 182 W.Va. 41, 385 S.E.2d 637 (1989) (requiring placement of two hearing-impaired students in a local school instead of an institution outside the county, even though there were only two such students in the county). For additional cases, see Rothstein, *Disabilities and the Law*, section 2.18.

24. 20 U.S.C., section 1412(a)(10)(A) (1997). It is obvious that there will be difficulties in ascertaining what the proportionate amount would be in some cases. The proposed regulations contemplate a system of consultation to determine which private school students are eligible for services, what services will be provided, how the services will be provided, and how evaluation of the program will occur. The local educational agency is given the final decision on these issues. 34 C.F.R., section 300.454(b) and (e), 62 Fed. Reg. 55094 (October 22, 1997).

25. 34 C.F.R., section 300.453 and .455 (March 12, 1999).

26. This is less likely to occur today because of the 1997 amendments clarifying that special education can be provided by the public agency at even a parochial school. It was just such a program that led to the Supreme Court's decision in *Board of Education* v. *Grumet*, 512 U.S. 687 (1994). The public school system's program of providing special education ser-

vices to students who were members of a Hasidic Jewish sect was to bus the students to the public school. The parents sought to require the school system to provide education at a neutral site because of religious concerns about undesirable acculturation. *Board of Education* v. *Wieder*, 72 N.Y. 174, 531 N.Y.S.2d 889, 531 N.Y. Supp. 2d 889 (Ct. App. 1988). The state of New York tried to resolve the issue by creating a school district that coincided with the Jewish community, a plan that was struck down by the Supreme Court as violating the First Amendment Establishment Clause.

The Supreme Court in *Zobrest* v. *Catalina Foothills School District*, 509 U.S. 1 (1993), addressed whether it violates the Establishment Clause for a public educational agency to provide special education services (a sign language interpreter) for a deaf student enrolled in a parochial school. The Court held that it is permissible. The facts in this case occurred before the 1997 amendments limiting the obligation of the public agency to provide special education services to students enrolled in private schools because of parental preference.

27. 34 C.F.R., section 300.456(b)(2).

28. 62 Fed. Reg. 55095 (October 22, 1997)(proposed regulations); 34 C.F.R., sections 300.461, 460.

29. 20 U.S.C., sections 1412(a)(3); (a)(10)(A)(ii) (1997). Proposed regulation 62 Fed. Reg. 55094 (October 22, 1997); 34 C.F.R., section 300.451.

30. 29 U.S.C., section 794 (1997).

31. 29 U.S.C., section 706(8)(B) (1997).

32. 29 U.S.C., section 706(8)(D) (1997).

33. 34 C.F.R., sections 104.31–.39.

34. 42 U.S.C., sections 12101 and following (1997).

35. 42 U.S.C., sections 12102(2), 12117(b) (1997).

36. 42 U.S.C., sections 12131–81 (1997); 28 C.F.R., part 35 (1997).

37. 42 U.S.C., sections 12181–89 (1997).

38. 42 U.S.C., section 12187 (1997).

39. 42 U.S.C., section 12181(7) (1997).

40. 28 C.F.R., section 36.304 (1997).

41. A few articles have focused on the legal analysis of these issues. These analyses all raise significant concerns about students with disabilities in choice programs, but few have addressed the 1997 amendments to the IDEA, the possible additional effect of the ADA on school choice and students with disabilities, or the concerns for the entire array of school choice options for students with disabilities. See Heubert, "Schools without Rules"; Jeff Neurauter, "On Educational Vouchers: Revisiting the Assumptions, Legal Issues, and Policy Perspectives," *Hamline Journal of Public Law and Policy*, vol. 17 (1996), pp. 459, 491; Julie F. Mead, "Including Students with Disabilities in Parental Choice Programs: The Challenge of Meaningful Choice," *West's Education Law Reporter*, vol. 100 (1995), p. 463; Wong, "The Implications of School Choice." One of the first articles to comment on the impact of the 1997 amendments is McKinney, "Charter Schools' Legal Responsibilities."

42. Although a child requiring speech therapy might cost slightly more than the average cost of providing regular education to a regular education student, those with significant sensory impairments can be the most expensive to educate. Wong, "The Implications of School Choice."

43. Nancy J. Zollers and Arun K. Ramanathan, "For-Profit Charter Schools and Students with Disabilities: The Sordid Side of the Business of Schooling," *Phi Delta Kappan* (December 1998), pp. 297–304.

44. *Bowers* v. *NCAA*, 974 F. Supp. 459 (D.N.J. 1997); *Ganden* v. *NCAA*, 1997 U.S. Dist. LEXIS 17368 (N.D. Ill. 1997). In May 1998 the NCAA reached a settlement agreeing to change its eligibility requirements for student athletes with learning disabilities. *Department of Jus-*

tice v. *NCAA*, settled May 26, 1998. See also *Cureton* v. *NCAA*, 1999 U.S. Dist. LEXIS 2359 (E.D. Pa. 1999). For a discussion of the experience of one charter school and a student with ADD/ADHD, see McKinney, "Charter Schools' Legal Responsibilities," p. 573.

45. Programs subject to section 504 of the Rehabilitation Act, 29 U.S.C., section 794, were to have engaged in self-evaluations of their programs by 1978 and were to have implemented a program of barrier removal. 34 C.F.R., sections 104.6(c), 104.22 (1997). For existing facilities, barrier removal was required that would make the program when viewed in its entirety readily accessible to individuals with disabilities. 34 C.F.R., section 104.22(a) (1997). In addition, new construction was to have met accessibility guidelines. 34 C.F.R., section 104.23 (1997). Schools have had at least two decades to work on the issue of physical environment accessibility.

Like section 504, the Americans with Disabilities Act, 42 U.S.C., sections 12101 and the following, requires public school programs subject to its provisions to engage in a self-evaluation and to remove barriers so that the program when viewed in its entirety is accessible. 28 C.F.R., sections 35.105, 35.150 (1997). This means either removal of barriers or providing alternative methods of complying, such as relocation of the classroom. An interesting question arises in a school system in assessing the "program in its entirety." Is the program the school or the entire school district? Based on judicial interpretations, it would seem that the answer is that the entire school district or at least schools within reasonable proximity to the student's residence should be considered in assessing physical access. In a case involving a student seeking to be placed in the neighborhood school where some ramping might be required for the student's wheelchair, the school might argue that because there is an accessible school in close proximity, the program in its entirety is accessible. Interestingly, the ADA and other discrimination laws have had a significant effect on the removal of barriers in schools. Events held in public schools by programs subject to the ADA can only be held there if the program is accessible within the applicable title. See *Bechtel* v. *East Penn School District*, 4 A.D.D. 677 (E.D. Pa. 1994) (student requested barrier removal under section 504).

In addition, federal voting accessibility laws, Voting Accessibility for the Elderly and Handicapped Act, 42 U.S.C., section 1973ee (1997), have required that elections be held at accessible sites. Because many schools are used as polling places, at least access in the parking lots and entrance to the facility have been affected.

Unexempted private schools are subject to Title III of the ADA, which requires that barriers must be removed to the extent it is readily achievable to do so (meaning without much difficulty or expense), and new construction is to meet design standards consistent with new construction for public schools. 42 U.S.C., section 12183(a)(1) (1997); 28 C.F.R., section 36.304.

It is worth noting that as a result of the ADA, there has been substantial attention to access issues related to facilities used by children, such as in day care centers and on playgrounds. 36 C.F.R., pt. 1191, app. A, 63 Fed. Reg. 2060 (January 13, 1998) (effective April 13, 1998).

46. In *Alexander* v. *Choate*, 469 U.S. 287 (1985), the Supreme Court held that while disability discrimination claimants were not required to prove intentional discrimination, neither would all policies and practices with a disparate impact on individuals with disabilities violate section 504.

47. Attorneys' fees are available to successful litigants, but many attorneys are reluctant to take all but the most clear-cut cases. In addition, attorneys with expertise related to disability law are not available in all areas.

48. *Cedar Rapids Community School District* v. *Garret F.*, 199WL 104410 (1999). See also Rothstein, *Disabilities and the Law*, section 2.24, notes 68, 70.

49. Rothstein, *Disabilities and the Law,* section 2.10.

50. The 1997 IDEA amendments allow interim placements for ten days for most discipli-

nary situations but as many as forty-five days for students carrying weapons to school or to school functions or for possessing, using, or selling drugs and controlled substances. 42 U.S.C., section 1415(k)(1)(A) (1997).

51. 42 U.S.C., section 1415(k)(8) (1997).

52. Zollers and Ramanathan, "For-Profit Charter Schools."

53. Heubert, "Schools without Rules?" pp. 334–38.

54. See citations in note 44.

55. Zollers and Ramanathan, "For-Profit Charter Schools."

56. Attorneys' fees and costs are reimbursed only if the plaintiff succeeds.

57. RPP International and the University of Minnesota, *A Study of Charter Schools: First-Year Report*, SAI 97-3007 (U.S. Department of Education, Office of Educational Research and Improvement, 1997). See also Zollers and Ramanathan, "For-Profit Charter Schools."

58. This issue is discussed in Wong, "The Implications of School Choice," pp. 851–53.

59. An excellent discussion of this issue is found in Heubert, "Schools without Rules?"

60. Private schools are subject to section 504 of the Rehabilitation Act of 1973, 29 U.S.C., section 794, and Title III of the ADA, 42 U.S.C., section 12181, unless the entity is subject to the religious organization exemption. The religious organization exemption means that a private school is not subject to Title III if the school is subject to the control of a religious organization. Even if the religious exemption applies, the program is still covered by section 504 if it receives federal financial assistance.

61. In addition, programs receiving federal financial assistance were subject to barrier-free design standards for new construction after the effective date of section 504 of the Rehabilitation Act of 1973. Most public school facilities constructed since the 1970s thus should be accessible.

62. Mary Zahn and Steve Schultze, "Children with Special Needs Often Get Teachers with Little Training," *Milwaukee Journal Sentinel*, May 24, 1998.

63. 20 U.S.C., section 1473 (1997).

64. Zahn and Schultze, "Children with Special Needs."

65. See the cases in note 3.

66. In August 1998, the parents of a five-year-old boy with cerebral palsy used the media instead of litigation to successfully challenge the school district's plan to bus him to a school fourteen miles away, while allowing his less impaired twin sister to remain at the neighborhood school. The school had planned to bus him to a school where there was a more specialized program and more students with disabilities. *School Law News*, August 21, 1998, p. 6.

67. For example, in the case of *Kennedy* v. *Board of Education*, 175 W.Va. 668, 337 S.E.2d 905 (1985), a school district in West Virginia, a state with limited resources, was required by the court to purchase a $40,000 four-wheel-drive vehicle to enable a student with a mobility impairment to get to school.

68. Sam Allis, "The Struggle to Pay for Special Ed," *Time*, November 4, 1996. See also *Maynard* v. *Heeren*, 563 N.W.2d 830 (S.Ct. S.D. 1997) (suit by parents of autistic child against alleged leader of taxpayer group opposed to expenses incurred by special education placement).

69. See Heubert, "Schools without Rules?" pp. 349–50.

70. *Department of Justice* v. *NCAA*, settlement, May 26, 1998.

71. *Pennsylvania Association for Retarded Children (PARC)* v. *Commissioner of Pennsylvania*, 334 F. Supp. 1257 (E.D. Pa. 1971); 343 F. Supp. 279 (E.D. Pa. 1972); *Mills* v. *Board of Education*, 348 F. Supp. 866 (D.D.C. 1972).

72. Laura F. Rothstein, "Special Education Policy Issues: Current Status and Impact on General Education Policy in the Twenty-First Century," *Kansas Journal of Law and Public Policy*, vol. 2 (1992), p. 75. Before the 1970s a key cost of public education, teacher salaries, was lower than the value of teacher services. Public schools were able to attract highly qual-

ified teachers in spite of these limitations because women seeking professional careers at that time had few options. With changes in the civil rights laws giving women more options, many of those who might have become teachers began seeking careers in law, medicine, and business. Teachers' salaries failed to respond to this competition for qualified individuals. The additional demands of public education, combined with inadequate funding, are certainly a substantial reason for the downhill trend in the quality of public education. Competition from private school choices and even from public school choices will not improve public education without an influx of substantially greater resources.

Contributors

Robert C. Bulman is a Ph.D. candidate at the University of California, Berkeley. His dissertation focuses on how families choose schools for their children.

William G. Buss is O. K. Patton Professor of Law at the University of Iowa College of Law. His teaching, research, and writing focus on education issues including labor law and collective bargaining.

Jesse H. Choper is Earl Warren Professor of Public Law at the University of California School of Law at Berkeley where he served as dean from 1982 to 1992. Author of numerous books on American constitutional law, he has been a commentator on the First Amendment and its relationship to education for over thirty-five years.

Jeffrey R. Henig is professor and chair of political science at George Washington University. A frequent writer and commentator on school reform issues, his 1994 book, *Rethinking School Choice: Limits of the Market Metaphor,* is one of the seminal works in the field.

Paul T. Hill is research professor in the University of Washington's School of Public Affairs and a senior social scientist with the RAND Corporation. His 1997 book, *Reinventing Public Education: How Contract Schools Can Transform American Education,* coauthored with Lawrence Pierce and James Guthrie, proposes an entirely new approach to promoting choice in our public schools.

Frank R. Kemerer is Regents Professor and director of the Center for the Study of Education Reform at the University of North Texas in Denton. He is the author of books on legal issues involving education and most recently was coprincipal investigator of a five-year study of public and private school choice in San Antonio funded in part by the U.S. Department of Education.

David L. Kirp is professor of public policy and former dean of the Goldman School of Public Policy at the University of California, Berkeley. He is the author of a number of books on education law and public policy, including the field's leading casebook, *Educational Policy and the Law,* with Mark Yudof and Betsy Levin. He is coprincipal investigator of a national charter school evaluation being carried out under contract with the U.S. Department of Education.

Betsy Levin was appointed by President Carter as the first general counsel of the U.S. Department of Education. She previously served as executive vice president and director of the Association of American Law Schools and dean of the University of Colorado School of Law. Levin has written widely on issues of equal educational opportunity, education finance, and the federal role in education. In 1999 she was distinguished visiting professor of law at the University of Baltimore.

Robert M. O'Neil is professor of law and founding director of the Thomas Jefferson Center for the Protection of Free Expression at the University of Virginia. A former president of both the University of Virginia and the University of Wisconsin System, he is the author of books on free speech and a frequent commentator on First Amendment issues in the academic community.

Laura F. Rothstein is Law Foundation Professor of Law at the University of Houston Law Center. She is the author of several books on disability issues including the treatise *Disabilities and the Law,* now in its second edition. She has long taught and published in this area of the law.

Stephen D. Sugarman is Agnes Roddy Robb Professor of Law at the University of California School of Law, Berkeley. He is coauthor with John Coons of *Education by Choice: The Case for Family Control.* Published in 1978 (and reissued in a new edition in 1999), the book is one of the first and most well-known works on school choice. In 1970 he, Coons, and William Clune published *Private Wealth and Public Education,* which laid the groundwork for the past three decades of school finance litigation.

Index